George MacDonald

WILLIAM RAEPER

A LION BOOK

Tring • Batavia • Sydney

Published by
Lion Publishing plc
Icknield Way, Tring, Herts, England
ISBN 0 7459 1123 4

Lion Publishing Corporation
1705 Hubbard Avenue, Batavia, Illinois 60510, USA
ISBN 0 7459 1123 4

Albatross Books Pty Ltd
PO Box 320, Sutherland, NSW 2232, Australia
ISBN 0 86760 871 4

First edition 1987

Front cover photograph of George MacDonald, possibly by Lewis Carroll, National
   Portrait Gallery

Back cover photographs:
Top left, Halloway House in Hastings

Top right, MacDonald at his writing desk, by Lewis Carroll

Bottom The MacDonald family in 1872, taken just before the American visit

Printed and bound in Great Britain
by Thetford Press

GEORGE MACDONALD

For my grandmother,
Euphemia Curran Bain Reid

CONTENTS

FOREWORD

George MacDonald is perhaps the most enigmatic of Victorians and this is a major reason why so little attention has been paid to him. I believe that it is time for MacDonald to take his proper place and for his ideas to receive the currency they deserve. While there can be no 'official biography' in one sense, I hope that this detailed study of his life and work, the first since Greville MacDonald's biography in the 1920s, will both generate and stimulate interest in a man whose remarkable spirit and unique view of man has much to tell us today.

Christopher MacDonald

ACKNOWLEDGEMENTS

This is my first book and during the time I have worked on it many people have helped me. I would like to thank some of them here.

First of all I would like to thank Julia Briggs who has read the entire manuscript and whose many suggestions and emendations have been invaluable. I would also like to thank Edmund Cusick with whom I have had many conversations on MacDonald, and whose opinions have heavily informed my own.

There is too little space to thank Freda Levson, George MacDonald's great-niece, who has been a great mainstay and critic over the last three years.

I would like to express my thanks to Professor Giorgio Spina of Genoa University and David S. Robb of Dundee University for their help with the chapter on the novels; to Geoffrey Rowell of Keble College for his help with the chapter on the theology; to Gillian Avery and Gwen Watkins for their help with the chapter on children's writing; and to Morton Cohen and Raphael Shaberman for their help with the section on Lewis Carroll.

The MacDonald family have helped me at all points they could, and I would like to express my thanks to Christopher MacDonald, Rosemary MacDonald, Ian and Roxanne MacDonald, Robert Ian MacDonald, Ina MacDonald and Ewith Plant and Margaret Troup.

Working on MacDonald has taken me to many places. In Scotland I would like to thank Morag Black of Greenkirtle (Huntly), the staff of the Brander Library, Huntly, and to make special mention of Madge Lobban, an authority on local history in Huntly, who died during the writing of this book. I would also like to thank King's College, Aberdeen and the National Library of Scotland.

In England I would like to thank the staff of the Bodleian Library, the British Library, Dr Williams Library, Manchester Public Library, the John Rylands University Library in Manchester, Cambridge University Library, Reading University Library, the Hampshire Record Office and the Broadlands Trustees.

In Italy I would like to thank Piero di Angeli of the Bibliotheca Nationale in Bordighera, Miriam Masterton of the Anglo-Ligurian Club, Guiseppe Bessone, and the Commune of Bordighera, for their warm welcome and generosity to me while I was there.

In America I would like to thank the Beinecke Library, the staff and students of the Yale Divinity School who appointed me a visiting fellow for the short time I was there, the Houghton Library, Harvard, the Huntington Library, San Marino, California, the University of California and Los Angeles, the Marion Wade Collection at Wheaton College, Illinois and the New York Public Library.

I would like to make special mention of Dan and Elizabeth Hamilton whose gracious support has helped me with the completion of this book. I would like too, to thank Glenn Sadler for allowing me to use his unpublished thesis on MacDonald, which contains much interesting biographical material, and for always being ready to answer my questions.

I would also like to thank the Ruskin Literary Trustees, for permission to quote previously-unpublished Ruskin letters; and A.P.Watt Ltd., who gave permission on behalf of the Trustees of the Dodgson Estate to quote from the published letters and diaries of Lewis Carroll.

Thanks are also due to the following for use of the pictures that appear in this book: Elizabeth Hamilton for pictures of The Farm and Trinity Chapel, Arundel; Rosemary MacDonald for the Lewis Carroll pictures, the drawing of George and the Dragon, the Edward Hughes portrait, MacDonald with his sons, Casa Coraggio, and the pictures of the MacDonalds in old age; Houghton Library, Harvard University, for MacDonald's bookplate; the Gordon Schools, Huntly, for the page of manuscript from *Sir Gibbie*; Freda Levson for the *Pilgrim's Progress* pictures and for the Casa Coraggio Great Room; and Guiseppe Bessone for the view of Bordighera.

There are many other people I have written to or met and there is not space here to thank them. They have all helped make this book a fuller account of MacDonald's life and work than any other that yet exists. What mistakes there are between the pages are, alas, only mine.

INTRODUCTION

To say that George MacDonald is an unjustly neglected writer has become almost a cliché. Nevertheless it is surprising how slow critics have been to document his life and assess his work. Up until about fifteen years ago critical work on MacDonald was poor and slight, and, though he is now beginning to receive more attention, there has, till now, been only one major biography of him — *George MacDonald and His Wife* by his son, Greville MacDonald, published in 1924 and two critical works — the idiosyncratic *The Golden Key* by Robert Lee Wolff (Yale 1961) and *George MacDonald* by Richard Reis (New York 1972).

The man who was the friend of John Ruskin and Lewis Carroll, who produced such startling fantasy works and fairy tales during his lifetime, and who perhaps only now in the late twentieth century can be read with any required degree of understanding, deserves more. While MacDonald's contribution to fantasy literature and children's writing has been taken for granted, critics have tended to look at his work through the prism of what has come after, rather than what had gone before. At the same time, MacDonald was, in his own day, a novelist of some distinction, a poet and a theologian, and these areas of his work have remained almost entirely untouched. If in the nineteenth century he was seen as an author of uplifting tales and a prophet, now he can be viewed as an explorer of the unconscious, a visionary ahead of his time whose imaginative power has kept many of his books on the shelves since they were first published.

Sixty years is a long time to lapse between biographies, and while Greville MacDonald's book is admirable in many ways, it does not treat his father's work in any detail, and much other material has come to light since it was written. This biography seeks to do two things: first of all it aims to provide a full account of MacDonald's life, using many letters and other documents which have previously remained unpublished, and secondly it aims to examine MacDonald's work in relation to his life and age, providing an introduction to his thought and ideas. Here I should like to mention the work of Stephen Prickett, Richard Reis, Roderick

McGillis and David Robb whose critical work on MacDonald I have found valuable and full of insight.

MacDonald's story is a moving one, and his ideas are compelling. As always in a biography of this length some passages will appeal more to some readers than others. It has often seemed to me a curious notion that a reader has to read *everything* in a book; on encountering those passages that are too specialized or detailed (though hopefully they are few), my advice is to pass them by and read on.

William Raeper
Oxford 1986

And lo! behind me was a great hole in the rock, narrow at the entrance but deep and wide within; and when I looked into it I shuddered, for I thought I saw far down the glimmer of a star. The youth entered and vanished. His guide strode back to his seat, and I lay in terror near the mouth of the vast cavern. When I looked up once more, I saw all the men leaning forward with head aside, as if listening intently to a far off sound. I likewise listened, but though much nearer than they I heard nothing. But I could see their faces change like waters in a windy and half-cloudy day. Sometimes though I heard nought it seemed to me as if one sighed or prayed beside me, and once I heard a clang of music, triumphant in hope; but I looked up, and lo it was the listeners who stood on their feet and sang. They ceased, sat down, and listened as before. At last one approached me, and I ventured to question him. 'Sir,' I said, 'wilt thou tell me what it means!' And he answered me thus. 'The youth desired to sing to the Immortals. It is a law with us that no one shall sing a song who cannot *be* the hero of his tale, who cannot live the song he sings, for what *right* hath he else to devise great things and to take holy deeds in his mouth. Therefore he enters the cavern where God weaveth the garment of souls, and there he lives in the form of his own dream, for God giveth them being that he may be tried. The sighs which thou didst hear were his longings after his own ideal, and thou didst hear him praying for the truth he beheld but could not reach. We sang because in his first battle, he strove well and overcame. We await the next.'

The Parable of the Singer
(*Within and Without* 1855)

CHAPTER ONE

The Blood-filled Glen

To cross Rannoch moor in the Scottish Highlands is to cross the face of another world. For the moor is an unrelenting landscape of peat and bog, stretching unbroken as far as the eye can see. It borders Glencoe, an impressive mountain pass eight miles long, which is both a fortress and a trap. It was in this place that the smallest branch of the Clan Donald settled. They were a proud tribe claiming descent from Conn of the Hundred Battles, High King of Ireland, from Colla, the Prince of the Isles, and from Fergus, the first ruler of the Scoto-Ireland kingdom of Dalriada. And it was to this sombre place that George MacDonald liked to trace his family tree.

In a letter to *The Spectator* in July 1867, MacDonald wrote: 'Surely it is one of the worst signs of a man to turn his back upon the rock whence he was hewn.'[1] He stuck to this maxim for the whole of his life, remaining first and foremost a Scot, and more than that, a Highlander and a Celt. He looked back with fondness to the great clan tradition, that had been swept away in the wake of Culloden and the Clearances, to a bardic people, ekeing their living out of the bare hills in the north and west of his native land. Despite the romance surrounding the Highlanders, these clansmen were regarded by the Scottish Lowlanders as little more than savages. 'The Gallows Herd' was their grim nickname, and as warriors and farmers they spent their time conducting raids, thieving and stealing cattle. MacDonald was passionately interested in his own ancestry and began his story on the night of the dreadful massacre which so shocked Europe at the end of the seventeenth century.[2]

For it happened that William of Orange had granted pardon to the clans who had fought against him during the Glorious Revolution, provided that they took an oath of allegiance to him by 1 January 1692. The clans hesitated, for they were Roman Catholic and the hated Dutch king was Protestant. They had already bound themselves to the Catholic Stuart James VII who was now in exile in France. Finally, when the indecisive James released the clans from their oath to him, there were only nineteen days left before the expiry date set by William. It was impossible, given the limitations on travel and communication that all the clan Chiefs could take the oath by the end of the old year. MacIain, Chief of the MacDonalds of Glencoe, unexpectedly reached Fort William to take the oath by 31 December, but was told sadly by John Hill, Commander of the garrison there, that this had to be done at Inverary. Delayed by bad snow and bad luck, he did not manage to reach Inverary until 6 January. This sealed the MacDonalds' fate. By 1 February, 120 men under Campbell of Glenlyon, a man with every reason to hate the MacDonalds as he had been reduced to penury by one of their more vicious raids, arrived in Glencoe with orders that his men be billeted, and also with assurances that he had no hostile intent. These men, according to the old Highland tradition of hospitality, were well looked after, and so it was that the Campbells and the MacDonalds rubbed shoulders together for nigh on a fortnight, wrestling together, tossing the caber, and playing *camanchd*, a particularly fierce kind of shinty. On 12 February 1692, Glenlyon received his fateful orders from Robert Duncanson:

'For His Majesty's Service, to Captain Robert Campbell of Glenlyon.

Sir,
  You are hereby ordered to fall upon the rebels, the MacDonalds of Glencoe, and to put all to the sword under seventy...'

After two weeks of peace the Campbell soldiers turned on their hosts without a hint of warning early on the morning of 13 February. Some forty MacDonalds were slaughtered, including the old Clan Chief Mac-Iain, who was pulling on his trews in order to fetch his guests some whisky to see them on their way with proper courtesy. The Campbell soldiers bayonetted men in their beds, or dragged them outside and shot them on the dungheaps. They drove cattle, sheep and goats from the byres, looted the houses and burned the thatch and timber. Fearing that the soldiers would return, the MacDonalds fled the glen. Some travelled to Appin, others hid in the caves and corries below the Pap of Glencoe, or else went beyond Kinlochleven to Keppoch's people on Loch Treig. Some went to Rannoch and their cold shielings on the Black Mount. As many as died in the massacre died of exposure in the bitter snow as they escaped for their lives from the bloodthirsty Campbells.
  One who was carried away as an infant, was called Ronald Mac-Donald. Little is known of him, save his name and that eventually he came to Portsoy, a little fishing town in the north-east of Scotland. There

Ronald settled, and his son began a business as a 'quarryman and polisher of Portsoy marble'.[3] This son in turn had a son — a red-haired man called William who became in time the Town Piper of Portsoy, playing every day at five in the morning and eight in the evening in an age when there were not so many clocks and watches.[4] It is said of this piper that he was blinded at Culloden[5] — that bleak, treeless moorland where Prince Charles Edward Stuart, the Young Pretender, met his final defeat on 16 April 1746. The battle was a brief one, lasting less than an hour, but it was a turning point in the history of Scotland. The Jacobite troops, hungry and tired after an all-night march, numbered some 5,000 men against the Duke of Cumberland's well-disciplined 9,000 troops, including artillery and mounted dragoons. A massacre followed, and in its aftermath the government showed no mercy towards the Highlanders. Their homes were burned and their cattle taken. It is a sad irony that there were more Scots in Cumberland's army than there were in the Prince's.

One of William's, the red-haired piper's sons was born three months before Culloden and was named Charles Edward after the Young Pretender. The story goes that this baby's mother died on the day of the battle when news of it reached her. But William escaped with the baby, and on their way through Nairn they were pursued by the townspeople[6], the blacksmith threatening them with a red-hot iron — yet somehow they managed to outrun the angry mob to safety. The pair hid among the caves of Portsoy for several months until the fuss died down and blind William was forgotten.

The baby, Charles Edward, the grandfather of George MacDonald, survived[7], grew up, and was educated at Fordyce School. Homeless and penniless this son of an outlaw and an exile made his way to Huntly, and with him a new and fascinating MacDonald saga began.[8]

CHAPTER TWO

The MacDonald Descent

When Charles Edward arrived in Huntly during the second half of the eighteenth century it was a town of only a few simple streets flanked by traditional gabled houses. The population at that time could not have been more than 600 people, including a mixture of outlawed Highlanders and Irish adventurers. Huntly itself lies forty miles north and west of Aberdeen in a fertile hollow, surrounded by a ring of hills. Its centre is the Square, composed of mainly seventeenth and eighteenth century buildings which later became shops. In the very heart of the Square are the 'Stannin' Stanes', probably remnants of a druid circle, which in time came to symbolize the power and influence of the Gordons. For the town lay very much in the shadow of its castle and the Gordon family had ruled there from the time of Robert the Bruce. The two rivers that form boundaries to the town meet close by the castle and then rush to the sea. While the Deveron was famed for its fishing, the Bogie was found to be good for bleaching, for a time the source of Huntly's wealth. It was through the efforts of one man, Hugh McVeagh, that the bleaching and linen trades opened up.

Charles Edward MacDonald began by assisting McVeagh as a clerk, but swiftly rose through the ranks to become an important part of the business. A man of extraordinary energy, he first became manager and then, when McVeagh died, proprietor of the firm. As the linen trade petered out and the factory had to be closed, he showed characteristic imagination and enterprise in opening a thread factory which he built in what is now MacDonald Street.[1] The thread produced by this factory was not only used for sewing in this country, but was exported as far afield as South America. When this factory too had to close, MacDonald immersed himself in other activities. He was the first man to introduce banking facilities into Huntly, becoming an agent of the Aberdeen Bank at a salary of £20 per annum and he set about developing the bleachfields. Despite his Roman Catholic name and parentage he always identified himself closely with the established church and remained there until the end of his life. This behaviour was, however, not too unusual as many Catholic Highlanders turned Protestant after Culloden. As an old man he used to sit in the elder's seat in the parish church and 'wear the tie wig, which was rare for those days, though round wigs were plentiful.'[2]

In 1778 Charles Edward MacDonald married a formidable woman — Isabella Robertson — George MacDonald's grandmother. She was a member of an old Drumblade family. Her portrait is vividly drawn in the character of Mrs Falconer in MacDonald's novel, *Robert Falconer*. As a girl she had been taught to read, but was forbidden to learn to write 'for fear she should write to the lads.' She began to teach herself to write, however, aged sixty. It was Isabella who destroyed much of the family history. She had, it is said, 'as fine a sense for the safety of valuables as for souls,' and, in need of a safe, she turned the traditional Chanter Kist to this use. This Kist was a huge oak-carved coffer which contained the piper's chanter and mouldy, old papers — in a typical family it might have held a family brooch, a gleaming cairngorm, a topaz or other jewellery, and perhaps a divining crystal, a rosary or even a sacred relic.[3] Isabella destroyed all these because, as she said, they were the wiles and snares of Satan. She was a vehement Calvinist, rigorous in her doctrine and consequently rigorous in her treatment of those around her. She burned a violin belonging to one of her sons because she believed that making such music was evil and her stern character is described powerfully in *Robert Falconer*. Mrs Falconer does not smile on greeting Robert:

> 'I think it was rather there was no smile in her religion, which, while it developed the power of a darkened conscience, over-laid and half-smothered all the lovelier impulses of her grand nature.'[4]

While her husband remained a member of the parish church, Isabella took herself and her family off to the Missionar Kirk, a zealous alternative to the established church. Built in 1801 and seating 700 people, the church had formed under George Cowie, a committed man whose ministry in the district lasted thirty-five years and under whom arose a small revival. His services could often last five or six hours and in the winter, without any heating, the congregation sometimes found the cold unbearable. But they were eager churchgoing folk. These Missionars derived their name from their support of missionary work overseas, and this nickname, though meant to be derogatory, was adopted with pride.[5]

Isabella did not initially attend the Missionar Kirk for any good religious reasons, however, but because the building belonging to the parish church was in such a bad state of repair that when the worshippers arrived one morning, they found the inside of the church filled with snow. Isabella was so incensed that she strode straight to the church of George Cowie.

At the age of ninety-two, in 1848, the year in which she died, she could still read large type with her glasses, despite her short sight. The newspapers that year were full of the revolutions taking place across Europe. 'Laddie,' she said, 'the newspaper is telling that amang a' the changes takin' place i' the warld they have gotten a guid Pope at Rome; an' I have been prayin' to the Lord a' nicht to gie him a new hert an' a guid wife!'[6]

Isabella gave birth to ten children in all. Three of her daughters and a son died in infancy, but the others survived. The most shadowy of her children is the eldest, William. He seems to have played no part in his father's business, but instead converted a disused bleachworks and became the founder of the Huntly Brewery. The manufacture of alcohol would certainly not have endeared him to his mother, who was so earnest in the cause of Temperance, and he seems to have spent much of his time estranged from the rest of the family.

The three other brothers, Charles, George and James, all became partners in their father's business. Their sister Mary married the Rev. James Spence, of Newport in the Isle of Wight. Charles, presumably the favourite, was bequeathed the bulk of the property and made senior partner.[7] The bleaching business was then still extensive and the Mac-Donalds had agents in every part of Scotland from Wick to Dumfries, and there was enough work for the brothers to share the duties of the business. James, the youngest, did all the travelling, sometimes covering sixty miles a day in the saddle — George supervised the work at the factory and Charles became the bank agent. He was personally responsible for advances made on behalf of the bank and soon found himself in severe financial difficulties — he may even have embezzled some money. In any case, Charles found himself in such straits that he fled from Huntly in 1831-2, abandoning his wife Helen and their two daughters, Mary and Helen. He died in New York in 1836, aged forty-one. Charles's wife only learnt of his death when she received a sum for the amount for which she had insured his life.[8]

When Charles disappeared he left his brothers, George and James, with the load of paying off his debts of £6,000. This sum took many years to clear, for despite being the leading family in the town, the MacDonalds' finances were always precariously balanced and there were several times when their business foundered.

Of the two remaining brothers, James became involved in the family business at the age of nineteen when his father died. A devout, committed and religious man, he was a keen member of the Missionar Kirk. George, father of the writer, the second son of Charles Edward and Isabella, began work as a handloom weaver, but went on to supervise work at the thread factory until it went to the wall in 1829. He had a reputation for being tolerant and devout; 'a finely built man — tall, square shouldered and handsome in appearance. He was exceedingly jovial and good-natured, and withal his personality was very winsome and attractive.'[9] In 1825 he had to have a leg amputated above the knee for white swelling, a condition associated with tuberculosis. His grandson recounted that:

'He refused the stupefying dose of whisky [used before the days of chloroform] and did not even have his face covered, preferring to watch the gory proceedings.'[10]

But the amputation of a leg is a serious business, especially when many died under the surgeon's knife. Thomas Ross wrote from Montrose on 7 September 1825:

'But the principal object of this letter is to request that you will speedily write me respecting my dear cousin G. MacDonald — poor fellow — I can scarcely think of him without shedding tears. Ah, the intensity of his sufferings at the time of his operation and since. It almost makes me shudder to think of it — If he is so much recovered that you can see him, I hope you will say how sincerely and deeply I sympathise with him in his present distressing condition.'[11]

George did survive, and so did his humour. The new wooden leg became the subject of many a joke. 'It is a fact, sir,' he was known to say, 'that I have a leg on each side of the Bogie' — and he boasted that 'The Defiance [the mail coach] runs between my legs every day.' His amputated leg had been laid to rest on the other side of the Aberdeen road in Drumblade churchyard.

But the most remarkable incident to give insight into his character happened on 8 April 1846 when his second wife was about to give birth to the youngest of their three daughters. This was towards the end of the worst of the three years of potato famine when everyone was desperate for food and rumour had gone round the town that the MacDonalds were holding a store of grain until prices, which were high, had risen even higher. Discontented, a number of people gathered outside The Farm to complain. George senior appeared to face them in his usual blue swallow-tail coat with gilt buttons, black and white check trousers and soft loose collar. The crowd was angry, but George senior managed to silence them, telling them that absolute quiet was essential if his wife was to deliver her baby safely. He pleaded with them to go down to the Square and tell him there what the trouble was about.

By the time he arrived there the crowd had swollen and grown ugly again. Their anger was near breaking-point. As a protest they had built a bonfire alongside the Stannin' Stanes with a clumsy effigy sprawled on top sporting a grotesque wooden leg. When the mob were just about ready to kindle the pile they had made, George senior burst out with, 'Bide a wee, lads...afore ye set the corp alow [aflame]. Ye've fastened the timmer leg to the wrang hurdie [hip].' And leaning on his stick he gravely added, 'Noo, ye's gang on wi' yer ploys wi' a guid conscience, an' burn yer auld freen!'[12]

The crowd was completely brought round and began to laugh and cheer him. Then, at his invitation, a few went back to The Farm with him to be convinced that its barn, like their own meal tubs, was empty.

George, the writer, portrayed his father's character in David Elginbrod:

> 'His carriage was full of rustic dignity, and a certain rustic refinement; his voice was wonderfully gentle, but deep; and slowest when most impassioned. He seemed to have come of some gigantic antediluvian breed: there was something of the Titan slumbering about him. He would have been a stern man, but for an unusual amount of reverence that seemed to overflood the sternness and change it into strong love.'[13] •

Certainly his reverence flowed at times into unconventional channels, even at the prayer meeting. On one occasion his prayer was full of the wonders of the microscope.[14].

George senior married twice. His first wife was Helen MacKay, the daughter of Captain Alexander MacKay of Duardbeg, Sutherland and sister of the Rev. MacIntosh MacKay, who was a friend of Sir Walter Scott, editor of the Highland Society's Gaelic Dictionary, and Moderator of the General Assembly of the Free Church of Scotland in 1849. She and George senior had six sons: Charles Francis, George, Alexander, John Hill and two others who died in childhood. Helen, like so many of her time, succumbed to tuberculosis in 1833, and a few years after her death, in November 1839, George senior married Margaret McColl, the daughter of the Rev. Donald McColl, RN, long resident at Tullochbeg, Huntly. She had three daughters: Isabella Ann, Louisa, and Jane Duff, and lived to be 102, not dying until 1906.

Family life apart, most of George senior's energy went into the business and the church. After the closure of the thread factory the MacDonalds turned their hands to producing flour and starch from potatoes. Machinery was erected on the bleachfields and elsewhere for this purpose. This factory continued until the potato famine of 1846.

After that the old factory in MacDonald Street was converted into a granary and the bleachfield mills were turned into meal mills. Thus it was that George senior and James were able to carry on a large trade as merchants and millers. The Glasgow spinning mills had dealt the death blow to the thread factory and then the invention of chloride of lime put paid to the bleaching. Annie Glass, whose mother was among the first workers at the thread factory, remembered that:

> 'They held a prayer meeting every week for the workers in the counting room of the factory from 7 till 8 o'clock in the evening. The meeting was conducted by Mr George in general and in his absence by Mr James — they were good Christian men, the MacDonalds.'

It also happened that George senior and James used to meet for prayer every Saturday evening at the close of the week's work.

George senior and James built a house in Bogie Street, on land belonging to their father. George senior brought his beautiful bride, Helen, there in 1822 and their two oldest children, Charles Francis and George, were born in that house. Soon after, however, the two brothers moved with their families to The Farm, and Charles, George senior's and James's older brother, moved into the Bogie Street house.

The Farm had formerly belonged to Hugh McVeagh and had been little more than a collection of farm buildings. Known as Upper Pirries-mill, McVeagh had the habit of referring to it as The Farm, and the name stuck. The MacDonald brothers built a house there near the river, nestling in some trees just outside the town. They christened it Bleach-field Cottage,[15] and it is a long-roofed building, built out of grey granite. George senior and James managed to acquire the tenancy of the property on the last occasion of the letting of all the farms on the 'Aucht-an-Forty'[16] as the lordship of Huntly was called. Within a few years the MacDonalds had reclaimed more bogland in proportion to the holding than any other tenant.

The Farm features largely in MacDonald's writing. It was an important reference point for his imagination. It was where his childhood was played out and his memories returned to it again and again.

CHAPTER THREE
The Little Gray Town

George was born in winter — on the tenth day of December 1824. His first two years were spent in the Bogie Street house that his father and uncle had built:

> 'What might be seen from this window certainly could not be called a very pleasant prospect. A broad street with low houses of cold grey stone, with perhaps the town drummer playing in the distance.'[1]

Isabella MacDonald, grandmother to baby George, lived just next door in a house on the corner of the street and there was a connecting door between her house and the other MacDonalds. As the baby grew he was well cared for by his able father and pretty mother. Helen MacDonald's health was never of the best and she worried that she could not give George enough milk, even farming him out at one point to a wet nurse. In a letter to Isabella, her mother-in-law, who was on a visit to Aberdeen she put down some of her anxieties on paper:

> 'My Dear Mother,
>   . . . I hope you will not be angry tho' I do not write a long letter. I am going to tell you something that will show you how little sense I have. Do you know I was almost angry on Saturday when your letter came to my dear G. about weaning our dear little Boy — for I was very unwilling to do it — and I always thought I would have been able to give him three months at least. But O! my heart was very sore when I saw that you, my dear husband, and Mrs Ross — and indeed all the rest — were so earnest about it — that I was forced to begin that very morning. And he has not got anything from me since. But I cannot help my heart being very much grieved for him yet, for he has forgot it: poor little fellow he is behaving wonderfully well as yet. He cryed desperate for a while the first night, but he has cryed very little since and I hope the worst is over now . . .'[2]

For George, growing up as a small boy amid all the bustle of two families

24

(his father's and his uncle's) sharing the same small house, his earliest recollections are not those of the rough and tumble of family life, but of something quite different. Early memories are usually a jumble, a con-certina'd pack of fragments from different times and places. But some things do stand out clearly, and as MacDonald was later to write:

> 'We cannot recall whence we came, nor tell how we began to be. We know approximately how far back we can remember, but have no idea how far back we may not have forgotten. Certainly we knew once much that we have forgotten now. My own earliest definable memory is of a great funeral of one of the Dukes of Gordon, when I was between two and three years of age. Surely my first knowledge was not of death. I must have known much and many things before, although that seems my earliest memory.'[3]

Though perhaps he was too young to associate the splendid melancholy of the funeral cortège with the reality of death, this memory may have served as a kind of omen, for death's shadow flitted in and out of MacDonald's long life, snatching many of his loved ones who died of tuberculosis — so much so that he came to refer to the disease as 'the family attendant'.

Certainly the most imposing occasion which took place in Huntly during MacDonald's early years was the funeral of Duke Alexander. The procession consisted of a number of carriages draped in black, with waving plumes and drawn by black Flemish horses in appropriate hous-ings. This was an unusual event. Huntly, like most small towns, was a place of routine and daily incident — a community where everyone knew everyone else and George began absorbing its features from an early age. Although the town had grown rapidly with the expansion of the bleach-ing and linen trades, these were already beginning to decline. Neverthe-less, the most striking sight still to be seen must have been the long webs of white cloth spread out on the fields on both sides of the Bogie. The streets of the town were constantly filled with the sharp clicks of handlooms. The town's everyday life ticked over under the baron baillie, Mr Gordon Cocklarch, and there were several Justices of the Peace both in the town and in the surrounding neighbourhood. Weekly and other markets were held in the Square selling, among other things, peats and turf brought from a moss five miles away. Cattle, not sheep, predominated in this part of the world. The town was in daily communication with both Aberdeen and Inverness by the Mail and Defiance coaches which linked it to the outside world. Roads were still unreliable and travel was difficult. Within the town itself the streets were not well kept, and poor drainage meant that pools and ditches lay all the year round, covered in summer in a horrible green slime. A double line of ashpits extended from end to end of each street, each house having its own. There was no street lighting at all.

In the countryside George would have seen the small, cultivated fields, their ridges crooked like a long drawn-out letter 'S'. The farm houses were thatched, each with its own kaleyard and the farmers had wooden ploughs drawn by eight, ten or twelve oxen. In the autumn bands of men and women with sickles did the harvest, reaping the oats and barley. The crops were often poor and frequently overtopped by a rank growth of weeds. These people had a simple, hard life with little romance in it. Oatmeal was their staple diet. Bread was a luxury. Butcher meat was never on the table except on a Sunday and then it came with the barley broth in which it was boiled. Few people had tea or coffee to drink. The MacDonalds were very well-off by comparison.

The church had its grip firmly on these people and in 1792 the local minister, Robert Innes, wrote that, 'The people in this parish, and, indeed in this district are certainly remarkable for their church going habits.' This was true, if only half the story. Calvinism was the doctrine that MacDonald had to imbibe from an early age. The Missionars were especially active in the local community and under John Hill, Sabbath Schools were established, attended by many, and the majority of those who went were children who actually belonged to the established church. The Missionar Kirk had the most prominent families in the town among its members and it was said that:

'It comprised the most energetic men in the locality — men remarkable alike for their religious zeal and activity in business. Although not a numerous body, they exercised greater influence on the community than did any other of the religious denominations. This may be accounted for partly by their strict observance of their religious duties.'

These religious duties were certainly strictly observed, and MacDonald in his turn must have had to observe them. The Missionars were Sabbatarian in the extreme, so much so that the sending out of a child to fetch milk on a Sunday morning was condemned — and while Sunday walking may have been disapproved of by other churches, among the Missionars it was absolutely forbidden. Alcohol, tolerated in some churches, was banned, as was card playing. John Hill, their minister, stamped out dances through his efforts from the pulpit and preached against drunkenness in the town's markets. He even wrote a 'Dialogue on the Causes, Extent and Cure of Drunkenness in Huntly'. The fire of these Missionars seemed impossible to quench. They were enthusiastic, exclusive and committed, banding together to protect their morals and worship their God.

Religious fervour marked only one section of the community, however, and, as is probably true of every community, under the veneer of outward respectability illicit practices abounded and often burst out into the open. There were regular stand-up fights at the markets and at other times. Of the two feeing markets held twice a year on Whitsunday and at Martinmas, the Rev. Innes wrote:

> 'They are for the hiring of farm-servants and may be described as unmitigated moral nuisances — not merely from the evils inseparably attendant on the congregating of large numbers of thoughtless young people of both sexes, with money in their pockets, and many of them with loose moral principles, but also from the utter destruction of those moral checks and mutual kindly feelings which ought to subsist between master and servant — the one class being hired generally without any regard to their character, as if they were mere beasts of burden, and the other feeling little welfare for those who are sure to leave them in half a year.'

The Total Abstinence Society came out in force to quell the consumption of alcohol, but the five inns and twelve public houses that served the small population stayed firmly open.

Huntly people also indulged in smuggling. Duty-free salt was brought in the bottom of fish wives' creels and many housewives had moulds and made illicit candles. Illegal distillation was carried on in all the surrounding parishes if not in the town itself. The Temperance societies only sprang up after distillation had been made legal, to counter a problem that had already existed for a very long time.

For the most part these people were poor and they lived in bad conditions. The best that any of the working people could hope for was a but-and-ben and bed-closet. George Gray, a native of Huntly, remembered that:

> 'Oftener the accommodation was shared by two families. There were no lathed walls and few plastered ceilings. The "but" end may have had a wooden floor and a sort of grate. There was no floor elsewhere in the "ben!" Except the hereditary eight-day clock and chest of drawers, the furniture was of the plainest description. There were no carpets and table cloths and every member of the family worked.'[4]

This then was the community that young George opened his eyes to — one of friendship and fights and routine and squalor. Yet the MacDonalds, though a cut above the other people in the town, did not look down on the poor, but held to the custom of giving oatmeal to beggars when they came round to beg, and remained both generous and popular.

In the individual memories and fragments of MacDonald's childhood his mother remains a presence rather than a character. In *Ranald Bannerman's Boyhood*, a book in which MacDonald recounted some of his earliest memories and adventures, Ranald remembers his mother bending over a baby — then, when he woke up, both the baby, his mother and the cradle were gone.[5] In this way, the young boy knew that the baby was dead. This is probably his only memory of his brother John who died in infancy. Helen was always tubercular, and Ranald remembers his mother being ill, and being told to stay out all day in order to keep the house quiet — almost paradoxically this was the beginning of his childhood freedom. He remembers his mother holding his head to her bosom and the comfort she brought him. These snatches are what one might expect a child to remember, coupled with the round of daily life on The Farm — riding the horses home from the plough in an age still free from machines; watching 'the grain dance from the sheaves under the skilful flails of the two strong men who belaboured them,'[6] and being fascinated by the winnowing machine:

'There was a winnowing machine, but quite a tame one, for its wheel I could drive myself — the handle now high as my head, now low as my knee — and watch at the same time the storm of chaff driven like drifting snow-flakes from its wide mouth.'[7]

Into this round erupted one event which did stay in MacDonald's memory all his life — the famous Moray Floods of 1829,[8] which occurred when he was four-and-a-half:

'At all events I do remember one flood that seems about as far off as anything — the rain pouring so thick that I put out my hand in front of me so as to try whether I could see it through the veil of the falling water. The river, which in general was to be seen only in glimpses from the house — for it ran at the bottom of the hollow — was outspread like a sea in front, and stretched away far on either hand.'[9]

That summer had been hot, killing off much of the vegetation and then suddenly on Sunday 2 August the rain started to fall — and it fell and fell. Enormous damage was done to both crops and property and people gathered to watch the carcasses of dead animals and other bodies floating past. In Huntly alone the water level rose twenty-two feet above its normal height. Houses were swept away and the Bridge of Spey at

Fochabers fell down. Eventually the flood subsided and life continued much as normal.

George was a lively, precocious boy. Once, when he was very young, he went 'strutting about in his first pair of trousers before his Uncle William, when the latter vowed he only needed a watch and a wifie to make a man of him. "I can do well enough wanting the watch — but — but — I would like that I had a wee wifie," ' answered George promptly.[10]

But play was often mixed with illness. George was a delicate boy despite his robust interests and outdoor enthusiasms. On one occasion he was kept in bed for four months and was bled from the arm, and there must have been many other days when he was forced to lie in bed and gaze either out of the window or up through the skylight, listening to the noises going on about him and longing for the freedom to go outside. He remembered the field at the back of The Farm vividly:

'Behind my Father's house there lies
A little grassy brae
Whose face my childhood's busy feet
Ran often up in play:
Whence on the chimneys I looked down,
In wonderment alway.'[11]

When he was not ill one of his special pleasures when he was still quite a small boy was to rush off to the Gordon Arms in the Square 'where shepherds and Highland drovers foregathered' and 'waiting behind a partition, he would collect all manner of information concerning shepherd and crofter life.'[12]

Like most boys, the time came when George had to go to school. Education in Scotland was much more widespread and egalitarian than it was in England and certainly after 1696, mainly due to the influence of John Knox, the parish school became a common feature of rural life. In Huntly, when MacDonald was a boy, there was not one, but two schools. The Parish School was in Church Street at that time and the schoolmaster was a man called Hay. This schoolmaster 'thought it a good diversion from his exacting duties now and then to look on and see two of his pupils at pitched battle, and to encourage them in giving each other black eyes or bloody noses.' But Hay, it seems, was a good teacher 'of quiet habits and fond of his constitutional walks by Bogieside.'

George and his brothers did not attend Hay's school, however, but the newer 'adventure school', mainly supported by the dissenting families of the town — especially by the Missionars. In a story MacDonald wrote called 'The Snow Fight',[13] he recalled something of his schooldays and stated that the boys of the 'high school', as it is called in the story, were admitted by 'possessing any of the names which gave the right of entrance...' and, 'On the whole they belonged to a higher social position than the boys who went to the other school.' This reinforces the probability that the Missionars' children mainly attended this school.

The syllabus of the two schools included Latin, Greek and Maths, along with learning portions from the dreaded Shorter Catechism — the bane of every schoolchild's life, taught on Saturday mornings. Containing a series of theological propositions beginning 'The chief end of man is to glorify God and enjoy him for ever', it is anything but short. The schoolchildren were set to learn it and if they failed to do so, then they were detained until they could. Saturday afternoons could either spell freedom or imprisonment therefore, and there seems to have been little mercy on offer.

For the first six years of his schooldays, MacDonald suffered under a brutal and tyrannical teacher called Colin Stewart. He belonged to Ross-shire and was a licentiate of the Church of Scotland. 'He was a man of fiery Celtic temper, and as we are told... he was only too free in his use of the tawse.'[14] The tawse was 'a long, thick strap of horse-hide, prepared by steeping in brine, black and supple with constant use, and cut into fingers at one end,'[15] which had been hardened in the fire.

Colin Stewart subjected his charges to the most astonishing brutality. Charles Francis MacDonald, George MacDonald's elder brother, re-membered that 'I have been more than once carried out of the school in a dead faint from his thrashings with the tawse and then I was under nine years of age.'[16] Once Stewart imprisoned nineteen boys for failing to learn their Shorter Catechism and forgot to come back for them — so they let themselves out by escaping through the classroom window. On the following Monday he flogged them all till the strap was covered with blood — so covered that he had to send little James Spence out to wash it. This man's cruelty was so intense that the children blamed him for the death of James MacDonald, one of the two brothers of George who died young, when he was only eight.

A typical school day would begin with prayer:

'The boys were still as death while the master prayed; but a spectator might easily have discovered that the chief good some of them got from the ceremony, was a perfect command of the organs of sound; for the restraint was limited to those organs; and projected tongues, deprived of their natural exercise, turned themselves, along with winking eyes, contorted features, and a wild use of hands and arms, into the means of telegraphic despatches to all parts of the room, throughout the ceremony.'[17]

Then there would be some kind of religious instruction before the master set the children the more academic tasks for the day. There was a break for lunch in the middle of the day from one till three and then the drudge continued until five:

'At five the school was dismissed for the day, not without another extempore prayer. A succession of jubilant shouts arose as the boys rushed out into the lane. Every day to them was a cycle of strife, suffering and deliverance.'[18]

Luckily for these schoolchildren, Colin Stewart left Scotland in 1835 when MacDonald was ten and emigrated to Australia. When Charles Francis MacDonald, George MacDonald's older brother, went on a visit to Sydney in 1857, the first face he met was that of his old schoolteacher. The man's immediate question was: 'And are the boys of Huntly always attending to their Shorter Catechism?'[19]

Stewart's replacement was a man of a different sort. Alexander Millar, aged twenty, a native of Huntly and a recent graduate, was a man of compassion and learning.[20] The 'energetic young teacher' who fostered in Ranald Bannerman a love for English literature, 'especially poetry', was undoubtedly modelled on him. Under Millar's humane regime, George began to make good progress, and, recognizing the boy's talent, Millar took him under his wing. Soon George outshone all the others in his class at expressive reading, and in a certain examination, at the request of one of the examining ministers, the boy read aloud a metrical composition of his own, handed in as an essay on 'Patriotism'.[21] Millar gave George help and some responsibility. He was set to teach others, then a fairly common practice as it was the custom that the Dominie, or schoolmaster, would appoint an older or more intelligent pupil to be a monitor to help supervise the other children and do some rudimentary teaching.[22] Mac-Donald's son Greville recounted that:

'Mr Millar would hold a morning class before breakfast and sometimes George, instead of going home, would go with a schoolfellow to his home... Mr Millar would invite him after school to go home with him, and their readings at times filled the hours till the boy must partake of the master's supper — potatoes and milk, oatcakes and butter.'[23]

After school fights often began, for 'there was a sort of standing feud between the two schools,' remembered one pupil. 'They were the "rats" and we were the "mice" and sometimes broken windows and broken heads were the result of our skirmishes. Now and then the rats — "rottens" as they were called — charged down the brae upon us, to our complete discomfiture, and we showed the better part of valour by retreating, to renew the fight another day.'[24]

George joined in all these fights just like the other boys, but Greville MacDonald said of his father that:

> 'My father had never been a good thrower — his chest ailments easily accounting for this, I think; and his duties lay chiefly in collecting and bringing into fighting ranks the ammunition. But his spirit soon got him acknowledged as the leader, and the charges at the head of his troop must have been full of "meikle micht."'[25]

'Meikle micht' — 'great strength' — or not, Ranald Bannerman's confession that 'I was ashamed of my own impotence for self defence...' strikes a truer chord, and MacDonald must have appeared to many at his school as sickly and self-absorbed. But the most formative event of his childhood was far removed from his experiences of school — it was the death of his mother when he was only eight. Helen at last succumbed to the tuberculosis that had plagued her so long, leaving only a miniature, a lock of hair, and a few fragments of memory. Time washed over his loss and there is a silence about Helen which is very deep and hard to penetrate. He could not have remembered very much about her:

> 'If I had been able to think of a mother at home, I should have been perfectly happy. Not that I missed her then; I had lost her too young for that. I mean the memory of the time wants but that to render it perfect in bliss.'[26]

He kept the letter his mother had written to Isabella about his weaning until the day he died. In one sense it was all he had left of her — that and a distant memory of her comfort — holding him to her bosom. Poignantly, he wrote of Ranald Bannerman's father:

> 'He rarely fondled us, or did anything in that manner to supply the loss of our mother. I believe his thoughts were tenderness itself towards us, but they did not show themselves in ordinary shape: some connecting link was absent.'[27]

There is a feeling, then, hovering about MacDonald's writing, that he was starved to an extent of love and affection as a boy. Robert Falconer too had 'no recollection of ever having been kissed.'[28]

One of the results of this emotional gap may have been to drive him to seek his own company and lose himself in the world of books. The narrator of *The Portent* writes that 'from my childhood I had rejoiced in being alone. The sense of room about me had been one of my greatest delights.' And then, like MacDonald probably:

'...in the long winter evenings, when I did not happen to have any book that interested me sufficiently, I used even to look forward with expectation to the hour when, laying myself straight upon my back, as if my bed were my coffin, I could call up from underground all who had passed away, and see how they fared, yea what progress they had made towards final dissolution of form.'[29]

This rather morbid, graphic interest in death is probably understandable in a lonely, bookish boy who has tasted death at an early age. Already his mother and one brother were dead, and another brother, James, was soon to die. That left Charles Francis and MacDonald's two younger brothers, Alec and the intelligent and moody John Hill.

The books in which MacDonald immersed himself during his long hours of reading would hardly serve as a diet for children today. He swallowed the heavy religion of Klopstock's *Messiah*, a poem translated from the German, and the gloomy verse of Young's *Night Thoughts*.[30] He knew Milton from an early age and Defoe's *Religious Courtship*, not to mention Boston's *Fourfold State* which was the torment of his life on a Sunday. On Sundays when he went to visit his grandmother to read and pray with her, he may also have read aloud portions of *Pilgrim's Progress*. These religious books were probably the only books allowed in the house, and MacDonald, through the mouth of Ranald Bannerman, reminded his readers that they 'must remember that there were very few books to be had then in that part of the country, and therefore any mode of literature was precious.'[31] And there was the Bible of course. The only children's book which MacDonald recalled reading occurs again in *Ranald Bannerman's Boyhood*:

'I had got the loan of Mrs Trimmer's story of the family of the robins, and was reading it with unspeakable delight. We had very few books for children in those days and in that far-out-of-the-way place, and those we did get were the more dearly prized.'[32]

Sarah Trimmer's book, published in 1818 and consisting of moral fables centred on a family of robins, 'Designed for the Instruction of Children' was enormously popular in its day.

Alexander Millar may have helped broaden George's literary interests while he was still at school, but it was not until later that he had the opportunity of immersing himself in the poets and writers of his day.

With even his reading diet religious in content, it is not surprising that religion rubbed off in many areas of his life. He took his duty seriously. When he was thirteen, his grandmother recorded in her diary for 1837 that:

> 'The Huntly Juvenile Temperance Society was begun by four young persons on Tuesday evening the fourth of December. On that same night the gas was first introduced into Huntly for preventing darkness to the town. The Juvenile Temperance Society was begun for preventing darkness to the mind.'[33]

George was the chairman of this august body and probably remained so until he left the town. Within a fortnight the Society had grown from a membership of four to twenty-two. Their declaration was: 'We agree to abstain from distilled spirits except for medicinal purposes and to discountenance the causes and practice of Distemperance.'[34]

Though duty may have weighed him down, it often gave way to play — kite-flying, holidays, trips to the coast, to Portsoy and the sea-side town of Banff where George's uncle George MacKay and his cousin Helen lived. It was thought that the sea might be beneficial to his health, for illness, as usual, was never far away. The first of George's letters to his father was written from Portsoy when he was nine:

> 'Portsoy 15th August 1833.
>
> My Dear Papa,
>   I return you many thanks for the kind letter I received on Wednesday. I am happy to hear that you are well. I have been unwell for two or three days, my throat was a little sore and my head very painful, but I am quite well now and have been in the sea today and like it very much. When I was down at the bathing I met a boy who was once a fellow of mine at Mr Stewart's school, and he showed me the carcase of a whale which had been cast on the shore. Mrs Morrison told me that the men at the green got a good deal of fat of it... Johnny [MacDonald's younger brother] is very amusing. He seems to be more frightened at the tub than at the sea. We are all quite well. Would you be so good as to come down and stay with us till we go home. Aunt makes me drink the water, but I am unwilling to do it. I am sorry that my writing is so bad, but my pen is very bad.
>   I remain, my dear Papa, your affect. son,
>   George MacDonald.'[35]

Even when not on holiday there was still a lot of freedom to explore the countryside — often on his grey mare 'Missy' whom he loved to ride. Riding was more than just a joy to him, it was a passion, and he was rarely off the horse's back. In 'A Story of the Seashore', for example, he wrote how 'once on a day, my cousin Frank and I' rode out on a horse, and how they:

> 'sought the coast, where deep
> waves foam
> 'Gainst rocks that lift their dark fronts to the north.'

Later in life he slipped a horse into many of his novels, and it is clear that from his earliest boyhood he was seized with a restless, intoxicating sense of adventure.

But these sorties were only respites from study and drudge and as he grew older the business of study grew more and more serious.

One interesting failure of his childhood — an academic one — was his inability to learn Gaelic. This must have caused him some shame as he made so much of his Celtic and Highland lineage. His Gaelic teacher was James MacDonald (no relation), a customs official and the father of John MacDonald, remembered as the most outstanding schoolmaster whom Huntly ever enjoyed. Joseph Dunbar recalled that:

> 'Mr MacDonald was a native of Invernesshire and a good Gaelic scholar. He used to take pleasure in reading Gaelic with students intending to come out for the ministry. One of those who took lessons in Gaelic from him was George MacDonald.'[36]

Later in life MacDonald wrote to his former teacher saying:

> 'If you did not succeed in teaching me Gaelic, it was my fault and my loss. I wish I had had the courage to go on with it. I should be reaping the benefit now. You were most kind to me. I trust all that was good in the feeling of clanship still survives — at least in remembering kindness. . . I can never forget the lessons I had from you in Gaelic. I wish I had continued the study of the language. I might have been the minister of a parish in the Highlands of Scotland.'[37]

Wishful thinking perhaps. Yet this odd failure, odd because MacDonald showed a flair for languages when he applied himself, was the only blot on his academic horizons. His teacher, Alexander Millar, was more than pleased with him, and remembered him as he was in his teenage years:

> 'At 14, George MacDonald was a tall, slight, delicate-looking boy, gentle, amiable and conscientious, and the very ideal of a true

gentleman. His nobility of character was very marked in some incidents of his school life. For example, one day, when in unusually high spirits he carried his fun into lesson hours, so as to distract the attention of all his class fellows. When he was called up to the desk I said, "George, I did not expect this from YOU, who have always been an example of good conduct." That afternoon, when school was being dismissed, he spontaneously came up to me and expressed his deep regret for not upholding his teacher's authority; and ever after, his whole-hearted application to study during lesson hours became an incentive to the others, so that the young teacher was cheered by seeing pupils enter with spirit into their work. George's general deportment was indeed so exemplary as to stamp its character on the school.'[38]

High praise indeed from a teacher. Millar went on to say that:

'Two of the English text-books on which the pupils had to pass weekly examinations were Dr McCulloch's "Series of Lessons" and "Course of Reading", and the answers had all to be given in writing, as weekly specimens of progress in English composition. I recollect being very much struck on one of these occasions by the marked ability evinced in George MacDonald's paper, and saying to him it was superior to many of the specimens of English composition which were appearing from time to time in the popular literature of the day. Forty years afterwards he told me in London, that it was THEN it first occurred to him that the world might possibly hear of him some day.

'Those of his fellow-pupils whose attainments came nearest to his, were always the readiest to acknowledge his decided superiority. In spare hours he might have been seen with a group of his class fellows around him entertaining them with stories of the barbarities which a not unreliable tradition tells us were practised in the dungeon of Huntly Castle.

'But a love of romance did not allure him from the great realities of life. His own heart in the right place, he used his talent of influence with his class fellows to interest them in foreign missions and his glowing words kindled a warm and practical missionary interest in the hearts of many of his school fellows.'[39]

There was, however, more form than conviction to the boy's belief. He squirmed during the long, gloomy judgemental sermons delivered Sunday after Sunday from the pulpit of the Missionar Kirk, and his distaste for the emotionally crippling doctrines of the Calvinism of that time found expression in many of the characters of his later novels — notably in Mrs

Falconer and Murdoch Malison, the schoolteacher in *Alec Forbes of Howglen*.

It is hard nowadays to feel the strain that these Calvinist beliefs inflicted on those who held them. The Missionars believed that Christ had died on the cross only for those who had been elected since before the foundation of the world — a limited number chosen capriciously by God with no reference to merit. The thought that people could have a hand in their own salvation was both presumptuous and abhorrent — God chose some and he simply did not choose others. Believers, therefore, had to examine their lives for some measure of God's grace working in them, and if there was no evidence of this grace then they believed that they were doomed to hell — a real hell filled with eternal fire and torture.

Based no doubt on MacDonald's own experiences, Annie Anderson in *Alec Forbes of Howglen* slips into the Missionar Kirk for the first time to find the following:

> 'The minister was reading, in a solemn voice, a terrible chapter of denunciation out of the prophet Isaiah; and Annie was soon seized with a deep listening awe. After the long prayer, during which they all stood — a posture certainly more reverential than the sitting which so commonly passes for kneeling — and the long psalm, during which they all sat, the sermon began... He chose for his text these words of the Psalmist: "The wicked shall be turned into hell, and all the nations that forget God." His sermon was less ponderous in construction and multitudinous in division than usual; for it simply consisted of answers to the two questions "Who are the wicked?" and "What is their fate?" The answer to the former question was: "The wicked are those that forget God"; the answer to the latter: "The torments of everlasting fire". Upon Annie the sermon produced the immediate conviction that she was one of the wicked, and that she was in danger of hell-fire... when the prayer, the singing and the final benediction were over, Annie crept out into the dark street as if into Outer Darkness.'[40]

This kind of experience left a vivid, indelible impression on the young MacDonald and like Robert Falconer:

> 'He made many frantic efforts to believe that he believed; took to keeping the Sabbath very carefully — that is, by going to church three times, and to Sunday-school as well; by never walking a step save to or from church — talking religiously — reading only religious books...all the time feeling that God was ready to pounce on him if he failed once.'[41]

MacDonald's standard plot of a young, academic boy who writes poetry and grows up to find God in his youth rather than in his boyhood is the pattern which was his own. It is borne out by what he says of himself:

'I have been familiar with the doctrines of the gospel from childhood. I always knew and felt that I ought to be a Christian, and repeatedly began to pray, but as often grew weary and gave it up. The truths of Christianity had no *life* in my soul.'[42]

Yet despite his weariness with the practices of religion, there was a restlessness about him. Like Robert Falconer his 'pondering fits grew in frequency and intensity' and probably too, like Robert:

'Little did Robert think that such was his need — that his soul was searching after One whose form was constantly presented to him, but as constantly obscured and made unlovely by the words without knowledge spoken in the religious assemblies of the land; that he was longing without knowing it on the Saturday for that from which on the Sunday he would be repelled without knowing it. Years passed before he drew nigh to the knowledge of what he sought.'[43]

He was already composing poetry, writing out his thoughts into verses to alleviate his discomfort, and thoughts of escape, too, filled his head. In a letter from his father to Thomas Ross the surgeon, dated 28 June 1839, George senior wrote:

'George is still at school but must leave soon. He is a boy of very superior talents, but he has taken a strange notion of going to sea. One of his uncles who has been for years at Sydney has expressed a wish that one of them should go thither and George would be willing to go if I would allow him but Charles hates the thought of leaving home.'[44]

Perhaps it was this uncle's prompting that caused George to write to his father that:

'It is now time for me to be thinking of what I should betake myself to, and tho' I would be sorry to displease you in any way, yet I must tell you that the sea is my delight and that I wish to go to it as soon as possible, and I hope that you will not use your paternal authority to prevent me, as you undoubtedly can. I feel I would be continually wishing and longing to be at sea. Though a dangerous, it is undoubtedly an honest and lawful employment, or I would scorn to be engaged in it. Whatever other things I may have intended were in my childhood days, so that you can hardly blame me for being flighty in this respect. O let me, dear father, for I could not be happy at anything else. And I am not altogether ignorant of sea affairs, tho' I have yet a great deal to learn, for I have been studying them for some time back. If it were not for putting you to too much trouble, I would beg an answer from you in writing, but I can hardly expect it, though I much wish it.

Your affectionate son
George.[45]

His health was such that any desire to be a sailor could never have been anything more than a pipe-dream. Certainly his efforts to ensure for himself a career at sea proceeded no further than this and the matter was quietly dropped. Besides, the MacDonald family had other things to think about. George senior was about to marry again — to Margaret McColl — and this event must have changed life at The Farm considerably. The marriage took place in November 1839, a month before George's fifteenth birthday. Margaret was a kind woman and a good second mother to the boys. She '...used to say that one of the first things that struck her in her new home was the fine manners and courtesy of all the boys. If one of their elders rose to leave the room, either George or Alec would always be beforehand to open the door. She could not drop a thimble or a ball of wool but it was instantly picked up for her. They were never allowed to speak broad Scotch at table or before their elders, though among themselves and social inferiors they would lapse into the vernacular.'[46]

Yet all this time the question of George's future must have been hanging in the air. Even at fourteen or fifteen boys were sent away to college, and for a boy of MacDonald's marked academic ability that was the obvious place for him to go. In MacDonald's largely autobiographical *Robert Falconer*, Mr Innes (the schoolteacher based on Alexander Millar) 'expressed a high opinion of the boy's faculties and attainments and strongly urged that he should be sent to college.'[47] Education was cheaper in Scotland and more readily available than it was in England. The brighter boys entered for the Bursary competition, and there were various awards to cover fees, fees and expenses, or simply part of the cost. Greville MacDonald wrote that: 'If a lad intended to enter for the Bursary Competition in Aberdeen, he would be sent to a grammar school for a few months to be coached, in Latin particularly.'[48] But the question was when. In *Robert Falconer* Mrs Falconer wishes to enter Robert at once for the competition, 'But the latter [Mr Innes] persuaded her that if the boy gave his whole attention to Latin till the next summer and then went to the grammar-school for three months or so, he would have an excellent chance of success.'[49] And so it was that MacDonald found himself in the position where 'He now wrote a version or translations from English into Latin five times a week and read Caesar, Virgil or Tacitus every day.'[50]

This learning continued week in and week out until MacDonald's head was stuffed with the required knowledge and then, one bright August day, 'Just as the sun rushed across the horizon he heard the tramp of a heavy horse in the yard, passing from the stable to the cart that was to carry his trunk to the turnpike road, three miles off, where the coach would pass'[51] and MacDonald found himself perched on top of the mail coach bearing him away to the great city of Aberdeen.

CHAPTER FOUR

The Crown of Stone

Aberdeen, the capital of the north-east of Scotland, is a graceful, granite city filled with the sound and smell of the sea. MacDonald arrived there aged fifteen, full of hopes of becoming a student, and lodged, like Robert Falconer, 'in a small house of two floors and a garret' at the top of the Spital Brae. He would have followed the custom of the time and taken with him a box full of provisions to see him through his months of study: 'At the top lay a linen bag full of oatmeal; underneath that was a thick layer of oatcake; underneath that two cheeses, a pound of butter and six pots of jam.'[1]

The Aulton (Old Town) Grammar School was a low, one-floored building with a long history dating back to 1256. One of its pupils, Alexander Whyte, wrote that: 'It was a small square house as plain and unclassical as possible, with benches like a church and a little desk in a corner, the place altogether capable of holding forty or fifty students.'[2]

Schoolwork began in earnest the moment MacDonald arrived:

'If the School work was dry it was thorough. If that Academy had no sweetly shadowing trees, beyond still was the sea and the sky; and that court, morning and afternoon, was filled with the shouts of eager boys kicking the football with mad rushings to and fro, and sometimes with wounds and faintings...'[3]

The long exercises were punctuated with play or solitary walks by the sea. He

'...would rush into the thick of the football game, fight like a maniac for one short burst, and then retire and look on... But sometimes, looking up from his Virgil or his Latin version, he would fling down his dictionary or his pen, and fly in a straight line, like a seagull weary of lake and river, down to the waste shore of the great deep.'[4]

Finally, after three months of hard studying, the great day came. Each student sitting the bursary 'was allowed a copy of Ainsworth's Dictionary — nothing else'. There is a vivid description of this exam in *Robert Falconer*:

'But when the sacrist appeared and unlocked the public school, and the black-gowned professors walked into the room, and the door was left open for the candidates to follow, then indeed a great awe fell upon the assembly, and the lads crept into their seats as if to a trial for life before a bench of the incorruptible. They took their places; a portion of Robertson's *History of Scotland* was given to them to turn into Latin; and soon there was nothing to be heard in the assembly but the turning of leaves of dictionaries, and the scratching of pens constructing the first copy of the Latinized theme. It was done — four weary hours, nearly five, one or two of which passed like minutes, the others as if each minute had been an hour, went by, and Robert in a kind of desperation, after a final reading of the Latin, gave in his paper and left the room.'[5]

As it turned out, MacDonald took twelfth place in the competition, winning the Fullarton Bursary of £14 per annum — enough to cover his fees and expenses for the five months session.[6] The results were announced in *The Aberdeen Herald* on 3 November 1840.

So MacDonald was a student at last and able to go and take up his studies at King's College in Old Aberdeen. In MacDonald's day Old Aberdeen was still very separate from New Aberdeen having its own corporation, provost[7] and town drummer. King's College, one of the two universities which the city boasted, is an old medieval building with a crown of stone set right in the heart of the old town.

Students entered the universities at a much younger age than they do today. In 1827 the average age was fourteen for King's and twelve for Marischal, the other University in Aberdeen, but by 1857 this had risen to seventeen years and nine months for King's and sixteen years and eight months at Marischal. MacDonald, entering a month before his sixteenth birthday, was therefore no unusual prodigy.

The degree of AM (now MA) lasted for four years, and each university session lasted from November through till the following March. In their first year, students were referred to as 'bajans' (bec jaune), in their second as 'semis', in their third as 'tertians', and in their fourth as 'magistrands'.

Many of the students themselves were poor. The cost of sending a son to university was the same as putting him in a small farm. Some students went as far as to live only on meal, laying out the rest of their money on books. As far as the curriculum went, although Chemistry and Natural

History had been established at King's in 1817, the students still had to plough through a good deal of Latin, Greek and Maths, the classical foundations of any education. For Latin, selections from Horace, Virgil and Cicero were studied, and for Greek, Xenophon, two Gospels and some Homer. In the classics there was a special emphasis on composition, Greek and Roman antiquities and Classical Geography. In Maths Euclid was studied, focussing on Practical Triangulation and levelling. On arrival students were taught the elements of Greek using traditional methods that the students found tedious.

The Greek and Latin classes took place mainly in the first and second sessions. In the third and fourth sessions, attention was switched to Natural History, Natural Philosophy and Moral Philosophy. In the examinations, a third of the marks obtained a pass, and a student who obtained more than a third in the majority of the subjects had a clause added to his diploma and one who did so in all the subjects 'graduated with the highest distinction'.

But student life was not all grind and no diversion:

'On Saturday evening, all work being laid aside, the students generally devoted themselves to amusement. . . [congregating along gas-lit Union Street] many of them were to be found parading in bands, visiting the places of amusement, or seated in certain of the hotels patronised by them.'[8]

MacDonald did not have much time or money for joining in such 'bands' though he showed an exact knowledge of wayward student life in writing about drunkenness and prostitution, and he was more than aware that college was 'a dangerous place for undermining good principles learned at home'.[9]

When MacDonald arrived at King's College, 'the professors,' according to Robert Troup, a friend, 'were rather boring and used to antiquated methods of teaching.' There was, however, one ray of light: 'Only the Professor of Natural Philosophy "Davy" Thomson who had just come fresh and vigorous from Cambridge, was beginning his work of University Reform and laying the foundation of Aberdeen's distinction in mathematics.'[10] The Chemistry class at that time had been flourishing for fifteen years and was the best attended chemical class in Scotland, and the famous William Gregory taught medicine and chemistry there from 1839−44 until he went to Edinburgh. MacDonald plumped for Chemistry, a strange choice perhaps for a future novelist and poet, and not an easy one for him to make. He wrote to his father at the beginning of his second session that 'I am in some doubts whether or not I should study

Chemistry.'[11] If his poetic yearnings were leading him in one direction then common sense and sound economics dictated another. As Mac-Donald wrote later of his hero Cosmo in *Castle Warlock*:

'The one profession he had a leaning to was that of chemistry, at the time receiving much attention in view of the agricultural and manufacturing prospects and offering a sure income to any man borne well in front upon its rising tide.'[12]

These are most likely the reasons why MacDonald chose to study this subject, though it probably did not sit easily on his sensibilities.

The young man was quickly assimilated into the life of the university, wearing the red gown all the students wore then and becoming familiar with the Humanity and Greek classrooms. Much of his time was spent on Latin composition or in solving difficult algebraic equations, but even so he composed verses steadily in his spare time right through the whole of his university career. Solitary in some ways, and coming from the country, he had to learn to mix with the other students:

'Some of the youths were of the lowliest origin — the sons of ploughmen and small country shopkeepers; shock-headed lads, with much of the looks and manners of year-old bullocks, mostly with freckled faces and a certain irresponsiveness of feature, soon to vanish as the mental and nervous motions became more frequent and rapid working the stiff clay of their faces into a readier obedience to the indwelling plasticity.'[13]

But he must have worked hard and done well after his arrival, because after two months of the first year's course, he was passed on to the work of the second year, being both a 'bajan' and a 'semi' in one session.

On the surface, MacDonald appeared both cheerful and orthodox, writing to his father:

'Aberdeen 5th January 1841.
My Dear Father,
    I am much obliged to you for the kind letter which you sent me some time ago. I hope I wish to serve God and to be delivered not only from the punishment of sin, but also from its power. Our potatoes and meal are almost done. Be so good as to send a fresh supply as soon as convenient... Mr Kennedy was at our Sabbath school soirée in the Old Town. He preaches most excellent sermons, and he never closes without saying something to the unconverted.'[14]

MacDonald's tune was soon to change. He still had too many problems which he had not resolved — problems of religion, problems of his future, and problems of his calling. These grew within him while he studied until they could no longer be ignored. Yet these inward questionings were not MacDonald's only concern. The events of the outside world must have impinged on all the students to some extent, and MacDonald took an active interest in all that was going on around him. There was the celebration of Queen Victoria's marriage to Prince Albert in 1840 and, more locally, the founding of the Aberdeen Philosophical Society. The Disruption, when the Church of Scotland split in two, occurred in 1843, and MacDonald could hardly have failed to take keen notice of this. His uncle, MacIntosh MacKay, was one of the leaders of this movement and in Huntly the 'Strathbogie Controversy' caused such a storm that soldiers were sent to maintain ministers in their pulpits. Cobden, one of the founders of the Anti-Corn Law League, visited Aberdeen in 1844 with other free trade speakers and in 1845 progress was such that the London mail was accelerated to reach Aberdeen in forty-four hours. That year also saw the founding of the Aberdeen Temperance Society. And there was Chartism, that swelling movement pressing for parliamentary reform. MacDonald wrote to his father:

'. . . I found all our friends well, and our lodgings very comfortable, although the lad who lodges along with us is not so much of a gentleman as we could wish; yet I hope he will not be any the worse in that respect for lodging with us. I saw a most splendid procession today of the Chartists going out to meet Fergus O'Connor. There were about two thousand of them in the procession, and there might have been fifteen thousand on the streets. The scene was really splendid.'[15]

MacDonald was a curious mixture of show and shyness. One of his contemporaries, William Geddes (later Principal of Aberdeen University) writing to him in 1865 stated:

'Though you did not mix much with the students at college, and, indeed, hardly cared to descend into the ordinary arena of emulation, your fellow students were not unaware of the talents which you possessed. I remember distinctly the universal impression regarding you, that you were master of powers which you had not put to the full measure of proof, but which were "touched to fine issues" and destined to yield great things.'[16]

MacDonald's shyness and withdrawal covered a deep, depressive brooding. He had rejected the aggressive, male God of the Calvinists and was looking for both a resolution and a meaning to the emptiness that was left within him. In *Weighed and Wanting* he wrote:

> 'I well remember feeling as a child that I did not care for God to love me if he did not love everybody: the kind of love I needed was the love that all men needed, the love that belonged to their nature as the children of the father, a love he could not give me except he gave it to all men.'[17]

MacDonald's outward studies became almost a veneer, hiding the inner shifts he was desperately trying to cope with:

> 'My books long days untouched have lain;
> The lecture hour is slow;
> For other thoughts go through my brain,
> Than those gowned bosoms know.'[18]

He did not know where his thoughts were going to lead him, and he worried that the study of science would damage his ability to write poetry. He did not know where to turn:

> '[The student's] intellect is seized and possessed by a new spirit. For a time knowledge is pride; the mere consciousness of knowing is the reward of its labour; the ever passing contact of mind with a new fact is a joy full of excitement, and promises an endless delight. But ever the thing that is known sinks into insignificance, save as a step on the endless stair on which he is climbing — whither he knows not; the *unknown* draws him; the new fact touches his mind, flames up in the contact, and drops back, a mere fact, on the heap below... The youth gazes on the fact of Science, cold, clear, beautiful; then, turning, looks for his friend — but alas! Poetry has fled.'[19]

This sense of abandonment grew worse before it grew better, but at odds with MacDonald's gloomy, reflective spirits there was a playfulness about him which the other students found either attractive or irritating. Geddes remembered that MacDonald 'was known as a youth of imaginative power, but like the typical Celt, dreamily careless of fame and class list positions. He was only two years senior in my classes and I remember the radiance of the tartan coat he wore — the most dazzling affair in dress I ever saw a student wear, but characteristic of the young Celtic Minstrel.'[20]

The lad who excelled at school at expressive reading could still make an impression if he wanted to. His love of finery was obviously a feature of

The Crown of Stone 47

his student days; and it remained with him for the rest of his life. Robert Troup recalled seeing him for the first time:

'I was in a room in College Bounds when a Magistrand who was at the window called out "Come and see that vain fellow George MacDonald going down the street in his fine velvet coat." I went to the window and saw a handsome young man walking pretty smartly, but with no appearance of vanity.'[21]

Greville MacDonald recounted that:

'Some years ago Mr John Christie, the archaeologist . . . wrote me that the student George MacDonald used often to visit Mr Christie's grandfather's house, and that his mother described the lad on one occasion as taking part in charades; how they rummaged out an old bottle-green coat for him; and how, it being buttonless, he cut a huge carrot into discs and sewed them on the coat — the effect being prodigious.'[22]

This almost childish love of dressing up extended to a fondness for jewels and other glittering things and caused one of his sons later to write about him that 'he was the gentlest, but the most persistent of the Dandies I have known.'[23]

The first session at university must have ended all too soon, and it was time to return to Huntly, changed a little and more distant from the familiar surroundings of his childhood. During the summer months students had two options open to them: either they worked on the land, and this MacDonald, owing to his delicate health, was unable to do, or else they tutored — usually for a richer family. Many of the students had to walk home — taking days to cover long distances through bad weather and poor conditions. Perhaps MacDonald with one or two others 'set out' like Robert Falconer and Eric Ericson in *Robert Falconer* 'on their journey of forty miles, with half a loaf in their pockets, and money enough to get bread and cheese, and a bottle of ale, at the far-parted roadside inns.' And no doubt when the young student arrived, 'it was time for supper and *worship*. These were the same as old: a plate of porridge, and a wooden bowl of milk for the former; a chapter and a hymn both read, and a prayer . . .'

Back in Huntly:

'He had fits of wandering, though . . . revelled in the glories of summer once more; went out to tea or supped with the schoolmaster; and, except going to church on Sunday, which was a weariness to every inch of flesh upon his bones, enjoyed everything.'[24]

Probably Alexander Millar helped him prepare for his studies in the second session. The year must have turned quickly enough and the student soon found himself back in the city and back at his books. He was, according to Troup, 'studious, quiet, sensitive, imaginative, frank, open, speaking freely what he thought. His love of truth was intense . . .'[25] He spent much of his spare time reading different writers.

By the end of MacDonald's second session it was clear that his family in Huntly were in financial straits. Smallholders were under severe economic pressure from which they never recovered and there was simply not enough money to pay for MacDonald's studies from 1842–43.[26] On top of that Charles MacDonald's debt still pressed heavily down on George senior and James at The Farm. Therefore, according to Robert Troup:

'After the second session he spent a year in a nobleman's mansion in the far north of Scotland perhaps doing tutorial work but chiefly, I think, in arranging and cataloguing the library.'[27]

This short period of MacDonald's life is tinged with mystery. Even his own son Greville was not able to discover where this 'nobleman's mansion' was or exactly how his father spent these months away from home and university. It is likely, however, that the place was Thurso Castle, the property of Sir George Sinclair, who had inherited it from his father, Sir John Sinclair, in 1835. Sir John Sinclair, the first President of the Board of Agriculture, had a link with the MacDonalds as his name appeared on an advertisement recommending the potato flour or 'Farina' which the MacDonalds manufactured for a time. Sir George Sinclair was a German scholar, having studied at Göttingen, and was well versed in ancient and modern languages. His library held a feast for MacDonald to gorge on.[28]

What must the young man have felt approaching Thurso Castle for the first time? He wrote in *Wilfrid Cumbermede:*

'When I reached the top and emerged from the trees that skirted the ridge, there stood the lordly hall before me, shining in autumnal sunlight, with gilded vanes and diamond-paned windows, as if it were a rock against which the gentle waves of the sea of light rippled and broke in flashes. When you looked at its foundation, which seemed to have torn its way up the climbing sward, you could not tell where the building began and the rock ended. In some parts indeed the rock was wrought into the walls of the house; while in places it was faced up with stone and mortar. My heart beat high with vague rejoicing.'[29]

In *The Portent* the hero, Duncan Campbell, is 'almost nineteen' (Mac-Donald's age at this time) and has two boys aged ten and twelve offered as pupils.[30] MacDonald described in close detail the library of the house — certainly almost exactly the library which he had to catalogue:

'Now I was in my element. I had never been by any means a bookworm but the very outside of a book had a charm to me. It was a kind of sacrament — an outward and visible sign of an inward and spiritual grace; as indeed, what on God's earth is not? So I set to work amongst the books, and soon became familiar with many titles at least, which had been perfectly unknown to me before. I found a perfect set of our poets — perfect according to the notion of the editor and the issue of the publisher, although it omitted both Chaucer and George Herbert. I began to nibble at that portion of the collection which belonged to the sixteenth century; but with little success. I found nothing, to my idea, but love poems without any love in them, and so I soon became weary. But I found in the library what I liked far better — many romances of a very marvellous sort, and plentiful interruption they gave to the formation of the catalogue. I likewise came across a whole nest of German classics, which seemed to have kept their places undisturbed, in virtue of their unintelligibility — I found in these volumes a mine of wealth inexhaustive.'[31]

This library introduced MacDonald to all that was to mark him and his writing for the rest of his life: romance, the sixteenth-century divines, romantic poetry and German literature. Here he could indulge his taste for modern literature and languages away from the classical and scientific restraints of the university. Perhaps it was at Thurso, using the recipe of a New Testament and a grammar, that he set himself to master the German language, doing so at a time when German was not a popular language for study. Through this language he was introduced to the strange, yearning, mystic writings of Novalis and the magic of Hoffmann. Beyond them he reached to the mystical writings of Swedenborg and Jacob Boehme. The writers he found in the library were the writers who were able to offer MacDonald the key to constructing a theology he could live with and submit to — introducing him to a God who expressed love and not judgement and whose character was to be seen in the workings of nature.

And perhaps he was able to indulge this love of nature at Thurso with lonely walks by the sea.

The image of the library is one that haunts MacDonald's fiction constantly, appearing in *David Elginbrod, Wilfrid Cumbermede, Phantastes, There and Back*, and especially in *Lilith*. In *Lilith* the library is a mysterious, mystical place, the beginning of adventure — and MacDonald, opening up his mind to new thoughts and ideas in the library at Thurso must have similarly felt at the beginning of a spiritual adventure.

After leaving Thurso MacDonald returned to Aberdeen where he taught arithmetic at the Aberdeen Central Academy from February to November 1843 'with great spirit and skill' in the words of Mr Thomas Merton, the school's headmaster, and he also managed to secure some private pupils.[32] Back in the swing of Aberdeen life he was 'an ardent if nervous speaker in the Debating Society', but his mind was still shifting and changing.

MacDonald's struggle with himself was a long one. Troup recalled that:

> 'On Sunday we went to Blackfriars Street Church, where the sermons were morning and afternoon, and between the services we often dined with him [MacDonald] and his brother [Charles Francis] as they lived not far from the church. At that time he was, I think, in spiritual difficulty caused by the doctrine of everlasting punishment and generally by the Calvinist teaching then all but universal in Scotland — sat by himself after the meal was over — silent and thoughtful and sometimes reading while others talked. His elder friends were anxious about his spiritual state. They knew he was all right morally, but...'[33]

On one level MacDonald's doctrinal concerns were shared by many of the young men round about him. On another level he was suffering much more profoundly than they knew. The church he attended, Blackfriars Church, was a place where there was much to admire and much to reject. The church itself had resulted from a secession from George Street Church and its first minister was James Spence, an uncle of MacDonald's, who had preached and ministered there for fifteen years.[34] After Spence's departure for the Isle of Wight, the congregation chose a young man of twenty-two, John Kennedy MA, the son of an independent minister of Inverness, to be their new pastor. He began his ministry on New Year's Day 1836 and soon this 'blue-eyed, rosy-cheeked young man' made his presence felt in the city. He was able, intelligent and gifted, drawing a growing congregation — especially from among young people and students. Both George MacDonald and his brother Charles attended there along with Robert Troup and Robert Spence and several other students who were all to become distinguished in their own way. On one hand Kennedy was a strict man and his pronounced Calvinism was evident 'in the discipline which he encouraged his office-bearers to exercise over the congregation: sinners were "excommunicated" with little chance for repentance; their sins or rather the fact that they had sinned seemed to indicate that they did not after all belong to the elect. He was also a keen advocate of Temperance.'[35]

But there was more to Kennedy than this. He was an active organizer and campaigner. As many as eight hundred children attended the two Sunday schools which were connected with the church, and in these schools MacDonald, Troup and Spence participated. Kennedy was active in speaking out for the emancipation of the negroes, against the Corn Laws, and in favour of the foreign Bible Society. He was a keen temperance reformer and 'one of Sheriff Watson's best and most unfailing helpers in his Ragged School work.'[36] It was through this man Kennedy that MacDonald had his first taste of social work and his first sight of the poverty and squalor of a big city. Perhaps it was as he worked with Kennedy that his concern for the poor grew and the realization came slowly that help had to come mainly through individuals and not through societies — and that these individuals had to offer practical help rather than pious words. This concern for the poor was one that stayed with MacDonald, though he himself rejected the idea of devoting himself to social causes. As it was, MacDonald knew Kennedy well. He coached a young man called John Park at Kennedy's house three times a week, and was active in the Sunday School as a teacher. Trouble loomed, however, when the Morisonian controversy broke in 1844.

James Morison of Bathgate, son of the Rev. Robert Morison, minister of the Secession Church of that same place, had become a minister and gone to the Cabrach, an area near Huntly, where a revival had taken place. While reading the first letter to the Corinthians Chapter 15, verses 3 and 4, Morison saw that Christ had died for *all* men and not just for the elect. Morison moved to Clerk's Lane Secession Church in Kilmarnock where he was soon summoned before the local Seceders Presbytery and asked to recant his unorthodox views. He refused and appealed to the Synod. His case aroused a good deal of publicity and one newspaper went as far as to say that 'a more important cause was never before tried in Scotland'. Morison was thrown out of the Church with his father and two others in 1843 — though their churches continued to flourish.

At a meeting in Kilmarnock on 16 May 1843, they formed the Evangelical Union which moved away from the Presbyterial idea of Church government and was not meant to be a denomination, sect or separate church. Kennedy felt that the truth was under fire and resolved in his own energetic way to protect his flock against Morison's heresy. He criticized the new movement vehemently from the pulpit — but found that its influence had taken deep root in his own ranks — notably on MacDonald, Spence and Troup. It was known that:

> 'These students had been carrying on a Sunday-school in the Town Hall in Old Aberdeen, where they gave active assistance in teaching during University Sessions. Those suspected of Morisonian leanings were first summoned to a friendly conference with the minister and the deacons, and when this proved ineffective, their services in the Sunday School were peremptorilydispensed with, and other teachers appointed to take their places. Thus ended MacDonald's experience in Sunday school teaching at this stage in his career.'[37]

Kennedy's moves backfired on him, however, and the school soon dwindled away to nothing. Other churches in the city, notably the Congregational churches at Blackhills, Skene and Printfield resolved to join the Evangelical Union, and their congregations grew, perhaps soaking up a number of the disaffected from Blackfriars. It is characteristic of MacDonald that although he did not approve of the doctrine, he stuck with the man. He continued at Blackfriars and went on corresponding with Kennedy even after he had left university.[38]

MacDonald's strange moods sometimes led him to display extreme behaviour. He wrote of Robert Falconer that: 'Often he would sink moaning on the floor, or stretch himself like a corpse, save that it was face downwards on the board of the bedstead. Night after night he returned to the battle, but with no permanent *success*. What a success that would have been!' But his own recorded behaviour is even stranger, even if Robert Falconer's actions are most likely a fair representation of MacDonald's own.

> 'One friend of his in the last two years of college was J. Maconachie, afterwards Rev. J. Maconachie of Dumrief who lived with his sister Mrs. J. Clark. MacDonald visited there a lot and felt at home with them. He hated the black Tom Cat, however and always said to Mrs Clark's daughter who opened the door to him, "Now Jessie, is the cat in the room? If so, please take him away before I come in."
>
> Mr Maconachie was an excellent singer and George enjoyed his music, favouring "Highland Mary". The two friends lived apart and could scarcely have walked together. But one wild stormy night Mr MacDonald called on Mr Maconachie about ten and invited him to go out for a walk with him on the links and the seashore. When Maconachie came back to his sister's at midnight he looked disturbed

and anxious and said, "I hope George MacDonald is not going out of his mind."

"What makes you suppose such a thing?"

"Well, when he got to the shore he walked backwards and forwards on the sands amid the howling wind and spray and with the waves coming up to our feet and all the time went out addressing the sea and the waves in the most extraordinary manner. I was really frightened at him."

"Oh," said Mrs Clark, "you are not to be afraid for George MacDonald. You know the saying, Genius and insanity are of a kind." '[39]

He was very depressed, maybe even close to the edge of a nervous breakdown. One of his few solaces was his relationship with Helen MacKay, his pretty cousin from Banff. Many of the verses he wrote while still at university were dedicated to her and copied into a book along with *The Rime of the Ancient Mariner*, portions of Shelley's *Wandering Jew* and extracts from other lesser poets. Helen remembered that 'he wrote many beautiful little things'. He was not sure what to do or what he was to become and she said that 'I was able to help him when he was puzzled and undecided as to what life was fit for'.

MacDonald's friendship with her was closer than just that of a cousin; there was some romantic attachment there, and it was to Helen that he confided many of his inmost thoughts. The resolution of this depression and uncertainty came slowly. His was no sudden and glorious conversion to a new form of faith:

'And for a long time I did not seem to make any progress, though my more intimate friends perceived a change in me. By and by I became more in earnest... But I could feel little or no abiding joy in religion. I looked to myself and not to the atonement. All I had been taught in my youth I required to learn over again. In my distress I could only cry to God to help me, and often in the midst of it felt assured he helped me. I set myself in some measure to do what was right. I began to see some of the beauty of religion, some of the grandness of the Truth. I read my bible and continued amidst much that was evil in thought and behaviour to cry to God. My unhappiness compelled me to it. The Truth has been slowly dawning upon me. I have seen I trust that Jesus is my Saviour though this has had little of the effect it ought to have upon me. I know I shall never be happy until my whole soul is *filled* with love to him, which is only a reasonable thing. I hope I am a Christian partly because in some degree I try to do the will of my Lord and Master. I wish to be delivered from myself. I wish to be made holy. My life is in God.'[40]

Yet though he had resolved his spiritual difficulties to some degree by the end of his time at university, he was no nearer to shaping a future for himself in any career. He confessed to his cousin Helen that he would like to become a doctor, but in 1845, when the potato famine held the country in its grip and the family business was about to shut down, there was no hope of any money to enable him to do this. He thought too of going to Giessen in Germany to continue his study of Chemistry under Von Liebig, but again lack of finance meant that MacDonald's hopes were thwarted.[41] There seemed no other course open for the present, but teaching.

He took third prize in Chemistry, came fourth in Natural Philosophy and in Moral Philosophy was seventeenth — a distinguished, though not a brilliant, performance — and on 29 March 1845 *The Aberdeen Herald* published among twenty-six candidates for the MA degree the name of George MacDonald.

CHAPTER FIVE

London

After graduating, MacDonald returned home to The Farm, to the squabble of relatives and the humdrum routine, and there, under his father's stern eye, began to ponder his future. Charles Francis, his elder brother, was already safely settled in business and now it was MacDonald's turn to choose a career. He talked at length to his father who tried to nudge him into the ministry, but as yet he was too undecided to plump for anything so definite.

In April he wrote to William Gregory,[1] his former Chemistry teacher at Aberdeen who had made a recent move to the University of Edinburgh, asking if there was any chance of a post as an assistant with him. Although Gregory was encouraging in his reply, he had to refuse because MacDonald did not possess the required qualifications. He suggested that MacDonald come to Edinburgh to pursue his studies, but the amount of money involved, meagre though it was, proved too much. Perhaps this was also an excuse. Although he was interested in Chemistry, MacDonald's passion was for poetry and literature, not for science. Poetry was not a realistic option. He had to *do* something.

Consequently, under pressure to make his own way, as his family could not support him, he went to London, following the flood of people who were moving from the land to increase the already overcrowded towns. In those days, steamer was the way to travel to London and as the boat made south from Aberdeen, ploughing through the thick swell of the sea, MacDonald's head was no doubt heavy with thoughts — of a new faith newly awakened, but not as yet certain, a faith that burdened him with the self-searching zeal of the newly-converted and pointed him towards a future that was in all honesty a blank. Behind him he was leaving all that he had known: Scotland, his friends, family, memories — and debts.

When the boat docked in London MacDonald found himself in a city of over three million people. It was a city blessed by the prosperity brought through expansion and industrial change and yet scarred by its slums and social injustices. Taking his first hesitant steps along its hurried streets, MacDonald found 'the universal roar'[2] deafening and hard to accustom himself to. He had for so long been used only to the sound of the sea and the wind on the hills. 'Fog and drizzle, and smoke, and stench composed the atmosphere'[3] — an unhealthy mixture for a delicate pair of lungs, and he found to his disgust that wherever he went he had 'to wade through deep mud even on the pavements'.[4] Short of cash and yet curious by nature, it is not hard to believe, like Robert Falconer, that he:

'...took to wandering about the labyrinthine city and in a couple of months knew more about the metropolis — the west end excepted — than most people who had lived their lives in it.'[5]

Though he was poor and without an income there was, nevertheless, a freedom in his situation which he enjoyed:

'He always carried a book in his pocket, but did not read much. On Sundays he generally went to some one of the many lonely heaths or commons of Surrey with his New Testament. When weary in London, he would go to the reading-room of the British Museum for an hour or two.'[6]

In fact, he spent a great deal of time reading his Bible and it was during this period of isolation that he worked out what he really believed in Christianity, trying to separate the wheat from the chaff with the might of his intellectual and spiritual muscle. He wrote to his father:

'I love my bible more. I am always finding out something new in it. I seem to have had everything to learn over again from the beginning — All my teaching in youth seems useless to me — I must get it all from the bible again.'[7]

But though he was inwardly isolated, he was not alone. There was church, for one thing. MacDonald began attending the fashionable Trevor Chapel in Brompton where the minister was Dr John Morison DD.[8] This man was an old friend of MacDonald's father, a kindly Scot who had once been apprenticed as a watchmaker in Banff. He took a warm interest in MacDonald and it was through his efforts that Mac-Donald secured his first post, a tutorship with the Radermacher family who were members of his church, and who lived at Park Cottage, Fulham. Though this job provided enough to live on, there was no excess, and MacDonald had to write dejectedly to his father at the end of the year that:

'I am sorry I am not yet able to send you any money — as my
Aberdeen accounts are rather heavy, and I shall not be able to settle
them quite this term. I may be able to send you some next time.'[9]

Knowing that his father thought little of his abilities in the realm of
household management, MacDonald was often at pains to impress on
George senior the tremendous cost of living in London compared with
the north-east of Scotland: 'You have no idea what it is to live in
London. I have paid £7 for boots and shoes since I came, and not a pair
but you would say is worn to the last.'[10] And so he had constantly to rely
on handouts from home. Meal, butter and sometimes even cakes were
despatched by steamer from Scotland and waited at the docks to be
collected.

As well as not bringing in much money, MacDonald's new duties did
not bring him much joy. He had to teach three boys the usual rudiments
of arithmetic and grammar, but the experience was wearing on his nerves
and far from rewarding.

He had to take them to the Trevor Chapel twice on a Sunday as well as
teach them and this he resented bitterly as it ate into what he saw as his
free time. There were two little girls in the family as well, and though
MacDonald could cope with their ignorance, shocked as he was at it, he
found their unruly behaviour very difficult to deal with:

'The worst bother is ill-brought up and noisy children — especially the
younger ones who scream frightfully.'[11]

But despite all these problems the Radermachers were kind, if not overly
generous, and MacDonald was grateful enough for the employment
which he had secured only by a thread.

There can be no doubt though, that MacDonald deeply detested this
work. The portrait of Hugh Sutherland in *David Elginbrod* who suffers
at the hands of the grasping Appleditches is a conflation of several
experiences in MacDonald's life, but the humiliation Hugh feels in
bending his talent to the employ of unworthy people is something
MacDonald felt profoundly at this period:

'They [the children] scorned the man whom their mother despised and
valued for the self-same reason, namely, that he was cheap.'[12]

Cosmo, the hero of *Castle Warlock*, has a similar tale to tell and is even
cheated out of his money. In reality the Radermachers were no such
caricatures. MacDonald even asked his father to send some oatmeal to
them, and occasionally Mr Radermacher would lend MacDonald money
if he needed it for a special occasion.

MacDonald made the commitment of being proposed as a member of Morison's church in November 1845, soon after his arrival in the capital. For him it was a big step to take and slowly he began to take a part in the life of the Brompton Congregation. He felt welcome and at home with the Morisons and was glad when they invited him to share in their Christmas dinner. This was a garrulous, clannish gathering of Scots with only 'one pure-blooded Englishwoman' seated at the table out of fifteen. But while MacDonald warmed to Morison as a man, he found difficulties in liking him as a preacher. Morison's method of singling out individuals for reproof during the sermon was the kind of conduct MacDonald found hard to accept and the sermons themselves fell short of what MacDonald wanted to hear. The young man found Morison a valuable though 'far from an intellectual preacher' and there were still many theological questions to be answered. He could admit to his father, 'I am a Christian, though one of the weakest', but he went on to confess:

'My greatest difficulty always is "How do I know that my faith is of a lasting kind such as will produce fruits?" I am ever so forgetful to pray or read God's word... But I trust that if God has led me to Christ he will keep me there. My mind is often very confused. I have made more progress — much since I began to pray more earnestly for the Spirit of God to guide me. Pray that I may not be that hateful thing, a lukewarm Christian.'[13]

It was to be a long time before this heaviness of attitude towards Christian commitment was dispelled. He was caught, wriggling on the jargon of the time, finding his nature at odds with the Calvinist God's judgemental frown. He wrote guiltily to his father:

'I have smoked a good deal since I came to London tho' not much lately. So I promise you never in this world to smoke again. I am equally bound by a promise as to snuff — so no more tobacco for me — Joy go with it.'[14]

There was more, however, to MacDonald's life in London than earnest introspection. He had an active social round. Apart from the Morisons and the Radermachers there was someone much closer to him already living in London — his beloved cousin Helen MacKay. She had come to the capital to attend finishing school in 1840 when MacDonald had set out for King's in Aberdeen, and in 1844 had been married to Alex Powell. She and MacDonald had naturally kept in touch, through letters and through Helen's occasional visits to Aberdeenshire,[15] but MacDonald's arrival in London must have set their relationship back on a more intimate footing and he was received often into their house in Stamford Grove, Upper Clapton. Through Helen and Alex it was inevitable that he should become acquainted with Alex's father and mother — James and Phoebe Powell — and their large family, who lived nearby in a house called The Limes in Clapton. The Powells loved entertaining and often had musical and theatrical evenings. James Powell was a prosperous leather merchant whose first wife had died leaving only one son. His second wife — Phoebe Sharman — was his first wife's cousin, and she bore him twelve children, four of whom died in infancy. This large number of children had left Phoebe Powell's health impaired and she was rather weak and frail. Consequently, responsibility for maintaining and running the household fell on her six daughters, especially on the eldest, Charlotte, whose singing voice outmatched her sisters' and whose boundless energy was spent in helping run such august institutions as the Society for Converting Roman Catholics.[16]

The Limes was an old Georgian house 'with good stabling and a three-acre garden'[17] and the bustling household was a mixture of liveliness and careful propriety.

The Powell family as a whole were fond of charades, and piano music too was often to be heard spilling out of the windows of their home. They were also Congregationalists — narrow in doctrine and pious in temperament — friendly, but genteel and shockable. Helen MacKay had already made her mark on the family with her more daring and free-thinking ways, causing wariness and astonishment, but when she introduced her cousin George to the company the gasps became audible. For MacDonald, even at his poorest and most depressive, was quite unlike the other young men who frequented the house. He had keen, eagle eyes and long hair. He sat and read poetry to the young ladies — Wordsworth and Tennyson and Browning's *Saul* and even his own, but he did not read as an amusement or a diversion.[18] Poetry was for him a serious business, as serious as religion itself. For the young Powell girls, who had been raised to believe that books were a mere leisurely stopgap to pass the time while their male counterparts carried on with the business of running the world, MacDonald's powerful recitation must have seemed awesome and enchanting. And not only did the young man read poetry in that declamatory Scots voice of his, fixing them with his dark northern looks and encouraging them to feel inspired by the words — he also looked like a poet — a romantic poet — ought to be. He had not yet grown a beard, for in the eyes of his pious associates this sign of affinity with the animal kingdom would have been going too far, but he entertained the family, and intrigued them, and taught them.[19]

One of the Powell sisters, Angela, was regarded as a bit simple by the rest of the family, and owing to her childish spelling was relegated to needlework. She later remembered that:

> 'He showed me new life in everything, understood me as an equal. This was very wonderful to me, as all my life I had been the fool of the family for my inability to spell and commit to memory. Great was my astonishment when he wished me to learn mathematics and began himself to teach me.'[20]

This was like a scene straight out of one of MacDonald's own novels, similar to the lessons between Hugh Sutherland and Euphrasia Cameron in *David Elginbrod* or Donal Grant and Lady Arctura in *Donal Grant* — for algebra is usually an essential ingredient in any MacDonald romance. This urge to teach and to teach woman was not just MacDonald the tutor displaying his skills in his spare time: it was part of his romantic ideal to elevate woman out of the drawing-room to stand beside man as an equal co-partner under God. In a letter he later wrote to Louisa Powell he said:

> 'I am much more disappointed in the news of George Searle's engagement. How could he do it? I hope he may not repent it. Just fancy — if she be as orthodox as her father! However perhaps he only wants her for a piece of house furniture, like a sofa or a carpet — not as a fellow-heir of eternal life.'[21]

This particular Powell sister was away from home when MacDonald first came to visit. Louisa — neither the youngest nor the eldest — had a thick nose and a wide mouth. She was, in a word, plain, with her hair severely parted in the middle and scraped tight behind her head. Small and slim she had, nevertheless, a twinkle in her eye and an enormous sense of fun, as well as an erratic temper. She soon fell under the spell of the young, dramatic visitor.

It did not take long for MacDonald and Louisa to realize that there was more than just cousinly affection between them, and their relationship developed quickly. His attentions were welcome and her plainness was not an issue with him. As he was to write in a later novel:

> 'I would advise any young man of aspiration in the matter of beauty to choose a plain woman for wife — if through her plainness she is yet lovely in his eyes; for the loveliness is herself, victorious over the plainness, and her face, so far from complete and yet serving her loveliness, has in it room for completion on a grander scale than possibly most handsome faces.'[22]

The earliest letter from MacDonald to Louisa is dated 27 March 1846 and was written from the Radermachers' house, Park Cottage:

'My dear Louisa,
Will you let the inclosed apologize for carrying off your thimble — I did not mean to do so — but I have not time to explain. I am sorry the bits of poetry are not more worth offering you, but perhaps I may succeed better some other time. Of course you will not put them in your book if you do not like them.'[23]

The thimble was needed as MacDonald was forced to mend and sew his own clothes. Writing to his stepmother, Margaret McColl, he told her proudly that 'I have pieced my trousers two or three times... I am quite independent.'[24]

Sharing poetry soon led to sharing confidences and in their deepening intimacy MacDonald began telling Louisa his problems:

'I am not yet going to write you a long letter, for indeed I am not very happy myself, having been struggling for some time with wrong and painful thoughts, which seem to take from me all right to look to Jesus. But I hope to be delivered from them, and triumph over them. Pray for humility for me, dear Louisa, and the feeling that my salvation is entirely owing to Christ Jesus.'[25]

For he was still agonizing over what to do. He could not remain with the Radermachers for ever, for that job was only to stave off starvation and give him time in which to make up his mind. Thoughts of the ministry were inevitably looming larger, as it was the only profession open to him that seemed (to those around him at least) to suit his talents and inclinations. But MacDonald was dogged about continuing with his poetry. In February 1846 he had his very first poem published, a rather sombre piece of blank verse 114 lines long called *David*, which may have drawn some inspiration from Browning's *Saul*.

And the tutoring was wearing him down further and further. In April 1847 he confessed to his father:

'I scarcely think however that I can stay another winter without they give me a fire in my room, for my illness is owing in a great measure to sitting in the cold.'[26]

Park Cottage was, he reflected, 'a strange house to live in — but God has blessed it to me very much, and though I have not been able to study much, I feel my mind strengthening and my views enlarging.' This letter to his father was something of a manifesto outlining his future plans. For he had finally decided to go to Highbury Theological College to train as a Congregational minister. This was the obvious place to go, for there was already a trickle of young men from Huntly who had studied there, including some members of the Spence family, one of whom was still at the college while MacDonald was thinking about his application, and James Legge,[27] another member of the Missionar Kirk, who had gone off to China as a missionary in 1839. Robert Troup was soon to arrive from Aberdeen where he was sharing lodgings with MacDonald's younger brother John, and both Kennedy, the minister at Blackfriars, and John Hill, minister of the Missionar Kirk at home in Huntly, were former students.

MacDonald resolved to delay going to the college until the autumn of 1848 as he wished to lay in a good stock of clothes and books, though he had invested what money he had in three volumes of Coleridge's poems and Lismondi's *History of the Literature of the South of Europe*. But his main reason for not being speedy with his application was:

'...that I wish my opinions and feelings and motives to *solidify* a little more — I wish to have more distinct and definite objects in view before entering on the work of the ministry, if God will accept of me for a workman. Perhaps I should wish also to overcome more the difficulties of my situation, which has so little in it to give me pleasure.'

He was honest with his father, warning him that:

'I did not wish you to understand me as having finally made up my mind as to the ministry. 'Tis true this feeling has been gradually gaining ground on me, and for a long time nothing has appeared to me of importance compared with that.'

But the crux of the problem was:

'One of my greatest difficulties in consenting to think of religion was that I thought I should have to give up my beautiful thoughts and my love for the things God has made. But I find that the happiness springing from all things not in themselves sinful is much increased by religion. God is the God of the Beautiful — Religion is the love of the Beautiful, and Heaven is the Home of the Beautiful — Nature is tenfold brighter in the Sun of Righteousness, and my love of Nature is more intense since I became a Christian — if indeed I am one. God has not given me such thoughts and forbidden me to enjoy them.'[28]

He shied away from becoming part of an institution that might cramp his freedom. But, cautious as he was, he pressed ahead with his application to the college and waited to see what the following months would bring.[29]

CHAPTER SIX

Highbury

As MacDonald had been a member of the congregation at Brompton for two years, Morison was more than happy to write a testimonial for him to the theological college noting that he 'has a remarkable gift in prayer, which has been specially observed in our Prayer-Meetings...' and John Hill, the minister from Huntly, told the college, 'I do not know a more serious young person, nor one of a sweeter or more teachable disposition.'

The testimonials had to be good, for Highbury was particular in the students it admitted, if not in matters of academic attainment, then certainly in the area of personal religion:

'Strict attention is enjoined to the duties of domestic religion: and, in the performance of family worship, morning and evening, the students are required to engage in rotation. A system of order and punctuality is established in relation to their studies, and to every part of their conduct — this is maintained by a set of regulations (printed and given to students) the due observance of which is enforced by small fines.[1]

It is hard to believe that these regulations produced an atmosphere congenial to the romantic, dreamy MacDonald. He worried about this.

The college itself was an imposing, classical style building with pillars. It had been founded in 1825 to continue the work of Hoxton Academy, one of the old Dissenting Academies. At that time the doors of Oxford, Cambridge and Durham were closed to the Congregationalists, and to all Nonconformists, though students at Highbury College were able to take London degrees after about 1840. In fact, the Dissenters were very proud of the level of education they could offer their young ministers and it is true that it was of no inferior brand.

There were forty students at the college in all, ten arriving and leaving each year, and the course was divided into two years of literature and two of theology, though the literature could be dispensed with if the candidate already had a degree. The teaching was worthy rather than inspiring and was conducted along narrow, doctrinal lines. Right thinking and not free-thinking was encouraged. Among the staff was the fearsome Professor

Godwin who taught Systematic Theology and New Testament Exegesis. This man's intellectual capabilities and rigorous faith terrified MacDonald who always stood a little in awe of him.

Each candidate for the college was required 'to write an account of his religious principles and experience: and also, of the motives which have induced him to apply for admission into the Academy.' Accordingly MacDonald had to submit to a twelve-point written enquiry, answering detailed questions on matters of faith and doctrine. He also had to prepare a discourse and write an essay, of which he only completed a part, on 'The Best Means of Promoting a Spirit of Piety in Students for the Ministry,' and 'these proving satisfactory it was resolved that he be received for the usual term of three months probation.'[2]

He was more than happy to give up his tutorship late in the spring of 1848 and sail north, home to Huntly for the summer, where he had not been for so long.[3] There was a new baby sister at The Farm whom he had not seen, and, of course, his father, who had been casting an anxious eye over his activities from a distance.

This was a happy, carefree visit and soon MacDonald found himself back in his old haunts, returning to the places of his boyhood, playing with his young sisters, going off riding, and then in the evenings having long talks with his father about his theological studies and perhaps even about his matrimonial plans. But his hardheaded and practical father was firm on one point: George had to be in a position to provide before he could marry, and this is why there was so long a delay before George and Louisa could finally become man and wife.

Robert Troup was also in Huntly during that summer working as co-pastor at the Missionar Kirk where his preaching pleased the Huntly congregation enormously. On the death of the pastor, John Hill, in September 1848, Troup was invited by the congregation to succeed him and this he did, after some soul-searching, remaining there for almost thirty years.

At the end of the summer, MacDonald had to leave the rivers and hills of his homeland once more and return to London. All the students at the college lived under one roof — the senior students on one side of the quadrangle and the juniors on the other. They ate all meals together and in this monastic environment MacDonald set to work.

1848 was a year of change. Revolt once again shook Europe to its foundations and the British, long afraid of a repetition of what had happened in France, feared that the violence would spread. After the threat of Napoleon had been vanquished, the country trembled at the thought of impending revolution and civil war. The 1840s had seen hunger spreading everywhere and famine in Ireland. A quarter of a million people a year were emigrating. In England Chartism had arisen with its radical demand for a vote for every man. This was the first large working-class movement of its kind, and no one really knew what the outcome would be — revolution or resolution. As it was, 1848 was the year its grip began to loosen, but it had nevertheless left a deep mark on the nation.

Such unrest was also a symptom of the deep changes Britain had been undergoing — the rise of large-scale engineering and machine tool industries had finally changed the Englishman from a countryman into a town-dweller, and the social problems associated with this move were enormous. Five thousand miles of railway had been built — the biggest leap forward in communications since Roman times, and as steam engines took people from town to town faster than they had ever travelled before, it seemed as if the whole of life were speeding up.

MacDonald was as aware of these changes as anyone else. He had already shown his concern for city problems in Aberdeen and the pressures he encountered in London helped shape his theology and poetic insight to an acute degree.

At college there was more Greek to learn, and Latin, as well as the new and fascinating field of Jewish antiquities. One of the first writing exercises that MacDonald set himself was not academic, however, and with a trembling hand he sat down to compose a letter to James Powell:

'I feel considerable embarrassment in writing to you and the only way I can get over it is to come to the point at once. . .'

Then impatiently he scored all this out and hurriedly wrote:

'Will you permit me to visit your daughter Louisa, with the hope of one day making her my wife?'[4]

Anxious hours passed as he waited for Powell's reply. Finally it came, and nervously he tore open the envelope. It contained good news. The relief MacDonald felt was obvious:

'As to the other part of your note, I hardly know what to say. I can only thank you again and say it is more than I thought of.'[5]

A couple of days later Louisa wrote to MacDonald with a barely concealed squeal of delight: *'Papa wishes me to write to you!!!'*[6]

There can be no doubt that the match was a good one as far as MacDonald and Louisa were concerned. They enjoyed a mutuality of affection that was both deep and enduring. When MacDonald wrote to her soon after their engagement: 'Surely few are able to call their wives their own as I shall call you if it please our God who made us and love',[7] he wrote with an assurance and faith which time proved true. For, if Louisa felt herself weak in intellect and in need of MacDonald's support, then he was often weak in body and in need of her nursing. In this way the one could not do without the other, and during their haphazard life together it was often Louisa's determination that carried them through. Because she had to rise to many difficult occasions throughout her long married life, Louisa became much less 'decorative' than other Victorian women in her position were forced to be and her character toughened considerably over the years. In the alchemy of love, MacDonald found some new resolution deep within himself and he was happier, clearer and more at peace than he had been for a long while. Perhaps it was as though his romantic ideal were coming true.

On 23 October, four days after their engagement, MacDonald wrote to Louisa — a long letter about love, and in this letter expressed many of the themes that were to surface later in his work. He presented a vision of heavenly love, at once spiritual and erotic, which would be the consummation of all their earthly desires:

> 'You and I love, but who *created* love? Let us ask him to purify our love to make it stronger and more real and more self-denying — I want to love you for ever — so that though there is no marrying or giving in marriage in heaven we may seek each other there as the best beloved. It is to heaven I look as the place where I shall have most enjoyment in you — both from my perfections and yours. Oh Louisa is it not true that our life here is a growing into life, and our death a being born — our true birth. And if there is anything beautiful in this our dreamy life, shall it not strive forth in glory to the bright waking consciousness of heaven.'[8]

So, in the love of Louisa, MacDonald found that the love of a woman and the love of God were different aspects of the same love and this belief formed a central part of the gospel he was to preach for the rest of his life. They exchanged long, daily letters, sharing deep thoughts and intimate domestic detail all through the period that MacDonald remained at college. It was usually late at night when everyone else was asleep that MacDonald would sit down at his desk beside the inky black window in his study and begin writing to Louisa. For during the day he was busy. Not only were there books to read and essays to write, but he also had to preach on some weekends, trying out his rhetorical skills in the pulpit. For this he was paid and the money was a welcome supplement to his meagre income. His love of public speaking carried over into the college where he was an active and earnest debater. When one of the students, Charles Green, read a paper on the 'Aesthetics of Public Worship' MacDonald joined wholeheartedly in the discussion, supporting Green vehemently in his 'condemnation of the general lack of any appeal to taste and natural sentiment in dissenting chapels'. And later he raised a few eyebrows by introducing a debate on the existence of ghosts. Writing from Huntly, Robert Troup noted: 'And so my friend G. MacDonald still holds to his old theory that ghosts exist. I never doubted the fact, but in regards to their visibility I am not so well satisfied.'[9] It is not surprising that MacDonald did consider ghosts as fact since his will to believe in the supernatural was intense and it is the strange mixture of the Gothic and the Christian which gives his novels their peculiar flavour.

Apart from his studies and his relationship with Louisa, MacDonald had time for other interests: his friends, for instance. There were Spence, Moir and Chancellor whom he had known before he joined the college, but there were new friends too, notably James Matheson, who later went to Nottingham, and who lived only a few minutes walk away from the college in Barnsbury Street. Through James, MacDonald met Greville Matheson, then working as a clerk in the Bank of England, who became his intimate friend, and with him he shared much of his feeling and his thinking — and his poetry. They both wrote reams of verse and sought help and criticism from one another. But when they were not locked together in earnest discussion they would take to the London night together, talking, having fun, and often visiting the theatre — the Olympic or Sadler's Wells — to see many of the plays of the day. It was during those Highbury years that both young men, sharing the same social concern, fell heavily under the influence of A.J.Scott whose lectures they attended at the Marylebone Institute in London.

Scott was an important influence in MacDonald's life. He had taken up the Chair of English Language and Literature at University College, London in November 1848 and was noted as something of a polymath, being interested in literature, languages, science and theology. He had moved into higher education from the ministry, for he had begun his career as a clergyman, and while preaching for McLeod Campbell[10] in 1829 in Port Glasgow, his sermons on the charismata in 1 Corinthians 12 had led to manifestations of prophecy and speaking in tongues among the congregation. In Scotland he had become close friends with Thomas Erskine of Linlathen and Edward Irving,[11] who invited Scott to become his assistant in London. Scott had received an invitation to become pastor of the Scottish Church in Woolwich in 1830, but found he could not subscribe wholly to the Westminster Confession of Faith. The sticking point was that 'none are redeemed by Christ but the elect only' and he sent a letter on this matter to the moderator of the London presbytery. In May 1831 he was charged with heresy before the presbytery of Paisley and deprived of his licence to preach — a sentence confirmed by the General Assembly. Notwithstanding, Scott remained at Woolwich until 1846, despite the ruling of the presbytery, where he was a popular pastor and minister of a small congregation.

Scott spent a lot of time working among the poor, teaching and preaching, and interested himself in working men's education and women's education. He helped found Queen's College, London, and was joint professor of Literature and Philosophy at Bedford College, London. Both of these institutions were for women, their aim being primarily to train teachers. The salient concerns of Scott's philosophy, his wider view of salvation, his love of literature, and his interest in working men's and in women's education as well as his concern for the poor, were all commitments which MacDonald shared and indeed became the hallmarks of the Christian Socialists who were beginning to gather steam at this time. It was said of Scott: 'As a lecturer he was engaging and inspiring, though too philosophic and profound to captivate a popular audience.'[12]

But MacDonald, for one, was captivated. Scott was the first man of authority whom MacDonald had met in whom he could place a whole-hearted faith. It may have been Scott who first introduced MacDonald to the writings of Dante[13] and he became something of a friend and mentor to MacDonald during his London days. After the staleness of college, Scott was a breath of fresh air. While MacDonald was lapping up Scott's lectures and pursuing his studies with, perhaps, less and less enthusiasm, he had turned his teaching energies from Angela to Louisa who was wilting under her new academic load. She could not follow Scott's lectures at all, and when trying to read Macaulay, she could mouth the words all right, but could not find the sense. It was very depressing, and her failure to enter the world of thought in which MacDonald seemed so at ease only served to deepen her sense of inferiority. MacDonald's efforts to turn his fiancée into one of his romantic heroines was having mixed results:

'But dear George need it be so, I have been hoping it is not a necessity. Can it not be that — often where my mind is unaccustomed to deep searching thought and *unable* too, cannot reach to understand yours my *heart* can feel for you — Your mind must and ought to be so much superior to mine that often I should not be able to see what you do, but may I not believe in this and love that it should be so, and almost feel for what I cannot comprehend, my love teaching me to feel what I could otherwise have no idea of.'[14]

Louisa's low spirits may have been linked as much to illness as to spiritual inadequacy however, for, like MacDonald, she was not robust and in May 1849 she went down to Hastings for a couple of months with her friends Josephine and Hannah Rutter to enjoy the air and use the bathing machines. Once out of London and settled on the coast Louisa loved the sea and the golden hue of the sun on the water. Away from The Limes there was little responsibility and she could holiday to her heart's content, walking along the beach, playing duets with either Josephine or Hannah, trying to read the impossible books MacDonald had given her and, of course, writing, writing, writing to MacDonald, for when it came to letters, Louisa's capacity and stamina were enormous. Often she would go down to the seashore and set herself on some rock and just write the morning away, sometimes sticking flowers or bits of seaweed on the letters. But as the days passed, Hastings became wearisome and the holiday freedom lapsed into a disagreeable sameness that Louisa hoped would soon be over. Unfortunately, MacDonald's letters only served to increase, not to lessen, her anxiety. He was depressed — as usual — and this time he was having problems with his preaching and what he called his 'heresy'. Congregations did not find him wholly acceptable — indeed, they found him difficult to understand at all when he preached — and this weighed heavily on him. And on top of that he was finding college more and more boring, laying his books to one side to write verse or else spending time translating Goethe and Schiller and other Germans. Louisa wrote worriedly to him:

> 'How sorry I was to find you so poorly and out of spirits as you were yesterday — don't sit up so late translating and Germanising. . .'[15]

MacDonald, with his moods and strange intensity, puzzled and even frightened Louisa, though she held onto him in love and believed that he was her superior. Often she signed her letters to him 'Your child' showing, in a poignant way, something of the relationship she felt towards him. In a way she was child and lover and mother all rolled into one:

> 'I am sure you have such a loving trust in Him and such an earnest holy love of Jesus that I could not be afraid as you think. I am not afraid of your *heresy*. I wish I could tell you just what it was I did feel afraid of but I am sure I cannot so shall not try as it would not be what I mean and you would only pity my ignorance and womanly sillyness.'[16]

MacDonald's father was less kind on the matter. Enthusing about the new minister Robert Troup, who had recently come back from a trip to Germany to take up his new duties, George MacDonald senior wrote:

> 'We are much delighted with our young minister. He is really no ordinary young man — so gentle, so prudent, so powerful and persuasive in the pulpit, so clear in his expositions of scripture that in this last especially I have never met with one who throws so much light into my mind. I wish you my boy, you could preach like him.'[17]

MacDonald was only able to visit Louisa once at Hastings and he managed the trip by borrowing some money from Mr Radermacher. He stayed for a few days and then came back. One of the reasons for going to see Louisa may have been to tell her of his plans for the summer, for Professor Godwin at Highbury had proposed that MacDonald should go to Cork in Ireland to fill a vacant pulpit for three months' supply preaching. This would give MacDonald experience as a minister and put money in his pocket. He needed it, for MacDonald told his father at this time that 'I am about three pounds in debt.'[18]

MacDonald left for Cork on 19 June 1849 and so he and Louisa spent a summer apart, which in the event might have been better spent together.

CHAPTER SEVEN

Home and Away

Ireland was a poor and hungry country, and MacDonald, out on horse-back much of the time, took stock of the state of its inhabitants and the reasons for their distress. Racked with famine and bitter with hatred of the British, Ireland was not an easy place to be, but MacDonald had a good stay there, though he suffered from the usual mood swings: 'My conscience has never been more at ease with regard to my studies. I am very glad I came here, to let me try myself a little...' But then doubts began to gnaw at him: 'I often fear I won't do for a minister, but God will guide me as will be best for me.'[1] He missed Louisa and was grateful to Carrie, her sister, when she sent Louisa's portrait to him by post.

In London, however, things were not going well for Louisa. There was a family crisis: Louisa's cousin, Charlotte Sharman, who lived at Welling-borough with her parents, had been lying insensible for days and was near death. Her condition brought the fact of death home to Louisa horribly and frightened her deeply. After days of anxious waiting it was not Charlotte but her mother, Louisa's Aunt Sarah, who died first at 2a.m. on the morning of 24 July, followed by Charlotte at noon of the same day. This double death shocked Louisa beyond words and she wrote to MacDonald: 'You can scarcely tell how very precious every letter I have from you is now to me.'[2]

For if Charlotte and Aunt Sarah could so easily be snatched from the world, then what of her own and George's future happiness? It was as if they were both walking a knife-edge and the terror that gathered in Louisa at the thought of such sudden death took many years to subside. In her panic she imagined that her father's love for her was 'all upset again' and she wrote to MacDonald asking him to 'pray that God would if possible humble my heart without rending it by some dreadful calamity and that at this time of sickness he may spare my life, for how could I die now? Is it wrong to pray so, my dear George?'[3]

The deaths brought such a gloom to Louisa's summer that she could take little pleasure in anything. She suffered from toothache — always a sign of stress with her — she tossed and turned in bed at night — and she was visited by strange dreams. At the first sign of illness in MacDonald, alarm set her heart beating wildly. When he was laid up with bronchitis and his spirits sank she wrote that he ought to have an angel to take care of him, 'but oh, how I should like to be that angel!' She sent out her stream of letters from a platform fixed in the fork of a strong oak tree in the garden of The Limes where she would retreat for privacy.[4]

Her cloud-hung days were lightened by visits from Greville Matheson, MacDonald's good friend, but when Charles Francis came down from Manchester to have a look at the woman his brother was going to marry, she found the meeting a trial. They met at Helen's, with whom Louisa was scarcely at ease anyway, and Charles Francis made himself so free with criticisms of her beloved George, and Helen appeared so coolly superior, that Louisa blurted out a few things she later regretted, and she retreated, feeling that her brother-in-law-to-be did not like her at all. MacDonald later wrote to her:

'. . . you only break out in thunder and lightning! I have a cold smile deep in my heart like a moth-eaten hole, when I feel really wronged.'[5]

Finally in August it was with deep weariness that Louisa sat down to write to Cork:

'Is it wrong, my dear George, but I have felt so tired the last few days and I often think what rest it would be to see you and sit quietly with you and grant that I may live to see you again, but I often think though perhaps there is not a whole fortnight before your return, I may not be alive then — If God lets me see you again it will be much more than I deserve.'[6]

But of course Louisa did see him again, and their reunion was a happy one, though MacDonald blotted his copybook on his return: he had grown a beard — an offence in the religious circles the Powells moved in. James Powell, on entering the drawing room and seeing the offending growth, gave him but one glance and walked out of the room again without a word. Poor George was forced by his future father-in-law's silent condemnation to go and shave it off immediately, this time — though later he grew one of the biggest and most majestic of all Victorian beards.[7]

The shadow of illness cast itself over the Powell family once again in September and while MacDonald was settling back into Highbury, Louisa and her sisters went to Lynmouth by the sea in North Devon with their mother who was recovering from a bad haemorrhage. There she spent a quiet and restful time in a cottage at the foot of a high hill, for the land there is very steep. The change must have done her good as Mrs Powell noticed that her daughter's cheeks were 'so fat they're standing up instead of hanging down'.

At Highbury MacDonald received news of the death of yet another member of his family — his cousin, Charles Edward, the eldest son of James senior who had grown up in the same house as he had, had fallen ill and died in Manchester. He was a promising young man of only twenty-three, and his loss was like that of a brother.

In the college MacDonald began to give his fellow students one free lecture a week in Chemistry. This may have been a mark of how bored he was with the college; he certainly did not charge his fellows for the privilege of listening to him and claimed only his expenses back from the college authorities. His mind was wandering further and further away from his prescribed studies into mysterious, mystic and obscure realms. From the haven of Lynmouth Louisa wrote encouragingly:

'I am so pleased that you are going to interest yourself with your loved chemistry again. I think it will make you much happier than anything else you could have just now.'[8]

And then the following day, Louisa wrote jocularly:

'I am so glad, dearest George, that you are really going to begin the wonders of your Cabalistic art — I hope at least if you discover the Rosicrucian secret of prolonging life you will find out it is more glorious to die than to live on, desolate, alone and not caring for anything around you... I shall not be afraid of the magic of your bottles and crucibles and liquids and essences and shall only be too delighted to be admitted into your mystic chamber or laboratory sometimes.'[9]

Louisa was doing more than just having a joke at her fiancé's interest in chemistry. MacDonald really was immersing himself in mystic and mysterious writers — in Swedenborg, the oblique Swede who spoke with spirits and wrote volume after volume of impenetrable, pseudo-biblical script, and in Jacob Boehme, whose mystical experience in 1600 had caused him to write the *Aurora* and *The Signature of All Things*, and whose works had influenced the German romantics and Coleridge and Blake. In following these lines of enquiry MacDonald was delving back to the roots of those writers who had most inspired him and so had chanced upon the mystics who represented the continuation of the alchemical tradition which had long ago died out. Alchemy combined both science and mysticism and gave birth to the study of chemistry which had been

MacDonald's subject at university. Whatever else college had done for him, it had given him time to set his ideas straight, though he was decidedly at odds with his surroundings there. He found many of the other young students dry and uninspiring:

> 'You ask whether all those young men are of the new ways of thinking — who are unsettled. Not one of them to my knowledge — but they are all dull fellows — or at least without anything marked about them — nothing much of their own — Yet tolerable specimens of Highbury.'[10]

It is significant that MacDonald left finally without taking his degree.[11]

As the year turned, MacDonald's thoughts turned to finding a charge, but who would have him? Confirmed in his 'heresy' he felt marked out as 'special' and 'different' and determined not to compromise his beliefs, but at the same time he had to have employment. His father insisted:

> 'I hope you will by and by be in circumstance to pay off your small debts, and make conscience of never venturing on taking a wife before then. If you begin thinking lightly of such a case, depend upon it, the carelessness will increase until none but yourself and such as are in similar circumstances can paint the agony it will entail.'[12]

George MacDonald senior did not approve of his son's dithering. In addition, it had always been at the back of his mind that George was perhaps too delicate to undertake any regular work and he grumbled that his son would probably do better with a nursemaid than a wife. He was crusty to George about not writing enough, but then MacDonald was often reluctant to communicate as he was not always the bearer of good news. His father, a mixture of gruff temper and good humour, was someone whom MacDonald wanted to appease, but in practice he found it difficult. Yet he battled on and it was at this time that Louisa chastised herself for being out of joint with everything in contrast to George's own 'peaceful, trusting faith'.

In February 1850 Charles Francis was married in Manchester to Jane McNee and MacDonald wrote to them:

> 'May you ever be as music set to noble words, as Tennyson has it. May you find the married state far better even than you expect it, and so do right and love each other that your souls may be ever coming into closer union.'[13]

And then MacDonald thought that he might have found a charge when he was asked to preach at Stebbing. His venture there, however, was not very successful, and just before he was due to set off there on a month's supply one of the deacons wrote to him 'that I had better not go as I was not acceptable to many of the people'. He sank into despair once more and confessed despondently to his father:

'...many say they can't understand me. I tried to be as simple as possible at Stebbing — but I fear many people think they understand phrases they are used to and not much more.'

But he was not to be beaten:

'I am more used to preaching. I must say that I think if people will try, I can make them understand me, — if they won't, I have no desire to be understood. I can't do their part of the work.'[14]

Yet when he was about to go to Chelmsford two weeks later, he reported to his father that 'my expectation of giving satisfaction is rather low'. If only someone would hand him a hundred pounds, he complained, 'then I will go out to Baron Liebig and have little fear of making a good chemist if not a good preacher.'[15] But no one did give him a hundred pounds and he did not go off to Giessen to study under Baron Liebig. Instead he went to Whitehaven to try out his preaching once again to see if he would prove any more acceptable to the people there.

While MacDonald was trying out different charges Louisa was left at The Limes struggling with Goethe and Carlyle — and worrying. Illness had returned to the family. Louisa's mother's health had not improved much, even after their holiday at Lynmouth and suddenly, after wavering for some time, it worsened. On 25 April, exhausted, she was laid on a board and bags of ice put on her chest. The 'family attendant' — tuberculosis — caused haemorrhaging again and this time the doctor feared that her heart was weakened too. Louisa sat up anxiously by her mother's bedside, reading German fairy stories to pass the time and watching the invalid's pale, pathetic face. MacDonald returned from Whitehaven into the midst of this crisis and watched Mrs Powell linger on, slipping further and further away, until finally, in the second week of June, she died. Louisa was distraught. Death had struck the Powell family once again. Yet it was precisely at moments such as these that MacDonald's assured, comforting words on the power and certainty of the love of God enveloped the family at its neediest. Writing from his own sickbed later in the year, MacDonald told Caroline, Louisa's sister:

'I cannot think of length of days as a blessing — but you must all be tired of hearing this same thing over and over again from me. Death is not an end — but a fresh beginning, the grandest birthday of all, the getting out of the lobby, into the theatre.'[16]

In line with many Victorians the Powells probably held to the belief that death was the entrance to an eternity of days, that is, that souls went on existing in endless time. Even at its best this seemed like a miserable doctrine for there was little joy in the thought of going on and on for ever. MacDonald was always at pains, however, to show how death was a birth into something *better* and so death was a hopeful sign, a sign of God's unalterable promise and unfailing love — a *good* sign.

That summer, perhaps to lighten the mood of the household, Mr Powell rented a house in Brighton and commuted backwards and forwards to London every day. Louisa, however, was troubled and in distress: 'This fearful night frightens me so and being alone, but if I were good I dare say it would not. . .'[17] She feared some dreadful punishment on account of what she saw as her bad character:

> '. . . if God will keep my heart pure by his Spirit I shall ever be able to love you and when I am ugly and commonplace and stupid, my love for you will still be of some value to you. After writing this I want to hide my face with your hands or arms.'[18]

One of the few compensations of that sombre summer was that MacDonald had been asked to preach at Arundel, a small town near Brighton, and had secured eight preaching engagements there. It was the usual course for a congregation to try out a prospective minister by asking him to preach several times and then to meet and decide whether he was suitable or not. From Arundel it was only a short hop to Brighton and so MacDonald was able to see Louisa quite easily and they were able to spend some time together.

As well as MacDonald's occasional visits to Brighton, Louisa, her sister Charlotte and her sister-in-law Helen went up to Arundel on the 27 August. What she found must have delighted her, for the small town, perched on a hill in the midst of the rolling Sussex Downs, was picturesque. Arundel was old and atmospheric, dominated by the Duke of Norfolk's castle looking out over the flat, wooded country around the town. As the Duke of Norfolk was the leading lay member of the Roman Catholic church in Britain, Catholic influence was strong in the town and the Nonconformists were on the edge of things. But Louisa was drunk with the beauty of the place. Beside the castle was the ancient parish church of St Nicholas, built in 1380, and Louisa was delighted by the swans gliding on the river Arun and gulls from the sea perching on the chimney-tops.

Louisa, Charlotte and Helen wandered through the streets to find MacDonald's lodgings, where his landlady Mrs New showed them round. No doubt they went to look at the Independent Church, built of red brick, a narrow-ended barn-like building with an impressive arched wooden door, the front of the church all studded with flint. This exciting day of exploration was marred for Louisa by Helen under whose tongue she was still smarting:

> 'And Helen gave me such a long lecture upon matrimony after we were in bed, and has made me afraid even more than before *for you*, not for myself. I wish she would in some things take the advice she gave me... How I wish I were as bewitching.'[19]

The following Sunday Mr Powell took Louisa to hear MacDonald preach and wrote swiftly to him before breakfast the following day: 'I ought perhaps to have commenced with saying how very much I was pleased with your professional services...'[20] Louisa busied herself for the rest of the month making up shirts and a stock-cravat for the young preacher and, slowly, excitement mounted as MacDonald waited to hear whether the congregation was going to invite him or not. He wrote to his father on 1 October that, 'I am informed tho' not officially that the church seemed to have but one mind at the meeting last night and that was that I should be their minister.'[21]

A couple of weeks later MacDonald accepted the invitation formally after being presented with the official documents which were signed by all except five who had not heard him preach and whom the congregation did not think ought to sign them. There were fifty-seven signatures to MacDonald's 'Call' in all. MacDonald settled down to his new duties right away, moving permanently into his lodgings with Mr and Mrs New towards the end of October. Suddenly it seemed the skies were clear. He was able to write at last to his father:

> 'We hope to be married in the spring — to which Mr Powell is quite favourable — and if you would receive us, we should like, if we could, to visit you then — perhaps in April. I should, of course, have much pleasure in letting you and Louisa know and speak to each other, and should like her to see the sky and the hills which first began to mould my spirit.'[22]

At last life seemed to be on a steady course and improving. MacDonald told his father at the end of October that the congregation was increasing, the midweek meetings were better — there was a prayer meeting on Monday and a lecture on Thursday — and he was running Bible Classes for young men and women. He was a pastor at last.

CHAPTER EIGHT
Arundel

When Mrs C.F. Alexander published her *Hymns for Little Children* in 1848 with a preface by John Keble and the famous stanza:

'The rich man in his castle,
The poor man at his gate,
God made them, high or lowly,
And ordered their estate.'[1]

she was actually living in a remote, feudal world, far away in Ireland, far from the towns and the upsurging commercial classes. For new people were making new money. In a more carefully layered society like Arundel where there really was a rich man in his castle, social differences may have been more keenly felt. The Independent Church in Tarrant Street could have been described in this way:

'Greengrocers, dealers in cheese and bacon, milkmen with some dressmakers of inferior pretensions and teachers of day schools of similar humble character formed the elite of the congregation.'[2]

These were the people who were coming into their own in Victorian England. They were little interested in culture, reading some poetry perhaps for its religious content, but certainly not for its beauty or its music. Probably many of them read nothing more than the local paper, though they would have such classics as *Pilgrim's Progress* and *Robinson Crusoe* on their shelves at home. Theatre and cards were regarded as of the Devil — novels were meant to instruct, *not* entertain or amuse, and these people's children would have their heads stuffed full of facts and worthy information.

The Congregationalists, whom MacDonald ministered to, formed a sizable slice of the church-going population and numbered 793,142 in the famous census of 1851, placing them numerically above the Baptists, but below the Methodists. Between 1830 and 1860 they had turned from a loose federation into something resembling a modern denomination. The Congregational Union had been formed in 1831, and this had cemented the self-determining congregations together — for each congregation was independent in function as well as name. There were neither very rich nor very poor in the Dissenting Chapels; neither aristocrats nor peasants were found in their pews. As Joshua Wilson told the Congregational Assembly in 1861:

'It is unquestionable fact, that our strength as a denomination lies in the large cities and towns, as our special vocation is to the middle classes of the people, who form the chief portion of their inhabitants.'[3]

The cream of the Dissenting Congregations was to be found in the towns, and that was one reason why MacDonald's brother Charles kept urging him go to Manchester, not just to keep the family together, but to go where 'the best congregations in Lancashire are.' It may have been that Arundel, while satisfactory, was hardly the best that MacDonald could have expected. While on supply there, MacDonald had been approached by a congregation in Brighton, but preferring Arundel he had settled with them.[4]

In the Congregational Church as a whole the stipends of its ministers varied widely. The best could expect between £500 and £700 a year, while in 1853 there were still ninety-seven Independent ministers who received less than £50 a year.[5] MacDonald was offered £150 by the people of Arundel which was an adequate amount for such a small town and a small congregation.

But, as MacDonald took up his duties, the Congregational Churches were being tested by a new threat. An insidious monster had sloped in from Germany: doubt in the form of biblical criticism. The *Leben Jesu* written by Strauss and translated by the young George Eliot had caused some impact, even among ordinary people, and so the sniff of anything German was tainted with heresy. And the congregations could not keep this 'heresy' from infecting their ministers. As these ministers were reasonably educated they could not seal themselves off from the intellectual doubts of the 1850s or be kept from the agnosticism of Emerson and Carlyle. Such educated dissenters stood on the far side of Congregationalism and their ranks included such people as James Martineau, Thomas Erskine, William Howitt and Mrs Gaskell. It is also true to say that in the fifties and sixties when many areas of science were opening up for study for the first time, many of the leading scientists came from Dissenting families. These new currents of thought eddied even into Arundel where, as the congregationalists decided their own affairs, the minister was at the mercy of his people and could easily be removed at a church meeting. This had already happened at Arundel where John Ashby, the minister there before MacDonald's arrival, had been accused of neglecting his flock and lecturing too much in Brighton, and had also been subject to a fuss caused by 'Some self-seeking persons I suspect — who would have something else in place of wine at the sacrament.' He had lasted four years. The minister before him had lasted three.[6] Somehow no one stayed very long at Arundel — yet ejections were fairly common in the Congregational Church so it is not fair to single out the chapel at Arundel for disapproval. But, at this time, these matters were for MacDonald like the dimmest of clouds on a brilliant summer's day.

While MacDonald was settling excitedly into Arundel as pastor, Louisa, who had been simmering for a long time under Helen's critical gaze, suddenly came to the boil. The matter of disagreement was the pocket books, filled with MacDonald's earliest poetry, which he had long ago given to Helen. Louisa had always been jealous of Helen, not just for her looks, but also for her former influence with George, and while Helen may have felt aloof and superior, she may, on the other hand, have found Louisa's behaviour only exaggerated and silly. As it was, Louisa made a journey to Helen's on the night of 23 October and there ensued a barely restrained row. The two young women talked for a long time about tact and then when Louisa raised the subject of the books, Helen pretended at first not to understand what Helen meant. When Louisa spelled out her meaning, Helen said, 'Very well, Louisa, I will make up a little packet for *him.*' Louisa wrote to MacDonald:

> 'I suppose she was afraid of my seeing your letters. . . I hope your pocket-books have not shared the fate of the poetry she told me was for no eyes but her own and was therefore put on the fire.'[7]

In Arundel MacDonald was still in lodgings with Mrs New and hoping that Mr Powell would give him enough money to rent a house. His plans were going smoothly and his ordination was fixed for 10 December, the date of his twenty-sixth birthday. Yet in a letter to his brother Charles, MacDonald confessed some of the genuine uncertainties that were plaguing him at the time:

> 'I don't think I am settled here for life. . . I hope either to leave this after six or more years, or to write a poem for the good of my generation. Perhaps both.'[8]

Louisa was longing to attend the ordination, but a long-promised visit to her aunts in Leamington stood in the way. Before either of these trips, however, she celebrated her birthday on 5 November at The Limes and her presents included a copy of *In Memoriam* copied out by MacDonald in longhand. Despite her protests, Mr Powell insisted that Louisa fulfil her promise to her aunts, and so reluctantly she left home on 7 November and took the train out of Paddington station for Leamington. She was slightly worried about George as he had been complaining about a cough. She tried to amuse herself on the journey by reading a volume of Ruskin, but then put that to one side to open a pencilled letter she had received from MacDonald just before she had left. It was the worst possible news — telling of a broken blood vessel and bad haemorrhage from the lungs. This was what she had been dreading. The attack might well have spelled the end of both marriage and the ministry. She leapt off the train at the first stop possible and hurried immediately back to London.[9] She wanted to rush off to Arundel and nurse him, but her family thought this was neither proper nor possible and so MacDonald was left in the capable hands of Mrs New, condemned to lie on his back with leeches feeding off his chest. Alex Powell made a hasty visit to Arundel and came back with better news, though the situation was fairly grim. When he was a little better, MacDonald was moved to The Limes and there saw Dr. Williams who told him that he could on no account preach for six to eight weeks. His lungs were badly affected and he had to take a dessertspoonful of cod-liver oil twice a day. Such helplessness was financially disastrous. After investing in books for the ministry, the young preacher had no money at all, and having to pay £2 a week for a substitute out of £150 a year would make his salary dwindle very quickly.

It was decided that as he needed somewhere to convalesce, and neither the air in London nor in Manchester was suitable for someone in his condition, he should go to his aunt, Mary Spence, at Newport on the Isle of Wight. Ironically, he had been due to go and preach there. She was good to him and there he was able to have the rest that he needed. To while away the time he began writing a poem — a long poem. He informed his father:

'I am busy in the evenings at a poem, but whether it will come to anything I don't know.'[10]

Though dismissive about this work in the letter to his father, MacDonald worked and reworked the poem, later to be entitled *Within and Without*.

He had to spend that Christmas as an invalid. Any preaching at all could have brought on an attack and he was forced to ease himself back into the parish slowly. It was not until January, and only after he had seen Dr Williams again, that he was allowed to begin work 'if I begin gently.'[11] He had finished the draft of his poem and spent the last ten days of his convalescence at Niton on the south coast. John Hill, his friend from Highbury, and son of the minister at Huntly, came to help him out with the evening service, and MacDonald resolved that:

'I will preach very briefly. Twenty minutes or so — and never mean to exceed half an hour after this — I still take the cod liver oil.[12]

Twenty minutes was brief considering that most Congregational churches were used to sermons of an hour or more.

MacDonald took up his duties again on 16 January 1851 and now his thoughts turned to marriage.

CHAPTER NINE
Marriage

The New Year saw both MacDonald and Louisa taken up with the preparation for their marriage and making domestic arrangements for their new life at Arundel. MacDonald wanted Caleb Morris, a free-thinking pastor friend of his, to marry them: 'I think I should like Caleb Morris better than anyone except Mr Scott.' But Louisa would have none of it. Her first meeting with Morris had not been a success. She had found him physically off-putting — 'so fat and rosy' — not at all what she had imagined, and they had talked awkwardly. MacDonald wrote ruefully, 'I suppose you would not like Caleb Morris to do it since he managed so ill.'

Apart from fixing on who was to marry them, MacDonald and Louisa had to decide on a house, but houses were hard to come by in Arundel and it was not easy to find one to rent. With some of Mr Powell's money behind them, however, they found a house in Tarrant Street, No. 48, just along the road from the church. It was a narrow, terraced red-brick Georgian house with access to the back, small for a large family, but big enough for two.

Time dragged by for Louisa, but gradually the great day drew nearer and nearer. The date was fixed for 8 March. Excitement mounted. MacDonald's brother Alec was able to come down from Manchester, along with Charles, but John was not able to visit until the following May when he planned to come and see the Great Exhibition in London, the wonder of that year.[1]

MacDonald himself planned to go up to London on the first Sunday in March and stay with his friends the Mathesons until the 8th. By then everything was arranged in their new home. The kitchen range was just right. The blinds were fixed. The furniture was installed, and finally, after so much illness and worry the day dawned and the pair were married at a chapel in Hackney known as 'The Old Gravel Pits' by the minister there, the Rev. John Davies. It was the chapel where Louisa and her brothers and sisters had been baptized. MacDonald wore a white satin waistcoat embroidered with sprigs of flowers, and Louisa, resplendent in white, stood demure beside him. At last they stood on the threshold of their dream:

> 'I have a feeling as if you were married and a vision of darkhaired children being made happy and the *blue eyes* and *dark eyes* playing together beneath the care of blue eyes and dark eyes. I have a vision of the sun-shine of youth adorning more sober middle age, a vision of husband and wife in the unselfishness of their hearts giving up and living for each other's happiness. I see you Louisa at the head of that beautiful family.'[2]

The wedding took place on a Saturday and the following morning MacDonald had to preach at Rugby, on their way to Leamington where Louisa's aunts had lent them their house for a honeymoon. As MacDonald unpacked the luggage at Rugby he found that his ever-present bottle of cod-liver oil had broken and soaked all the way through to the pair of trousers he was due to face the congregation in.[3]

MacDonald's wedding present to Louisa was a love poem, later printed as part of *Within and Without*. Called 'Love me, Beloved', it pursues MacDonald's preoccupation with love in death leading to a union which is at once spiritual, erotic and eternal:

> 'Love me, beloved; Hades and Death
> Shall vanish away like a frosty breath;
> These hands, that now are at home in thine,
> Shall clasp thee again, if thou art still mine;
> And thou shalt be mine, my spirit's bride,
> In the ceaseless flow of eternity's tide,
> If the truest love thy heart can know
> Meet the truest love that from mine can flow.
> Pray God, beloved, for thee and me,
> That our souls may be wedded eternally.'[4]

MacDonald and Louisa settled down in contentment in Arundel, enchanted with the countryside. His only complaint was that the town was a place 'where I can have no *society*, and no books of any kind except what I have of my own...' Their life was regular, punctuated by visits from relatives and friends from London. Much as he would have liked to have shown his new bride to his father, MacDonald was ordered by his doctor to remain in the south, so the hoped-for trip to Huntly had to be postponed indefinitely.

MacDonald later put down many of his experiences at Arundel in his novel *Annals of a Quiet Neighbourhood*, and some of the characters, such as Old Rogers, whom the vicar, Mr Walton, meets on the bridge, were drawn straight from life. Though MacDonald made Walton an Anglican vicar, setting his church at St Nicholas's, much of what Walton does is reminiscent of MacDonald. It is easy to imagine MacDonald facing a congregation, such as Walton did, and finding the following:

'The people had dined, and the usual somnolence followed. So I curtailed my sermon as much as I could, omitting page after page of my manuscript; and when I came to a close, was rewarded by perceiving an agreeable surprise upon many of the faces round me.'[5]

MacDonald followed the usual Congregational method of delivering his sermons extempore — that is, he wrote out what he was going to say, learned it up, and then preached from the pulpit, apparently without notes. As a preacher would often have to preach for an hour and then pray aloud for half an hour, the congregation would have felt alternatively let off lightly or short-changed by MacDonald's shorter sermons. His lungs were still weak and could not be too heavily relied upon and it was impossible for him to preach at length even if he had wanted to.

Like Walton, much of MacDonald's work involved visiting and helping people. He enjoyed the ordinary people in his congregation and the young, and it appears that they enjoyed him. He was certainly different from the other ministers they had had. Walton read Wordsworth's ballads to the people and one can imagine MacDonald doing the same:

'For I thought with myself, if I could get them to like poetry and beautiful things in words it would not only do them good, but help them to see what is in the Bible, and therefore to love it more.'[6]

Walton gives an evening lecture on Sir Philip Sidney as probably Mac-Donald did, and, like Walton, MacDonald had to deal gently with the little points of theology and conduct that came up in day-to-day life. MacDonald enjoyed going out for long walks in the country, especially on a Monday after the concentrated duties of Sunday were over. After being shut up in a church for most of the day, MacDonald loved to wander free:

'For I have always found the open air the most genial influence upon me for the production of religious feeling and thought.'[7]

MacDonald's ordination took place in June 1851 and Professor Godwin from Highbury arrived for it. Charlotte Powell, Louisa's sister, had also been invited, and MacDonald's brothers, John and Alec, were able to make the journey. It was the first time that MacDonald had seen John for six years. For Godwin and Charlotte it was an important meeting — the first stirrings of love — and they were married by MacDonald two years later.

After the ordination John and Alec paid a visit to Huntly while, in Arundel, MacDonald and Louisa enjoyed a stream of visits from the various Powell sisters and from old friends from college days, the Mathesons. These were happy interruptions, though MacDonald was in a weak state for a lot of this time. Often he and Louisa had to rely on gifts of food from different members of the church, some of which would arrive mysteriously and anonymously on the doorstep. During this time his father urged him to throw himself fully into his work as a minister and:

> '. . . give over the fruitless game of poetry, and apply yourself to the preaching of the gospel and the instruction of your people. A nervous temperament and a poetical imagination are too much for a frail clay tabernacle, as witness your hypochondriac Cowper and many such like.'[8]

This was depressing advice to receive as MacDonald felt that he had so little support to follow his *true* vocation which was that of a poet. And now his father had raised *his* voice against him.

Occasionally either MacDonald or Louisa or both would have a day in London, seeing the Powells or the Mathesons and, of course, they visited the Great Exhibition. Robert Troup, in London to see the Exhibition, 'found them happy in each other and in their work, church and surroundings.'[9] But though many of the people were charmed, if a little astonished, with their new pastor, the richer, more important tradesmen who were the deacons of the church were a group whom MacDonald found repellent. They were only typical of their times:

> 'The same man who was on Sunday a pious and devout Christian pillar of the Church, supporter of foreign missions, distributor of Bibles, on Monday was the tough businessman and hard bargainer whose creed was "Each for himself. . . The devil take the hindmost, O!" '[10]

MacDonald believed strongly in the retarding power of riches. 'Riches indubitably favour stupidity,' he wrote, 'poverty, mental and moral development.' MacDonald's son remembered that:

> 'In later years he was once preaching at the most fashionable church in Glasgow, the congregation mainly of the wealthiest. In the course of

the sermon he remarked: "One may readily conclude how poorly God thinks of riches when we see the sort of people he sends them to." '[11]

But from the deacons' point of view a pastor who wrote poems and hymns was a little suspicious. Too much book learning was frowned upon and even the simple exhortations MacDonald delivered to his flock from the pulpit by no means pleased everybody:

'He would tell the well-to-do people of his congregation that in giving help to the poor in the way of clothing they ought not to be content to hand them worn out and threadbare garments which they could no longer use themselves but should give such as had still good measure of wear and warmth. That and similar preaching. . . gave offence to some of the "good folks" of his congregation.'[12]

His youthful poetic effusions were often above the heads of many of his listeners and even if those people had been able to follow him it is not likely that they would have warmed to his message. MacDonald himself was patient with them and eager to bring them round to his way of thinking. He told his father:

'I firmly believe people have hitherto been a great deal too much taken up about doctrine and far too little about practice. . . forgetting that the more perfect a theory about the infinite the surer it is to be wrong.'[13]

MacDonald was adamant that he stood apart from any action or belief that smacked of sectarianism: 'I am neither Arminian nor Calvinist. To no system could I subscribe.'[14] Only, in a congregation holding firm sectarian views, such liberality and tolerance of opinion was regarded as subversive. There were murmurs, but as yet they did not disturb the peace in Tarrant Street. Louisa sowed seeds in the garden and, pregnant, awaited the arrival of their first child. And, as a special Christmas present for some of their friends, MacDonald was hard at work translating 'Twelve of the Spiritual Songs of Novalis', poems which had gripped his imagination while he was still a student. He spent much labour on these, consulting Greville Matheson and his own brother John on points of translation and metrical arrangement. John was so enthusiastic about the project that he sent £9 to help towards printing costs. MacDonald was in a philosophical frame of mind during these days:

'I hope to be of some use in the world, and I think I may be let remain in it for a little while. This illness or rather weakness may be but part of my training for future years of usefulness.'[15]

And he was racing to have his pamphlet of Novalis's translations out in time. 'I have run myself up short,' he complained to Greville Matheson, 'and wish to have them out by Christmas Day.'[16] In the event, he succeeded, and was able to distribute the poems to such friends as Greville Matheson, his brother John, A.J. Scott, and Thomas Lynch,[17] the hymn writer, whose publication of *The Rivulet*, an innocuous collection of verse, later led to a storm over his orthodoxy. But it was Christmas, and in keeping with Christmas, there was goodwill to all men.

CHAPTER TEN

New Year, New Problems

The New Year, 1852, brought a new arrival in the shape of the Mac-Donalds' first baby — a healthy, bouncing girl. She was named Lilia Scott or Lily after the mother and daughter in the long poem *Within and Without*[1] which MacDonald had composed during his convalescence on the Isle of Wight, and after A.J. Scott, MacDonald's mentor from his Highbury days. The usual joys and sorrows of new parenthood attended the baby's advent, and MacDonald commented ruefully to his father in a letter that: 'She is a much larger child than I expected and seems to have a good pair of lungs.'[2]

Aside from this happy event good news came that his friends were more than pleased with the translations of Novalis. Thomas Lynch wrote to MacDonald and told him:

'...Any one who will give not perusal only but re-perusals to your Songs of Novalis will understand how every line may to author and translator have gleamed with that peculiar magnetic light of which literature as well as Science knows something, which is not for all eyes, nor for the eyes sensitive to it at all times, or without darkened privacy and discipline of patience...'[3]

A.J. Scott thanked him and said that Novalis was 'an old friend' and John, George's brother in Sheffield, the most enthusiastic of all wrote: 'I have read them till I have them nearly by heart' and promptly decided to study German. Louisa, who was often at her piano, realizing that they were *Songs* of Novalis, set them to music and sang them.

In Manchester Charles and his wife Jane were prospering quietly, while Alec, who had never given much trouble to anybody, suddenly found himself in deep water. He was a straightforward man who lacked the talent (and the melancholy) of George and John. He had kept himself quiet and was advancing slowly in business in Manchester. He attended the Cavendish Street Chapel where Charles was a deacon and it was there that his eyes lighted on Miss Hannah Robertson, daughter of a distinguished surgeon who attended the chapel. Alec was smitten, but his situation was hopeless:

> 'It was not till the night of a soirée among the Sunday School children that he resolved to speak his mind. He walked home with her and made a manly declaration of love, telling her plainly that he had nothing to depend on but his own resources. He was received in the most gentle and ladylike manner, but was disappointed in hearing that she never had the remotest idea of his attachment...'[4]

Hannah Robertson was Alec's first love and the anguish at being refused, even though it had been so gently done, either coincided with or caused a downward turn in his health and he began to spit blood, as MacDonald had done in 1850. From this time on he began to decline. He came to Arundel in March 1852 to be nursed and Louisa looked after him as best she could. But it was no good. His condition did not improve at all and he made the long journey home to Huntly to be near his family.

In Arundel, the pastor's orthodoxy was about to be put to the test. Whispers behind MacDonald's back were growing in number and volume, for it seemed, unbelievably and shockingly, that the young pastor thought that animals would share a place in heaven and what was worse, much worse, that the heathen would have some period of probation in the after life — Purgatory in fact. In a Roman Catholic stronghold such as Arundel, the congregation must have felt especially sensitive to this issue. Popery and heresy could not be tolerated at any cost. What complaints MacDonald received he kept to himself or communicated only to Louisa. So soon settled, it would not have done to say that he had landed his family in trouble already.

When the deacons of the church visited him formally at the end of June he was not ready for them, and the meeting came as something of a surprise. When they told him that they could not go on paying him as much money as they had been doing, MacDonald thought that it was something to do with his wish for a larger house and said, 'I am sorry to hear it, but if it must be, why, I suppose we must contrive to live on less.' The deputation, confused and embarrassed, withdrew and it was only when Louisa was out making some calls among the congregation that she realized they wanted MacDonald to resign. This was a hard and unexpected blow — but the complaints came only from one faction within the church. Nevertheless the practice of that time was for the minister to appear before a meeting of the whole church and answer charges.

Accordingly, MacDonald prepared a statement:

'It having been represented to me that a small party in the church has for some time been exceedingly dissatisfied with my preaching, it has become my duty to bring the matter before the assembled church. My first impulse was at once to resign, as the most agreeable mode for me to be delivered from the annoyance. On mentioning this to some of my friends in the church, the proposal was met with no opposition, although it drew forth expressions of sorrow, and the declaration of benefit derived from my labours. But from the advice of two of my friends engaged in the same work, and from the awakened perception in my own mind that, as I came at the invitation of the whole church, it would be unfair to the other members of the church to resign unconditionally on account of the dissatisfaction of a few, I resolved to put it in the following form: Will you, the Church, let me know whether you sympathize or not with the dissatisfaction of the few? Such a communication from you will let me know how to act: I put it thus from the feeling that this is my duty. With my own personal feelings I have nothing to do in this assembly. I retire and await your decision.'

This grand rhetoric was delivered at a meeting held on 5 July at which there were only twenty people present. As fifty-seven people had signed the call and 117 had turned out when the census of 1851 was taken, such a small proportion of the church could not sway MacDonald to leave. Their resolution, however, was only what could have been expected:

'We do not sympathize with the statement which has been made that "there is nothing in his preaching." But we do sympathize with those who were dissatisfied with the statement from the pulpit "that with the Heathen the time of trial does not (in his, the Revd. G. MacDonald's opinion) cease at their death," which certainly implies a future state of probation. And this Church considers such a view is not in accordance with the Scriptures and quite differs with the sentiments held by the Ministers of the Independent Denomination.
  'It is by no means our wish that the Revd. G. MacDonald should relinquish the office of Pastor of this Church; such a course would cause much regret. But if on reflection he continues to hold and express such an opinion it is evident that it will cause serious difficulties in the Church.'5

But his salary was cut from £150 to £115, and he was naïve not to see that serious consequences would inevitably arise from voicing such views.

After the financial blow, which was a hint to encourage them to leave, MacDonald and Louisa had to make plans to supplement their income — taking in paying guests for example. Louisa's sister Carrie came to stay with them and her money helped keep the household afloat. Then Louisa hit on the idea of forming a school:

> 'Mrs MacDonald is desirous of receiving into her family two or three pupils, young ladies, from the age of eight to sixteen.'[6]

Louisa had already done some teaching, though she had not enjoyed it much, and MacDonald could help with some subjects. They rallied such referees as Caleb Morris and Thomas Binney, a well-known clergyman in London, and planned to charge sixty guineas a year. Advertisements were placed in the *Christian Patriot*, but there were no takers. More and more they had to rely on handouts from friendly members of the congregation. Mrs Alphaeus Smith was especially kind, leaving cream and cheese and fruit and vegetables for them. It was not a happy situation, though MacDonald tried to continue much as normal. He exchanged pulpits with the ministers round about, including with his friend Mr Ross of Brighton who was having similar difficulties with his congregation. Then, in the summer, he took some time off and went on a visit to The Limes, going from there up to Manchester where he stayed with Charles and met the bewitching Hannah Robertson. Of the difficult events of that summer, all he reported to his father was:

> 'I have been very much occupied with one thing and another —
> particularly with some annoyance given me by some members of the
> church who are very unteachable. I thought it not unlikely at the time
> that I should have to leave — but it has brought out on the other hand
> expressions of attachment and benefit, which have more than
> comforted me for the opposition of a few.'[7]

MacDonald chafed against being at the mercy of a group of tradesmen 'in which they regard you more as *their* servant than as Christ's' and nursed vague hopes of going to Australia where Alec his brother had even vaguer hopes of becoming a sheep farmer.

Louisa was left with Lilia and her sister Carrie at Arundel to suffer the mixed bag of substitutes who came to preach — and the flirtatious maid. Louisa never could establish easy relationships with her servants and the maid had to go. There were visits, of course, including one from Mr Bull who was sorry not to have been of more use at the church meeting:

> 'He proposed a "resolution of attachment and affection" which was
> most warmly responded to, until someone referred to your sermon. I

told him if such words (from the chapel) had come before, you would be feeling quite differently about your position.'[8]

Sadly MacDonald's position was becoming more and more difficult and it was clear that he could not go on much longer.

He missed home dreadfully. It had been so long since he had last been there, and his fresh troubles must have sharpened his longing to be in Huntly once again. Thanking his half-sister Isabella for the Christmas present she had sent him, he wrote to her:

> 'How much I should like to spend a winter at home again, a snowy winter, with great heaps and wreaths of snow; and sometimes the wild storm howling in the chimneys and against the windows and down at the kitchen door — And how much I should love to spend one long summer day in June, lying on the grass before the house, and looking up into the deep sky with large white clouds in it. And when I lifted my head I should see the dear old hills all round about; and the shining of the Bogie, whose rush I should hear far off and soft, making a noise hardly louder than a lot of midges. It would be delightful if I could go to sleep here some night, and waken there with Louisa and my little Lily, all at home.'[9]

In April 1853 Alec, who had been haemorrhaging badly since the previous summer, finally died and was laid to rest in the little walled churchyard at Drumblade. MacDonald had not seen him again, but Charles had hastened to Huntly just before the end to attend his brother's bedside where Alec gave him a weak smile and said, 'Never mind, Charles man! This is nae the end o' it!'

The family mourned him and it was with a mixture of sorrow and nostalgia that MacDonald remembered running through the fields with him on a summer evening when they were boys, trying to catch the cornscraich until reprimanded by their father for trampling down the long grass. Again, at the moment of a death, MacDonald became his most poetic and comforting. His certainty, or at the very least, optimism, drove out sorrow and mourning as he turned the black night of death inside out and showed it as a glorious dawn:

> 'Surely God that clothes the fields now with the wild flowers risen from their winter graves, will keep Alec's beauty in his remembrance and not let a manifestation of himself, as every human form is, so full of the true, simple, noble and pure be forgotten.'[10]

As the inevitable resignation at Arundel drew nearer, MacDonald wrote to his father:

'Oh, I know a little now and only a little what Christ's deep sayings mean about becoming like a child, about leaving all for him, about service and truth and love. God is our loving true self-forgetting friend.'[11]

Unfortunately behaving like one of the lilies of the field did not go down well with the family. What was MacDonald to do? He had to do something. He had failed, but his situation was not irretrievable, though he did not seem willing to improve his position. Both fathers sighed again. Mr Powell became distinctly less cordial and MacDonald's father despaired once more. It was left to Professor Godwin, MacDonald's old tutor, to advise him, but this MacDonald dreaded:

'Mr Godwin seems very anxious to see me — I wish that interview were over. We are very unlike, and the meeting of the unlike, even with the kindest feelings, is unpleasant to one of my nature.'[12]

But MacDonald did harbour some thoughts of his own about his predicament and wrote to his brother Charles:

'The rein of my heart, as far as earthly condition is at present concerned is to go to Manchester. I am willing to live on next to nothing for a while, and might find ways of making up a little by giving lessons. My desire from God is that he would give me a place to speak freely and work freely in — and Manchester would be my choice before any. I am sure I could help such as you. What do you mean by the *opening* you expect in a few months? Is it a chapel built and deserted, or to be built? Begin me in any way in Manchester. I will not try, I hope, to draw a congregation, but to speak God's truth boldly.'[13]

First the interview with Godwin had to be endured. It was true that he was critical, thinking that MacDonald had done little to ensure the success of his ministry in Arundel, but his bark was worse than his bite. He raised his eyebrows at the collection of books MacDonald had amassed, but he did advise him to go somewhere where he could minister to young people who would understand him. This was solid, practical advice, but MacDonald was not open to considering 'practicalities' in this way. He had no wish to be 'successful', at least as a preacher — his only desire was to preach the gospel he was brimful of and which taught that God would provide his every need. In clinging to these beliefs he appeared hopelessly unworldly to his family and irritating beyond measure. He finally resigned his charge at the end of May 1853 and the only bright spot at all on the horizon was that he had an article published in the *Monthly Christian Spectator* entitled 'Browning's Christmas Eve'.

Though MacDonald had quit his church he could not yet quit his house. Louisa was expecting another baby in July and she needed to stay in one place. Finished at last with the church, MacDonald wrote to Godwin:

'. . . for me it is recreation enough to be delivered from relationships that are a burden and a weariness. This is over here.'[14]

Now he had to try his fortune elsewhere. In Manchester.

CHAPTER ELEVEN
Manchester

Faced with the prospect of having no work and supporting a wife, an eighteen-month-old child and another as yet unborn, MacDonald found himself subject to a curious mixture of moods. On the one hand his situation was romantic and daring: he was a pilgrim battling against the odds with only God for his staff and guide. On the other hand, the necessity of paying the bills and finding accommodation pressed urgently on him. Yet he was comforted by the fact that the men whom he admired most found themselves in positions similar to himself. A.J. Scott had been charged with heresy and now, in London, F.D. Maurice, a man whom MacDonald greatly admired, had caused a storm with the publication of his *Theological Essays*, which led to his expulsion from his chair at King's College, London, later that year. It seemed almost as if MacDonald were in the vanguard of a new kind of reformation.

There was no question as yet of MacDonald giving up the ministry and so he cast his eyes round for a charge — half-heartedly admittedly — for he felt that he could not fit in anywhere, and rather than be at the mercy of another congregation he had resolved to form his own church where he could teach and preach what he wanted. But for the moment, at least outwardly, he stayed with the orthodox channels. Manchester attracted him, firstly because his brother Charles was there and eager to help, but secondly and more importantly, A.J. Scott had moved to Manchester in 1851 to become principal of the recently established Owens College.

Once in Manchester MacDonald sent his card to A.J. Scott who later came to see him. When Scott arrived he asked if MacDonald was to be in Manchester for long. MacDonald answered: 'For a fortnight now, but I hope to get here permanently, for my heterodoxy has driven me out and I have nothing to do.'[1] Scott was kindly and understanding and asked MacDonald to come and see him the following Sunday afternoon. They had a long talk then and Scott promised to introduce MacDonald to his colleagues and assured him of finding some tuition at least.

That same Sunday evening, MacDonald was invited to preach at Dr

Halley's chapel, but as far as MacDonald was concerned the evening was not a success.[2] Dr Halley was less helpful than Mr Scott. He said that he did not know of any vacant charges except Robert Spence's in Liverpool. Spence was a cousin of MacDonald's, a very studious man, who had been at Highbury around the same time as him and had recently moved to a new post in Dundee.[3] It seemed that MacDonald had more chance there than anywhere else, and after contacting the church, was able to secure eight preaching engagements for later in the year. Liverpool was a promising place as Alex and Helen Powell had moved there, and Flora, one of Louisa's sisters, had married Joshua Sing and was living there too.

On 23 July 1853 Louisa gave birth to her second child, Mary Josephine. She remained in Arundel until she was well enough to travel to The Limes where she stayed for seven weeks. Unfortunately she missed her sister's wedding. Charlotte and John Godwin were married in August, a union whose sudden announcement surprised the family. Stern John and indomitable Charlotte had both found their match: they were made for each other. MacDonald came down from Manchester to marry them, his problems forgotten in the delight of family revels. It was a strange irony that had turned Colin Stewart, the schoolmaster in Huntly whom he had feared, into an uncle (as he had married a sister of MacIntosh MacKay), and now John Godwin, the tutor whom he had feared, into a brother-in-law — but as brothers rather than tutor and student their relationship began to improve. Lilia was at the wedding, brought up to London by another of Louisa's sisters, and she enjoyed herself well enough to have her first taste of champagne.

Far away in Sheffield MacDonald's brother John was packing up his things. The life of a schoolmaster did not satisfy him, and, though he was looking for something, he did not know what. He could not share the Christian certainties of his brothers, and so he had decided to taste adventure instead. That August he set out for Moscow to see what life in another country would bring him.

MacDonald's visit to London was but a happy interlude before facing the double problem of packing up house at Arundel and finding some work. When MacDonald returned to Manchester and saw Dr Halley once more he found that the Newington Chapel where he was about to preach had already found a new incumbent and that they only wanted him for the preaching. But he was 'not at all sorry I am not going there'. The idea was fixing itself more and more in his mind that he ought to form his own church:

'I feel more and more doubtful about getting a church here, but hopeful about raising one.'[4]

Charles, his brother, did the best he could:

> 'He is very encouraging and good too about my position and seems
> uneasy and troubled if I am not well. I suppose Charles Edward's and
> Alec's deaths have made him so.'[5]

Unfortunately each of Charles's efforts seemed to run into the sand.

Louisa was busy packing. Her father had agreed to pay the removal
expenses, but it was difficult to dismantle a home and leave with nowhere
to go. In the meantime her father had promised that she and George
could store their furniture in his firm's warehouses. But much had to be
sold — the piano as well as many of the books. That was a bitter pill to
swallow. It was beyond their means to hire a carriage to take everything
away and so they hired a barge instead to sail off down the river, leaving
Arundel behind forever.

So the autumn deepened till winter began to chill the Manchester
streets. Two of Charles's friends had talked of the possibility of using a
disused carpenter's shop as a meeting-place — but then it was pulled
down. With the hope of finding a church dwindling daily, MacDonald
applied for the post of librarian and clerk at Owens College. He was
desperate. The salary was only £100 a year, but the duties were not
strenuous. MacDonald knew about libraries, after all: 'The chief difficulty
will be my inexperience in Book-keeping, but I have been studying that
and Charles says I could do it quite well.'[6] MacDonald was up against
stiff opposition for the post. There were about forty applicants in all, but
it was a straw to cling to. Another fragile hope was that it looked likely
that a London publisher called Freeman would publish his long poem,
Within and Without. He had been sending it quietly to different publishers in the hope that someone would accept it and now it looked as
though the weary round of rejections was over. Godwin told him: 'You
are at one of the turning points of your life and I pray you may be led in
the right path'[7] — for to become a librarian would be to abandon the
ministry; of this Godwin and the rest of the family did not approve.
MacDonald replied as honestly as he could:

> '. . . as I have no resources I must at once try and get some teaching in
> Manchester, and so be in some measure independent. This is the more
> necessary — manifoldly because I know my ways of thinking as so
> very different from those of any churches, that, it is doubtful whether I
> shall ever find a church already formed that will choose me. If one
> should, I shall hold myself in readiness to be turned out very soon. At
> the same time as far as now shows itself to my mind, preaching is my

work, and preach I will somehow or other. That which is gradually bringing to my mind a great eternal peace and hope I will try to give to others — but it is and must be very different from what is commonly accounted religious teaching.'[8]

Even after he had applied to Owens College, MacDonald reaffirmed this:

'Preaching I think is in part my mission in this world and I shall try to fulfil it. But I wish to raise a church for myself or rather to gather around me those who feel I can teach them to their profit.'[9]

After a week of anxious waiting he learned that he had not been successful in his application to Owens College: 'My friends are commonly glad — no — some of them only — that I have not succeeded.'[10]

As it happened, the publisher also let MacDonald down after reading his work and decided to withdraw from their agreement. MacDonald seemed further away from recognition than ever. All he could do was waver between Liverpool and Manchester, missing Louisa and looking for work.

Finally Louisa went up on 10 October to stay with Helen and Alex in Liverpool after being placated by a letter from her sister-in-law. MacDonald, though, warned her: 'Do not be led into confidences about ourselves which you might afterwards repent.' Louisa settled down there as best she could and then in a letter written shortly after her arrival remarked on the death of F.W. Robertson, the remarkable preacher at Brighton whom they had heard and whose theology was so like MacDonald's:

'He died, Mr Griffith says, of a broken heart from what he has endured from persecution. He has been hunted to death for his liberality and goodness. Is it not fearful to think of the piety of the churches? I am, my very dear Husband, heart and soul and life yours.
P.S. — I would rather be with you on a starvation diet than anywhere without you but with all the luxuries of creation.'[11]

MacDonald joined his family in Liverpool in December and there they spent Christmas. Although it was a happy time, they must have felt uneasy about the precariousness of their situation.

January came and with it the hope of a new church:

'Most probably I shall have to preach at Rusholme [in Manchester] next Sunday. Mr Harrison thinks I shall be able. I know not what significance is to be attached to my preaching there then — but it will be a beginning. . . .'[12]

Harrison was his doctor, and there was a strong possibility that Rusholme would invite him to be their minister. But then the wintry chills as usual began to wear down his health and he was reduced to sitting by the fire in the gaslight wrapped up in blankets. His brother Charles fussed round him:

'Charles is very kind. It was quite a picture to see him about four this morning in his shirt and drawers like a cricketer, with his handsome bearded face bent down making poultices for his sick brother.'[13]

Dr Harrison had to be called and 'lanced my mouth gum. I nearly fainted after it was over. But I am much better now, though still feverish.' Yet though MacDonald was in a weakened condition he could not bear to be apart from Louisa and the children for much longer and besides, though Alex and Helen had no children of their own and had a spacious house in Liverpool, they could not keep their MacDonald lodgers for ever. George and Louisa resolved to find some temporary lodgings in Manchester:

'Yes, dearest, I think we will try lodging here for a while, and if our money is spent, and nothing to do, then it will be time to think of your going somewhere else. Though if we could get just enough food to keep *us* alive and the children quite happy, I would rather be half-starved together than well-fed asunder. Tomorrow afternoon I mean to go to Rusholme to look for some lodgings.'[14]

He agreed that:

'It is rather a sad time for us to begin housekeeping with our little means for everything... and war threatening, which will raise everything. But if we are doing right, it is all the same to the rich God whether we begin with ten pounds or a thousand. *Appearances* are nothing, if *realities* are on our side... I am very rich in my wife and children. I wish I could support them. Perhaps I shall soon.'[15]

War was in the air. The Crimean war between Russia and Britain was about to break into the open — and John, MacDonald's brother, was in Moscow. George MacDonald senior waited at The Farm for news of his youngest son.

Louisa and the children were able to come to Manchester in February 1854 where they spent two or three days at the Scotts. It was there that MacDonald heard: 'All is over at Rusholme, and I am glad of it for I do not think I should have felt comfortable there.'[16] MacDonald went off to Birkenhead to preach, but the effort was too much and he was laid up for three weeks with lung trouble and the serious possibility of another haemorrhage. He stayed with a Mr Rawlings who also opened his door to Louisa and the two little girls. They were generously treated there, with a carriage at their disposal. But the illness was serious and MacDonald was warned not to preach for several weeks and so the family's principal source of income was cut off.[17]

An immediate solution to their problem came through the kindness of a Miss Ker, Mrs Scott's sister. She lent the MacDonalds a farmhouse at Alderley, twelve or fifteen miles outside Manchester, which she had rented, and allowed them to stay there for nothing. The house was prim, but comfortable with a 'large, low stone-floored, four-doored room' and a piano and books and everything else they might wish. The family were originally meant to stay there only a fortnight, but MacDonald's illness was such that they did not leave until the end of March.

MacDonald petitioned his father to send another cask of oatmeal as the previous one had been lost in the move from Arundel, and begged for some barley too. This oatmeal was more than just a reminder of home. When MacDonald stated that 'My unwellness is attributed by my medical man to overmuch mental action,' that may well have been true. Certain foods brought him out in a nervous rash and he found that he could not eat them. When he was ill only oatmeal would do.

But letters to and from Huntly had become strained. MacDonald's father complained to George and Louisa that they were being 'presumptuous' in their actions, and wanted them to settle down to some stable, regular employment as soon as possible. After all, it was now nine months since MacDonald had quit Arundel, and in that time, apart from piecemeal preaching, he had done nothing except mouth fine sentiments about the lilies of the field. Louisa worried that she was to blame:

> 'My wife has taken it into *her* head that you have taken it into *yours* that she is a fine lady who does not know how to help herself and is rendered miserable by the absence of anything to which she has become accustomed.'[18]

There may, of course, have been more than a grain of truth in this, but it was MacDonald's insistence on his own heterodoxy and his unwillingness to play servant to another congregation that had prevented him from finding work. He admitted to his father that 'everything of late has failed' but firmly added: 'Not that I think anything I have tried has failed from the higher point of view.'[19] He tried for another job at Owens College — as head librarian this time — but was turned down once again.

Mr Powell agreed to pay the rent for a house and finally on 4 May they moved into 3, Camp Terrace, Lower Broughton, 'a nice house, large, and in some respects handsome' for £35 a year. Arthur Morley Francis, an old friend of MacDonald's from Highbury days, came to lodge with them and his ten shillings a week was all the income they had. MacDonald decided to give lectures on English literature to young ladies to raise money. This kind of work was easy to pick up. And Louisa's sister, Carrie, came from London to live with them. Soon she was on her knees stitching carpets and curtains with Arthur Francis helping her.

Manchester was a complete contrast from quiet, rural Arundel. Smoky and industrial, its streets hurried with workers making their way to the mills. It was not the healthiest of places, but George and Louisa were surrounded by friends there, and there was opportunity for work that MacDonald could do. But it was not a place he found attractive:

'Tis a poor drizzly morning, dark and sad,
The cloud has fallen, and filled with fold on fold
The chimneyed city; and smoke is caught,
And spreads diluted in the cloud, and sinks,
A black precipitate on miry streets
And faces gray slide through the darkened fog...
...Slave engines utter again their ugly growl...
...the organized whole
Of cranks and bells and levers, pinions and screws
Wherewith small man has eked his body out,
And made himself a mighty, weary giant.'[20]

His father sent the cask of provisions, including some beef, and MacDonald began to work on his lectures, 'A whole world of reading lies before me for that.' And so began a round of teaching, calling on people, and using the Free Library where he became friendly with the librarian, Mr Edwards. Soon he was able to write to his friend Alphaeus Smith in Arundel:

'Now at length we are settled in a house of our own, and I hope
soon to have a large hall in Manchester for preaching in on
Sundays... It is an easy thing to be as honest as society requires of
one, but it is not easy to be pure, to be in what are counted little
things thoroughly, divinely upright. May God teach me in this.'[21]

Their income began to grow slowly from the teaching MacDonald could scrape up, and this was not all that was growing. MacDonald had made a serious new addition to his personage. He wrote playfully to his father:

> 'You seem amused and somewhat indignant at my wearing a
> beard. Don't imagine it a foot long though in place of an inch; and
> believe that I feel nearer to nature, yes, seriously nearer to
> God's intent when he made man in his own image by doing so.'[22]

The beard was one expression of individuality, and in June 1854 MacDonald finally started his own 'church' in Renshaw Street. Some friends of his paid rent for the room and gathered round week after week to hear him preach freely without any fear of reprisal. It was good to be able to talk of the heart of God's love and to mix poetry and theology with people who understood him, and to meet on a basis of equality, for there were no such things as seat rents in MacDonald's 'church' nor any kind of distinction between rich and poor. But the income to be had from the little band, mainly personal friends, who gathered every week to hear him, was negligible, and the numbers attending did not increase. This was disappointing, even though MacDonald claimed that he was not interested in worldly success.

Yet even if his income was not stable, he was using his talents in several different directions, managing a hand-to-mouth existence. Money was still short, however, and would become shorter as Louisa was expecting another baby. MacDonald began to give lectures to young ladies and soon had twenty-five regular attenders all paying a guinea each for a course of twelve on such subjects as *Macbeth*, *King Lear* and the *Modern Poets*. He also took on some private pupils whom he taught for three hours a day, usually boys, and these he coached in arithmetic and mathematics.

That summer John was trapped in Russia, where the situation had become more dangerous and the family were worried as to how he would escape. News came from him in July that he was safe, but nothing more. No one knew what adventures he might be having.

MacDonald continued to worry about pleasing his father. Even with his teaching, he was scarcely distinguishing himself: 'My principal temptation to desire success,' he wrote, 'is that you should one day have the pleasure of seeing your son honoured before you die.' He was pleased that his father liked his contributions to the *Monthly Christian Spectator*. MacDonald had contributed poems, articles and some stories. In August 1854 the prose story *The Broken Swords* came out in that magazine.

Then in September the railway finally reached Huntly. It was heralded with due pomp and ceremony, slicing through George MacDonald senior's land just in front of the house. While he was accustoming himself to the noise of the engines whistling past his windows into the station close by, in Manchester his granddaughter Caroline Grace arrived, bawling her way into the world, between five and six on the morning of 16 September. 'What a wonder it is — this miracle that happens every day and every hour!' wrote MacDonald excitedly. Louisa was disappointed at producing another girl, but MacDonald was delighted: 'Not I, I like girls best,' he declared.[23]

Louisa's sister Carrie had taken Lilia to London before Grace's birth and Angela, another sister, came up to help with Louisa's confinement. It was not long before she found herself drawn to Arthur Morley Francis, who seemed eager to help her with the housework, and the two were soon firmly attached.

MacDonald went south again in October, preaching at Coventry and not able to move a step further till they paid him; only when they did could he complete his journey to London and there find Lilia who was not feeling well. He went from there to Barnsbury Street where the Mathesons received him heartily. He and Greville attended F.D. Maurice's inaugural lecture at the Working Men's College on the evening of the 31st. He managed to find some preaching — preaching for Caleb Morris a couple of times — and then daring to preach in a Unitarian Chapel. He wrote to Louisa:

> 'Your papa looked very funny at hearing it was a Unitarian Chapel, shrugging his shoulders — but not a whit less kind.'[24]

It was a relaxing time. He went out on horseback with Phoebe Powell, riding in Hyde Park and calling on the Godwins and the Mathesons. He went with Carrie to the Crystal Palace, and waited for Louisa and the girls to join him at the Powells for Christmas.

Soon after Christmas MacDonald was back in Manchester. He was excited at the opening of the new Ladies' College. This short-lived institution had been started by two sisters whom MacDonald met through A.J. Scott and the new work it provided brought in more money, while his lectures at Camp Terrace were also going well. 'I have a great many ladies,' he boasted, but he needed them. Bills piled up. The coal bill was enormous — £4 — and he had to borrow £5 to help do up the nursery before Louisa's return. He asked Louisa to greet Caleb Morris for him: '...what we should do now without the money he and his friends have given us I don't know.'

'Our father in heaven knows what we need and sends it to us as we require it — only keeps us always somewhat short that we may look for more — the part that is wanting being the connexion with the infinite supply in God's California — we must be taught to go there for it always.'[25]

He delivered his first lecture at the College on 31 January and took on another class of two pupils there. He planned more and wrote home to Huntly, asking his father to send down John's science books.

Then, like a bolt from the blue, there was good news. Macmillan had refused MacDonald's long poem, but in February Longmans agreed to publish it. MacDonald was overjoyed. It seemed his honour was to be fully recovered at last:

'I send back by this post to Mess. Longmans of London the signed agreement between Longman's house and me for the publication of my poem. They expect to bring it out in April.'[26]

In fact they brought it out in May. On 18 May 1855 *Within and Without* was finally published.

CHAPTER TWELVE

Within and Without — MacDonald's Poetry

Within and Without was not written overnight; it was the fruit of many years' work and was MacDonald's first important artistic statement to the public at large. To understand the man it is necessary to understand his poetry and to chart his advance from the first few youthful scribblings to this first major publication in 1855, and beyond.

The boy who used to sweep and tidy the nursery at the age of eight and then take down a copy of *Pilgrim's Progress* to read, had begun composing poetry at a very early age. But the young George MacDonald wrote down none of these verses. Instead he used to walk around with his early pieces of poetry held only in his head. When he turned ten, however, his grandmother used to help him write down what he had rhymed that day. Later he remembered not being satisfied with the grammar of one particular word, even though the rhyme was all right. MacDonald's early exposure to literature was fairly slight — when he ventured as far as reading one of Walter Scott's *Waverley* novels, his father took it away from him, though later regretted doing so.[1] It was only when Millar arrived at the school in Huntly that MacDonald began to read more deeply and, even as a young adolescent, he experienced the current feelings of 'romanticism' without really understanding them.

The power of nature, sacramental and sanctifying in its effect, lies at the very heart of MacDonald's poetic vision and this effect is something he began to feel when he himself still idled in the bleachfields:

'The fact is I was coming in for my share in the spiritual influences of Nature, so largely poured on the heart and mind of my generation. The prophets of the new blessing, Wordsworth and Coleridge I knew nothing of. Keats was only beginning to write. I had read a little of Cowper, but did not care for him. Yet I was under the same spell as they all. Nature was a power upon me. I was filled with the vague recognition of a present soul in Nature — with a sense of the humanity everywhere diffused through her and operating upon ours. I was but fourteen, and had only feelings, but something lay at the heart of the feelings, which would one day blossom into thoughts.'[2]

The catalyst which eventually changed those feelings into thoughts was probably MacDonald's encounter with the library at Thurso Castle while he was still a student. The rows of books in English and German caught him up and baptized his imagination anew. Feeling was the key word. The feelings MacDonald found in the poems he read corresponded with what he himself felt and hungered after, and forced him to read further. Thus he immersed himself in both the English and the German romantics — in Wordsworth and in Coleridge, in Goethe and in Schiller — and in Novalis who, above all, was his touchstone in these important matters of feeling and poetry. The life and thought of Novalis so gripped MacDonald that he returned to him again and again, finding some deep affinity in the spiritual, sad and simple poetry of the afflicted German.

Novalis's best known works are *Hymns to the Night* and *Heinrich von Ofterdingen* written in 1799 and 1800. While Novalis was writing these works he was already ill with consumption and died in March 1801, almost four years to the day after his beloved Sophie, his idealized and doomed love. He died firm in the faith that once his soul had escaped his body he would meet with her again face to face.

Novalis's mysticism and piety, expressed in disturbing and beautiful symbols, was one which appealed strongly to MacDonald. For Novalis appeared to be able to integrate heart and soul, longing after a 'new' Christianity, 'the basis for the projective force of a new world-edifice and a new humanity.' Of all the German romantics he alone had the strength and experience to put into poetry what religion and Christianity meant to him. His *Spiritual Songs* were revelations of the new religion, of the deification of the universe and of his yearning love for eternity. He thought that the classical religion of Ancient Greece, rooted in the here and now, held a deep terror of death, while Christianity by contrast had reconciled the world to the idea of death, because of Christ's resurrection and the defeat of death. Friedrich Schlegel wrote to Novalis: 'Perhaps you are the first person in our age to have an artistic sense for death.' And this taste of death, 'good death', was a taste which in turn quickened MacDonald. With his restless roving along the sea-shore, his sitting motionless in crowded rooms and uttering time after time 'I wis' we were a' deid!' MacDonald found a glorious liberation in the thought that death was merely a higher form of life and that the soul, shuffling off the fetters of the body, would rise free and unbounded to bliss.

MacDonald had translated Novalis's *Spiritual Songs* into simple, hymnal English for the Christmas of 1851 in Arundel, heralding the arrival of the new religion in Sussex.[3] Later he also translated *Hymns to the Night*, along with some other works from German in a volume entitled *Exotics*, later reissued in *Rampolli*. These books did not sell and twice MacDonald brought out the *Spiritual Songs* at his own expense. It was his task to bring Novalis before the English reading public though in fact he would never become popular with more than a faithful, influential few.

Novalis's novel *Heinrich von Ofterdingen*, however, influenced Mac-Donald in a different way. The story of Heinrich and his journey to Augsburg, along with his search for the mysterious blue flower, is a symbolic parable. The book is an 'Erziehungsroman', that is, it is about an individual's education and thus resembles *Phantastes*. The mining scenes anticipate *The Princess and the Goblin*. The whole, rather than the separate parts of the book, symbolizes the step-by-step upward ascent of man and his deliverance from the bonds of earthly life.

Heinrich von Ofterdingen is deliberately set in the removed but recognizable past: 'An idyllic poverty adorned those times with a peculiarly earnest and innocent simplicity.'[4] Novalis believed that:

'. . . between the rough and crude times of barbarism and the modern age abounding in wealth, art and knowledge, there was a reflective and romantic period concealing a higher form under a simple garment.'[5]

And this love of the past which the English romantics no less than the Germans deployed to paint mediaevalism in high colours was the same love which MacDonald used to paint scenes of past peasant life in Scotland. The truth was very far from the poetry, but the quaint pictures of the peasants living close to the soil in harmony and natural justice stem from the same impulses as moved Novalis and his brother romantics.

Heinrich von Ofterdingen is regarded as a definitive example of early romanticism and the ideas that flowed through it flowed into the pens of other writers. For example, Schleiermacher said, 'Whenever I gaze upon my inward self, I am immediately in the realms of eternity. I behold the activity of the spirit which no world can change, which time cannot destroy, which itself creates both world and time.' Tieck declared that: 'Not these plants, not these mountains, do I wish to copy, but my spirit, my mood which governs me just at this moment.' Schelling summed up all their feelings when he announced that 'Every true work of art is a manifesto of the absolute world unity expressed in perfect form.'

They were prophets of a new consciousness, a turning-point for the poet, transforming him into a being who primarily feels and whose feelings are of primary importance. Poetry thus became an expressive vehicle, an alliance of philosophy and music and, in the wake of recent events in France, a revolutionary force. Across the sea, Wordsworth and Coleridge began promoting this 'romantic' revolution in English.

In England its manifesto was the Preface to the *Lyrical Ballads* of 1800. In it Wordsworth claimed that poetry was 'the spontaneous overflow of powerful feelings' and thus tipped the balance towards the expressive theory of poetry which had already gained so much ground in Germany. Previously, poetry had been regarded as mimetic, a kind of painting of nature drawing its *raison d'être* from classical criticism; now the analogy shifted more to music, with the poet as both instrument and player. Earlier the most admired forms of verse had been epic and tragedy but these were now displaced, clearing the ground for the lyric and ballad, more suitable vehicles for emotional intensity. Further, because of their deep roots in the folk tradition of the country they could be thought of as somehow more 'natural' and nearer the people.

Yet MacDonald had other models besides Wordsworth. Being a Scottish rather than an English poet he looked to Ossian and to Burns, the archetypal ploughboy-peasant poet, for inspiration, and there found a love of the past and a love of nature.

The love of nature remained all-important, and in *England's Antiphon*, MacDonald's guide to the history of religious verse in England, he wrote:

'The divine expressions of Nature, that is, the face of the Father therein visible, began to heal the plague which the worship of knowledge had bred.'

In this realm Wordsworth remained very much the ideal. MacDonald wrote of him:

'The very element in which the mind of Wordsworth lived and moved was a Christian pantheism... Now, Wordsworth is the high priest of nature thus regarded. He saw God everywhere; not always immediately, in his own form, it is true; but whether he looked upon the awful mountain-peak, sky-encompassed with loveliness, or upon the face of a little child, which is as it were eyes in the face of nature — in all things he felt the solemn presence of the Divine Spirit. By Keats this presence was recognised only as the spirit of beauty; to Wordsworth, God as the Spirit of Truth was manifested through the forms of the external world.'[6]

The romantic pattern for a work of art remained MacDonald's own:

'A work of art is essentially the internal made external, resulting from a creative process operating under the impulse of feeling, and embodying the combined product of the poet's perceptions, thoughts and feelings. The primary source and subject matter of a poem, therefore, are the attributes and actions of the poet's own mind.'[7]

Yet for MacDonald a work of art had to be more than this. He was not just a poet, but a teacher and theologian too and the didactic element in his work is strong.

To teach and delight were both fundamental aims of MacDonald's poetry and it should come as no surprise that later in his life he issued an anthology of the writings of Sir Philip Sidney (with whom he felt some kinship), taken mainly from the *Arcadia* and bound in an attractive little volume called *A Cabinet of Gems*.

According to the expressive theory of poetry, the poet changed, not just from painter to musician, but also from craftsman to creator. The creative power of the imagination became all-important and, just as God had made the universe out of nothing, so the poet formed the poem as a second creation. The strain of ideas underlying this view ran all the way back, not so much to Plato's Demiurge in the *Timaeus*, but rather to the neo-platonic Greek philosopher Plotinus and the *Enneads* which formed the source of many of MacDonald's ideas, theological as well as poetic. Plotinus had given a high position to the arts, contradicting Plato who saw art merely as an imitation of an imitation:

'Still the arts are not to be slighted on the ground that they create by imitation of natural objects; for, to begin with, these natural objects are themselves imitations; then, we must recognise that they give no bare reproduction of the thing seen but go back to the ideas from which Nature itself derives, and, furthermore, that much of their work is all their own; they are holders of beauty and add where nature is lacking.'[8]

So the arts have their part to play in making the world better, and as the source of the poem is ultimately the same as the source of the tree or the flower, so there exists a unity of which man is but a part. It is the task of the poet or philosopher to guide men towards such a right-seeing and hence the importance of Sidney's axiom of poetry having to teach as well as delight, especially for a poet like MacDonald who had deep-seated theological interests.

In MacDonald's eyes, if Wordsworth was the seer, then Coleridge was the sage, a man who combined philosophy, poetry and theology drawing

on the ancient tradition that stemmed from Plato and Plotinus. Mac-
Donald wrote:

> '. . . yet Coleridge had much to do with the opening of Wordsworth's
> eyes to such visions; as, indeed, more than any other man in our times,
> he has opened the eyes of the English people to see wonderful things.
> There is little of a directly religious kind in his poetry; yet we find in
> him what we miss in Wordsworth, an inclined plane from the
> revelation in nature to the culminating revelation in the Son of Man.
> Somehow, I say, perhaps, because we find it in his prose, we feel more
> of this in Coleridge's verse.'[9]

There were many people in the nineteenth century who could make little
sense of Coleridge, but he had his devoted disciples of whom MacDonald
was one and F.D. Maurice, the influential theologian, another. Stephen
Prickett comments that, 'Through Maurice's *Kingdom of Christ* Coleridge's vision became a challenge to the Church of England which it has
neither been able to live with, or to do without.' Such a transmutation of
Coleridge into a distinctively theological challenge was one, of course,
which MacDonald was eager to take up, and did so. Prickett goes on to
say that:

> 'It was Coleridge's great and lasting contribution to the nineteenth
> century and no less to our own time, to have rediscovered and
> re-affirmed the complex symbolism that transforms the language of
> religious experience from easy platitude and comfortable doctrine to
> ambiguity and tension, to fear and trembling.'[10]

Coleridge claimed that, 'An IDEA, in the *highest* sense of that word,
cannot be conveyed but by a symbol,' in other words, by a work of art,
and in *Aids to Reflection* he insisted that, 'For if words are not THINGS,
they are LIVING POWERS by which the things of most importance to
mankind are actuated, combined and humanized.' In this way Coleridge
postulated an organic thought process of which each work is but the part
of a whole and saw the imagination as a creative faculty, at the same time
bringing the two levels of experience, inner and outer, together as a
coherent whole. MacDonald shared this view. For him Imagination:

> '. . . is, therefore, that faculty in man which is likest to the prime
> operation of the power of God, and has, therefore, been called the
> *creative* faculty and in its exercise *creation. Poet* means *maker.*'[11]

The role of poet as creator imitating the Creator was one MacDonald
saw as a divine gift and just as Coleridge thought in 'wholes', so

MacDonald's work too has a remarkable unity, the same preoccupations and images flowing into different genres of writing. If MacDonald succeeds most neatly in turning the inside outside in his fantasy writing, the rules nevertheless hold good for his own poetry.

MacDonald's preoccupation with Wordsworth and Coleridge was intense. He wrote on Wordsworth in a collection of pieces called *Orts* as well as on Shelley, and in his novels his heroes often have a volume of the poet's verse in hand. In *David Elginbrod*, for example, Hugh Sutherland's tutelage of Margaret Elginbrod includes reading from Coleridge's poems, 'smaller pieces' from Wordsworth and selections from Ossian. As a poor tutor in London MacDonald invested some of his meagre income in Coleridge's verse and later in life lectured on *The Rime of the Ancient Mariner* many times. He was obsessed with the poem:

'He prayeth best, who loveth best
All things both great and small:
For the dear God who loveth us,
He made and loveth all.'

In the strange and alien symbolism of Coleridge's haunting poem Mac-Donald paradoxically found both a home and a meaning.

Few of MacDonald's early poems survive. Most were written in the book he gave to his cousin Helen MacKay and of these only some fragments remain. The earliest of them was probably written when he was seventeen:

'Like a boat on the wave
When a storm is in the sky, —
Like the rose o'er a grave
When the winter is nigh, —
Like a star when it streams
Through the clouds in their flight, —
Like the fabric of dreams
'Mid the slumbers of night...'[12]

There is nothing very remarkable about this slight and rhythmical verse, but its picture of the fleeting transience of this life (as opposed to the eternal solidity of the next) is one of MacDonald's perpetual themes.

From his earliest days MacDonald employed the lyric form and a simple, musical language in such a way to express what he saw as important truths. As the poems were expressions of his own state of mind, and MacDonald's mind was often steeped in gloom, his gloom was inevitably projected into the language and the imagery of his poems. He could write:

'Bury me, bury me deep
In some lonely cove on the wild sea's shore.
There none o'er my grave will come and weep:
But the maddened waves' tempest roar
Will soothe this spirit when, shrouded in gloom,
It visits its rough and unlettered tomb.'[13]

His concerns were always the same — to escape the maddening round of everyday life into a rest which is always depicted as sleep or death, the only place where he can find an erotic and spiritual consummation and hence a purgation of all that is troubling him. His poems of this period are deeply sexual, deeply religious and deeply troubled. Nature, though a divine power in herself, can only reflect the poet's mood:

'The mysterious night.
When but a tip of the low hornèd moon
Looks o'er the crest of a peaked cloudy height,
Edging it with a glory — fading soon:
A few pale stars are through the cloud-rifts strewn,
And the low wind is running to and fro,
Like a forsaken child that knows not where to go.'[14]

Such a projection fits in with MacDonald's own poetic theory — 'For the world is — allow us the homely figure — the human being turned inside out.'

If Wordsworth's manifesto was the *Preface to the Lyrical Ballads*, then MacDonald's was his essay: *The Imagination: Its Functions and Culture* where he deals with the romantic theory of the imagination, interpreting it according to his own theological concerns. For the world is not merely seen as a projection of the poet's own feelings and wishes, there is already latent in Nature a meaning given by God:

'For the world around him is an outward configuration of the condition of his mind; and inexhaustible storehouse of forms whence he may choose exponents — the crystal pitchers that shall protect his thought and not need to be broken that the light may break forth. The meanings are in those forms already, else they could be no garment of unveiling.'

And as God is the source of everything, Man included, then Man's imagination and faculty to create can only be secondary:

'If we now consider the so-called creative faculty in man, we shall find that in no *primary* sense is this faculty creative. Indeed, a man is rather *being thought* than thinking, when a new thought arises in his mind. He knew it not till he found it there, therefore he could not even have sent for it. He did not create it, else how could it be the surprise that it was when it arose?'

Here MacDonald is using his own intuition to arrive at a theory of how God inspires. A fervent believer in the supernatural, he was definitely anti-Kantian in his acceptance of the surprising intervention of a loving God...as well as of things that go bump in the night:

'...the fact that there is always more in a work of art — which is the highest result of the embodying imagination — than the producer himself perceived while he produced it, seems to us a strong reason for attributing to it a larger origin than the man alone — for saying at the last, that the inspiration of the Almighty shaped its ends.'

Such a view of poetry as divinely inspired places it very close to prophecy and revelation — MacDonald certainly believed that poetry was a divine breaking-through into the present world to reveal something of the lasting truth of the universe. After all, 'This outward world is but a passing vision of the persistent true,' and poetry, close to the source of speech, retained for MacDonald a *symbolic* aspect while prose represented poetry worn out through over-use and slipped downwards into mere *signs*. Poetry was the unifying element in the Platonic dichotomy, as it was the unifying element in the apparent division between poetry and science, for MacDonald argued that science could not be allowed as the sole interpreter of nature:

'Every experiment has its origin in hypothesis; without the scaffolding of hypothesis, the house of science could never arise. And the construction of any hypothesis whatsoever is the work of the imagination. The man who cannot invent will never discover.'

The imagination is necessarily at the basis of every human activity. Writing at a time when, in the church at least, many people regarded the imagination as a dangerous and disagreeable thing, MacDonald had to stress that the source of the imagination was God and hence good.

If the theory underlying MacDonald's poetry is coherent and exact, what of the execution of the poems themselves? Of MacDonald's early works, only two bear closer scrutiny. One, 'David', was MacDonald's first poem ever to be published, in February 1846. It deals with King

David and his dead son Absalom. The theme of fathers and sons is one which occupied MacDonald throughout much of his work: he had a close relationship with his own father and saw such a bond as a human reflection of God's relationship with Christ. His thoughts on the matter became most explicit in the Dedication to the 1857 collection of *Poems*:

'Take of the first-fruits, Father, of thy care...
Thou hast been faithful to my highest need;
And I thy debtor, ever, evermore,
Shall never feel the grateful burden sore.
Yet most I thank thee, not for any deed,
But for the sense thy living self did breed
That fatherhood is at the great world's core.'

Though not published until 1846, 'David' was originally written in the book MacDonald gave to Helen MacKay and so was probably composed some time between 1840 and 1842. As in all his early work it has a gloomy preoccupation with death and ghosts — the very stuff of Gothic — and the descriptive parts of the poem have a morbid, languorous lushness:

'The sun was down; the wan-faced moon uprose,
Like the pale spectre of a former sun.'

Through the night King David walks 'like a solitary ghost among the tombs.'

Reduced to a spectre, rather as Euphra in *David Elginbrod* and Julian in *Within and Without*, David makes his way to Absalom's tomb and remembers the lost, happy days before his son went astray. David himself is implicated in Absalom's sin, for it was he who taught the young man how to hold the bow. But sadly the mourning king soon wakes out of his reverie and the dream is gone:

'And then a solitary gust of wind
Swept o'er the trees, and they did moan with him;
And a lone cloud, that just then past o'erhead,
Wept o'er the grave a few big drops of rain.
And then he slowly rose, and hasted home;
And ne'er a word with his bright tears there fell,
Save, as he turned, "Oh! Absalom, my son!"'[15]

Here the pathetic fallacy is at its most explicit, accompanied by morbidness at its most extreme, as the trees moan and the cloud weeps with the mourning king. It is redolent of the romantic writers at their most melancholy and also of much of the Gothic writing. It is certain that

MacDonald read the gothic novel *The Castle of Otranto* and he surely must have devoured other such texts.

Another early, but unpublished work is an unfinished two-act blank verse drama called *Gennaro*,[16] written in 1845–46, after MacDonald had come to London and was working for the Radermachers. The poem opens, set in: 'A gothic library, with stained, ivy-grown windows. Gennaro alone on a couch.' Gennaro, a young student, invokes a spirit with whom he makes a kind of Faustian pact. Yet the similarity to Faust lies only in the outline and not in the content of the story, for Gennaro asks:

> 'Wilt thou give me the power to know the thoughts
> That people every world of consciousness
> *Whose* outward image moves before me?'

In this Gennaro resembles not so much Faust as Solomon, though it is undeniable that Goethe's *Faust* lies at the well-spring of the inspiration of this poem, as it did for many of the romantic writers. As a work of the spirit and the imagination, *Faust* held an indescribable appeal for MacDonald. In *Gennaro* the spirit answers Gennaro's request by saying, 'That I can never do.' Instead he gives Gennaro the ability to read the heart from actions and then takes him invisible, from his body, on a journey. They see a girl drowning on a wrecked ship and then approach the city where sounds rise like 'exhalations'. The spirit then takes Gennaro to another young girl who is 'past all feeling save of misery'.

> 'If she is conscious of a wish, it is
> A feeble longing after nothingness.'

Act One closes at a dance, where the spirit whispers the name of the desolate girl into the ear of a pale youth who is seated on a couch by a dark girl. The youth starts guiltily, rises and goes. Gennaro exclaims with vehemence:

> 'I will disclose it to her. She shall never
> Wed infamy; for this is not the being
> Whom she doth love; and did she know his love
> Her soul would loathe him; and she would but weep
> That a fair form had vanished from the world.'

In Act Two the scene shifts to 'A ledge of rock running out into the sea: Gennaro alone.' The spirit takes Gennaro out to a vessel to see:

'...one who hath known the weariness
and the delight of being...
...his name
Was on men's tongues, and their inmost souls,
A name of wonder and deep reverence.'

This man is a kind of Christ-figure. The spirit then leads Gennaro back to the city where images of degradation and poverty well up before him:

'...the wretched one
Who, clasping to her bosom her pale child
Lifteth up to him eyes where supplication
Hath taken its last refuge.'

Finally Gennaro complains, 'Oh! Spirit, I am lost in this wide place.' Then he hears a sound:

'Let us join the worshippers
Spirit: The worshippers!'

Gennaro shows MacDonald's interest, first of all, in blank verse drama as a vehicle for poetry. Though gothic and fantastic in content, it marks a move away from simple introspection towards an attempt to use poetry as a vehicle for ideas. The poem is marked off from MacDonald's other early work, not just by its length but also by its intent. Neatly and painstakingly copied out, it must have taken him many hours to compose and recompose — and it paved the way for the writing of his major poem *Within and Without* begun four years later during his convalescence on the South Coast in 1850−51.

MacDonald spent more time and care on composing *Within and Without* than on any other of his works. It is a monument of patience and labour, a lengthy verse drama published after several years of waiting, and served as the turning-point in MacDonald's life — from his period in the wilderness into the beginnings of a literary career. Few people bought it or read it, and he received only £20 for writing it, but it was a moderate success in its way, running to two editions. It is a long and curious poem, standing strangely in the climate of the times. For the debates of the middle of the nineteenth century were between faith and doubt, science and religion. The pace of life had altered and the old certainties had gone for ever. Though German poets ·such as Herder, Novalis and Goethe wrote of springtime, renewal and birth, the Victorians were searching for something to believe — they believed that there was something to believe, but they could not find it. Amy Cruse in *The Victorians and their Books* wrote:

'Men were waiting for a new revelation that would clear away the doubts and perplexities that the discoveries of science and the controversies concerning religion had raised. Some went to the poets for help and found in them sympathy and consolation and soul refreshment. But the poets themselves had but a clouded vision; they too were troubled and anxious.'[17]

Matthew Arnold for one complained in the introduction to his 1853 collection of poems of 'the bewildering confusion of the times,' and Kingsley added despondently, 'few of us deeply believe anything.' But by far the most influential doubter, who set the tone of the age, was Tennyson whose poem 'In Memoriam',[18] published in 1850, summed up the feelings of his generation:

'Behold we know not anything;
I can but trust that good shall fall
At last — far off — at last, to all.'

MacDonald held Tennyson in very high regard and in *England's Antiphon* classed him with 'the noble band of reverent doubters' whose poetry almost reached the high status of religious. Of Tennyson, MacDonald claimed:

'. . . he has written *the* poem of the hoping doubters, *the* poem of our age, the grand minor organ-fugue of *In Memoriam*. It is the cry of the bereaved Psyche into the dark infinite after the vanished love.'[19]

Thus in *Within and Without*[20] the monk Julian's tortured mind, seeking after a revelation of the true God, is quite in keeping with the spirit of the age. The very title *Within and Without* sums up the concerns of the expressive theory of poetry and exposes MacDonald's own metaphysical preoccupations. It is a long, five-act blank verse drama, but falls into three parts. Five is an obviously biblical number, the number of the books of the pentateuch, as well as the usual number of acts in a play; MacDonald claimed that he spent forty days writing the poem, the number of days Christ spent in the wilderness. Some revelation must be at hand.

The whole poem is dedicated to Louisa and written 'weary with sickness and with social haze'. The first part opens in a monastery cell where Julian, the Count Lamballa, has spent four years after fleeing from an unsatisfactory love affair with the beautiful Lilia. In contrast with the other monks who are content to lead a jolly life, Julian is earnestly seeking after the true God but cannot find him, 'My prayers fall back in dust upon my soul.'

Though Julian's sincerity stands out sharply against the greed of the abbot or the empty theological speculation of another monk, Stephen, the monks are displeased at Julian's philosophizing and label him an atheist and a troublemaker. Gradually feeling grows against him. But Robert, a friendlier monk, tells Julian that he has met an old woman lying ill at an inn who has told him about Julian's love affair and its fateful outcome — 'But false play came between.' With Robert's help Julian escapes from the monastery and makes his way back to his own castle where his old nurse tells him that Count Nembroni has become the only creditor to Lilia's father, and to flee his embraces Lilia has gone to lodge with an honest old couple in the town. Julian slays Count Nembroni and nurses Lilia through a serious illness. She is horrified to discover that he is a monk, but nevertheless agrees to run away with him. Together they set sail in Julian's leaf-like boat for England, leaving an angry crowd behind them, who have come to punish Julian for his 'heresy'.

This could easily have been the ending of the whole poem, and in itself is the stuff of conventional melodrama. But MacDonald did not leave the story there. The next part of the drama opens five years later in London. Julian has made peace with God, though he is too much distracted by poetry and theology from the business of everyday life. There is a child of the union, Lily, who is a typical MacDonald embodiment of goodness — angelic, simple and wise. Julian is deeply attached to the child:

'Come as a little Christ from heaven to earth,
To call me *father*, that my soul may know
What *father* means, and turn its eyes to God!'

But all is not well. Lilia, despite her beauty, is cold, distant and sad. For the love between them has lost its warmth. Julian muses:

'I am afraid the thought arises still
Within her heart, that she is not my wife —
Not truly, lawfully. I hoped the child
Would put that thought at rest; but now I fear
She fancies I have begun to think the same,
And that it lies a heavy weight of sin
Upon my heart.

And Lilia too is troubled by the same thoughts.

The middle section of the drama unfolds a tale of suffering with a compassion unique in MacDonald's work. The poignant description of love growing cold between two people is deeply moving. The passage has, perhaps, some biographical significance — the distracted husband; the put-upon wife — and Julian does at one point read 'Love me, beloved', the lyric MacDonald gave to Louisa on her wedding day. Whatever the case, the passage answers Gennaro's wish to know the workings of the hearts of men and women.

Lilia is tempted to elope to Italy with Lord Seaford, but refuses. She has, however, already sent Julian a letter saying she has gone. To increase his misery, Lily the child dies and it is only when Julian is near death that Lord Seaford hurries to Julian's side and is able to tell him the truth.

'Your wife is innocent,' he whispers, and with this aweful knowledge, a light burns up in Julian's eyes and he dies.

Again, MacDonald could easily have finished the drama there — it is a fitting and moving climax. But, he pursues his characters even further, up to heaven itself, where he stages a grand, cosmic reunion. The setting for the final part of the poem is 'A world not realized'.[21] Lilia is standing in front of a crucifix dressed in black, a guardian angel hovering unseen behind her. Julian arrives and dismisses the angel.

Then the scene shifts to the summit of a large mountain. The earth is invisible beneath a sea of vapour and only rocky peaks pierce through the clouds. Julian is finally at peace. At that moment Lilia rises out of the fog and Lily, resting on a bar of cloud, swoops down like a bird to help her. Mother and child climb up the rock:

> 'At last Julian reaches his hand. They stand beside him, and the three are clasped in one infinite embrace.'

Julian says:

> 'O God, Thy thoughts, Thy ways are not as ours;
> Yet fill our longing hearts up to the brim.'

> 'The moon and the stars and the blue night close around the three; and the Poet awakes from his dream.'

The poem on any level is imaginative and fantastic, but its taut musical verse has been honed to tell a story and at the same time be a powerful theological instrument. Julian, contrived as an Italian count with a German mother in order to display the necessary emotions, is a convincing hero, but as in much of MacDonald's work, the poem's strength lies not so much in its art as in its sentiments. Many people read MacDonald not for the beauty of his verse, but for his insights into human nature. Yet *Within and Without* possesses a grandeur greater than any other poem MacDonald ever wrote. And, though it in some way contains in embryo form the themes he was to develop later in his work — man seeking after and finding God; the intervention of the supernatural; the discovery of erotic love and the consummation at death — the middle section stands apart and gives *Within and Without* an important place in the MacDonald canon.

By September 1855, 300 copies of the poem had been sold — not many, but enough, and contemporary reviews were favourable. The *Athenaeum* commented, 'Seldom have spiritual abysses been more thoroughly sounded, — seldom has despair had a more eloquent voice, — seldom has mystic sentiment been more beautifully interpreted...' though the reviewer went on to complain, '...the whole, nevertheless, is inexpressibly painful... Nature and existence are not all clouds and rain, but attended with sunshine and honest pleasures.'[22] *Fraser's Magazine*, however, commended the poem for its honesty, 'I have at last found an honest poet, one of the most thoroughly genuine I have met with for years.'[23] It was this quality of sincerity that compelled people, despite finding deficiencies in his art, and which in the wake of the publication of the work, brought him several influential admirers.

MacDonald's other verses are fragmentary in comparison with the monument of *Within and Without*. He published a collection of *Poems* in 1857, *The Disciple and other Poems* in 1867, *Diary of an Old Soul*, privately printed in 1880, *A Threefold Cord* with poems by his friend Greville Matheson and his brother John Hill MacDonald also privately printed in 1883, and finally he had all his verse reprinted, including the poems contained in his novels and stories, in two volumes of *Poetical Works* in 1893.

Out of all these volumes there are only two substantial poems apart from *Diary of an Old Soul*. One is 'The Disciple' which MacDonald forged from several different poems contained in the 1857 collection using 'A Boy's Grief' as his nucleus. 'The Disciple' contains the usual journey to God ending with:

'Here thou hast brought me — alone now
To kiss thy garment's hem,
Entirely to thy will to bow,
And trust thee even to them.'

The other poem 'A Hidden Life' tells a circular story, the idealized ending taking place when the young student returns to work his father's land.

MacDonald's own preference was for the lyric, the ballad and the sonnet. He set out his recipe in the introduction to *England's Antiphon*:

'The earliest form of literature is the ballad, which is the germ of all subsequent forms of poetry, for it has in itself all their elements: the *lyric* for it was first chanted to some stringed instrument; the *epic* for it tells a tale, often of solemn and ancient report; the *dramatic*, for its actors are ever ready to start forward into life, snatch the word from the mouth of the narrator, and speak in their own persons. All these forms have been used for the utterance of religious thought and feeling. Of the lyrical poems of England, religion possesses the most; of the epic, the best; of the dramatic, the oldest.'

George Herbert was MacDonald's ideal in the realm of religious verse — apart from the 'shape' poems which he found affected — for Herbert managed to combine form and sentiment perfectly, as well as remaining a model pastor. The lyric and the ballad, as well as being traditional forms, and hence close to the people, were musical forms; the analogy of music to poetry was important to MacDonald, drawn as it was from the theorizing of the Germans, and it is no surprise to read in *Robert Falconer*:

'The man whose poetry is like nature in this, that it produces individual, incommunicable moods and conditions of mind, — a sense of elevated, tender, marvellous, and evanescent existence must be a poet indeed... I suspect, however, that for such purposes it is rather music than articulation that is needful — that, with the hope of these finer results, the language must rather be turned into music than logically extended.'[24]

So the mood can be created through the sound rather than through the sense. In this way meaning dissolves into communion and the relationship between the reader and the poem becomes a mystic and sanctified bond. Like Wordsworth, MacDonald used to subject his poems to long and exhaustive revision. This was not a sign of the poet's inadequacy, but of his dissatisfaction with earthly, verbal forms and his striving after the Ideal.

MacDonald's minor poems are often sonnets dedicated to people who were important to him such as A.J. Scott and F.D. Maurice; they also explore a number of biblical themes. For example there is a series on 'The Gospel Women' in the 1857 collection, and another on the beatitudes in

The Disciple and Other Poems. And there are others marked by Mac-
Donald's usual pastoral and theological inclinations such as 'The Hills':

> 'And now, in wandering about,
> Whene'er I see a hill,
> A childish feeling of delight
> Springs in my bosom still;
> And longings for the high unknown
> Follow and flow and fill.'[25]

There are also poems such as 'The Homeless Ghost' with its beautiful,
female shade who would seem to have a home in a fairy story or a later
romance.

Two other kinds of poetic form that MacDonald uses are worth some
attention — the Scotch ballads and the children's poems. His homeland,
the north-east of Scotland, was steeped in the ballad tradition, and the
Scots language had a literary tradition of its own, maintained in the
poetry of Burns whom MacDonald loved. In the poems at least, Mac-
Donald's Scots is a careful variety, one English people can understand,
and the ballads show a theologizing of traditional themes. 'The Earl o'
Quarterdeck', for instance, has a rhyme scheme and content similar to
that of 'Sir Patrick Spens', but unlike the traditional ballad it is moralistic.
Where the ballad is normally interested only in telling a story, Mac-
Donald must insert a meaning:

> 'Then up and spoke the king himsel'
> "Haud on for Dumferline!"
> Quo the skipper, "Ye're the king upo' the land —
> I'm king upo' the brine."'[26]

The king receives his come-uppance when he finds out that his temporal
power is limited — he cannot rule the waves — nor can he rule the heart
of his daughter who decides to have the skipper for her king at the end of
the poem.

MacDonald often falls into the mawkish, sentimental and ridiculous.
There is a fair amount of Victorian sugar in many of his poems. The end
of 'Ower the Hedge', instead of being touching, is merely comic:

> 'Crutch awa' he flang it
> Clean forgot his hairms
> Cudna stan' withoot it,
> Fell in Mally's airms.'[27]

The musical aspect of MacDonald's verse is nowhere more clearly integral than in the children's poems, though even here a moral is sometimes spelled out, as in 'King Cole':

> 'And the king rose up and served them duly
> And his people loved him very truly.'[28]

Many of the children's poems seem musical 'nothings', mere childish babblings which are hard to justify. It is as though MacDonald had taken Wordsworth's edict of 'spontaneous overflow' too literally and uncritically deluged the reader with wanton doggerel. But while some of the poems such as 'What the Owl Knows' are merely trite, even here there is a theological device at play. The babbling is deliberate, a babbling from the source of life, from the source of language itself and this locates truth as close to the childlike and holy. Just as Wordsworth could see an old woman or an idiot boy as fit matter for his sermons, so MacDonald held to the doctrine that the foolish things of this world are close to the heart of God and shame the wise. The figure of the 'Holy Fool' is important to him, indeed it was one he had to play in real life. The fool in a short story like *The Wow o' Rivven* is therefore not an object of mockery, but a source of inspiration. The poem which Diamond (another 'Holy Fool') and his mother find on the beach in *At the Back of the North Wind*, 'No End of No Story', holds a meaning that neither of them understand:

> 'and over the shallows
> with all the swallows
> that do not know
> whence the wind doth blow
> that comes from behind
> a blowing wind.'[29]

Its sound, like an endless stream, is purifying and healing, creating a mood without giving any particular sense. It is a poem which is essentially anti-rational, whose words are not there to create meaning but somehow mystically and intuitively can change hearts.

MacDonald's only other notable poem is *Diary of an Old Soul* (1880), which was printed only on the right-hand page, leaving the left for notes. It is a devotional poem divided into twelve sections for the twelve months of the year, with a stanza to be read every day. It ruminates on relatives and friends long and recently dead and concentrates on how God has dealt with the author through all his sufferings. In the poem, as in *Within and Without*, the verse is pared down to express theological meaning, and it is intended to be read as a spiritual exercise and not as an evening's entertainment. The entry for 1 October is especially poignant and shows how readers came to turn to MacDonald for consolation and to help them with their own spiritual needs:

> 'Remember, Lord, thou hast not made me good,
> Or if thou didst, it was so long ago
> I have forgotten — and never understood,
> I humbly think. At best it was a crude,
> A rough-hewn goodness, that did need this woe,
> This sin, these harms of all kinds fierce and rude,
> To shape it out, making it live and grow.'

MacDonald turned from writing verse to prose through economic necessity. And if verse was not the best vehicle for his imagination, he nevertheless cultivated an image of himself as a poet, for he saw that as the highest calling and even won some of his admirers round to his view. William Geddes, a fellow student with MacDonald, and later principal of Aberdeen University, published an article after Tennyson's death in March 1891 in *Blackwood's Magazine* called *George MacDonald as a Poet*.[30] Its intention was to arouse interest in the possibility of Mac-Donald becoming Poet Laureate — but the honour fell to Alfred Austin instead.

Much of MacDonald's verse is unmemorable, but the themes which throbbed through its lines were to take other forms, notably in fairy tales and romances, and these were fated to remain compelling and enduring.

CHAPTER THIRTEEN
North Again

As MacDonald was anxiously counting the days till the publication of *Within and Without* his mind was distracted by the news that his half-sister Bella, then aged fourteen, had fallen ill with tuberculosis and was not likely to improve. In June 1855 her health grew much worse and it became clear that MacDonald had to travel up to Huntly if he wanted to see her before she died. In the meantime Robert Troup, now the pastor of the Missionar Kirk, had become engaged to MacDonald's cousin Margaret, who was more like a sister to George, and the couple were anxious that MacDonald should marry them. MacDonald had not been to Huntly since his own marriage: hardship and illness had prevented it, but now he had the opportunity. He knew that he would be in favour this time as he had at last done something — he had written a poem. He devoured reviews and wrote enthusiastically of the one he had read in the *Brighton Review*, sent to him by his friend Dr Ross:

> 'I have peeped at it and have seen some names with whom mine is coupled enough if I am not mistaken in my hurried glance, to satisfy the wildest ambition.'[1]

No doubt MacDonald's father was also scouring the newspaper columns for reactions to his son's literary effort. Mr Powell was certainly won over. A few days after the publication of the poem, MacDonald and Lilia crept silently into The Limes as a surprise, only to find old Mr Powell weeping over it. The publication of *Within and Without* substantially altered the way the family treated him. They became more understanding of his difficult circumstances, recognizing his temperament more fully as that of a 'poet'.

MacDonald left for Huntly on 1 July 1855, not by steamer this time, for by now the railway had reached The Farm. So, face pressed eagerly against the carriage window, he watched the scenery grow more and more rugged as he rattled all the way up to Edinburgh to spend the night.

It was the first time that MacDonald had ever visited the graceful city of Edinburgh, 'The Athens of the North', and after downing some tea and a steak he went out to wander through the narrow streets of the old town. He stepped down the Royal Mile and gazed at Holyrood Palace. But after 'our orderly *clean* commonplace well-behaved Manchester', parts of Edinburgh came as a shock. The filth and grime of the city took MacDonald aback as did the conditions that many of the people had to live in:

> 'Some of the dark *closes* and entries look most infernal, and in the dim light you could see something swarming, children or grown people perhaps, almost falling away from the outlined definiteness of the human. It was more like some of the older parts of Aberdeen than anything I had seen, but worse, much worse.'[2]

MacDonald continued his journey the next day, but had to stop over with his cousin James at Aberdeen as he arrived too late to catch the last train to Huntly. He wrote lovingly to Louisa that night:

> 'Perhaps you will come yet and see my dear home this year. Get as much of the table done as you can without hurting yourself.'[3]

There had not been enough money for Louisa to accompany MacDonald on his long journey and she had taken it into her head that if she decorated a table for her brother Alex (who would pay her £5 for it) then she might be able to join her husband later in the summer. It was a hopeless dream, however, as the drudgery of everyday life, looking after the children and coping with Charlotte, the maid, whom Louisa could not abide, soon pulled her down.

The last leg of the journey by train was full of excitement:

> 'I am seated alone, a few miles on my way to Huntly. I have passed in the distance the stone crown which tops the square tower of my old college, and the pagoda-looking towers of the cathedral — and beyond lies the sea...'[4]

The train sped on through Inverurie past the grass-grown ancient burial mound and through Insch under the shadow of the vitrified fort standing open to the sky, round the side of the Clashmach, soon to bloom purple rich with summer heather and past the gates of The Farm into Huntly station where it stopped with a hiss of steam and a screech. MacDonald's sisters were there waiting for him and as he stepped off the train greetings and embraces were exchanged and together the family, united once more, walked the few short yards along the line from the station back to The Farm. To be back in the open countryside and at home was marvellous for MacDonald. One of the first things that he did was to rush out and sit on the grass in the sun with the Bogie bubbling at his side. The only shadow on the day was that:

> '...down in the nursery lies my poor thin sister, very quiet — or rather sits, for she sits in bed with her knees up and her head leaning upon them — so thin is she. Yet there is no incongruity between them — I mean this outside and that inside for she lies like a seed waiting for the summer to which this summer is but a winter.'[5]

The grief melted a little at his father's kindly welcome — much fuller than expected — which waylaid all MacDonald's fears. He talked often about the book with pleasure and MacDonald felt that he had found some understanding and acceptance at last. Indeed his father was so pleased to see him that he offered his son a cigar:

> 'I smoked a cigar last night with my father's permission, and being the first for nine years I was very ill after it, and have not quite recovered [from] it today.'[6]

This was a greater welcome than he had been expecting, for not only was he still wary about turning up with no money — he was wary about turning up with a beard and a moustache and feared criticism. He told Louisa:

> 'My father is so kind and liberal — more so even than I expected — he has no objection at all to my moustache, though he would like it off to make me more acceptable, but he does not seem to care much.'[7]

MacDonald's beard caused him some anxiety over the following few days — first of all in going to a prayer meeting where Troup asked him if he would preach at church the following Sunday. No comment was made. MacDonald wrote with relief to Louisa, 'My beard is safe, I think.' The first hurdle was over. Pleased as he was at being invited to preach, he was a little impatient with the people: 'The prayer-meeters keep on praying for the spirit, and never recognize it when it comes.' Then, angrily, MacDonald reported:

> 'My uncle offered me a guinea for my moustache tonight, seriously though funnily. If he knew how bitterly hurt his own son was at his compelling him to shave, he would not have risked it. If fathers knew how liberality makes their sons love them, they would exercise it oftener. But my noble old father told me that for his part *I might let it grow till I stuffed it in my trousers*.'[8]

This irritation was, however, but a grain of sand in the most placid of oysters. The days spun on happily. MacDonald drank milk and bitter beer to gain strength, read Beaumont and Fletcher and Shakespeare and sat having long talks and playing backgammon with Dr McColl. He spent much time with his father too, walking out with him under the warm sun through fields of flowers. A rusty nail through the foot hampered MacDonald's movements for a few days, but soon he was out again — on horseback — riding free through the empty countryside around Huntly. One day he galloped for eighteen miles and came home talking of:

'...some delightful feelings floating into me from the face of the blue hills. And the profusion of wild roses on some parts of my road. The heather is just beginning to break out in purple on the hillsides. Another week of warm sunshine will empurple some from base to summit.'[9]

Slowly the possibility that Louisa would join him slipped away. She was stuck in Manchester, beleaguered by ailing children and almost at her wits' end. She was pregnant again. The table stood unpainted and the best way out of the misery seemed to be to take up the invitation to go and stay with her sister Flora (Mrs Joshua Sing) in Liverpool. Accordingly she packed up the house and set off. As usual, Louisa was ill-at-ease depending on the kindness of others, though the rivalry she felt with Flora took a different form from that with Helen. Mr Powell came to Liverpool to stay on a visit, and, though it was pleasant to see him again:

'...I have been out a little with Papa. I do not think he will say anything about our pockets. Everything is too bright and glowing and rich and plentiful here to think of such words as 'no money' or *getting on*.'[10]

— there were some familiar sadnesses: 'But I find it difficult to bear the much greater love Papa has for Flo than me.'[11] MacDonald understood his wife's nervousness and wrote to her soothingly, 'Dear Love, I fear you are having a very hard life of it just now,' and 'You have a harder trial than the others dear, both from your husband being — what he is — and poor besides — but perhaps that may be made up to you some day.'

News came that John had left his position as tutor in the family of the Chaplain to the British Embassy in Moscow and, despite the dangers, had arrived safely in Leipzig. He did not talk of coming home, but had resolved to find a situation in Germany, and failing that, to sail to America.

In Huntly, as the wedding between Robert Troup and Margaret MacDonald approached, MacDonald became aware of petty jealousies dividing the church. This came as a shock because as a boy such complaints had passed over his head. He was upset to find that he was one of the objects of discontent:

> 'I have more and more cause to rejoice that I am not connected with any so-called church under the sun. A good many seem annoyed for instance at the minister marrying my cousin.'[12]

The great day came and went and with it MacDonald's reason for staying on in Huntly. His family pressed him to stay longer and he gave in a little, but he knew that he must soon journey south again. With Robert Troup and Margaret on honeymoon, his anxieties increased as he feared that he would not be asked to preach again owing to his 'heterodoxy'. He was right — he was not asked to preach again, but the reason was not wrong belief:

> 'The objections made by a few — My uncle among the rest — not for their own sakes — but for others forsook to my *beard* has been the reason why I have not been asked to preach.'[13]

MacDonald stayed on at The Farm for another two weeks, gathering material for stories, and drinking in the scenery, now in full bloom. But he had to go. He and his sister Bella exchanged presents. He gave her a book of *Grimm's Fairy Tales* in red boards with woodcuts which he had asked Louisa to send up, and she bought him something to take away out of the little pocket money she had:

> 'She had nearly a pound — and today she gave me two sets of flannel for the winter, which I should think took all she had. Her little body will be cold before I wear them.'[14]

He added grimly to Louisa, 'It will be our turn sometime most likely to go through this.'

Then, as Louisa was determined to dismiss her maid, Margaret McColl MacDonald pressed a young girl called Elsie Gordon on MacDonald and urged him to employ her. Her wages were £7 a year. So the pair, man and girl, prepared for the long trip south. MacDonald's last act was to go on a pilgrimage with his father to see his brother Alec's grave at the church-yard at Drumblade:

> 'I have been with my father to see Alec's grave, five miles away. He lies beside my mother and two brothers. I thought — oh there is room

for me between him and the wall. But I must be where you are my own, only I should like if we could both lie in that quiet country churchyard.'[15]

Gifts of money came from various quarters to tide him over, and MacDonald's father paid the fares south. After a long journey they arrived in Manchester early in the morning and Elsie at once settled happily into family life.

Work began again — lecturing mainly — which brought in £3 a week and the MacDonalds hoped to have an Owens College student to board with them to give a slice of extra income. But the squeaky cheap furniture and heavily darned clothes still broadcast a tale of want and hard economy. A piece of good news, however, was that MacDonald had found a congregation enthusiastic about his ministry. He wrote to his father:

'I am glad to tell you that I was unanimously invited last Sunday by a company of 70 seat-holders to preach to them. I agreed to do so for a year to see how it will do. I was never treated with such respect.'[16]

He had had so many disappointments before, that he proceeded cautiously, but the Albert Place Chapel in Bolton proved a friendly place:

'I shall let you know as soon as any further steps are taken at Bolton. I should not wonder if it come to an agreement, nor should I wonder if the contrary. I think I should only make the engagement for a year, with the understanding that except renewed on both sides it would terminate then.'[17]

But his relationship with the largely working-class congregation of this church was good and he enjoyed his contact with them. He had no pastoral or administrative duties to attend to, but only appeared on a Sunday to preach. It was something to be so accepted and in addition swelled his pocket a little further.

Within and Without continued to cause little ripples. A.J. Scott told MacDonald that he had heard that it had been well received in the best literary circle in London and reviews still appeared, some good, some bad. Then, letters of appreciation began to make their way to Manchester. Early in the summer the famous Christian Socialist and writer Charles Kingsley had written, while MacDonald was in Huntly, saying how much he had enjoyed the poem, and in September MacDonald received 'a gratifying letter from Maurice'. Both these men shared the same spiritual concerns as MacDonald and were much admired by him. It must have been gratifying to receive such encouraging praise. One interesting admirer whom MacDonald attracted was Lady Byron,[18] widow of the poet:

> 'I have heard several things about my book since I returned — the principal of which is the interest Lady Byron, the widow of the poet, has taken in it. It seems to have taken a powerful hold on her.'[19]

She was soon to turn her admiration for MacDonald into philanthropic actions for his benefit.

Lady Byron was a lady of stern beliefs. One critic wrote, 'A strong sense of duty, shown in a rather puritanical precision, led unsympathetic observers to regard her as prudish, pedantic and frigid.'[20] After her separation from the tempestuous Lord Byron in 1816 she had been sorely buffeted by scandal. She settled eventually in Brighton where she 'took an interest in the religious questions of the day, and spent a large part of her income in charity.' She was fond of theology and mathematics and had written one or two poems herself. Phrenology was also a strange passion with her. While in Brighton she had become familiar with F.W. Robertson the preacher, whom she relied on heavily and missed when he died. The only other man she became close to towards the end of her life was George MacDonald.[21] Perhaps the description of the estrangement between Julian and Lilia in *Within and Without* touched a nerve in her, but more than that, the sentiments in the poem were close to those of F.W. Robertson and this similarity was noted by others as well as Lady Byron. The *Brighton Herald* of 27 June 1857 writing on *A Poet-Preacher in Brighton* commented:

> 'On Sunday morning we had the pleasure of hearing a sermon from Mr MacDonald, at the Pavilion Chapel, Church Street. It was a brief, and probably almost unstudied extemporal address; but we have heard nothing approaching it from the local pulpit since the late F.W. Robertson. Of that gifted preacher's style it reminded us strongly.'

In MacDonald then, Lady Byron saw shades of her former mentor and was drawn to him accordingly. The young poet was more than flattered by her attentions — he became sincerely attached to her and she confided some of her story in him, and often sent him gifts of money. She had some reservations however, criticizing the public readings of his poetry and finding the excess of emotion 'intolerable'. She feared that he would never succeed as a lecturer. But these criticisms did not wound him, and she probably kept most of her worries to herself.

MacDonald drew her as Lady Bernard in *The Vicar's Daughter*[22] and dedicated *David Elginbrod* to her after her death — 'There are few rich who...enter in to the Kingdom of Heaven in spite of their riches. She to whom this book is dedicated is — I will not say was — one of the noblest of such.' This was proof of devotion and gratitude indeed.

Suddenly at the end of that summer John, MacDonald's brother, returned to England, throwing up his plans for staying in Germany or sailing to America. He was very out of spirits, so much so that he found it hard to put pen to paper. Restless as ever, he was thinking now of going to Dresden to give private lessons. He found lodgings near MacDonald and Louisa. Meanwhile Louisa fell ill and went to Liverpool to stay with friends called the Hendersons. The doctor recommended sea-bathing.

And then Bella died on 24 August, fading like a withered flower out of the world. The family grieved, but they were glad the waiting was over. MacDonald wrote to his stepmother:

'Schiller says "Death cannot be an evil because it is universal." God would not let it be the law of His Universe if it were what it looks to us.'[23]

MacDonald carried on with his lecturing and preaching, but as autumn bit he was struck down by the worst haemorrhage from the lungs that he had had so far. He lay close to death for many days and the doctors were unable to stop the bleeding. He had to lie completely still, without coughing or moving, bags of ice weighing heavily on his chest. Louisa was unable to cope with such nursing, and her sister Angela came over from Liverpool to help. Greville MacDonald recorded:

'The two Miss Kers, Mrs A.J. Scott's sisters, came one or other of them to his bedside to read or sing to him for hours together. Dr Harrison declared that he had never known any patient who, fully aware that he might be dying, looked death in the face with such perfect equanimity.'[24]

Slowly, the bleeding did lessen, and after being bled at the arm, the blood spitting stopped and did not return.

As usual MacDonald's illness had set back the family's finances a long way, but Mr Powell had paid the last quarter's rent though they were still £25 in debt. The congregation at Albert Place was waiting patiently:

'The people at Bolton are willing to wait *any* time for me. Their only dread seemed to be that I should give up the idea of going back to them.'[25]

But this would take time. Phoebe Powell, Louisa's sister, was soon to be married to Joseph King on 20 February and Mr Powell was willing to subsidize two or three months' convalescence in Devon after that.

Gifts came from unexpected quarters. On New Year's Day three gentlemen, an Independent, a Churchman and a Unitarian, brought £30 and some of the Bolton Congregation called with a quarter's salary in advance. Then the post brought an unexpected £5 bank order from Ann Ross, a relative in Huntly. MacDonald penned a long reply to her:

'Please to receive my warm thanks. I was suddenly laid aside from work. And my family was dependent on my daily labour in teaching, lecturing besides preaching, but such has been the kindness of my friends, some of whom I had never known to be friends before, such the generosity of my congregation at Bolton, and such your goodness that we are in the meantime free from all anxiety. And if by this time we have not learned to "cast *all* our care on him who careth for us," I think we are getting to learn it. I have so much hope along with a little faith that I have not been troubled — scarcely at all. I see more and more that nothing will do for anybody in my circumstances but an absolute but an absolute enthusiastic confidence in God. It will be some time before I am able to work again. We are going to Devonshire or somewhere in the South for a while. It will probably be the month of May before we return here.'[26]

Just two-and-a-half weeks later MacDonald summoned up the strength to scribble a hurried note to his father:

'I am too tired with writing notes to do more than tell you that I have a son at last. Before ten last night he arrived. Louisa behaved so courageously. He is a great boy — might be three months old they say!'[27]

The boy — the first son and fourth child — was named after one of MacDonald's oldest and dearest friends, Greville.

CHAPTER FOURTEEN
North and South

As soon as Louisa's period of confinement was over, Mrs Scott spirited MacDonald away to their house on Cheetham Hill where he was nursed into better health, leaving Louisa to be taken care of by her sister Angela and a friend, Mrs Andrew. MacDonald lay reading, writing and waiting for visitors. While listening for his brother John to arrive (who in the end failed to show up), MacDonald wrote to Louisa:

> I was left quite alone, and spent the time meditating in spite of stupidity — and in *reading Hoffman's Golden Pot again.*'[1]

When he was finally able to get out of bed there were a few hectic days making their house ready in order to leave for an indefinite time. They found a man and his wife who were happy to live there rent free, and they moved to the Scotts before travelling down to The Limes for Phoebe's wedding. Several gifts of money from friends sped them on their way.

The wedding was a splendid family occasion and the couple set sail for Italy, to Naples and Rome on their honeymoon, but these exertions took their toll on George and Louisa. MacDonald's lungs were clear at last, but he was told by his doctors to rest for six months. So, early in March, MacDonald and Louisa with Lilia and the baby journeyed to Kingswear in Devon, but hardly had they moved into their house on the hill when MacDonald began haemorrhaging again. Louisa ran to the local vicar for help and his family sent for the doctor. As a result of this emergency the two families became friends. MacDonald was laid up in bed again and the cruel east wind kept him from a quick recovery. Soon, however, he was lying on the sofa, 'Looking out from the window through the mouth of the river Dart (as Jonah might through the jaws of the whale) into the great Atlantic.' It was here that F.D. Maurice paid the invalid a visit, reading to him out of Ruskin 'the scene on the shore of the Galilean lake,' and here, after much talking, MacDonald was able to go out to dinner with friends of Maurice's.

They moved a week later to Little Ravenswell where the garden ran down to the sea-wall and MacDonald spent much time on the shore; he also copied out his poems in a neat edition inscribed 'Kingswear, Lynmouth, Lynton', which he later gave Louisa as a present. He asked his father that same month:

> 'Will you please give up the Rev. to me. I never liked it. I only say *please* — if you have no particular reason for doing so.'[2]

Though Little Ravenswell was a good spot, Louisa was eager to press on to Lynton and Lynmouth where she had been on holiday with her mother eight years previously. They travelled there by steamer and took up residence at Mrs Appleby's lodgings. MacDonald found:

> '. . . a most romantic country; crowded hills, with wood climbing up to the top of some from the bottom of the valleys — while others are as bare as any in Scotland.'[3]

While they were staying in this haven on the North Devon coast they arranged a trip to Huntly. At long last Louisa was about to meet George's family. She went back to Manchester first while MacDonald travelled north by sea.

They spent three happy months at The Farm clasped in the bosom of George's family. MacDonald regained strength slowly and wrote to Charlotte Godwin:

> 'I scarcely do anything but read German stories and work a few verses now and then.'[4]

For the first time Louisa was able to gaze on the Clashmach and walk by the Bogie and the Deveron. All the things that George had told her so much about, all the people she had come to know through descriptions and letters — at last she came face to face with them all.

But as the sun grew colder and winter beckoned, friends urged a move south again. MacDonald's lungs were simply not up to the excesses of the Scottish climate. One friend who urged a move very particularly was Lady Byron who offered a solution as to where they should spend the winter that they had neither looked for nor dreamed of.

CHAPTER FIFTEEN
Algiers

As a suitable wintering-place for someone with weak lungs Lady Byron suggested Algiers — a place where sunshine was guaranteed. She agreed to pay travelling expenses and provide introductions to friends whom she knew would be staying there. George and Louisa were enthralled. Neither of them had been abroad before and the thought of an exotic adventure in the North African sun opened up exciting vistas before them. They gathered at The Limes in October. MacDonald had been unable to meet Lady Byron owing to an illness which had forced her to leave London, and he had to postpone that treat until his return.

The Scotts sent £50 to help them on their way. As a preparation George and Louisa went to the zoo for the first time, perhaps to spot the animals that they soon expected to see wandering unhindered round the Algerian streets.

Lilia was to be left with Aunt Charlotte Godwin at Belsize Road and Grace and baby Greville were to lodge with their grandfather and their Aunt Caroline at The Limes. Only frail, waifish Mary was to accompany her parents on the trip. After affectionate goodbyes and much kissing — they set off on 31 October 1856.

Travel was slow. It took seven hours to cross the English Channel. Then began the long journey down through France to Marseilles. First they spent a couple of days at Rouen, and then moved on to Paris where they spent Louisa's birthday looking round the city. It was so bitterly cold that MacDonald could not stay out of doors for very long and had to beat a retreat back to the Hotel Folkstone in the Rue Castilliane where they were staying. They did manage a visit to Versailles, however. After a few days in Paris they pressed on, but were delayed a week in Valence owing to MacDonald suddenly suffering a bout of bronchitis. Avignon pleased them and finally they arrived in Marseilles where they saw the Mediterranean and the shore, 'rocky and grand'.

By now they were weary of hotel life and longed to settle in one place, but they were detained in Marseilles for a week 'for not knowing rightly about the steamboats'. MacDonald was coughing again and a lump appeared in Louisa's throat at the thought of 'the dreaded going on board' for she was not a good sailor. But go she had to. They left finally on the *Osiris* on Saturday 22 November at noon and arrived in Algiers at the same time the following Monday. Forty-eight hours of sailing! Louisa's only comment was 'Seasickness is humiliating.'[1]

On arrival Algiers was 'white and dazzling' and full of marvels. By the blue edge of the Mediterranean there stood trees 'with many yellow oranges' and hedgerows of cactus. The streets thronged with a glorious mix of people: Arabs, Jews, French, 'Moorish' women, Negroes 'as black as soot' and children with purple hair. Mixed in with the heat and the flies and the dust, donkeys roamed. They saw muzzled oxen yoked by their horns, beautiful Arab horses — and camels.

MacDonald was still not well and had to languish much of the time in his hotel room with the shutters firmly bolted to keep the too-bright sun at bay and the unbearable noise locked outside:

> 'The town is full of French soldiers in all variety of uniforms; and what with their infernal drums and trumpets, and the noise of French and Arabic and the waggons and horses with bells — and, beautiful in themselves, the fountains before the door, we long for quiet.'[2]

When he did venture out he donned his Rob Roy plaid and Glengarry bonnet, thus adding to the colour already crowding the Algerian streets. He nosed around the town with delight:

> 'The lower part of the town is French, though tinctured with Arabesque; but above, you might fancy — what with narrow passages, the only streets, what with arched ways, and houses projecting till the walls touch, and a constant succession on either hand of courts with Moorish arches, and stairs up and down — that you were in the time of the pirates!'[3]

The hotel life could not last long, however, as their money would soon dribble away and by Christmas they had found rooms in an old Moorish house set on a hill fringed by olive groves, a little way inland from the western suburb of St Eugène. The house looked out over the Mediterranean. It was spacious enough, but damp — the floor paved with tiles of many colours and the walls two-and-a-half feet thick. There was a piano which Louisa always needed to soothe her and that was a great bonus.

The MacDonalds soon fell into contact with the Leigh-Smiths, who were there with their three daughters. Leigh-Smith himself had lately been MP for Norwich.[4] The ill-health of one of their daughters, Anna, was the reason that the family were holidaying in Algiers. First impressions, however, were a little strained:

'They are fast, devil-may-care sort of girls, not altogether to our taste, but very pleasant, and they seem to draw and paint well.'[5]

Lady Byron had asked them to befriend the MacDonalds and together they became part of the little expatriate group that met regularly in one another's houses, drinking tea and talking, and every so often when the weather was exceptionally pleasant, setting off on a picnic. The Mac-Donalds too contributed towards the entertainment as Louisa recorded:

'. . . We gave a soirée the other night and with flowers made the room quite pretty — great boughs of lovely scented acacia and lots of hawthorn and dear dark rich roses and wild pimpernels, large dark blue ones, and though they were all people with lots of money, I think they enjoyed themselves without wine or delicacies.'[6]

The Oliphants were also there, with their son and daughter. Oliphant was the son of the Edinburgh publisher. As this family possessed the only large china teapot (along with six teaspoons) of any of the expatriates, they were very much in demand at social occasions.

This group of people met and remet almost daily, whiling away the hours in genteel and quiet activity. Apart from their company the MacDonalds thirsted only for the mail which arrived by boat twice a week and MacDonald even asked his father, 'Could you send us an Aberdeen or Banff paper now and then?' It was about this time that Louisa fell pregnant again.

On the next floor up of the house where the MacDonalds were staying lived Archdeacon Wix and his family. They were friendly and they saw a lot of each other. On Christmas Eve MacDonald wrote almost gleefully to his cousin James:

'I should go to high mass at midnight tonight, which I do not think would shock Archdeacon Wix and his lady so much as they will be shocked when they find out, if ever they do, that I count *the* church as much a sect as the independents or the Mormonites.'[7]

Life, however, did not consist entirely of social visiting and picnics. MacDonald was still ill and had to spend much of his time alone indoors. This meant that he had leisure for 'writing rather than seeing' and much of the 1857 collection of *Poems* were written at this time. 'Abu Midjan', a playful, mocking ballad, is the piece most obviously coloured by his stay in Algiers. He was pleased to learn too that Longmans wanted to bring out a second edition of *Within and Without* in the spring. Before he had left England he had heard that there were only sixty copies left from the first printing:

'A second edition of my book is called for. In going over it again, I find it very faulty, but I can do little to improve it. I hope my next may be better.'[8]

He felt hampered by his lack of movement and wrote to Caroline Powell:

'When I am able, I hope to spend more time in prowling about the streets and seeing what the inhabitants are about.'

He had time to make some observations, though:

'Meantime I have learned something of the face of nature and the face of man — very little of the face of woman though. I do look as keenly as I can through the thin Manchester stuff over the Moorish faces, but I see almost invariably a sickly, thin countenance — at least in appearance through the veil, with soft black eyes — always black, over it, and often made hideous by stained eyebrows, meeting in Moorish arches over the nose.'[9]

The new year brought the worst weather for thirty years, 'thunder, hail, rain, wind and strong seas', but the weather was not cold enough to confine George and Louisa to the house. It did his lungs no good, however, and he had two attacks of bronchitis and spat blood once more. To add to their problems Mary contracted an eye disease which took many months to clear.

March brought trees in leaf, peach blossom and a wind from the desert that was said to lead to suicide. News came in that month that Mac-Donald's brother Charles, whose business had become hazardous in Manchester and who had had to rely on his father to settle his debts, was on his way to Australia. With the arrival of spring came the feeling that they ought to be on the move before the landscape was burnt up in the blistering summer heat.

MacDonald and Louisa began their long journey back to Britain at the end of April. The crossing to Marseilles was rough and again Louisa suffered terribly, but they were back safe and sound at The Limes by the middle of May. MacDonald's first concern was to hand in his collection of poems to Longmans as they were eager to publish them quickly; his next was to find somewhere to live. A return to Manchester was ruled out on medical grounds and though it seemed sensible for a writer to remain in the literary orbit of London, MacDonald's bronchitis pushed them to look for a place on the south coast, at least for the following winter.

But first MacDonald went north to Manchester to tie up loose ends and say goodbye to his congregation at Bolton as well as to the Scotts — and especially to his brother John who was now teaching at Barrow Hall near Warrington. On his return to London he at last met Lady Byron and this severe ermine-cloaked lady made a great impression on him:

'I have been to see Lady Byron. She is the most extraordinary person, of remarkable intellect, and a great, pure unselfish soul.'[10]

She made a proposal that MacDonald edit some letters in her possession, probably as a disguised way of giving him more money.

Then MacDonald went to Huntly on a short visit. As usual he had a good time:

'Mother has given me such beautiful drawers and flannels, and is going to get some shirts made for me. Perhaps I am going to the sea-side to the neighbourhood of the old castle on the sea-shore, for a day this week.'[11]

But at The Limes Louisa and her sister Annie were having their differences. It was the old, old story. Louisa felt in the way. MacDonald had to write:

'We must be saved from ourselves by very unpleasant things, and have no choice whether it shall be toothache or living on other people's means. I do not relish the thought of St. Leonard's at all, but I don't care. I have no suggestions to advance, and therefore ought not to have any oppositions. I am very useless and feel it.'[12]

On his return to The Limes Louisa was still very depressed, perhaps as a result of her pregnancy, and MacDonald wrote back to his father, 'We find it useless to try anything till we have a house.' A scheme for having a young man to live with them for a year on the basis of giving him bed and board and three hours of lessons a day for £100 fell through, partly because there was nowhere permanent to put him. The need for somewhere of their own to live grew steadily more vital.

MacDonald dined alone with Lady Byron in Dover Street a day or two before his new daughter was born. She asked him to tell her the truth about his circumstances, saying, 'I hope it is no disgrace to me to be rich as it is none to you to be poor,' and adding, 'If I can do anything for you, you must understand, Mr MacDonald, it is rather for the public than yourself.' A few days later she sent him a cheque for £25 and promised another £50 at Christmas. She was not keen on Hastings on the south coast as a choice of residence, fearing it would not yield good pupils, as the more fashionable place was the nearby Brighton. Nevertheless,

Hastings was chosen, but as the MacDonalds made their preparations for the move there was another death. Louisa's sister-in-law, Mrs George Powell, died on 20 August. Even though she had had heart disease and had been in bad health for a long time her death came as a severe shock and her husband's grief was terrible. After MacDonald's long illness and convalescence here was another reminder for Louisa that death could swoop down unbidden and carry any loved one away. On 31 August another baby was born, a girl called Irene.

The MacDonalds left The Limes at the end of September 1857 and stayed with the Rosses in Brighton till they could move to their new home in Hastings. The house they had chosen stood on the Tackleway and was named Providence House. The MacDonalds renamed it Huntly Cottage; it stood near East Hill House where Lady Byron had spent some months. Hastings was a watering-hole, tucked into the folds of coastland hills with good, fresh sea air and little society — though a few minor literary figures lived there. It was within easy reach of London which made for good communications with relatives and friends. Huntly Cottage had thirteen good-sized rooms and cost only £35 a year. There was space enough for pupils to come and be taught, while its first-floor drawing room was large enough for lectures. By 15 October MacDonald was able to tell his father:

'We are in our own house at last, and our landlady has let us have the use of her furniture till our own arrives, so that we can manage pretty well, having only two of the children and a nurse with us.'[13]

Louisa was distracted, however, that she had no help with the children, 'except that of a girl of fourteen or fifteen, with joints like a Dutch doll and a brain like a Dutch cheese. Louisa is often worn out.'[14]

When the furniture arrived at last, battered by its storage and travels:

'Its unpacking, thanks to the cayenne pepper used to keep the moth away, gave the master a severe attack of asthma and bronchitis; so that, till sorting and cleansing were over, he fled to friends in Brighton for a week.'[15]

In the absence of pupils to teach, MacDonald turned to writing with a will and told his father, 'I had hoped to have a fairy tale or something of the sort ready by Christmas, but that has been quite prevented by my illness.'[16] A month later he informed his father:

'I am writing a kind of fairy-tale in the hope that it will pay me better than the more evidently serious works. This is in prose. I had hoped that I should have it ready by Christmas, but I was too ill to do it. I don't know myself what it will be worth yet.'[17]

This book took MacDonald 'two months to write without any close work' — 'was a sort of fairy tale for grown people' — and it was to prove one of the major works of MacDonald's whole life. Its name — *Phantastes*.

CHAPTER SIXTEEN
Phantastes

The New Year of 1858 opened with the whole family in good health for once, perhaps owing to the mild winter weather. The MacDonalds found that they liked Hastings best of all the towns they had lived in — it certainly suited Louisa far better than Algiers had the previous winter. The household fell into a regular routine, MacDonald scribbling in his study and the children being well-regimented by Louisa and the nurse. MacDonald reported to his father that, 'I have carefully revised and partly rewritten *The Spiritual Songs* and sent them to Longman.'[1] Though nothing seems to have come of this venture, a more successful outing in London found him a publisher for *Phantastes*. He visited Lady Byron there and saw Caleb Morris, as well as F.D. Maurice, who suggested Smith, Elder and Co. as possible publishers of MacDonald's new work. After handing the manuscript in to them, '. . . two days after had £50 in my hands for it. It will be out by and by but I mean to try and improve it first.'[2] The end result is one of the strangest and most wistful productions in the whole of English literature.

Phantastes claims to be 'A Faerie Romance' for grown men and women. Though it contains shades of Spenser and echoes of Bunyan, it draws most of its substance from German romantic literature where the fairy element was more fully developed and treated more seriously. The title *Phantastes* derives its name from Phineas Fletcher's poetic allegory *The Purple Island* of 1633. Here Phantastes or Fancie is one of the three counsellors of the mind. Fletcher was directly inspired by a scene in Spenser's *The Faerie Queene* where Phantastes is an endless spinner of fantasies, locked away in a dark chamber within the House of Temperance. Whatever the derivation, the word itself has some connection with the imagination, and, written so closely to the Greek spelling, brings to mind the classical definition of the imagination as a 'making visible' or 'showing forth'.

If *Phantastes* has a single source it is surely *Heinrich von Ofterdingen* by Novalis, and, just as that book takes the form of a quest, so *Phantastes* too is a quest, of an inward nature. MacDonald's theory of art involved turning the inside outside, and this is most surely done in *Phantastes*, a book written so quickly that it might almost qualify as a stream of consciousness (or rather unconsciousness) novel. But *Phantastes* is not a novel in the accepted sense. It is a novel without a plot; a story without characters. MacDonald imbibed many German tales throughout his long convalescences. He loved Hoffmann's *Golden Pot* and De la Motte Fouqué's *Undine*, which he regarded as the most perfect of all fairy tales. Though fairy tales were in MacDonald's blood, there were powerful reasons why he chose the fairy form for his first long excursion into prose: psychological reasons — fairy tales clearly reveal the workings of the human mind; and spiritual reasons — there is room for the wondrous and the marvellous in them.

MacDonald prefaces *Phantastes* with some quotations from Novalis, one of which reads: 'A fairy story is like a disjointed dream-vision, an ensemble of wonderful things and occurrences, for example, a musical fantasy, the harmonic sequences of an Aeolian harp, nature itself...' *Phantastes* then, as a fairy story, is like a dream, exploring first and foremost the unconscious inner meaning of the soul, as MacDonald had attempted to do through the character of Julian in *Within and Without*. But, as in a dream, MacDonald does not have to obey normal conventions, for a dream is a place in which rules are broken, and where the laws of the actual are deliberately transgressed. Such a text is open-ended in a way that a conventional novel is not. A novel tells a story about certain characters in given situations, but *Phantastes* has no such comforting stability; there is merely a series of encounters, as in a night of dreams, and the question lingers — what does all this mean? *Phantastes* challenges its readers to discover something that it does not immediately give — that is, a meaning. This challenge is heightened by the inherent ambiguity of the 'characters' who people the text. In such a protean landscape as Fairy Land in *Phantastes*, where things change their shape and habit from one line of text to the next, the reader is disturbed into examining the text more closely. In effect, the text calls attention to itself, for in all its ambiguity it is calling attention to things normally left hidden.

As MacDonald believed that there was always more in a work of art than the artist put in, he was happy to believe that there were levels of meaning in his own work that even he did not understand. In response to a letter from a woman who had written expressing admiration for *Phantastes*, Louisa wrote:

'He bade me tell you that he has no key to his little work but he is sure that in your appreciation of it, you must have felt some meaning and he has always told his friends to take any meaning they themselves see in it.'[3]

But MacDonald was to a certain extent conscious of the unconscious. He knew what he was about. Stephen Prickett in his book *Victorian Fantasy* writes:

> 'It is only with the works of George MacDonald, possibly the greatest fantasy writer of that (or any other) period, that something like a fully balanced artistic theory emerges.'[4]

MacDonald orchestrated his fairy story to achieve certain conscious ends and this is part of his distinctiveness as a fantasy writer. The three elements that fed romanticism at the turn of the nineteenth century — the Gothic, the revival of religious mysticism, and the revulsion against the social conditions caused by the early industrial revolution — are all present in his work, but there is a further scheme. What tale there is in *Phantastes* tells of Anodos who wakes up the day after his twenty-first birthday to open a cabinet which has long lain undisturbed and was left to him by his father. The name 'Anodos' is often taken to mean 'Pathless', though, like so many things in the book, it is capable of various interpretations. It could also mean 'Aimless' as the Wise Woman whom Anodos meets on his travels describes him as '. . . wandering now without an aim'. Anodos finds more than he bargains for in the cabinet, for out hops a fairy being to whom he is instantly attracted, but who rebuffs him with, '. . . a man must not fall in love with his grandmother, you know.'[5] Her appearance at once aligns faery with the feminine and this emphasis is carried on throughout the book, for it is Anodos' grandmothers and not his grandfathers who have fairy blood in them. In one of the many cottages Anodos stays in in Fairy Land, for example, the father seems quite impervious to the enchantment around him, while the mother of the house is descended from a princess who was changed long ago by a wicked fairy into a white cat. Anodos exclaims:

> '"When I looked out of the window this morning," I said, "I felt almost certain that Fairy Land was all a delusion of my brain; but whenever I come near you or your little daughter, I feel differently."'

This suggests that Anodos, as well as having some fairy blood in him, also has some femininity and so his asexual name may also suggest androgyny. In Fairy Land the earth is strongly feminine and the book is scattered with images of mothering and nursing: 'I fell asleep in this cradle, in which mother Nature was rocking her weary child.' The desire for a return to the womb, for union with the mother, is strong in this magical place.

Anodos' fairy grandmother promises him entry into Fairy Land and, next morning when he awakes, he finds that:

'I became aware of the sound of running water near me; and looking out of bed, I saw that a large green marble basin, in which I was wont to wash, and which stood on a low pedestal of the same material in a corner of my room, was overflowing like a spring; and that a stream of clean water was running over the carpet, all the length of the room, finding its outlet I knew not where. And, stranger still, where this carpet, which I had myself designed to imitate a field of grass and daisies, bordered the course of the little stream, the grass-blades and daisies seemed to wave in a tiny breeze that followed the water's flow...'

Slowly Anodos' bedroom transforms into a woodland scene:

'I happened to fix my eye on a little cluster of ivy leaves. The first of these was evidently the work of the carver; the next looked curious, the third was unmistakable ivy; and just beyond it a tendril of clematis had twined itself about the gilt handle of one of the drawers. Hearing next a slight motion above me, I looked up, and saw that the branches and leaves designed upon the curtains of my bed were slightly in motion...'

When Anodos finally leaps out of his bed, his feet touch grass. He is outside. Or rather, he is *inside*, because he has become part of a dream landscape where anything can happen. The transformation of his chamber is an illustration of art being liberated into life — or imitation being changed into reality — in effect the same kind of transformation Anodos must undergo in order to become fully adult, the indication being that though he is twenty-one in years, he is not yet fully grown in maturity. And the spring-board into the magical country of Fairy Land is none other than a Victorian bedchamber — a place where dreams can take place, and where the pretty self-designed furnishings take on a life that Anodos did not intend for them. In one sense, Anodos has entered the obverse side of the mind, and having done so, the mind plays tricks. He finds that he can no longer trust his senses:

'...although my glance often fell on some object which I fancied to be a human form; for I soon found that I was quite deceived, as the moment I fixed my regard on it, it showed plainly that it was a bush, or a tree or a rock.'

Anodos is alien and rational in an intuitive, unpredictable world and needs to be brought into harmony and communion with his surroundings. In Fairy Land even the medium of language dissolves, changing Anodos' grasp of reality, bringing him into contact with the things themselves and leaving him with only impressions that he can but imperfectly convey to the reader:

> 'In the fairy book everything was just as it should be, though whether
> in words or something else, I cannot tell. It glowed and flashed the
> thoughts upon the soul, with such a power that the medium
> disappeared from the consciousness, and it was occupied only again
> with the things themselves.'

Such experiences are repeated again and again, especially with songs which Anodos hears but finds that he can never perfectly put into words. Just as words slip, so the distinction between reader and text shifts. Anodos reads about the knight Percival in a book and then later comes face to face with him. In a different way, in the library of the Fairy Palace, Anodos becomes the protagonist of every book that he reads and as he becomes Cosmo when reading Cosmo's story, so MacDonald expects his readers to 'become' Anodos as they read his story. For Anodos is a type of Everyman and his quest is our quest.

Anodos' quest is not as deliberate as Heinrich von Ofterdingen's to find the blue flower; indeed his path is haphazard and only ever followed intuitively. He is not sure what he is looking for — at least till he finds the marble lady — only that he must go on. What he is looking for is, if anything, a kind of nirvana — a spiritual union of death and bliss where perfect rest is found. When Tolkien wrote that 'Death is the theme that most inspired George MacDonald' in his essay *On Fairy Stories* he meant exactly that. Though death is a theme central to Victorian literature, MacDonald does not treat it as a problem, but rather as the aim of all existence. Death is what gives meaning to life. It is something to be longed for, most clearly expressed perhaps in Diamond's death in *At the Back of the North Wind*, and at the end of Mossy's and Tangle's pilgrimage in *The Golden Key* where death is only more life.

If there is one unifying thread of story which links the encounters in *Phantastes* then it is Anodos' pursuit of the marble woman whom he awakes from a cave with the power of song newly granted to him on his entry into Fairy Land. She flees from him and in his haste to find her again he mistakes for her the dreaded Alder-maiden who pretends to be his beloved ideal, but seduces him just as she has previously seduced the knight Percival. After this 'fall' Anodos is stricken with grief. As a result of his encounter, Percival's armour becomes rusty and he has to perform deeds of valour and bravery to restore it to its former pristine condition.

In his search for the lady, his most important and sinister encounter in this odd landscape is in the Church of Darkness where an ogress with long teeth reads from a book a passage on darkness which describes exactly the opposite of what MacDonald believed. It is an inversion of the first Chapter of John's Gospel. Darkness and not light is the overcomer. It is in this place that Anodos first meets his shadow. Anodos opens a cupboard and finds that it has no back:

> 'As I gazed, I clearly discerned two or three stars glimmering faintly in the distant blue. But suddenly . . . a dark figure sped into and along the passage from the blue opening at the remote end . . . I looked round over my shoulder; and there, on the ground, lay a black shadow, the size of a man. It was so dark, that I could see it in the dim light of the lamp, which shone full upon it, apparently without thinning at all the intensity of its hue.'

The shadow soon makes his presence felt by emptying the world round Anodos of all its beauty and poetry. Flowers wither where he falls, 'a lovely fairy child' changes into 'a common-place boy, with a rough broad trimmed straw hat' and his wondrous toys become ordinary. Similarly the shadow causes Anodos to break a young girl's magic globe which utters a lovely harmony when touched. She flees weeping through the forest.[6] Then, to his horror, Anodos finds that he grows pleased with his new companion:

> 'But the most dreadful thing of all was, that I now began to feel something like satisfaction in the presence of the shadow . . .'

Shadows slip in and out of fairy tales of this period. There is Hoffmann's *The Devil's Elixirs*, for example, Andersen's *The Story of the Shadow*, Adalbert von Chamisso's *Peter Schlemihl* and also, the examples of Faust and Mephistopheles, Frankenstein and his monster, and Jekyll and Hyde. But in this case the shadow is not some hideous manifestation of a deep-seated repression — it is quite the opposite. It sucks the beauty from the world precisely because it forces Anodos to see as 'real' men see. As this is Fairy Land where things are turned upside down, everyday 'reality' appears as a shadow, but has a blighting effect. MacDonald is pointing out that we need more than just our five senses to appreciate the world. But is he saying just that — or more than that? The shadow is undoubtedly evil, and acts as some vengeful *doppelgänger* — it sticks like sin — it darkens the senses, but there is more to it than just one meaning.[7]

The tough kernel of MacDonald's work lies in the variety of archetypal symbols he presents to the reader. As *Phantastes* is a psychological work, these symbols must have a psychological meaning and as the romance has a transcendent dimension, pointing the reader towards God, these same symbols must also have a spiritual meaning. That one symbol can have a multiplicity of meanings prohibits tying the 'meaning' down to a one-to-one allegorical correspondence and to try to do so is damaging. Like the girl's globe they shatter and only black vapour remains. Instead, MacDonald's symbols are constituted of elements of meaning. The reader perceives and receives the symbol, but any attempt to articulate the meaning of the symbol leads to failure. How is this possible?

If these symbols need some key to help unlock their power, then the two figures most intimately associated with the exploration of the unconscious, Freud and Jung, must be invoked. Freud was interested in fantasies; Jung was interested in myths. Freud saw dreams as a kind of code and believed that to crack that would enable the analyst to examine his patient's fears, desires and neuroses. It is possible to apply such an analysis to *Phantastes* and to trace many of the classical Oedipal and other neurotic symptoms in the persona of Anodos, but it is more rewarding to look for more universal elements in MacDonald's symbolism. Jung went a stage further than Freud, admitting that although sexual drive was important, it did not explain everything. Jung preferred to take dream symbols at their face value and saw them not so much as pictures of neurosis, but as important and permanent aspects of the human psyche. As Freud had done, Jung saw that fairy tales exposed such symbols in a vulnerable way in which more 'realistic' texts did not. He wrote:

'Being a spontaneous, naïve and uncontrived product of the psyche, the fairy tale cannot very well express anything except what the psyche actually is.'[8]

In other words, both the good and bad elements in a fairy tale are aspects of our own personalities. Indeed the fairy tale attempts to resolve questions and desires which it would normally be blasphemy to utter, as it reveals the unconscious workings of the psyche. Anodos' first great blasphemy is to attempt to seduce his grandmother, transgressing psychological laws; his second is to discover that God is a woman, thus transgressing the spiritual. 'Man's worst sin,' wrote Jung, 'is *unconsciousness*.'[9] MacDonald exposes the psyche and plunges us into a world that we have to come out of — changed.

One of Jung's major discoveries in his psychotherapeutic work was that certain symbols occur spontaneously at different times in history and in different cultures:

'The fact is that certain ideas exist almost everywhere and at all times and can even spontaneously create themselves quite independently of migration and tradition.'[10]

They spring from what Jung termed the 'collective unconscious' which is the psychic reservoir of the whole of mankind. Jung isolated certain recurring symbols such as the anima or woman, the shadow, the child and the wise man and charged them with a universal significance. Interestingly many of Jung's symbols correspond closely to MacDonald's. The anima in Jung, for example, is all that is 'feminine' in man, projected on to some female figure. She can be creative or destructive, old or young, witch, saint or whore, good fairy or bad fairy.

The classic anima projections in MacDonald are the Wise Woman in *Phantastes*, with her four-doored cottage, Lilith, the embodiment of sexual evil, and Irene, the great-great-grandmother in *The Princess and the Goblin* and *The Princess and Curdie*. Irene is not just a grandmother or even a *great*-grandmother, but a *great-great*-grandmother implying age, stature, majesty and immortality. She and the Wise Woman constitute the obverse of the harsh Calvinist male God whom MacDonald repudiated, appearing as motherly goddesses of nature, gentle, loving and wise. The child, often seen as walking along the border between this world and the Other, corresponds to Anodos who somehow has to reconcile his experience in both worlds. Jung believed that the emergence of the ego and its splitting off from the unconsciousness is a rift that somehow has to be healed. He called the process whereby a person went in search of this wholeness 'individuation', that is, a return to the state where one is 'undivided'.

'On the other hand, the fairy tale makes it clear that it is possible for a man to attain totality, to become whole, only with the co-operation of the spirit of darkness, indeed that the latter is actually a *causa instrumentalis* of redemption and individuation.'[11]

In such a journey the ego is lost, only to be recovered again integrated with the whole self.

Jung's view on the necessity of evil is hard to accept perhaps, but it accords to a large extent with MacDonald's. MacDonald believed that even the devil himself would be redeemed and so God must have some reason why he was still allowed to run around the world causing harm. In MacDonald's eyes such harm is only a result of seeing in the wrong way. Turn harm inside out and there is a blessing lurking there:

'What we call evil, is the only and best shape, which, for the person and his condition at the time, could be assumed to be the best good.'[12]

Therefore even evil contributes towards redemption.

In his pursuit of the marble woman Anodos comes to a fairy palace where he finds his name emblazoned on a chamber door, reminiscent of *Beauty and the Beast*. He stays there for a while, spending time in the palace library and seeking his beloved. He finds her by singing to her, but loses her again by trying to grasp her and so breaking the rules of the palace. Dashing through a door he finds himself lost on a windswept plain. The woman is reminiscent of the woman revealed to Julian in *Within and Without* and is surely modelled on the marble statue referred to in *A Story of the Seashore* which MacDonald used to gaze at as a young boy on his visits to Cullen.

Soon Anodos enters a rocky domain populated by goblins, the same goblins who would later make a more substantial appearance in *The Princess and the Goblin*. Plunging into a sea after enduring their taunts, he surfaces near a cottage where an old wise woman lives who nurses him. The wise woman sings him back to health and, after excursions through each of the four doors set in her cottage walls, Anodos goes on his way only to fall in with two brothers who are hammering armour into shape in order to meet three giants in battle. After the battle Anodos is the only one left alive and he continues his journey until he meets Percival again and becomes his squire. At some strange religious gathering they attend Anodos becomes suspicious that 'something worse than the ordinary deceptions of priestcraft' are taking place. Smuggling himself to the front of the crowd he casts down a wooden idol and a large wolf jumps out of a hole hidden beneath the figure. Anodos grasps the animal by the throat and in the ensuing turmoil is killed. But Anodos does not stop existing with his death. Deep in the ground, he is aware of the knight and his lady, who is the lady Anodos loved, weeping for him, and his soul rises up into a primrose which the lady plucks before he floats up even higher onto a cloud. It is then that Anodos' great realization is confirmed within him:

'I knew now, that it is by loving, and not by being loved, that one can come nearest the soul of another . . .'

Almost at that moment he experiences a terrible shudder and awakes back on earth in the early morning before sunrise. He has been gone, he finds out, for twenty-one days, one for each year of his life, and has learned more in that short time than in all his other years put together. 'Thus I, who set out to find my Ideal, came back rejoicing that I had lost my shadow.'

Anodos' experiences are not escapist: he is reborn into this world, unlike Anselmus in *The Golden Pot* who ends up living with Serpentina on their 'Freehold in Atlantis'. Anodos' sisters greet him with 'joy mingled with awe and respect' because they see that he has indefinably changed. And, though he has come back safely from Fairy Land:

> 'I have a strange feeling sometimes, that I am a ghost, sent into the world to minister to my fellow men, or, rather, to repair the wrongs I have already done.'

One of MacDonald's favourite sayings came from Novalis: 'Our life is no dream; but it ought to become one, and perhaps will.' And there is always a tension between what is real and what is dream in MacDonald, especially at the end of *Lilith* where Vane no longer knows if he is awake or asleep. This is especially true as Fairy Land is much more 'real' than everyday reality and reality is simply the shadow side of something greater to come.

At the end of *Phantastes* all the images of the mother — the earth, the beech tree and the wise woman — blend harmoniously as Anodos realizes that evil is simply one shape of good and the leaves whisper 'A great good is coming — is coming — is coming to thee, Anodos,' and he realizes that this message is true.

What one remembers from *Phantastes* is not the flimsy thread of the story or descriptive prose passages, but the encounters: the marble lady, the evil Alder-maiden, the shadow, the rusty knight and the old, wise woman spinning in her cottage. They are not people, but symbols, the symbols Jung identified and MacDonald used to powerful effect. These symbols remain, working their way into us after we have finished reading the book. In one sense we never finish reading it because we can never fully mine the meaning of any one symbol. When the thistles laugh at Anodos and say: 'Look at him! Look at him! He has begun a story without a beginning, and it will never have any end...' they are also laughing at us, just as Jung too acknowledged that the process of individuation could never be completed.

The lesson MacDonald learned from his poetry was that two apparently contradictory things can be at one and the same time true, held in a poetic tension. This is how he combines naturalism and Platonism, and there is a similar tension present in his use of symbols. The marble lady, for example, is an Ideal, the perfect woman and an example of spiritual perfection, but Anodos also conceives of her in erotic terms and the song he uses to sing her into visibility in the Fairy Palace is highly sexually charged. Later in the tale she appears human, as the knight's lady, a little altered, but made of flesh and blood as well as marble. Anodos' wanderings are thus a wandering through MacDonald's mind, through Mind itself and also through the domain of the spiritual. His combination of the erotic and the spiritual is at once daring, disturbing and exciting — yet MacDonald firmly believed that the love of God could be mediated through the love of woman and that enjoyment, whether of nature or God, could take place at a level where the distinction between the spiritual and the sexual no longer existed.

MacDonald's purpose was to open our eyes to the Fairy Land all around us and to kindle a longing in our hearts for what Anodos achieves at the end of the book. Jung complained that without symbols man was a lost orphan. MacDonald gives us symbols, a myth to live by that nourishes us and protects us and helps to integrate minds fractured by the defeating rationalism of the Enlightenment and the darkness of the Industrial Revolution.

Despite a savaging by the critics, MacDonald believed in the worth of his work and it has come to be perceived over the last century as a classic of its kind.

CHAPTER SEVENTEEN

Another Farewell

January 1858 brought about the completion of *Phantastes*, that book about 'good death', and, swift on its heels, February brought the news that MacDonald's brother John was seriously ill. The old family disease was at work again. John's upper left lung was badly affected and he was much weakened. He was able to make the journey south to Huntly Cottage at Hastings for nursing early in April, but despite good care and constant attention he did not seem to recover at all. MacDonald planned to take his sick brother up to Huntly when he was well enough to travel, but Dr Hale, the family homoeopathic doctor, shook his head at this and said that John must do nothing but rest for eight to ten months. He lay, white-faced, while Louisa read to him and George sat by his bedside to talk to him. So it was that John's world slowly shrank to a curtained bedroom.

MacDonald inevitably made friends of his doctors as he had to see so much of them and Dr Hale proved a good companion in distress. Writing to his father, MacDonald enthused:

'The Doctor attends him as my friend and charges nothing. I think he will be interested in him for his own sake. I am very glad to have him with us; for we understand each other so well. And as to expense — never think of that. Thank God He takes all anxiety off us. The more we want the more we have and shall have. Things are looking well for us — but God is the giver — and He has plenty. It is very sad for those who cannot trust in Him: it is miserable slavery.'[1]

It was at about this time that Charles Francis, MacDonald's brother, returned from Sydney with high hopes of making his fortune. But they were soon to be tumbled. Greville MacDonald remembered:

'He assured my mother that in a few months he would be able to write her a cheque for a thousand pounds and never miss it. Though his intentions were honest and generous, his brother [George] throughout his long life had constantly to supplement his precarious supplies.'[2]

But though Charles' return was welcome after his long trip to the other side of the world, all eyes were on the invalid, John. Yet even as John was sinking, MacDonald's life was beginning to mushroom after his own long convalescence. He began giving lectures in the drawing-room of Huntly Cottage and though they were very badly attended, they scraped in a little money. In May he dined once again with Lady Byron, who introduced him to many of her friends including the Recorder of London, Russell Gurney and his kind wife Ellen who were to become stalwart friends.[3] Soon Ellen Gurney was busy organizing lectures for MacDonald to give in London. 'I must be working for my bread somehow,'[4] commented MacDonald to his father.

Momentarily, like the sun coming out from behind a cloud, John seemed to improve:

'His cough seems to us less, and certainly his pain is *very* much less. He is decidedly more cheerful, and eats better, though doubtless he is in a precarious condition still.'[5]

But he was no sooner better than he had a bad turn in June and his condition became critical again:

'We both read to him when we can, but he is only able for a bit of a story at a time and is soon tired even of that. He is certainly in a very doubtful conditon...'[6]

Even though he was so weak, John was determined to see Huntly again before he died and somehow, like a salmon slipping upstream, he was able to board the steamer for Aberdeen, probably looked after by his brother Charles, and reach home. MacDonald must have known that he would never see his brother alive again when he bade him that last farewell and it was only a few short weeks later that John died in Huntly on 7 July, aged twenty-eight. Melancholic, restless John had finally found rest.

'In the hush of noon he died,
The sun shone on — why should he not shine on?
Glad summer noises rose from all the land;
The love of God lay warm on hill and plain;
'Tis well to die in summer.'[7]

'A few days after the burial,' records Greville MacDonald, George MacDonald senior 'was at dusk going out at a little gate that opened from the farm precincts to a back road running up on to the moor, and saw a figure coming towards this gate. He stepped back within the gate. The figure passed on, but then turned, and my grandfather saw it was

John, with plaid over his shoulder in his customary manner. The old man hastened after, but because of his lameness, failed to overtake the wayfarer before he disappeared at a bend of the ascending road.'[8] When George MacDonald senior reached the turn, the figure could not be seen. Troubled, he returned to his wife, unable to explain his experience at all. He felt that it signified something, but he did not understand what.

A few weeks later on 26 August,[9] George MacDonald senior walked round the farm as usual in the long summer twilight. Everything was as it should have been. As he went indoors through the dusky light he felt a violent stab of pain in the left side of his chest. He collapsed and his brother James was immediately called for and also the doctor, who hurried to him, poulticing him all night with some relief.

> 'At eleven o'clock in the morning little Jeanie, then twelve years old, came to the room to ask her mother something. He was then lying in bed, the child's mother sitting by his side. He turned his head to see who was at the door, looked straight at his little daughter and smiled to her. But her mother then saw a death-like change pass over his face and called out to the child to run for the doctor; but he died immediately.'[10]

John's death was expected; George MacDonald senior's was not. Plummeting out of the blue, MacDonald received the awful telegram:

> 'Your father after fourteen hours sickness died today at noon. You will hear further by post.'[11]

Without any delay, MacDonald rushed northwards to comfort his stepmother and help with the arrangements for the funeral which was set for 31 August at noon, when the old man would at last be laid in Drumblade Churchyard beside the other members of his family. MacDonald arrived to find his stepmother in a terrible state. Despite stout friends like Robert Troup whom she could lean on, her grief was unassuageable and for days after her husband's death 'she would pace the meadows with bowed head, clenching and unclenching her hands held to her bosom in mute appeal against the inexorable. . .'[12] George MacDonald senior was a well-liked and notable figure in the town. His death caused shock-waves throughout the community. George wrote to Louisa:

> '. . . My mother seems a little more cheerful today. Charles and I went to see some poor people this afternoon. It is very pleasant to hear how they all talk about my father. You would almost fancy that he had been a kind of chief of the clan. . . I am glad my father got through. I love him more than ever.'[13]

For MacDonald, the death of his father was the closing of a significant chapter in his life, for his father had been brother as well as father to him, and despite their differences, confidant too. MacDonald had long sought his father's approval and eventually won it, even though he may have liked the old man to have seen his son rise even higher. The imprint of the deaths of father and brother on MacDonald, falling so close to one another, and cutting so deep, came out in his writing. Death was at the very heart of MacDonald's writing and thoughts on relatives who have slipped into its sleep are threaded in and out of *Diary of an Old Soul*. But it is in the strange poem 'Somnium Mystici: A Microcosm in Terza Rima' that father and brother most definitely appear:

'Worn out I lay
With the death struggle,'

writes the poet, when his chamber door opens and his brother appears, leading him out as the spirit in *Gennaro* had done, through streets and even over water to:

'The ancient earthly childhood when we shared
One bed, like birds that nestled in one nest.'

Then he goes on to write of his father:

'Father — ah, brother, how he used to teach
Us children in our beds! A temple-hall
Became, when he sat there, the common room —
Prone on the ground before him I did fall,
So grand he towered above me like a doom.'

This father erupted even into MacDonald's dreams. He told his step-mother:

'I dreamed last night I saw my father. I felt I loved him so much and was clinging to him, when to my surprise I found he was so much taller than I, that I did not reach his shoulder. There is a meaning in that, is there not.'

Perhaps the answer lay in that:

'Thus I find
That Memory needs no brain, but keeps her store
In hidden chambers of the eternal mind;
And from the floor of that remembrance, I
Went back to years all full of mystic signs

Unreadable, while yet my soul did lie
Closed in my mother's.'[14]

MacDonald went back through the years again and again to nourish his writing with 'mystic signs' from his childhood, and the final monument to his father is the towering figure of David Elginbrod in the novel of the same name who, like MacDonald's father, vanishes abruptly from the story while it is only half-finished.[15]

The widow, Margaret McColl MacDonald, was in turmoil as to what to do. MacDonald offered her Hastings as a retreat to come to live in, but she refused. She was determined to leave The Farm. Perhaps relations with her brother-in-law James would not have gone at all smoothly, for she would not have been able to support herself at The Farm now that her husband had gone. Perhaps she could not bear to remain in the same surroundings without him who had given such colour to her life. Back in Hastings towards the end of September MacDonald wrote to his step-mother, 'Whatever good things we can fancy for ourselves, God has better than that in store for us.'[16]

Margaret McColl MacDonald did not know what God had in store for her, but she left the old home with her two daughters and the £1,100 bequeathed to her by her husband at the end of the year.

CHAPTER EIGHTEEN

From Hastings
to London...

When MacDonald returned to Hastings after the deaths of both his brother John and his father, he found Louisa almost ready to give birth to another child, but this time without the usual accompanying toothache and frayed nerves. 'I do not think she ever got so far as this without much more discomfort than she has experienced this time,' he wrote to his stepmother.

On 28 October 1858, *Phantastes* was published and MacDonald eagerly scanned the papers for reviews. 'The Reviewers are on the whole behaving very well to me as yet,' he wrote, but at the same time he found it hard to veil his disappointment at the harsh and unsympathetic treatment of his work in the press. As the day of Louisa's delivery approached, the children were bundled off to their Aunt Charlotte's and there, in the unaccustomed quiet of Huntly Cottage, Louisa gave birth to her fifth and last daughter, Winifred Louisa. Mercifully it was an easy birth, and she was a good baby. It was not long however before the family stormed back and the house was filled with laughs and howls once again.

The new year came and the month of February, usually a miserable time of year, was lightened by various visits of the whole family to London. MacDonald gave four lectures at the London Institution during that month, perhaps the ones that Ellen Gurney had arranged for him, but they were aimed at increasing his reputation rather than making money. Perhaps this scheme worked, for he was invited to lecture at the Royal Institution in Manchester in May and at the Philosophical Institution in Edinburgh in August later that year.[1] The family presumably stayed mainly at The Limes while they dallied in London, and often Lady Byron would send round her carriage inviting them to lunch or to 'tea-dinner'. Louisa found herself becoming slowly better acquainted with this kindly though fearsome woman. After some successful lectures in Hastings in March,[2] MacDonald planned to give some more lectures in London in April and so moved into Lady Byron's house near Regent's

Park for two weeks. It was during this stay that Lady Byron disclosed some of her own history to MacDonald, confidences which he kept unbroken for the rest of his life. They discussed his future too, as well as matters of spiritual interest, and it was perhaps through these conversations with his elderly patron that MacDonald began to think of moving from the south coast to London, to try to enter the world of London literary life. Lady Byron offered to help the MacDonalds find a suitable house in the capital and so, with new plans buzzing in his head, MacDonald returned to Louisa and the children.

In April of that year, 1859, Henry Crabb Robinson, the famous diarist and friend of Wordsworth, Coleridge and Lamb, recorded in his diary:

'April 16 (Brighton). I called on Lady Byron at three and found a very interesting man, a Mr MacDonald author of a poem *Within and Without*, which I must read. He is an invalid and a German scholar. The talk was altogether interesting. He will call on me.'[3]

MacDonald must have made a deep initial impression on Crabb Robinson as straightway on his return to London he subscribed to Mudie's library and took out a copy of *Within and Without*. He found it, however, 'A jumble of sentimentality and speculation.' Undaunted, he decided to attend a course of MacDonald's lectures in Brighton, but looking round at the audience he lamented, 'but thinly attended — chiefly ladies... MacDonald has to manage his voice which is disagreeable from overloudness... I was made uncomfortable by the feeling that I was unable to render others the services I wish.'[4]

The next lecture was worse attended than the one on Scott, and MacDonald 'read so low that he was not audible...but I fear the general impression was not favourable.'[5] The following lectures on Shelley and Keats were scarcely more successful. The final nail in the coffin from Crabb Robinson came a year later when he complained that, 'MacDonald's lecture...hardly authorised the sacrifice I made to attend it.' It was on Tennyson.[6]

Though there was no doubt a want of judgement in the way MacDonald presented himself to the public — he slid easily into excess of one kind or another — Crabb Robinson did witness him at his nadir, for the lectures at Brighton were a dismal failure and had to be cancelled. So bitter was MacDonald over this experience that he resolved never to preach or lecture at any south coast watering-place again.[7] As usual he left with firm sentiments, but an empty pocket. It must have been painful for him because that year he had been striving hard to provide for himself and his family. With no income to speak of, but three publications to his name, he marshalled some testimonials from A.J. Scott, Russell Gurney, F.D. Maurice, and his newly-acquired friend David Masson[8] and applied in June to the Royal Literary Fund, a body set up at the end of the eighteenth century to help authors in need. On 15 July he acknowledged receipt of £70. In these straits and with a move to London imminent he had to set about finding himself some kind of employment. Here Crabb Robinson did lend a hand, if an unwilling one, for the old man was acquainted with Elizabeth Jesser Reid who had founded Bedford College for Ladies in 1849. MacDonald had met Mrs Reid through Anna Leigh-Smith whom he had met in Algiers. Mrs Reid was a tireless and persistent campaigner for women's education and Bedford College was the first institute of higher education for women, differing from Queen's College founded by F.D. Maurice in 1848 in that it was meant to be more than just a training college for governesses. While Queen's was an Anglican foundation, Mrs Reid, a staunch Unitarian, wished Bedford College to remain firmly non-sectarian. She had also included women on the governing body. But there was a problem: remuneration for the teachers at the college was small. There were no women available who had the right kind of education, and scholars seemed unwilling to ally themselves with the place. Most of the professors had to find two or three posts in different places in order to make ends meet, and this was unsatisfactory. When MacDonald heard that the college was looking for a professor of English Literature he was interested in applying for the post, hoping that it might lead to something better.

Meanwhile, Crabb Robinson called on Mrs Reid, 'and stayed late. We talked about MacDonald and the professor's chair he seeks and I have no doubt will have if it is worth possessing.' But Crabb Robinson thought the prize 'a mean one' which would not cover the difference in the cost of living between Hastings and London. As it turned out, MacDonald was delighted to hear from Miss Swanick on 15 July that he had been elected professor at the Ladies' College. Probably at that stage any boost to his confidence was welcome.

MacDonald received only thirty to fifty guineas a year as professor at the college, and earned half a guinea per lecture. Professors were paid by the number of classes and pupils, and were not given a set salary in those early years. MacDonald's connection with the college lasted until 1867 when he resigned in protest at the Council's insistence on an external report on the teaching of the college being made by James Bryce, one of the assistant commissioners on the Royal Commission into Middle Class Education.

Soon after his appointment, it was necessary for MacDonald to travel up to Edinburgh and then to Huntly for a rest and to see his relatives. Weary after the long journey he scratched some slow sad words to Louisa:

'The beauty of this place — the central beauty is gone. I see his spectacles lying. My mother wears them now. It makes one feel that it is all passing. But God is rich who has all persons as well as thoughts and things in him.'[9]

Even at a distance worries pressed on him — to dispose of one house and move into another. George and Louisa agreed to meet in Liverpool:

'I am very tired dearest Louie and must go to bed. I shall be at work at my *play* tomorrow I hope. Perhaps I have been sent here that I may write a good one, by having nothing at all to take me from it. But I feel it is difficult. I never felt this so much with anything else I have tried.[10]

After *Phantastes* which had not been a commercial and popular success, MacDonald turned to writing a play. As an avid theatregoer he saw hundreds of people crammed into their seats being moved either to tears or laughter by what they saw and the preaching instinct in him was aroused. Thus he set to work on *If I had a Father*. He was serious and enthusiastic about the project, writing to Lady Byron:

'I hope it will be wicked enough to please you — if not, I shall try one in the style of *Titus Andronicus* or *The Jew of Malta*.[11]

But after writing and rewriting the piece many times he could not make it come alive and Smith, Elder and Co. refused to publish it. MacDonald's only rueful comment was, 'I doubt whether it would tell on the stage.' In the event the play was turned into a story and published in *The Gifts of the Christ Child and Other Stories* in 1882.

In London Lady Byron hoped to secure the house of her friends the De Morgans at 7 Camden Street for the MacDonald family. Despite lavish plans for improving the house her offer was bettered without warning and the deal fell through. Then Lady Byron fell ill and had to leave London. The MacDonalds found themselves stranded. Having disposed of the Hastings house they now had nowhere to live.

Fortunately they managed to find a house in Bloomsbury — 18 Queen Square — and moved in for six months. There the girls were happy dancing and curtseying round the statue of Queen Anne in the Square garden, and Greville helped the gardener pick up dead leaves for the bonfire.[12] This house served as a good resting place from which they could go house-hunting. In their travels round London MacDonald's eyes lighted on a

Victorian Gothic house tacked on to the end of a Georgian terrace in Albert Street, Camden, called Tudor Lodge.[13] The house captured Mac-Donald's imagination — it was both romantic and Gothic — and he decided to take it. It was a tall narrow house with small rooms, not suitable for a large family, but angels propped up the sills of the church-shaped windows, a weeping ash garlanded the garden which was a riot of marigolds, wallflowers and weeds and at the back of the house there was a large studio suitable for lecturing in, reached by a small steep stairway leading down through a door at the end of the hall. It had been built by the historical painter Charles Lucy, and Thomas Lynch the hymn-writer, whom MacDonald had known, had lived there.[14] After a brief move back to Hastings, to St Anne's Cottage on Castle Hill on 25 April, the family finally moved into Tudor Lodge on 6 August. It was a happy house, though cramped.[15]

While these moves were taking place and MacDonald was struggling with his play, he still found time to publish *The Portent*, serialized in the first year of the *Cornhill Magazine* in May, June and July of 1860. It tells a spooky tale of Highland second sight and a mysterious sleepwalking girl. In 1864 it was published in book form with a significantly different ending.[16]

Finally, after a long illness, Lady Byron died in her sleep on 16 May 1860. Her frequent gifts of money ceased and at this time it seemed that MacDonald was making little headway on the literary front. Greville MacDonald remembered:

> 'Now followed very anxious days, and publishers all refused his play. How many weeks or months it was after Lady Byron's death I do not know; but my mother would tell us how one day she had started out to buy certain necessities, and in the omnibus had lost her purse with the very last sovereign in it. They did not know where to turn next for help, and there was hardly enough food in the house for the children's dinner. Only Lily, with her instinctive understanding realised how bad things were, and found her own appetite was providentially indifferent. Then, my mother said, as the evening closed in, she and my father were standing hand in hand as if waiting some answer to their prayers. It was in the little front drawing-room of Tudor Lodge, and the rain poured down upon the weeping ash that overspread the tiny garden. The postman walked up the steps, dropped a letter in the box, and with his double knock woke them from their quietude. The letter was from Lady Byron's executors enclosing a cheque for £300, a legacy of which they had not been advised.'[17]

But to say that life in London for the MacDonalds was over-shadowed by despair would be to be misleading. New opportunities were gradually opening up for the whole family. Already introduced into notable society by Lady Byron, they were now able to enjoy their new friends. Through the Russell Gurneys they met Maria Price La Touche whom MacDonald helped with her tract *The Cry of Esau*. She became especially intimate with Louisa, always referring to her as 'Mother Brown-bird'. The writer Mrs Oliphant was an old friend and she introduced MacDonald to her friend Dinah Mulock, now famous as the authoress of *John Halifax, Gentleman*. They also met Charles Kingsley and Matthew Arnold. George Murray Smith, the publisher, actively encouraged MacDonald through this difficult period of his life and at his dinners MacDonald met James Greenwood, G.H. Lewes, Leslie Stephen, Leigh Hunt, James Payn and Henry S. King.[18] Flattered though he was to meet such people, MacDonald had a mixed reaction to these gatherings:

> 'The merely professional literary party was an abhorrence to him. He said it made him feel sick — he could not help it. He took more pleasure in smoking a pipe now and then with an old cobbler somewhere about the Theobald's Road than in the evening with the most delightful literary society that London could furnish.'[19]

But his circle was not just a literary one. The MacDonalds also knew Dr Elizabeth Garrett, the first woman doctor, and Josephine Butler, the famous nineteenth-century reformer. In fact, the family became so infected with talk of women's rights and education that Greville MacDonald remembers:

> 'My parents' intimacy with such protagonists of the feminist movement as the beautiful and devoted Josephine Butler, Madame Bodichon of Girton renown, Mrs Reid, Principal of Bedford College, Anna Sidgwick, Miss Buss and Miss Beale, no doubt made deep, if forgotten impressions upon me. The power of suggestion, though not yet formulated, thoroughly convinced me of my sex's inferiority. I distinctly remember wondering how it could be that my adored mother had ever married my father who, in spite of his splendour, was only a man!'[20]

MacDonald did not move in the most glittering circles of the day, but in two interlocking and interesting ones: religious and artistic. He knew many of the minor notables of his time, people whom he came across naturally in the pursuit of his literary life, but the two artists he was closest to were Alexander Munro the sculptor and Arthur Hughes the painter. Munro was a friend from Hastings days and introduced Hughes to MacDonald. Both artists had been influenced by the Pre-Raphaelite movement, and Hughes is regarded as a Pre-Raphaelite painter, though he never officially became a brother. Both men knew Ruskin well and were friendly with Millais, Morris, Holman Hunt, Burne-Jones, Rossetti and the rest of that group. In time Hughes became MacDonald's illustrator and their partnership was a fruitful one, matching illustration to text as aptly as Tenniel to Carroll. Both Munro and Hughes had a deep, though private, faith. So it was that MacDonald was ensnared and influenced by the romantic moral earnestness of the Pre-Raphaelites and began to move among them.

At the same time MacDonald's religious centre became St Peter's, Vere Street, a fog-scarred church just off Oxford Street, where F.D. Maurice was appointed preacher in July 1860. It was a controversial appointment and the man responsible was William Cowper, stepson of Lord Palmerston, and then chief commissioner of the Board of Works. He and his wife, later to become Lord and Lady Mount-Temple, were zealously religious and became close friends of the MacDonalds, sharing his broad views. Despite an attack by the influential *Record*, Maurice was duly instituted and 'read himself in ' on Sunday 9 September 1860. There was no parish work attached to the church — Maurice simply rolled up to preach, and did so, apart from an upset in 1862, when he almost resigned over a controversy concerning Bishop Colenso and the *Pentateuch*, until 1869 when he had to relinquish the post on grounds of ill-health. By then he was Knightsbridge Professor of Casuistry, Moral Theology and Moral Philosophy at Cambridge, and the weekly journey to London was too strenuous for him.

MacDonald cherished the opportunity of sitting at the feet of one he held in such high esteem and, when he was not preaching himself, St Peter's became his spiritual home in London, and so it was that at last the Dissenter entered the Church of England. St Peter's was a fashionable place and MacDonald felt at home with the upper-middle-class reformers who shared his own broad views of the church and its duty.

Among Maurice's congregation was a young girl of twenty-two, full of vitality and with a maturity beyond her years. Her name was Octavia Hill.[21] From her earliest years Octavia Hill had been raised on ideas of reform. Her mother, an independent woman, had come to work for Maurice and the Christian Socialists soon after they began their work setting up co-operatives in London. Her father, James Hill, had been a corn merchant and a banker noted for his good work in municipal and educational reform, and had worked wholeheartedly with Cobden and Bright for the repeal of the Corn Laws. Her grandfather, Dr Thomas Southwood Smith, was an authority on fever epidemics and sanitation. In

1852 Octavia Hill began work at the Ladies' Guild, a co-operative association promoted by the Christian Socialists of which her mother became manager. The young girl was soon put in charge of a branch teaching children how to make toys and she had to supervise their work, find business, and do all the accounts herself. She fell under the spell of Maurice while he was still chaplain at Lincoln's Inn and he was drawn to the strange young girl and her sister, Miranda. Octavia possessed her own copy of Maurice's *Theological Essays* which she underlined heavily and re-read many times. In 1853 she met Ruskin who aided her in her artistic training and was later to help her with her schemes for improving tenements. When the MacDonalds met her she was still young, with most of her impressive work ahead of her. She and the MacDonalds became firm friends and her connection with the family lasted fifty years. In 1856 she became the secretary for the classes for women at the Working Men's College in Great Ormond Street where MacDonald soon found himself lecturing on poetry.[22]

On 27 October Louisa gave birth to another son, Ronald, and so another child was squeezed into the narrow house. But if there was not much privacy, there was a lot of fun. Greville scratched away on his violin, Lilia and Mary were sent out for singing lessons, and Grace learned to play the piano. With relatives so near at hand, Mr Powell and Carrie were frequent visitors in the evenings, as well as the Godwins and the Mathesons. Louie, MacDonald's sister, now joined the horde, fresh down from Huntly, and began attending Bedford College. She provided welcome help with the children. Even in those days the family delighted in theatricals, and Sir Johnston Forbes-Robertson remembered:

> '... You will remember, of course, how he [George MacDonald] enjoyed the children's parties your mother gave in the great studio and how he used to cover himself with a skin rug, and pretend to be a bear to the great delight of us all. Arthur Hughes used to join in with great gusto. I recall that on the walls of the studio were some casts of the Parthenon Friezes, which at a Christmas party were all lit up with small candles artfully stuck about, a most beautiful effect.'[23]

MacDonald family life was a muddled affair, with MacDonald himself sprawling over it like some great biblical patriarch. They rose early and breakfasted at about half past seven — usually on porridge. Then the day would begin in earnest. MacDonald spent his mornings writing, secluded in his study, and ventured forth in the afternoons to lecture or to call on friends. The evenings varied, dining out or in, with or without friends — usually with, and sometimes as a special treat there was a trip to the theatre. Whist evenings became popular, but when there were no guests MacDonald liked to retreat and play with his own toy soldiers. He was the proud owner of a collection to which he added throughout his life. On quieter evenings the girls sewed or made up their own games like Smiling Mary, a card game like whist, while Lily or Louisa read aloud the latest novel. And no doubt the family kept to the Victorian pattern of family prayers, hands clasped together, morning or evening or both, with grace before meals. Politeness was paramount. The rule of the house was 'Thou shalt not call thy nurse a *Beast*.'[24]

Though Sunday was a different day — there was roast mutton and apple pudding to eat instead of cold boiled beef and rice — MacDonald was not a strict Sunday observer and church-going was not enforced on the children; Greville succeeded in excusing himself sometimes with a feigned or induced headache to avoid driving in 'a four-wheeled cab smelling deliciously of dirty stable-straw' down to Vere Street. On Sunday evenings the family had musical gatherings and laid out cold joints, hot potatoes, milk puddings, bread and cheese — there were no formal invitations — and both the guests and the children joined in the washing up afterwards.

In the midst of all this bustle MacDonald was very vague about organizing education for his children. Perhaps he vainly believed that given the right surroundings they would educate themselves. 'Lessons,' wrote Greville, 'were given by my mother in any accidentally spare hours,'[25] though sometimes there was a governess. Whatever the case, there was never enough money to send the boys away to school and most of the educating was done at home, save for Greville who became a chorister at King's College and suffered mercilessly on account of his deafness, long hair and Pre-Raphaelite appearance. His bohemian non-conformity, it seems, extracted nothing but taunts and cruelty from the other boys.[26]

Greville adored his mother:

> 'Thus I recall the blessedness of sitting on the floor, my head against
> my mother's lap, while she told us a never-ending story of two
> children and their rainbow-coloured glass balls, each marvellous and
> magical.'[27]

But he feared his father: 'He stood for the Inexorable.' And it is true that MacDonald seems to have had two distinct sides to his character in family life. On the one hand he was gentle, loving, full of fun and genuinely liberal:

> 'So far as was possible, he never refused me anything I asked. I
> remember his saying that his own father, poor though he was, had

never denied him anything, and that he hoped his own children would be able to say as much of him.'[28]

But he demanded passive obedience from his children and was a strict disciplinarian:

'... when appeal to an undeveloped moral sense failed: corporal punishment, sometimes severe, was inevitable.'[29]

With a houseful of children rasping each other constantly — Greville pulling Irene's hair, or the usual squabbling over toys — MacDonald was not averse to beating his children, especially boys, when occasion demanded:

'I do not know that my sisters were ever punished. That girls were far above boys in goodness was always impressed upon me.'[30]

And if pushed he was capable of tying a child's hands behind his back and frog-marching him along the street and home to bed.

Finally, when it came to Latin, Greville gave up:

'My father began to teach me Latin when I was nine, I think. The initial lesson dealt with the opening lines of the Aeneid. He first translated them, and tried to make me feel their metric thrill, then I had to commit them to my impossible memory. But I did not understand him; and the words had no more meaning than if he himself invented them just for a lesson. Such a system might be good for a clever boy; but it was worse than useless for me.'[31]

But despite its ups and downs there was a great security in the MacDonald family, emotionally and spiritually if not financially, and they were all close to one another and sympathetic to outsiders.

One frequent visitor in these days loved the rough and tumble of large family life — he came from a family of eleven himself — and was soon nicknamed by the MacDonald children as 'Uncle Dodgson'[32]. He was to be better known to the world at large, however, as Lewis Carroll.

CHAPTER NINETEEN
Lewis Carroll

When Charles Dodgson, the shy mathematics don from Christ Church College, Oxford[1] was thinking of taking holy orders, he wanted to cure the stammer which so afflicted him in conversation with adults. He therefore consulted the greatest authority of the day, Dr James Hunt Ph. D., editor of the *Anthropological Review* and author of *Stammering and Stuttering*. Dr Hunt lived at Ore, near Hastings, and was a good friend of MacDonald's homoeopathic Dr Hale, and it was through this medical connection that the shy don and the exiled Scot first met. Outwardly they were so different, but inwardly they had much in common. They may have met that April while the MacDonalds were back in Hastings between houses, though Greville remembered their friendship as 'dating from the days of the Tackleway.'[2]

Dodgson, later famous for his friendships with children, first met two of the MacDonald children, Greville and Mary, at the studio of Alexander Munro, the sculptor, in London. Greville, aged five, was posing for the 'Boy with a Dolphin' fountain later to be placed in Hyde Park.[3]

'"They were a girl and a boy, about seven and six years old — I claimed their acquaintance, and began at once proving to the boy, Greville, that he had better take the opportunity of having his head changed for a marble one. The effect was that in about two minutes they had entirely forgotten that I was a total stranger, and were earnestly arguing the question as if we were old acquaintances." Mr Dodgson urged that a marble head would not have to be brushed and combed. At this the boy turned to his sister with an air of great relief saying, "Do you hear *that*, Mary? It needn't be combed!" And the narrator adds, "I have no doubt combing, with his great head of long hair, like Hallam Tennyson's, was *the* misery of his life. His final argument was that a marble head couldn't speak, and as I couldn't convince either that he would be all the better for that, I gave in."'[4]

Dodgson afterwards penned a sketch of Greville, in his kilt, with the marble head in his hands, and Munro, hair and beard standing on end with fright, fleeing away in terror.

Dodgson soon found himself caught up in MacDonald family life and made Tudor Lodge a regular stopping place on his visits to London. Greville MacDonald recounts:

'Our annual treat was Uncle Dodgson taking us to the Polytechnic for the entrancing "dissolving views" of fairy-tales, or to go down in the diving bell, or watch the mechanical athlete *Leotard*. There was also the Coliseum in Albany Street, with its storms by land and sea on a wonderful stage, and its great panorama of London. And there was Cremer's toy-shop in Regent Street — not to mention bath-buns and ginger-beer — all associated in my memory with the adorable writer of *Alice*.'[5]

Though Dodgson spoke first to Greville, Mary, sprightly and dark-haired, quickly became his favourite, and he often took her or her and Lily out to tea or to play croquet. When they were a little older he sometimes took them both to the Olympic Theatre to see the Terrys act,[6] but more often he watched the MacDonalds' own theatricals:

'I spent the evening with the MacDonalds to see the children act *Cinderella*. Mary was Cinderella, Lily and Miss Netty Smart the two sisters, Grace the fairy, Irene was "Lord Lovel" dressed in a suit of Greville's clothes, and Miss J. MacDonald, Greville, Winifred and Ronald appeared at the Ball. Mary acted very well, but Lily was far the best: she has evidently a talent for it.'[7]

Mary, whom MacDonald called 'my blackbird' on account of her singing voice, was fond of sport but it was not an interest held in high esteem in the MacDonald household. Wilfred Dodgson, Charles' brother, taught her how to box and because of her agility and deftness nicknamed her 'The Kensington Chicken'. And when he was not in London, Dodgson sent letters full of quirky humour with which he regaled the girls. To Mary, the earliest and first of all his child friends, he wrote:

'This hot weather makes me very sad and sulky. I can hardly keep my temper sometimes. For instance, just now the Bishop of Oxford came in to see me — it was a civil thing to do, and he meant no harm, poor man: but I was so provoked at his coming in that I threw a book at his head, which I am afraid hurt him a good deal.'[8]

There are delightful echoes of the White Queen's boast later in this letter that she could believe 'as many as six impossible things before breakfast' and it may come as little surprise therefore to find that in *Through the Looking Glass* Lilia is transformed into Lily, the White Pawn and daughter of the White Queen, while Mary's cat Snowdrop makes an appearance as Alice's white kitten in the same book.

When Dodgson made friends it was not long before his photographic equipment appeared and he would insist on their posing. At ease in the world of children, his stammer disappeared, only to reappear when confronted with adults, and his photography seems to have been one way of easing his discomfort in adult relationships. He made arrangements to stay with the MacDonalds at the end of July 1863 in order to photograph them and some of their friends. At that stage the family were lodged with Mr Powell who had relinquished his religious principles enough to grow a beard[9] and so soften his crisp features at over the age of eighty. Powell had finally moved from The Limes to Elm Lodge in Heath Street, Hampstead in the summer of 1862. Dodgson's first night there did not go to plan however, for after an evening on the town:

'...it was about ½ past 12 when I left the theatre, and ½ past 1 when I got to Elm Lodge, where I failed in waking any one, and after more than half an hour of knocking and singing, ended by walking into London again in search of a bed. I found one at last at Windsor's Coffee House, near the Euston and got to bed about three.'[10]

What apologies and laughter there were the following day when Dodgson came crawling back can only be imagined, but he had his bed safe enough the next night and then went with the MacDonalds to Vere Street on the Sunday morning where he often attended when he was in London. In fact the following day 'Mr Maurice came for luncheon and sat for his picture',[11] so Dodgson at last captured the great man on negative. This was the first of two photographic sessions at the MacDonalds in 1863, the second was the following October when, among others, the Hughes family came to sit.[12] After a busy week, on 31 July Dodgson recorded, 'I have now done all the MacDonalds...' and that afternoon he took Mary along to see Hughes who wanted to put her into a painting. This was to be *Beauty* and Dodgson finally saw the finished canvas at the Royal Academy on 5 July 1865.[13] But Mary, though the favourite beauty, was not the only one, as Dodgson commissioned an artist called Darvall to colour in oils a photograph he had taken of Irene MacDonald in 1864.

A few months before seeing Mary's picture hung, Dodgson hoped that his brother Wilfred might be able to board with the MacDonalds for a while as he had to spend some months in London.[14]

Though Dodgson's connection with the MacDonald family was a long one, he was probably closest to them in the 1860s when the girls were young, around the period when he wrote *Alice in Wonderland*. The famous river trip to Godstow with Alice, Edith and Lorina Liddell took place on 4 July 1862. It is interesting that only five days later on 9 July Dodgson records:

> 'First down to the Great Northern to see Frances and Elizabeth off for Croft. Then to Tudor Lodge, where I met Mr MacDonald coming out. I walked a mile or so with him, on his way to a publisher with the M.S. of his fairy tale *The Light Princess* in which he showed me some exquisite drawings by Hughes.'[15]

For its humour — and lightness — it is the story which approaches most closely the work of Lewis Carroll, and shows how both works grew out of shared ideas. Henry Kingsley, picking up the manuscript of *Alice's Adventures Underground*, was impressed and urged Dodgson to publish it, but Dodgson was not sure and so sent his story to MacDonald and Louisa to test out on the children.[16] Greville MacDonald wrote:

> 'I remember that first reading well, and also my braggart avowal that I wished there were 60,000 volumes of it.'[17]

The MacDonalds' enthusiastic reception tipped the scales for Dodgson and he decided to go ahead and publish. MacDonald may even have influenced Dodgson to some extent in his choice of Tenniel as illustrator, as he had previously produced an edition of *Undine* which MacDonald had much admired. Certainly, when Dodgson was looking for an illustrator for *Through the Looking Glass* in April 1868, he asked MacDonald to give him an introduction to Sir Noel Paton whom he met several years later, with the aid of another note from MacDonald, in Edinburgh. Paton complained that he was too ill for the undertaking and urged 'that Tenniel is *the* man'.

MacDonald's long friendship with Dodgson was more than just a criss-cross of people and events, however. They shared more than high spirits and good humour, though there was plenty of that. Greville remembered:

> 'How happily could my father laugh over this loving humourist's impromptu drawings, full of absurdities, mock-maxims and erratic logic so dear to the child-heart, young or old!'[18]

Dodgson's serious side, however, and his religious commitment were very important to him.

He had a strong sense of personal unworthiness and it may have been this rather than his stammer which prevented him from advancing in the church.

Both Dodgson and MacDonald had a deep-rooted faith and both were stuck with the title 'Reverend' which neither of them much wanted. MacDonald gave up using it and Dodgson never proceeded from deacon to priest, remaining in a kind of cloistered limbo at Christ Church. While MacDonald reached his avowed non-sectarianism through slipping off the Calvinist high road, Dodgson's church background could not have been more different. His father had been a High Church Archdeacon, and while at Oxford Dodgson was close to Liddon, a High Churchman and leading light in the Oxford Movement. Dodgson believed, as Mac-Donald did, that the centre-point of the Christian message is that God is a God of love; he had a distaste for the sects and forms of ritual that distracted from this simple, central message. In the debates then raging between faith and doubt, science and religion, these two men who had come to divinity from a scientific background must have had much to talk about.

Doctrinally then, MacDonald and Dodgson were close and their theological interests led to other shared interests. Both were passionate about the theatre, for example, and Dodgson became an avid fan of the MacDonald family theatricals.

Dodgson laid out his ideas in 'The Stage and the Spirit of Reverence' in *The Theatre* of June 1888, believing that 'The stage is...an engine of incalculable power for influencing society.' He saw the object of acting as to raise the mind above itself. Their common interests also stretched further to the world beyond, for spiritualism had taken a strong hold from the mid-nineteenth century onwards. It should not perhaps be seen so much as a dabbling in the black arts as a subject arising from the scientific curiosity that pervaded the era. To prove that there was a world beyond, using scientific means, was a prospect that attracted many Victorians; but it was also the case that the crumbling of the church, attacked by science from without and the new criticism from within, meant that its members fell into all manner of fringe activities and superstitions.

As a member of The Society for Psychical Research Dodgson found himself in company with Conan Doyle, Gladstone, Ruskin, the painter G.F. Watts, Mrs Oscar Wilde and other leading Victorians. He was also a member of the Ghost Society. It was a fashion of the times. His interest in ghosts and spirits, in the thin shimmering veil that separates this world from the next, and in the dream-like quality of this life compared with what was seen as the solid reality of the next, all preoccupied Dodgson, and were all concerns that he shared with MacDonald.

MacDonald pooh-poohed spiritualism in *David Elginbrod*, but later came into close contact with it through his friends the Mount-Temples and through Ruskin. MacDonald was also fascinated by magic and mesmerism, and while he was living in Hastings had been to see a demonstration by a Pole called Zamoiski who had made Greville Matheson forget both his Christian-name and surname. MacDonald used this hypnotist in *David Elginbrod* where he appears as the sinister Von Funkelstein.

An interest in the occult was not the only thing to unite MacDonald and Dodgson. MacDonald was a convinced homoeopath and though Dodgson had lampooned homoeopathy in *The Rectory Umbrella*, he changed his mind and began taking homoeopathic remedies, noting which ones he found effective, soon after he met the MacDonalds. Their love for nature and natural things went further — into a hatred for vivisection. Part of MacDonald's novel, *Paul Faber, Surgeon* was reprinted as an anti-vivisection tract, while Dodgson went to the touching lengths of inventing a painless mousetrap.

As well as sharing so many interests, Dodgson's and MacDonald's imaginations informed one another at a profound level and they both held a common vision.[19] Before Dodgson met MacDonald he showed no sign that he would one day set himself to writing fairy tales — for that is how he regarded *Alice*. He had only published a few poems and short stories and in those days his chief influences were Tennyson and Hood.

There can be no doubt that some of the themes at the heart of *Phantastes* reappeared in *Alice in Wonderland*, though of course Dodgson never attempted any moral or religious allegory in the story. Alice, like Anodos, finds herself wandering in a strange, unpredictable land where things can change their shape from moment to moment. Like Anodos, she descends underground and the world she enters is a distant echo of the one presented so startlingly in German Romantic literature which MacDonald was to explore again in *The Princess and the Goblin*. Alice is not travelling in search of a white lady as Anodos is, but a white rabbit, whom she meets at the beginning of her journey. Many critics have sought the origin of the white rabbit, from Landseer's painting of *Titania* to the hillsides of Wales, but whatever its origin, there is a white rabbit partly fitting Carroll's description in *Phantastes*:

'. . . a large white rabbit cantered slowly up, put one of its little feet on mine, and looked up at me with its red eyes, just as I had been looking up at the flower above me. I stopped and stroked it; but when I attempted to lift it, it banged the ground with its hind feet, and scampered off at a great rate, turning, however, to look at me, several times before I lost sight of it.'[20]

The landscape which Alice finds herself in has the same effect as the worlds which Anodos and Vane enter. She loses her sense of identity:

'"Who are *you*?" said the Caterpillar.
"I-I hardly know, Sir, just at present — at least I know who I *was* when I got up this morning, but I think I must have been changed several times since then."
"What do you mean by that?" said the Caterpillar sternly. "Explain yourself!"
"I can't explain *myself*, I'm afraid, Sir," said Alice, "because I'm not myself, you see."'[21]

Dodgson wrote of Alice: 'For this curious child was very fond of pretending to be two people,' and whatever was true of Alice, it was certainly a fact that Dodgson had neatly divided himself into two people: Charles Dodgson and Lewis Carroll — one a shy, rational mathematician, the other full of fun and games and subversive humour. The split in the personalities may represent a split in Dodgson's mind to the extent that Alice, like Anodos, finds herself on the far side of the mind, and has to wander through a great deal of illogicality before coming back to a sense of self-awareness. What Alice is in search of is an Eden-like garden, unlocked by the same golden key which Mossy and Tangle use in MacDonald's story to unlock the rainbow and so enter paradise.

Crossing over into *Through the Looking Glass*, the mirror that Alice passes through has the quality of transforming the ordinary into the extraordinary, as Cosmo noted in *Phantastes* ('All mirrors are magic mirrors'). Later it is, of course, a mirror that Vane passes through in *Lilith* written in 1895. But the crux of the book is when Alice discovers the Red King snoring under a tree:

'"He's dreaming now," said Tweedledee: "and what do you think he's dreaming about?"
Alice said, "Nobody can guess that."
"Why, about *you*!" Tweedledee exclaimed, clapping his hands triumphantly. "And if he left off dreaming about you, where do you suppose you'd be?"
"Where I am now, of course," said Alice.
"Not you!" Tweedledee retorted contemptuously. "You'd be nowhere. Why, you're only a sort of thing in his dream."'[22]

'Our life is no dream, but it ought to become one, and perhaps will,' wrote Novalis, and this quote is one which MacDonald used again and again. Life as a dream was central to the wisdom of both Dodgson and

MacDonald, and the tension felt at the end of *Through the Looking Glass* as to whether the Red King is part of Alice's dream or vice versa — 'Which do *you* think it was?' — is felt keenly at the end of *Lilith* when Vane is no longer sure whether he is awake or asleep. His life really has become a dream. In MacDonald's essay on 'The Imagination' he wrote, 'Indeed, a man is rather *being thought* than *thinking*, when a new thought arises in his mind.'[23]

In the same year that MacDonald first published his essay on 'The Imagination', Dodgson contributed 'Bruno's Revenge', a short story, to a magazine. He then continued to work the story up over many years into two books: *Sylvie and Bruno* (1889) and *Sylvie and Bruno Concluded* (1893). They were a struggle to write, and Dodgson confessed to Winifred MacDonald that he had put more 'real thought' into them than into the *Alice* books. These books take the theme of life as a dream. After dozing a while, the narrator wakes with a start to ponder:

> '"So, either I've been dreaming about Sylvie," I said to myself, "and this is the reality. Or else I've really been with Sylvie and this is a dream! Is Life itself a dream, I wonder."'[24]

Sylvie and Bruno is made up of fragments of dreams and conversations interspersed with measures of morality and Christian teaching. It is much nearer MacDonald's work than anything else Dodgson ever wrote, and the double story may have been suggested by Diamond's adventures in *At the Back of the North Wind*. Dodgson presents two other worlds — Elfland and the burlesque Outland — while MacDonald only ever has one and it is doubtful whether he would have approved of Outland as he disliked satire, finding it a degenerate genre. It is certain that MacDonald would have been charmed by Sylvie and Bruno however, for their sentimental characterization was of the kind close to MacDonald's own heart.

Dodgson for his part certainly knew MacDonald's novels and read them with delight, chatting over *David Elginbrod* with him soon after it was published and noting that Annie Anderson in *Alec Forbes of Howglen* was 'one of the most delightful [characters] I have ever met with in fiction.'[25]

Forrester's last-minute marriage, in *Sylvie and Bruno*, and his sacrificial entry into the plague-ridden village only to undergo an inevitable death and resurrection are familiar devices to any one who has ever read any of MacDonald's novels.

For all its long years in composition, *Sylvie and Bruno* never caught the public's imagination. It has been long since eclipsed by the less didactic *Alice* and is seldom read nowadays.

Dodgson's relationship with the MacDonalds stretched on into the 1890s, though their friendship began to slip as the children grew up. But in those early years of their friendship, just after the MacDonalds had moved to London, and Dodgson came to call, there was one ambition fixed in MacDonald's mind that kept eluding him: to be published.

Even though he was unable to get anything published after *Within and Without* and *Phantastes*, MacDonald continued to write and write. Greville MacDonald records:

'He wrote with tireless, minutely painstaking energy, although often laid up by bronchitis, asthma and wretched headaches. I remember more than one grave attack of haemoptysis in the early sixties. Once he fell in alighting from an omnibus, and cut his forehead terribly, arriving home covered in blood.'[26]

After the refusal of his play *If I had a Father*, the publisher George Murray Smith took MacDonald to one side and said:

'. . . if you would but write novels, you would find all the publishers saving up to buy them of you! Nothing but fiction pays. Yet I will publish any of your poetry.'[27]

Straight away MacDonald began work on *Seekers and Finders*, only to abandon the manuscript after he found that no one would take it. He was stuck and searched desperately for a new idea. Greville remembered:

'One evening at an informal supper of oysters, beefsteak pudding and bottled stout, he [Smith-Williams] and James Greenwood, my father and others were consorting, when George MacDonald's attention was arrested by hearing Manby Smith, the gifted journalist, then writing regularly for the *Leisure Hour*, *Chambers Journal*, etc., reciting a certain Scotch epitaph he had heard somewhere. "What's that, what's that?" my father exclaimed, as though catching sight of some living thing that might evade him: "Say it again, Mr Smith!"
The latter repeated:
Here lie I, Martin Elginbrodde;
Hae mercy o' my soul, Lord God;
As I wad do, were I Lord God,
An' ye were Martin Elginbrodde.'[28]

These lines suddenly unlocked MacDonald's imagination. He went home and began to write, finding himself released. The epitaph grew and grew in his mind, shaping itself into his novel *David Elginbrod*. After finishing the book he parcelled the manuscript up and sent it off, but again, as with *Seekers and Finders*, it seemed as if no one wanted it.

Meanwhile, insult was added to injury by the *Cornhill Magazine* sending back a Scotch[29] ballad merely because it was Scotch. This was in January 1862. That spring Louisa had to travel down to Hastings with her father, Mr Powell, and Charlotte Godwin to nurse their youngest sister who was dangerously ill with rheumatic fever. The family was separated and George was left to cope with all the children in London. While Louisa was busy nursing, Dr and Mrs Hale arranged for two readings for MacDonald — a fairy tale of his own and selections from Spenser's *Faerie Queene*. Their success made it possible for the whole family to have a change down by the sea-side.[30]

On 15 July 1862 Louisa gave birth in the cramped surroundings of Tudor Lodge to another son named Robert Falconer after MacDonald's ideal character in *Seekers and Finders*, later to have a novel named after himself. With the entry of yet another child into the household it was decided that another move was necessary. So the MacDonalds put on their hats and went house-hunting once again. They eventually found a house in a large imposing Georgian row in Kensington, 12 Earles Terrace, and made ready to pack their things. But there were other reasons, apart from the growing family, for the move. It was thought that the gravel of Kensington would be better than the red clay of Regent's Park for MacDonald's impaired lungs, and the new house was more conveniently situated for those who attended his classes and lectures. In his customary manner MacDonald escaped during the move and went to stay with Louisa's cousin Mark Sharman at Wellingborough. The move was completed on 12 September 1863.[31] One of the friends who came to call on them soon after they had moved in was Charles Dodgson. Sauntering through Kensington he could not find the house at all and went on instead to Holman Hunt's. He wrote afterwards to Louisa from the sculptor Munro's house in Belgravia:

'Late as it is, I will write one line to tell you that I have made an effort (not on a Friday, but yet a failure) to find your new house. I found an Earl *Street*, but the aborigines themselves didn't know of anything else beginning with 'Earl.' I mean to start again soon, taking a bag of provisions, an axe, and the other essentials for a traveller exploring in unknown regions.'[32]

Luckily he found the house the next time he passed by.

David Elginbrod had been refused by many publishers and now, on the point of failing to place his second novel, MacDonald's frustration was growing. But somehow the book fell into the hands of his friend

Margaret Oliphant, a novelist of some standing, and a fellow Scot, who read it and was entranced:[33]

> 'She always spoke of it as a work of genius, and quoted it as one of the instances of publishers' blunders, for when the M.S. came to her it came enveloped in wrappings that showed how many refusals it had suffered.'[34]

She took it to Hurst and Blackett, her publishers, and virtually ordered them to publish it which they did without delay. Writing to Blackwood, editor of the famous magazine, late in 1863, Margaret Oliphant pleaded:

> 'I am very glad you like *David Elginbrod*, and my anxiety to get the article admission I may explain by telling you that it was at my urgent recommendation (having read the M.S. and made such humble suggestions towards its improvement as my knowledge of the literary susceptibility made possible) that Mr Blackett published it; and that the author is not only a man of genius but a man burdened with ever so many children, and, what is perhaps worse, a troublesome conscientiousness; so please, if you are persuadable, let me have my way this time, and I will assault or congratulate, haul down or set up, anybody your honour pleases hereafter.'[35]

David Elginbrod finally appeared in January 1863.[36] After its publication MacDonald never had any difficulty in placing another book.

CHAPTER TWENTY

David Elginbrod — the Novels

With ninety pounds in his pocket for *David Elginbrod* MacDonald was finally a novelist. At a time when Charles Dickens was making £10,000 a novel this first payment was modest, but the Victorian era was one of great rewards and disappointments for writers. The novel was the literary form of the age, read by an eager audience, from Prime Minister to housemaids (and one Prime Minister, Disraeli, was even a novelist). The number of novels being published to meet the unquenchable demands of the reading public was ever increasing. Better education had made people able and eager to read and novels were often serialized in newspapers and magazines or widely available through Mudie's circulating library or from the railway bookstalls of W.H. Smith. Novelists jostled for prominence — their pictures were pasted in omnibuses or on the walls of depots — and a bestseller could take the country by storm. But many of the best known writers of the day have long since been forgotten. A writer could find a niche and survive, however, provided that he (or very commonly she) could supply what the public wanted. Amy Cruse in her book *The Victorians and their Books* records that:

'George Borrow in his *Lavengro* published in 1851, tells how he offered to a publisher some old ballads and a romance in the German style, and was told that such things had no chance of success with the readers of that day.

"Don't you think you could write a series of evangelical tales?" said the publisher.

"Evangelical tales, sir?"

"Yes, sir, Evangelical novels...something in the style of *The Dairyman's Daughter*."

"I never heard of the work till the present moment."

"Then, sir, procure it by all means. Sir, I could afford as much as ten pounds for a well-written tale in the style of *The Dairyman's Daughter*; that is the kind of literature, sir, that sells at the present day." [1]

By the time MacDonald had begun writing novels, a flood of novels that were at once entertaining and instructive had saturated the market, and he followed suit. There is no doubt that it was financial necessity which drove him from poetry to prose. In an interview given in 1893 MacDonald reflected that:

> 'As to myself...I had no choice. I had to write for money, and prose pays the best; and I have had to write hard, too. I am a busy man. I have always two novels on the stocks at once — I used to manage three.'[2]

It was a time of prolific novelists and writers whose works were forgotten almost as quickly as they were written, though even the great names of Victorian literature such as Dickens, Ruskin, Kingsley or Matthew Arnold seemed tireless in their ability to bring volume after volume of their writing rolling off the presses:

> 'The explanation lies partly in their optimism — their confidence in the power of the mind to resolve every problem and of the individual to influence the course of events regardless of political or economic forces; and in their deep conviction that a critical age of transition and an uneducated democracy required immediate guidance in many areas.'[3]

The catchphrase of the Victorian era was that they were living through 'an age of transition', moving from a certain past to an uncertain future. The swell of the cities and increasing industrialization, bad conditions, strikes and unrest shook the Victorian gentleman in his castle from without, and from within he was assailed by the many '-isms' of the day — Socialism, Puseyism and scepticism — as the traditional foundations of faith were slowly gnawed away. It was a worrying time and the Victorians were great worriers. As the pace of life increased and the glittering network of railways joined town to town in a way that had never been possible before, so the Victorians found themselves trapped in the quickening pace of urban life, harking back nostalgically to the time before the railways, the Edens of rural, undisturbed places. Such strains of thought run deeply through the novels of George Eliot, Thomas Hardy and others and MacDonald was inevitably tinted with the same nostalgia. Although they were puzzled and bewildered, the Victorians also believed that there were answers to their problems, and so it was an age of preaching and preachers, of prophets and theories — the age of Carlyle, Ruskin, Matthew Arnold and William Morris. Carlyle, the first of the Victorian 'prophets', was a Scot, and in his writings he attacked the assumptions of the *laissez-faire* society using notions drawn from German romanticism and transcendentalism.[4] For Carlyle, the great enemy was mechanism, and MacDonald, who read deeply in Carlyle and imbibed the same German influences, wrote under his shadow, espousing many of the same theories.

In such an age as this, when Victorian novelists sharpened their pens they did so with a purpose. Perhaps more than any other novelist Charles Dickens graphically presented the squalor of inner-city life and pricked the Victorian conscience towards change. For the Victorians, fiction existed not only to entertain, but also to instruct — to instruct in the business of living, in the business of religion, and in the business of education. Many other novelists were mainly theological in their purpose. First and foremost stood Charles Kingsley whose novels *Alton Locke* and *Yeast* caused a stir with their depiction of social conditions and their marriage of religion and politics. At the other end of the spectrum, the genteel Charlotte Yonge captured the country with her novel *The Heir of Redclyffe* in 1853.

Sir Guy, hero of *The Heir of Redclyffe*, was a hero in an age that needed heroes. The achievements of Nelson and Wellington were long past and, in their anxiety, the Victorians of the mid-nineteenth century craved not only theories, but models whom they could emulate. Carlyle himself wrote that:

'In all epochs of the world we shall find the Great Man to have been the indispensable saviour of his epoch.'[5]

And Walter Houghton in *The Victorian Frame of Mind* comments:

'To the Victorians a hero might be a messiah or he might be a
revelation of God, but he was certain to be a man of the highest moral
stature, and therefore of enormous importance to a period in which the
alarming increase of both the commercial spirit and religious doubt
made moral inspiration a primary need.'[6]

The two characters towering over MacDonald's fiction — David Elginbrod and Robert Falconer — are both examples of such great men. They embody MacDonald's answer to the Victorian dilemma, for MacDonald was also prophetic in his writing and his novels served as the pulpit from which he could deliver his message. His watchcry was 'Art for truth's sake'[7] in defiance of all his opponents, and years later his son Ronald MacDonald wrote:

'Once I asked him why he did not, for change and variety, write a story
of mere human passion and artistic plot. He replied that he would like

to write it. I asked him further whether his highest literary quality was not in a measure injured by what must seem to many the monotony of his theme — referring to the novels alone. He admitted that it was possible; and went on to tell me that, having begun to do his work as a congregational minister, and having been driven. . .into giving up the professional pulpit, he was no less impelled than compelled to use unceasingly the new platform whence he had found that his voice could carry so far.'[8]

So, spinning together the two strains of theology and romance, Mac-Donald eventually produced a sizeable *oeuvre* of some twenty-six novels, quite apart from his poetry, children's books and religious works. These novels, though sharing many of the characteristics common to Victorian novels, have a distinctiveness that is hard to classify, unless it be that of theological romance. The novels fall into two groups: Scottish and English, and it is generally agreed that the Scottish novels are livelier, contrasting with the flat domesticity of their English counterparts.

In fact, MacDonald's first published novel, *David Elginbrod*, contains many of the features that occupied him throughout his prolific career. The book falls into an English part (Arnstead and later London) and a Scottish part (Turriepuffit). It is part-theological, part-Gothic, part-romance, part-autobiography and represents the root from which the other novels grow. It tells the story of young Hugh Sutherland, who, in one of the vacations from his university, comes to Turriepuffit to work as a tutor for Lord Glasford. While working at the big house he meets the crofter and ploughman David Elginbrod, his wife Janet and their daughter Margaret. They are an idealized family possessing all the noble virtues that MacDonald associated with old peasant Scotland, and which are also to be found in Scott's novels.

It is hard to appreciate now the spell that Walter Scott's *Waverley* novels cast over the nineteenth century. They conjured up an historical and romantic Scotland peopled with exotic characters such as Rob Roy MacGregor, the same Scotland which emerges in Robert Louis Stevenson's *Kidnapped*. There was a general awakening of interest in Scotland and things Scottish at this time — even Queen Victoria had wrapped herself in the Scottish myth, retreating to Balmoral and having a piper play under her window every morning. The truth was somewhat different. The grim carnage associated with the Gallows Herd had gone, but the Highlands had been cleared for sheep and the Clyde Valley was now reeking with mills — the Industrial Revolution had transformed Scotland almost overnight. If Turriepuffit is a figment summoned from MacDonald's childhood, it is a world suffused with the glow of Burns and Ossian and

Wordsworth — literally a Glamour-town enchanted by the transforming magic of nostalgia — a world that had slipped away forever. Turriepuffit, the distant, Scottish idyll is more than a description, it is a place where nature is able to exercise her charms unhindered and Wordsworthian sentiments flow out of every hill and fir-tree.

Such a romantic view of nature as a divine educative mediator is central to MacDonald's vision and encounters with nature are always key points in the development of MacDonald's characters. One interesting aspect of such encounters is that they always occur in association with particular texts. After Hugh Sutherland begins teaching her poetry, Margaret Elginbrod, who has been presented to the reader as a child of nature communing with God in the natural church, the forest, finds that:

> 'Not only was the pine wood now dearer to her than before, but its mystery seemed more sacred, and, at the same time, more likely to be one day solved.'[9]

The supreme example of this kind of encounter comes in *Robert Falconer*. Robert, who is suffering from a lame foot, stumbles into a Cottar's home, where a young girl, Jessie Hewson, cares for him, seeing that he is injured. By chance he finds a copy of the *Arabian Nights* in the cottage which he reads and which sets his imagination alight. After resting and reading Robert finds that it is time to go home, and the romantic encounter with the girl, coupled with the text, has done its work. Robert is prepared to experience the power of nature in a meaningful way:

> 'As he reached the middle of the field, the wind was suddenly there with a low sough from out of the north-west. . . . When he looked to the north-west, whence the sky came, he saw nothing but a pale cleft in the sky. The meaning, the music of the night, awoke in his soul; he forgot his lame foot, and the weight of Mr Lammie's great boots, ran home and up the stair to his own room, seized his violin with eager haste, nor laid it down again till he could draw from it, at will, a sound like the moaning of the wind over the stubblefield. Then he knew that he could play the Flowers of the Forest.'[10]

MacDonald intended his reader to feel what Robert felt and through doing so to open his portals to the benevolent influences of nature, and beyond nature, God. What is interesting is that Robert needs a text to do this to act as a 'key' to open nature's mystery to him. The romantic element is also very important. Duncan Campbell in *The Portent* finds that he can read Spenser only after falling in love with Lady Alice and the description of Robert Falconer's violin as a 'bonny leddy' is applied to the lovely Mary St. John. Indeed, when Robert catches sight of Mary St. John walking in the garden it springs into his mind that his violin is in fact a woman. But it is primarily through poetry that MacDonald's heroes enter into these experiences. One of the prevalent images in his writing is that of the library, a place filled with books, a 'bookscape' as it is called in *There and Back*, and hence a place filled with knowledge and mystery. Just as in *Phantastes* Anodos climbs into different adventures through the books he finds in the library of the fairy palace, so many of MacDonald's feelings about nature come from the poets and other writers he read, and not just from his childhood experiences. He had had to be schooled to appreciate nature and as a result the interaction of text and experience is to be found everywhere in his novels.

In the setting of Turriepuffit the figure of David Elginbrod, modelled on MacDonald's own father, but mingled with poetry and romance, is shown as one of nature's true aristocrats — in stark comparison with the Glasfords, who may be aristocrats in the eyes of the world, but who suffer from mean and suspicious natures. David Elginbrod's comment on Mrs Glasford is:

> '"She does na come o' a guid breed. Man, it's a fine thing to come o' a guid breed. They hae a hantle to answer for 'at come o' decent forebears."'[11]

David has a purity, an ancestry, that the worldly Glasfords lack. He has 'a seer-like look' and it is into his mouth that MacDonald places all his own pronouncements on faith. Elginbrod's 'natural' religion expresses itself through everyday imagery bypassing the frequently 'affected' style of preachers and evangelists. It is a religion of the spirit welling up from within, not grafted on through books and learning from outside:

> '"We ken no more, Maister Sutherlan', what we're growin' till, than that neep-seed there kens what a neep is, though a neep it will be. The only odds is, that we ken that we dinna ken, and the neep-seed kens nothing at all aboot it. But ae thing, Maister Sutherlan', we may be sure o' that whatever it be, it will be worth God's makin' an' our growin".'[12]

MacDonald allowed Elginbrod to go further than this, permitting him to touch on dangerous doctrines, and gently introducing the idea of purgatory for example:

> '"It wad be an ill day for a' o's, Maggy my doo gin he war to close his een to oor sins, an' ca' us just in his sicht, what we cudna possibly be just in oor ain or in ony ither body's, no to say his."'[13]

Such ideas are explored further in other novels — a notable example being Robert Falconer's plan for emptying hell. The boy protests to his grandmother that the souls of the wicked and the blest are in either hell or heaven through no merit of their own and asks why those in heaven could not bend down to bear the sins of those languishing in hell and help find remission for them. He finishes his speech with tears, so overcome is he at the effort of expressing himself to his fearsome grandmother. Her response to him is to beat him. As with many Scottish novelists, Calvinism is the scapegoat for much that was rigid and harsh in the Scottish temperament, but Mrs Falconer is finally revered rather than rejected. She represents a co-existence of conflicting temperaments and the tradition out of which young Falconer has grown. After the beating:

> 'His grandmother, herself weeping fast and silently, with scarce altered countenance, took her neatly folded handkerchief from her pocket, and wiped her grandson's fresh cheeks, then wiped her own withered face; and from that moment Robert knew that he loved her.'[14]

And MacDonald is always careful to distinguish between Calvin the man and his followers:

> 'They take up what their leader, urged by the necessity of the time, spoke loudest, never heeding what he loved most; and then work the former out to a logical perdition of everything belonging to the latter.'[15]

But MacDonald also found time to paint a lighter side of Scottish religious foibles. The blackness is tinged with humour and MacDonald, not notable for his humour, brings life to his depiction of Scottish scenes and characters. In *David Elginbrod* there is 'a noisy little stream, that obstinately refused to keep Scotch Sabbath, praising the Lord after its own fashion' and in *Alec Forbes of Howglen* there is a classic encounter between Cupples, the cynical and drunken librarian who is carrying a purple foxglove, and the ponderous and hypocritical shop-owner Robert Bruce:

> '"I'm surprised to see ye carryin' that thing o' the Lord's day, Mr Cupples. Fowk'll think ill o' ye."
> "Weel, ye see, Mr Bruce, it angert me sae to see the ill-faured thing positeevely growin' there upo' the Lord's day, that I pud it up 'maist by the reet. To think o' a weyd like that prankin' itsel oot in its purple and its spots upo' the Sawbath day! It canna ken what it's aboot. I'm only feared I left eneuch o't to be up again afore lang."
> "I doobt Mr Cupples, ye haena come unner the pooer o' grace yet."'[16]

This preoccupation with preaching in a pastoral setting was characteristic of the Victorian Scottish novel and can be ascribed to other novelists apart from MacDonald, most notably Margaret Oliphant who mined her Scottish childhood for all it was worth. Many of her novels, such as *Passages from the Life of Margaret Maitland*, compare with MacDonald's in their idyllic settings and interest in church affairs. The church was a source of drama: the Great Disruption of 1843 had been a major event in Scotland, splitting the Church of Scotland into two. It ensured an abiding public interest in the life of the parish. F.R. Hart in *The Scottish Novel* comments:

> 'And the symbolic locales of Scottish fiction remain centred on the manse, the minister, his ally or rival the schoolmaster, and his patron (or enemy) the local laird.'[17]

These three characters figure largely in MacDonald's novels. Though Turriepuffit is held in contrast to the more sophisticated (and less desirable) Arnstead, MacDonald drew a vivid portrait of the community of his childhood in *Robert Falconer* and *Alec Forbes of Howglen* and to some extent in the fishing village of Portlossie in *Malcolm*. Rothieden and Glamerton are thinly veiled portraits of Huntly and many of the population are drawn from MacDonald's memory. But the Scotland that MacDonald presents is also one based on the Christian chivalric values of charity under siege from the *nouveaux riches* who have grown fat on the profits culled from commercialism. As in every picture of Eden — there are snakes. Robert Bruce, the shopkeeper in *Alec Forbes of Howglen*, is anxious that every one should think he is lineally descended from the old King, but in fact he bears more resemblance to the spider:

> 'He stood on the watch in his shop like a great spider that ate children; and his windows were his web.'[18]

And he is a hypocrite and a cheat, stealing Annie Anderson's five pounds and pocketing it for himself. Symbolically, at his unmasking he crawls out of church on all fours in the dark like an animal, his power broken. In *What's Mine's Mine* Peregrine Palmer has bought an estate for grouse shooting and is seen as an insidious English influence planted beside the upright Macruadhs. MacDonald's portrayal of the Macruadh clan is one of a noble people forced into poverty, but retaining their dignity, who leave *en masse* for Canada at the end of the novel, only to return to Scotland some years later to reclaim their land. Theirs is the grandeur associated with paintings such as *The Monarch of the Glen* or sad Jacobite ballads, but far removed from the realities of life.

The realities of life, however, are only too vividly portrayed in the scenes of school life in *Alec Forbes of Howglen*. Children wincing under the lash of Murdoch Malison and the miserable Saturday morning sessions where they are forced to learn their Shorter Catechism are true to life — entertaining and gruelling by turns. Murdoch Malison strides centre stage of the book like some monstrous figure of Vice from a morality play and it is sobering to think that his original in life, Colin Stewart, was, if anything, worse than the portrayal in the book:

'Murder Malison, as the boys called him, turned with the tawse over his shoulder, whence it had been on the point of swooping upon Annie, and answered him [Alec] with a hissing blow over his downbent head, followed by a succession of furious blows upon every part of his person, as it twisted and writhed and doubled; till, making no attempt at resistance, he was knocked down by the storm and lay prostrate under the fierce lashes, the master holding him down with one foot, and laying on with the whole force of the opposite arm.'[19]

Luckily Alec Forbes lives to fight another day. Malison aims to become a minister of the Church of Scotland and, though his failure in the pulpit brings about a change in his personality, the link between violence and religion has been made. The violence that the children suffer to their bodies at school is inflicted on their spirits at church. After listening to the sermon at the Missionar Kirk, Annie Anderson fears that:

'A spiritual terror was seated on the throne of the universe, and was called God — and to whom should she pray against it? Amidst the darkness, a deeper darkness fell.'[20]

MacDonald's idyll is a dualistic one, possessing both light and shade, and alongside Alec's and Annie's pleasant pursuits in the building of the boat, throwing snowballs, clapping sods of turf on chimneys as a joke and burying Bruce's shop half in snow, there is both cruelty and darkness. *Alec Forbes of Howglen* opens grimly with a funeral and in the violence of the flood later in the book Tibbie Dyster dies and Murdoch Malison is swept away trying to save Truffey, a pupil whom he has previously crippled through his over-enthusiasm with the tawse. Though Malison dies in a redeeming act, it is a terrible moment. MacDonald's small communities are nevertheless peopled with memorable characters: the theological and often comic conversations of Thomas Crann and George Macwha in *Alec Forbes of Howglen*, for example; Tibbie Dyster, the old blind woman whom Annie Anderson befriends; and, in the narrow streets of Rothieden, the collection of gossipping men supping their drink at the Boar's Head each Friday — Dooble Sanny the drunken shoemaker and Shargar, the waif whom Mrs Falconer takes in. The characters are all drawn with humour and conviction.

MacDonald's thirst for accuracy sometimes caused trouble when the characters in his novels were too easily recognizable. Mrs Falconer (MacDonald's grandmother) did burn a violin, but one belonging to her reprobate son Charles, and she did take in four bastard children of Sir Andrew Leith Hay of Leith Hall near Huntly. One of those sons grew into a prosperous if greedy shopkeeper and was pilloried by MacDonald as Robert Bruce in *Alec Forbes of Howglen*. This novel gave the shopkeeper and his family such a blacking that they had to move away from Huntly to Aberdeen. The character of Thomas Crann was based on James Maitland, a well-known local evangelist, and John Hill MacDonald, MacDonald's brother, had all Ericson's doubts; and there was also a Banffshire religious revival as described in *Malcolm*.[21] Up in Huntly MacDonald's uncle James read an instalment of *Robert Falconer* serialized in the *Argosy* with mounting horror and, throwing the magazine to one side, drove with all speed the twenty miles to Banff to persuade the editor of the *Banffshire Journal* not to review it. On arriving home he took out his pen and wrote grimly to his nephew:

'The veil cast over various of the characters in Falconer's life is so transparent that no living person here can be at a loss for a moment to identify them... Who can doubt the person meant by the owner of the Bleach green and the factory house, and yet the allusion to the latter is connected with the fact, painful to me to this day, that her *three* sons became insolvent 36 years ago, and it was in consequence of that the house was on the market for several years... Admiral Gordon's family are in similar circumstances with Lord Rothie... I am sorry to say it has distressed us all young and old, and I hope and reasonably beg that in the farther progress of the story, these printed allusions may be discontinued...'[22]

MacDonald, poles apart from his uncle in temperament, ignored his advice and the story stood, not just as a record of memory, but possibly too as an instrument of revenge. Perhaps MacDonald was summoning up the ghosts of his past in order to exorcise them. Maybe he thought that some of the people in Huntly were at last getting what they deserved.

The Scottish portion of MacDonald's writing, however, is more than a comment on the people of Huntly. MacDonald's is an important contribution to Scottish Victorian literature and stands as part of the uneasy

tradition linking Scotland and England, Scottish and English. For Mac-
Donald can be seen as a traditional 'lad o' pairts' hailing from a poor
background, passing through university on a bursary, and then hitting
the high road to England to make for fame and fortune. It is an almost
legendary path and, arriving in London, MacDonald would have found a
swarm of Scottish writers rubbing shoulders with each other and a
publishing business that was dominated by Scots.

The Scots have always claimed that the departure of the Scottish court
in 1603 for England when James VI of Scotland became James I of
England ended artistic patronage in Scotland, thus removing an important stratum of society; and the departure of the Scottish parliament a
century later in 1707 furthered the rot.[23] What Scotland was left with that
was distinctively Scottish were the church and the law and an atmosphere
of hard-headed Calvinism. The Reformation, which changed the church
in Scotland far more than in England, introduced a version of the Bible
translated into English, not Scots. This served to undermine the Scots
language, never a full dialect, but rather a separate literary language
paralleling the development of Chaucerian Middle English, which developed into what is now called Standard English. Scots was demoted to a
half-foreign regional dialect which had to be expunged as one moved up
the social scale. MacDonald is well aware of the Scottish literary tradition
and shows a corresponding ambiguity towards the Scots language.[24] In
Alec Forbes of Howglen he wrote:

> 'I do not allow however that the Scotch is a *patois* in the ordinary sense
> of the word. For had not Scotland a living literature, and that a high
> one, when England could produce none, or next to none — I mean in
> the fifteenth century? But old age, and the introduction of a more
> polished form of utterance, have given to the Scotch all the other
> advantages of a *patois*, in addition to its own directness and
> simplicity.'[25]

The Makars, Dunbar and Henryson, were the flowers of fifteenth-
century Scottish literature, and later, while Edinburgh had been flourishing as the Athens of the North, Burns had emerged, writing in a Scots
which the London public seemed able to read with pleasure. MacDonald
had no compunction therefore in putting large stretches of Scots into his
novels, but he displays a characteristic Scots inferiority in his attitude
towards it. He himself had been taught to speak English at table like most
'well brought-up' Scottish children and it is a telling point that when
Margaret Elginbrod begins to receive the benefits of learning, Mac-
Donald noted:

'It will be observed that Margaret's speech had begun to *improve*, that is, to be more like English.'[26]

And both Alec Forbes and Robert Falconer follow an odyssey through from Scottish to English as they grow up and go to university:

'My reader may have observed a little change for the better in Robert's speech. Dr Anderson had urged upon him the necessity of being able at least to speak English, and he had been trying to modify the antique Saxon dialect they used at Rothieden with the newer and more refined English.'[27]

In a similar way Malcolm in *The Marquis of Lossie* decides to speak only in English when he arrives in London and indeed MacDonald translated his own boyhood into English in *Ranald Bannerman's Boyhood*. Such an ambiguity in relation to Scots is another example of the light and shade, the extraordinary dualism to be found in the Scottish character. The Scots speak not one language, but two — a refined English and a 'natural' Scots, for Scots remains the language of emotion and ancestry.

MacDonald's characters always lapse into Scots at emotional high points. Dr Anderson, Robert Falconer's mentor (who has reconstructed a traditional peasant's room as his bedroom in his fine Aberdeen house) falls into Scots, the language of his forebears, on his deathbed. Similarly both Robert Falconer and Mrs Forbes break into Scots the moment they break into anger. As a more 'natural' language Scots expresses their feelings more completely; it embraces the ideas expressed by Wordsworth in his preface to the *Lyrical Ballads* of a poetry written in a natural language for natural people, close to the common forms of speech. MacDonald wanted to combine a traditional written Scots with the spoken language he knew from his own boyhood.[28] In *Malcolm*, for example, there are many humorous exchanges among the inhabitants of Portlossie, and Miss Horn, whose proud claim is that 'I hae nae feelin's', is yet able to display anger towards the nasty witch-like Barbara Catanach:

'"What mean ye?" demanded Miss Horn, sternly and curtly. "I ken what I mean mysel', an' ane that's no content wi' that, bude [behoved] ill be a howdie [midwife]. I wad fain hae gotten a fancy oot o' my heid that's been there this mony a lang day; but please yersel', mem, gien ye winna be neebourly."'

MacDonald had a profound philological interest in Scottish speech, selling out to his English readers only so far as to translate a few words here and there.

The Farm, just outside Huntly, where MacDonald spent his childhood.

Thurso Castle. This is probably the 'nobleman's mansion', where MacDonald worked as tutor in 1842, and which housed the library that was to haunt his future writing.

Trinity Congregational Church, Arundel. MacDonald resigned as minister of the church in 1853, over allegations that his views were 'not in accordance with the Scriptures'.

Louisa and George MacDonald, taken by Lewis Carroll at Elm Lodge in 1863. This is the earliest photograph of the MacDonalds together.

From left to right: Louisa MacDonald, Greville, Mary, Lewis Carroll, Grace, Lilia. Taken in the garden of Elm Lodge in July 1863.

Mary MacDonald, one of
Lewis Carroll's earliest
'child friends',
photographed by
Carroll in 1863.

This drawing by Arthur
Hughes is of George and
the Dragon, with Mary
MacDonald portrayed as
Alice.

This original sketch for MacDonald's bookplate is derived from Blake, showing death giving way to new life. It includes the family motto (an anagram of 'George MacDonald'): 'Corage! God mend al!' From this, the family named their house at Boscombe 'Corage', and the house in Bordighera 'Casa Coraggio'.

Below left. A portrait of George MacDonald by Edward Hughes.

Below right. George MacDonald, caricatured for *Once a Week,* November 1872.

The MacDonalds' Italian Home, Casa Coraggio, at Bordighera.

MacDonald pictured with his sons in the 1880s.

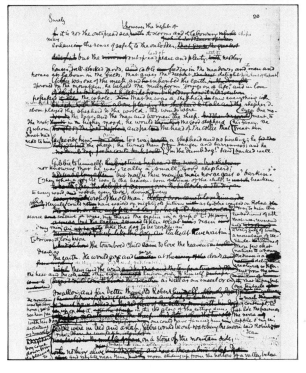

A page of manuscript from *Sir Gibbie* (now at the Gordon Schools, Huntly)

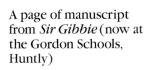

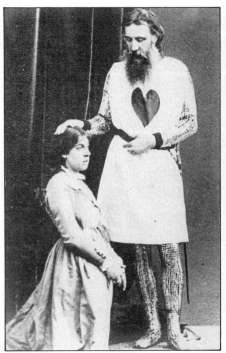

A scene from a MacDonald performance of *Pilgrim's Progress.* George appears here as Greatheart, with Lilia as Christiana.

MacDonald as Evangelist, in a scene from *Pilgrim's Progress.*

The MacDonald family scrubbing the floor at Casa Coraggio. In the Great Room, pictured here, the family mounted plays, concerts and tableaux. The room seated 250 (or 400 standing) and was built especially by MacDonald for this purpose.

George MacDonald in old age.

Bordighera in the 1880s. The area had a reputation for good health, and many wealthy Britons stayed there for the winter months.

The declining years: George, Irene and Louisa MacDonald outside Casa Coraggio in the 1890s.

But if the use of Scots may have put some readers off, it was the pictures of Scotland that drew many people to MacDonald's books. Critics have tended to hop from Scott to Galt to the 'Kailyard'[29] school without so much as a glance at MacDonald but this was not what his contemporaries saw. MacDonald was compared to Margaret Oliphant and William Black in the *Edinburgh Review* of April 1876 and linked to the Kailyard by David Christie Murray in *My Contemporaries in Fiction* in 1897 when he wrote:

'When one calls to mind the rapid and extensive popularity achieved by the latest school of Scottish dialect writers, one is tempted to wonder a little at the comparative neglect which has befallen a real master of that *genre*, who is still living and writing, and who began his work within the memory of the middle-aged.'

Of the Kailyarders, three Scottish novelists who were very popular towards the end of the nineteenth century, Crockett and Maclaren are now largely forgotten, but J.M. Barrie is still remembered for *Peter Pan*. Their books sold by the hundred thousand. *Beside the Bonnie Brier Bush* sold a quarter of a million copies in Britain and half a million in the States. Their popularity, if short-lived, deeply affected the Scots' view of themselves and their fiction provided the cosy fireside sentimentality that still persists in such publications as *The Sunday Post* and *The People's Friend* today. Such a charge, however, could not be laid at MacDonald's door. Though his view of Scotland is undoubtedly romantic, his descriptions of Rothieden and Glamerton have a cutting edge. As he moved from Scotland to England straight after finishing university, he had no first-hand experience of industrialized Scotland. The railway did not reach Huntly until ten years after MacDonald had left home and even today Aberdeenshire is a largely agricultural region. Unlike the Kailyarders, MacDonald was passionately interested in social conditions and the gin-soaked women, shrivelled babies and street urchins of underworld London are presented very starkly to the reader. Even when propriety inhibits MacDonald from writing too explicitly about violence or prostitution there is never any doubt as to what he is talking about:

'Of some of the places into which Falconer led me that night I will attempt no description — places blazing with lights and mirrors, crowded with dancers, billowing with music, close and hot, and full of the saddest of all sights, the uninteresting faces of commonplace women.'[30]

No doubt if MacDonald had gone to Glasgow instead of London he would have written about what he would have found there.

If MacDonald's contribution as a mid-Victorian Scottish writer has been too easily passed over, it is nevertheless true that he was never in the front rank of novelists. He did not reach the heights of Dickens or George Eliot, but though never became a bestseller, many of his novels passed through several editions and his sales were good. The *Cornhill Magazine* launched by George Murray Smith in 1860 with Thackeray as its editor, to which MacDonald contributed *The Portent* in its first three issues, was a triumph and spawned other magazines such as the *Argosy, Once a Week* and *All the Year Round. Robert Falconer* was serialized in the *Argosy* while more overtly theological works such as *Annals of a Quiet Neighbourhood* and *The Seaboard Parish* came out in the *Sunday Magazine.* The long sermons in the latter two books were therefore written for an audience who felt the need to be improved on the Sabbath and through the sermons of Walton, the Vicar, MacDonald rammed his points home. At his height MacDonald was paid £800 to £1000 for a novel — a good price.

Contemporary reactions to his novels were mixed. Most reviewers favoured his sentiments above his style:

> '. . . it is high praise indeed to say of his works that it is impossible to read them without being benefited. . .'

wrote one reviewer, though the same reviewer detected 'a slight smack of the schoolmaster'[31] which is certainly true. J. Knight in the *Fortnightly Review* complained that:

> 'Each succeeding volume has become increasingly didactic. . . there is a lamentable falling off in artistic method and purpose.'

But the same reviewer was drawn to MacDonald's descriptions of Scotland, which most reviewers singled out for praise:

> 'The command of humour and pathos Robert Falconer displays is wonderful, its descriptions of Scotch life and character are admirable; it has great power of characterisation and psychological analysis, and its style is throughout picturesque and musical — the prose of a poet.'[32]

Most of these criticisms are true enough. The novels do smack of the schoolmaster and often lapse into pedantry and compilations of facts. But MacDonald was unrepentant about his didacticism. In a letter to Lord Mount-Temple in 1879 he wrote of his novels that he wanted:

> '. . . to make them true to the real and not to the spoilt humanity. . . I will try to show what we might be, may be, must be, shall be — and something of the struggle to gain it.'[33]

And in one of his books for children, *Gutta Percha Willie*, MacDonald declared:

> 'I don't care to write about boys and girls, or men and women, who are not growing in the right way. They are not interesting enough to write about.'[34]

As he spent much of his life teaching women, it is not surprising that he was read mainly by women, for they more often had the leisure to pore over his romances and creaking theological plots. But his novels are not easy to read today. The prose is like syrup, affected and latinate, full of pulpit oratory. Many of the novels were written as though delivered straight from the pulpit. MacDonald wrote quickly but agonized over his manuscripts, crossing and recrossing his handwritten lines. He never seemed happy with his books in any form and they changed radically from edition to edition. For example, the 1882 edition of *Adela Cathcart* lost three of the best stories from the 1864 edition and gained *The Snow Fight*, while *Robert Falconer* seemed to have been almost completely rewritten in its passage from serialization in the *Argosy* to a three-volume novel.

In many ways, MacDonald's plots (when there is a plot) echo his sentences, advancing by fits and starts as MacDonald pauses to make asides to his audience. The audience was probably as happy with the asides as anything else, for they are often kernels of MacDonald's thought expressed concisely in an aphoristic manner, but such digressions do not make for good novel writing. In *Robert Falconer*, for example, MacDonald is at pains to show that Robert is responding to nature and not to books, though in fact the opposite is the case:

> 'It is good that children of faculty, as distinguished from capacity, should not have too many books to read, or too much of early lessoning. The increase of examinations in our country will increase its capacity and diminish its faculty. We shall have more compilers and reducers, and fewer thinkers; more modifiers and completers and fewer inventors.'[35]

Point taken, but that is what it is, a point in a lesson, and the novel itself becomes a lesson book showing MacDonald's heroes faring well or ill in the school of life on their way to 'the gran' schuil o' the just made perfec'[36] with *Pilgrim's Progress* and the *Prodigal Son* as the archetypal models. His books are filled with schools and schoolmasters from the memorable Murdoch Malison in *Alec Forbes of Howglen* to Alexander Graham in *Malcolm*. There may be no governesses in MacDonald's novels, as there were in English novels of the period, but Donal Grant and

Hugh Sutherland are their Scottish male equivalents and the reader follows them on their path towards God learning many lessons on the way.[37]

What he has done in *The Seaboard Parish*, for example, is to press a series of sermons into a three-volume novel and use them, as he used all his novels, to address the theological and social questions of the day. In *The Seaboard Parish* he addressed the 'woman question', in *Mary Marston* he voiced his moral disgust at the marriage market, there are rambling discourses on how to bring the gospel to a commercial inner city area through the enlightened character of the Rev. Fuller in *Guild Court*, MacDonald's most Dickensian novel, while *There and Back* includes John Tuke, a socialist book-binder. As always, these questions are woven into a distinctively theological fabric. More often than not, MacDonald's characters become mere pegs to hang sermons on and this results in an indifference towards the plots of the novels which can be both bewildering and irritating.

The business of education in MacDonald's novels tends to work its way even into the business of love. What MacDonald hero is not ready with a copy of Euclid in his hand? Teaching a young woman algebra is an important step in the stages of modern courtly love. It is through a question of Italian grammar that Euphrasia Cameron snares Hugh Sutherland in *David Elginbrod* and the schoolroom gives birth to romance both for Duncan Campbell and Lady Alice in *The Portent*, and Donal Grant and Lady Arctura in *Donal Grant*. Beauchamp, Alec Forbes' rival, weans Kate Fraser away from him by pretending a liking for Byron.[38]

For MacDonald, learning and loving go together and are spiritually tied; real life is often less tidy. The leisured middle classes of MacDonald's day may have lived well-regulated lives and consumed novels voraciously, but they were assailed from without by the forces of industrial expansion leading them into an unknown future, and from within by doubt and turmoil. They wanted to believe, but many of them found that they — or worse, their children — simply could not.

This peculiar tension created a novel of anxiety — the sensation novel — which flourished in the 1860s and drew much of its inspiration from the Gothic novel which had flowered at the end of the eighteen century and was also the product of a turbulent age. Writing on the sensation novel in *Blackwood's Magazine* in May 1862, Margaret Oliphant claimed that the complacency of 1851, the year of the Great Exhibition, had been shattered as wars, such as the Crimean War, had broken out, and industry had turned to producing weapons of death rather than instruments of peace. The sensation novel dealt with the invasion of crime or the supernatural into an ordinary domestic setting. It gave an injection of excitement into a dull existence — and the Victorians thirsted for excitement. The Newgate novel of 'low life' titillated them, as did the sensational journalism and sensational trials of the day. Stage melodramas drew the crowds (and presumably MacDonald was often among the audience) and the novels of Dickens had a powerful effect on the Victorian imagination. Novels such as *Uncle Silas* (1864), *Lady Audley's Secret* (1862) and *East Lynne* (1861) were all written during this decade and enjoyed enormous popularity. The queen of sensation novels was Wilkie Collins' *The Woman in White*, published in 1860. MacDonald smuggled plot elements from that novel into his own work — the fiddling of the marriage registers in *Wilfrid Cumbermede*; the abduction of Lady Arctura in *Donal Grant*; and the villain in *David Elginbrod*, Count Von Funkelstein, who may owe something to the towering (and infinitely more charming) figure of Count Fosco, a villain whose type runs back through the Gothic and melodrama to the Jacobean theatre.

The anxiety of the age was also demonstrated in the craze for trying to prove the existence of the next world through pseudo-scientific means. This was the age of spirit-rapping, ghosts, magic and mesmerism. Both Kingsley and Dickens experimented with mesmerism and many people in the mid-Victorian era sat down to their first seance. In August 1860, a month after *The Portent* ended in the *Cornhill Magazine*, an article appeared in it entitled 'Stranger than Fiction'. Its premise was:

'If we have lived for thousands of years in a state of absolute unconsciousness of the arterial system that was coursing through our bodies, who shall presume to say that there is nothing more to be learned in time to come?'[39]

The article then goes on to describe a seance: floating chairs, ghostly arms and a flurry of poltergeist activity:

'The semblance of what seemed a hand, with white, long, and delicate fingers, rose up slowly in the darkness, and bending over a flower, suddenly vanished with it.'[40]

MacDonald may well have read this article; his imagination was certainly kindled by the current craze of spirit-rapping. The description of the seance in *David Elginbrod* is detailed enough to suggest that MacDonald dabbled in such activities himself, even if he remained sceptical about them. When David's name appears as a result of the spirit's intervention, MacDonald immediately interjects: 'Do I then believe that David himself did write that name of his? Heaven forbid that any friend of mine should be able to believe it!'[41]

David Elginbrod reflects the thirst for sensation that ran through the 1860s; mesmerism, somnambulism, crime, revenge and spiritualism are all components of the plot. It has often been criticized because the main character dies half-way through the book without the reader knowing anything about it, but the sudden introduction of Von Funkelstein with his seances and evil mesmeric plot is just as dramatic and bewildering. The reader enters a different world.[42] Some authors of the 1860s felt duty bound to include such supernatural elements in their work, and Mac-Donald, fascinated by the supernatural, carried on with ghosts and somnambulism and intrigue for the rest of his writing career.

David Elginbrod is MacDonald's purest attempt at the sensation novel. Von Funkelstein is presented as an archetypal villain. He demonstrates his power early on by making a pass at a cat with his hand which kills it stone dead from a distance, and, as a German, fits the prevailing fashion for such villains. His charlatanism is never really in doubt, for though Euphra believes him to be Count Halkar, MacDonald hints that he is only a trumped-up criminal clerk. He is after a crystal ring which will magnify his mesmeric powers and, in a complicated scheme, holds Euphra in his thrall, forcing her to act the part of a ghost to enable him to accomplish his dubious ends. His power over her is clearly sexual and has overtones of a vampire and his victim. When he meets Euphra secretly he orders her to:

> '"Put your arms round me."
>
> She seemed to grow to the earth, and drag herself from it, one foot after another. But she came close up to the Bohemian and put one arm half round him, looking to the earth all the time.'[43]

As in all MacDonald's works these sensational aspects of his writing are suborned to a specifically theological purpose. The supernatural phenomena are mere trickery — after Hugh Sutherland catches a glimpse of the glorified face of Margaret Elginbrod at the seance the reader learns that he did in fact see Margaret who is now working as a servant in the house. MacDonald also contrasts the shallowness of Arnstead with the full-blooded spirituality of Turriepuffit and Mrs Elton's theological niceties are held up against David Elginbrod's simple and true faith. The comparison is between nature and sophistication, singled out in the characters of Margaret Elginbrod and Euphrasia Cameron. Euphra, a fascinating, though shallow coquette, is conquered by Von Funkelstein through the exercise of her own charms. She is caught in her own web and comes to enact the part of a ghost because in spiritual terms that is what she is. She has no real substance. The motto of the novel is: 'Wo keine Götter sind, walten Gespenster' from Novalis' *Die Christenheit* ('Where Gods are not, spectres rule), so Euphra, lacking faith in God, is no better than a ghost and so becomes one, possessed by the phantasms of another man's mind. In her struggle for faith she fights against Von Funkelstein's influence until finally she breaks free, and dies in the attempt. As Euphra, likened to a ghost, becomes a ghost, so the stuff of fantasy emerges into what is a supposedly realistic novel and metaphor becomes embodied fact.

Behind the sensation novel stands the Gothic novel — the literature of haunted castles fringed with bats, pale heroines set on by terrors too dreadful to name, villains, vampires, werewolves, ghosts and monsters.[44] The Gothic novel with its portrayal of a crumbling medieval world influenced the romantic writers to a great extent. The dark side of medieval romance — courtly knights in search of the grail — was demons damning the soul of the questing hero to perdition. Man is presented as an eternal victim and the Gothic paradigms most often employed are Dr Faustus and Prometheus, two overreachers who are punished for their arrogance; and in Gothic writing their drama is played out over and over again.

MacDonald was well aware of the Gothic tradition. The tales of Edgar Allan Poe are specifically mentioned in *David Elginbrod* and there is a reference to *The Castle of Otranto* in *Wilfrid Cumbermede*. Leopold Lingard in *Thomas Wingfold, Curate* cries:

> 'I am like the horrible creature Frankenstein made — one that has no right to existence — and at the same time like the maker of it, who is accountable for that existence. I am a blot on God's creation that must be wiped off.'[45]

MacDonald believed in redemption rather than damnation, however, and adapted the Gothic conventions to his own ends. Nevertheless, many of the preoccupations of the Gothic novel are MacDonald's own — its horror of and fascination with sex, the obsession with the supernatural and immortality, the exploration of the divine and demonic potentials of the human spirit, and the whiff of charnel-houses and graveyards. MacDonald's fascination and revulsion with putrefying corpses may have been intensified by the influence of Calvinism which held that sin was deeply rooted in the flesh and so set about repressing the sexual instincts.

Alongside the Gothic the ghost story sprang up as a popular form of Victorian literature and, if such fiction may be regarded as the literature of repression, it is not surprising that if one part of the mind is repressed it will eventually resurface and 'haunt' you. Ghosts became a fashionable vogue and the divided consciousness at odds with itself and fearful of the world about it resulted in the double, a powerful symbol of conflict.[46]

For the Scot, Calvinism had a demonic vitalism that could cleave a soul in two; and it found a symbol in the city of Edinburgh, setting the elegant splendour of the new town, a monument to eighteenth-century rationalism and empiricism, against the steaming graveyards and squalid tenements that clutched at the skirts of the castle. It was a city of churches and brothels, of Deacon Brodie and of Burke and Hare. The Manichee in the soul of the Scot is all too clearly seen in two of the most powerful of nineteenth-century novels on this theme: Hogg's *Confessions of a Justified Sinner* (1824) and Robert Louis Stevenson's *The Strange Case of Dr Jekyll and Mr Hyde* (1886). That the appropriately named Hyde has been repressed is clear from the fact that he is smaller than Jekyll and not so well-developed, but gradually he gains strength until each time that Jekyll falls asleep he wakes up as Hyde. *William Wilson* by Edgar Allan Poe is another famous instance of the double and it is interesting to note that both Poe's father and stepfather were Scottish with similar backgrounds to Hogg, Stevenson and MacDonald.

The most notable instance of the double is the shadow in *Phantastes*, but in *Alec Forbes of Howglen*, Patrick Beauchamp emerges to some extent as Alec's double. In fact both Alec and Beauchamp can be seen as figments of MacDonald's psyche, revealing a split in MacDonald's own mind. While Alec follows MacDonald's own course to faith through school and university, the arrogant Beauchamp displays a dazzling taste in dress and an obsession with his Highland ancestry which MacDonald also shared. Beauchamp appears at several key points in the story to thwart Alec. He is the cause of the crowd's anger when they chase Alec from the Dissecting Room and he steals Kate Fraser away from him. After a cry of:

'Beauchamp,' said Alec, 'You are my devil...'[47]

Beauchamp stabs Alec and Alec soon after turns to drink and prostitution, sliding downhill fast. A similar relation can be traced between Wilfrid Cumbermede and Geoffrey Brotherton in *Wilfrid Cumbermede* and in this novel Brotherton actually marries Wilfrid's love Mary Osborne. In *The Flight of the Shadow* there are identical twin brothers who believe that each has killed the other, but whose paths cross and recross (confusing their niece, the heroine Belorba Day) until they finally meet as through a mirror at Versailles.

That such a pattern is evident in both the realistic novels and the fantasies shows MacDonald's use of the Gothic mode as a bridge to explore the unconscious. His preoccupation with dreams, for example, is a testimony to this, as he pushes the text towards probing the inner workings of the mind. If the crux of romantic poetry was to turn the inside outside and this same crux underpinned nineteenth-century fantasy writing, it is not surprising that MacDonald strains towards expressing the same vision in his realistic novels. Fantasy changes metaphor into image and gives expression to the underlying nineteenth-century need for transformation. It is supremely the literature of transition, for one thing actually changes into another, though the fear was that one could become either an angel or a beast. One of Darwin's legacies was a fear of the bestial nature within. The vampire and the werewolf are obvious figures for the beast within. In MacDonald the constant association of women with predatory cat-like creatures reaches its purest expression in *Lilith*, who actually possesses the ability to change herself into a leopardess.

MacDonald's imagery reveals both his own fears and the fears of the age. Many of his characters have been pushed towards an unnatural state of mind: Lady Alice is a somnambulist; Harry in *David Elginbrod* has a neurotic compulsion to step on every third diamond of the carpet; and both Charley Osborne in *Wilfrid Cumbermede* and Kate Fraser in *Alec Forbes of Howglen* commit suicide. MacDonald's symbols for woman — corpse, ghost and cat — expose his own inner anxieties, but, according to a Jungian model, they can be applied to the human psyche at large. His fascination with sex and death is hard to ignore. On one level some of his characters are obviously autobiographical figments — the theoretical and useless article writer Mr Raymout in *Weighed and Wanting* is a negative portrait of himself, while the positive, practical and attractive Dr Christopher is a rosy wish-fulfilment on MacDonald's part. Robert Falconer moves from autobiography to icon, becoming both a doctor and a social worker, two dreams MacDonald never fulfilled, while Alec Forbes returns home to his roots and the arms of Annie Anderson. But deeper than that there is a series of symbols in Gothic trappings which Mac-Donald works on again and again, fashioning his *oeuvre* into a kind of kaleidoscope, where each symbol gains a particular resonance both when associated with other symbols and also with itself as it recurs in other books: the castle, the horse, the flood, the cave and the beautiful ghost return again and again to 'haunt' the text and they do not lose their power, but gain a special significance. Thus the horse appears as a demon horse in *The Portent*, a jewel-filled ornament in *Castle Warlock*, and a fountain in *St George and St Michael*. There is no point in tying these symbols to a strict allegory. To say that the castle is the soul, for example, is at best only partly true — though it is often an extension of the human personality. In *Castle Warlock*, for example, Cosmo finds that: '... the house was almost a part of himself — an extension of his own body, as much his as the shell of a snail is his'[48]; and the recess of the psyche is amply illustrated in *Donal Grant* where the body Donal and Arctura discover chained to the four-poster bed in the hidden chapel is referred to as Arctura's 'dead self'.

To interpret MacDonald's novels merely as Christian fables is to do them a disservice. Rather his symbols have to be emotionally perceived and absorbed into the consciousness of the reader. These symbols meet the reader at a level far removed from plot or character and begin a process which acts on the unconscious mind of the reader. MacDonald asks his readers to interact with the text in a way which is significantly different from the approach needed for most novels — this perhaps helps to explain why some readers have found in MacDonald's work a richness that they find in no other writer. Supremely a writer of unconscious, the alchemy of his writing transforms the minds of those who read him. The longing for transformation that many of his readers feel finds fulfilment in the movement from unbelief to belief, in peasants becoming noblemen, in women becoming corpses, witches, angels or saints. The world of *Phantastes* bubbles through fissures in the text and the reader is compelled to read the novel according to the rules (or lack of them) of a fantasy and not of a realistic novel. The world of the unconscious is opened up and laid bare before the reader.

MacDonald's writing gives expression to the unconscious by transforming his characters, often based on figures from myths and folk tales, into projections of his own psyche. Such projections reveal a deep-seated dualism. MacDonald's women are generally divided into saints and coquettes: the 'natural' childhood friend of innocence such as Annie Anderson in *Alec Forbes of Howglen* is set against the dangerous city sophisticate such as Euphrasia Cameron in *David Elginbrod* or Lady Lufa in *Home Again*.

An elevation of womanhood is usually accompanied by its shadow. As Jung has pointed out, the creation of the Madonna begets the unconscious reaction of the witch. So in *David Elginbrod* Euphra is the witch, constantly referred to as 'fascinating' and 'bewitching'. Hugh Sutherland stops short for a moment when 'a vague suspicion crossed his mind that she was bewitching him'[49], though this does not prevent his falling hopelessly in love with her. Her indeterminate age ('she might be four-and-twenty; she might be two-and-thirty') aids her indefinable and fascinating charms. She tries to capture Hugh and hold him in her affections as though she were casting a spell over him. Such 'fascinating' women appear frequently in MacDonald's fiction. There is the flirt in the library who drives Cupples to drink in *Alec Forbes of Howglen*, Clara Coningham in *Wilfrid Cumbermede* and the destructive Lady Lufa in *Home Again*. Opposed to them are the women who exemplify natural goodness: Annie Anderson in *Alec Forbes of Howglen*, Belorba Day in *The Flight of the Shadow*, Kirsty in *Heather and Snow* and Ethelwyn Walton in *The Vicar's Daughter*.

Many of MacDonald's negative women are early sketches for his later Lilith. These culminate in the character of Lady Cairnedge in *The Flight of the Shadow*, written probably after some early drafts of *Lilith* had already been completed. She is a wholly evil and unnatural woman, repudiated by her son and in a vivid passage she is described as one of the Undead:

'She lay asleep, lovely to look at as an angel of God. Her hair, part of it thrown across the top-rail of the little iron bed, streamed out on each side of the pillow, and in the midst of it lay her face, a radiant isle in a dark sea. I stood and gazed. Fascinated by her beauty? God forbid! I was fascinated by the awful incongruity between that face, pure as the moonlight, and the charnel-house that lay unseen behind it. She was to me, henceforth, not a woman, but a live death.'[50]

In *Lilith*, Lilith herself is really a corpse whom Vane sleeps with to bring back to life. The association between corpses, women and sexuality is a constant and disturbing one in MacDonald's writing. Necrophilia plays an important part in his vision. We can see it first in his early ballad *The Homeless Ghost* in which a young man is frightened off by a lonely and erotic shade. In *David Elginbrod*, Euphra, held in the grip of Von Funkelstein's power, is forced to act the part of a corpse. Von Funkelstein lays a bet with Hugh that he cannot spend the night in a haunted chamber of the house. Hugh agrees to do so, but the wine laid out for him is drugged, thus heightening the terrifying effects of what he is about to experience. The ghost enters:

'But there was one sign of life. Though the eyes were closed, tears flowed from them; and seemed to have worn channels for their constant flow down this face of death, which ought to have been lying still in the grave, returning to its dust, and was weeping above ground instead. The figure stood for a moment, as one who would gaze, could she but open her heavy death-rusted eyelids. Then, as if in hopeless defeat, she turned away. And then, to crown the horror literally as well as figuratively, Hugh saw that her hair sparkled and gleamed goldenly as the hair of a saint might, if the aureole were combed down into it.'[51]

One of MacDonald's many obsessions is a preoccupation with hands and feet. Both Robert Falconer and Wilfrid Cumbermede, for example, are lamed in association with a sexual wounding and in *David Elginbrod* Euphra constantly hides her feet, covering them up with her dress which she refuses to lift. Finally, they are revealed, and Hugh's sexual arousal is never in doubt:

'When she had gone half-way to the door, Hugh, lying as he was on a couch, could see her feet, for the dress did not reach the ground . . . Not a sign of the tomb was upon them. Small, living, delicately formed, Hugh, could he have forgot the face they bore above, might have envied the floor which in their nakedness they seemed to caress, so lingeringly did they move from it in their noiseless progress.'[52]

Soon after this appearance a carriage runs over Euphra's ankle and she is lamed, an injury from which she finally dies:

'Blood was flowing from her foot; and it was so much swollen that it was impossible to guess at the amount of the injury. The foot was already twice the size of the other, in which Hugh for the first time recognised such a delicacy of form, as to his fastidious eye and already snared heart, would have been perfectly enchanting, but for the agony he suffered from the injury to the other.'[53]

MacDonald highlights the sexual fascination of the feet as they are parts of the body (along with the hands) which can be decently naked, but he charges them with an intense eroticism. This motif of hands and feet connected with laming runs through his writing to the leopardess leaving a trail of blood from her wounded paw in *Lilith*.

Many of MacDonald's images appear to characters in dreams, the realm of the unconscious. Dreams are important to MacDonald for they can be signs, messages and prophecies. He went so far as to append a note to the last chapter of *There and Back* stating that 'Barbara's Dream' in which she dreams of her heavenly father, was a real one. But dreams bring more than spiritual insight. It is through a dream that Donal Grant and Lady Arctura in *Donal Grant* discover the hidden chapel in which they find a four-poster bed with a dead woman chained to it and an infant slain upon the altar, and it is also through a dream that Cosmo comes to find the hidden treasure that will save his ancestral home in *Castle Warlock*. Dreams often come true or are otherwise used to comment on the progress of the story and on the characters' state of mind.

Wilfrid Cumbermede is a novel *full* of dreams and is probably the most intensely written of all MacDonald's novels.

In this particular novel stands the dream of all dreams — the vision of Athanasia — the appearance of Death as a beautiful woman.[54] Wilfrid dreams that he is wandering in a great palace — 'From hall to hall I went, along corridor and gallery, and up and down endless stairs.' Passing from room to room, Wilfrid notices that there is always something left there — a glove, or a handkerchief — and the rooms are 'scented with a stange entrancing odour'. Finally at the end of his wandering, he comes face to face with Athanasia herself, a veiled figure who slowly lifts her veil for him, revealing the face of a beautiful woman: '"I am Death — dost thou not know me?" answered the figure, in a sweet though worn and weary voice.' She opens a door to a beautiful landscape with a river running past, steps outside, pulls the door to — 'and left me alone in the dark hollow of the earth. I broke into a convulsive weeping and awoke.'

This dream brings together so many of the images scattered through MacDonald's writing that it is charged with an unusual intensity and is like approaching the centre of a web. The more MacDonald a reader has read, the more power will this passage wield, for Athanasia is the unconscious beckoning the reader to go forward and meet her. His vision of Athanasia haunts him for the rest of the book:

> 'Once and only once, I found myself dreaming the dream of *that* night, and I knew that I had dreamed it before. Through palace and chapel and charnel-house, I followed her, ever with a dim sense of awful result; and when at last she lifted the shining veil, instead of the face of Athanasia, the bare teeth of a skull grinned at me from under a spotted shroud through which the sunlight shone from behind, revealing all its horrors.'[55]

Death and sex and corpses. Horror and fascination. Desire and revulsion. MacDonald's is a divided consciousness, revealing a Victorian delight and disgust with sex. This is revealed also in his attitude towards some eighteenth-century literature. He condemns *Tristram Shandy* in several of his books. It is burned in *Adela Cathcart* and in *Alec Forbes of Howglen* Cupples speaks out against it as 'A pailace o' dirt and impidence and speeritual stink.'[56] This was presumably because the eighteenth century had fewer scruples about describing the mechanics of sex, while the Victorians repressed such descriptions out of prudishness.

Sexual explicitness surfaces only in the pornography of the period or else emerges coded in dreams and in fantasies, as in MacDonald.

The physicality of love is displaced and many of MacDonald's characters forsake an earthly union for a mystical and spiritual one after death. Ericson and Mary St John in *Robert Falconer* pledge their love to one another before he dies, and she goes on to be a self-appointed nun working chastely among London's poor, side by side with Falconer. Donal Grant and Arctura in *Donal Grant* make a marriage pact and become man and wife on Arctura's death-bed when it is clear that this is a marriage for heaven only, while in *The Portent* Duncan Campbell and Lady Alice, in the first version of the story, do not find each other again until after death. But sexuality, no matter how much it is displaced, returns in dreams — sometimes nightmarishly as in Belorba Day's encounter with the phallic worm that never dies, a monster that coils itself about her in a sexual embrace:

> 'The red worm was on the bank. It was crawling toward me. I went to meet it. It sprang from the ground, threw itself upon me, and twisted itself about me. It was a human embrace, the embrace of someone unknown who loved me.'[57]

Thus the unknown depths of human sexuality can take forms that tantalize and terrify the heroes and heroines of MacDonald's novels. As in his pure fantasies, conventional rules dissolve, and even the boundaries of gender are transgressed as male and female identities are united. Delving into *Wilfrid Cumbermede* it appears that Wilfrid and his friend Charley Osborne have an apparently homosexual relationship, though Wilfrid's love is later transferred to Charley's sister, Mary Osborne. In the Alps after a storm Wilfrid takes refuge in a house where he is dressed in girl's clothes and asks the mother and daughter of the family to comb his hair out like a girl's. When he is ill Charley nurses him 'more like a woman than a boy' and afterwards: 'The best immediate result of my illness was that I learned to love Charley Osborne more dearly. We renewed an affection resembling from afar that of Shakespeare for his nameless friend...'[58] At one point he goes as far as to declare to Charley that 'I love you more than ever'. They share a room and sleep together, after which Wilfrid injures his foot with a knife. Such lameness is always a sign of sexuality in MacDonald's writing. At school their exclusive friendship arouses hostility from the other boys and from their teachers, Mr Forest and Mr Elder (whose emblematic names are at least suggestive of nature and wisdom) and finally they are parted by the heavy hand of religion in the form of Charley's father, the uncompromising Reverend Osborne whom Charley rejects along with his religion. In *Mary Marston*, in a less anguished way, Mary goes to act as a voluntary servant to Hesper Redmain because: 'The chief attraction to her, however, was simply Hesper herself. She had fallen in love with her — I hardly know how otherwise to describe the current with which her being set towards her.'[59]

Both Wilfrid Cumbermede and Mary Marston cross the normal boundaries of love and other sexual transgressions are repeated throughout the novels. In *Weighed and Wanting* Hester Raymount is a picture of Lilia, MacDonald's eldest daughter. At the end of the book she is close to marrying Dr Christopher, a wish-fulfilment portrait of MacDonald himself and so the novel finishes with a hint of incest. Wilfrid Cumbermede finds his aged grandmother strangely attractive, a motif which occurs strongly in *Phantastes*: 'How shall I describe the shrunken, yet delicate, the gracious, if not graceful form, and the face from which extreme old age had not wasted half the loveliness?'[60]

Such notions of incest are made most explicit in *Lilith* where Vane is seduced by his bride's mother, the child-devouring demon Lilith. It is clear, therefore, that MacDonald has thrown conventional notions of human sexuality into the melting-pot. Perhaps he was uneasily seated in his own sexuality. Many of his young male characters show feminine streaks: for example, the young soldier in *The Broken Swords*, the very title of which suggests emasculation. MacDonald's own bookishness and illness as a child may have heightened feelings of his own femininity and he certainly preferred little girls to little boys as his own family testified. The two best-known Victorian figures with whom he is associated, Lewis Carroll and John Ruskin, were both drawn to very young girls and MacDonald's unfailing sympathy which he extended towards them may have included some feelings of kinship.

One disturbing aspect of MacDonald's sexuality as expressed in the novels is its link with violence. Just as violence is linked with religion in MacDonald's thinking and religion is linked with sex, so the trinity is completed and violence is linked with sex. Alec Forbes, beaten by Malison, and Robert Falconer, beaten by his grandmother, are both victims of a Calvinist urge to punish, but in *Paul Faber, Surgeon* Juliet Meredith slips off her nightdress and kneels shivering before her husband after handing him a whip: 'Whip me and take me again,' she begs, but Paul Faber tosses the instrument to one side and strides out of the room. MacDonald leaves the reader in no doubt that Faber has made the wrong decision:

'Had he struck once, had he seen the purple streak rise in the snow, that instant his pride-frozen heart would have melted into a torrent of grief; he would have flung himself on the floor beside her, and in an agony of pity over her and horror at his own sacrilege, would have clasped her to his bosom, and baptized her in the tears of remorse and repentance; from that moment they would have been married indeed.'[61]

In MacDonald's day God was often pictured as a refining fire, a purifier, a judge doling out punishment for people's sins. MacDonald moved away from the idea of an eternal hell towards purgatory, a place where human beings would be purified before entering heaven. With such notions in mind it becomes more understandable why repentance and tears follow on so closely after beatings in MacDonald and why the lash of the whip is used to turn people towards good. In *Weighed and Wanting* Mr Raymount whips his wayward son Cornelius as well as his wife Amy, who bursts through a window in order to defend him, but the whipping results in the whole family being reunited after a great deal of discord.

The apparent instances of sexual sadism in MacDonald's novels remain uncomfortable episodes, but set within a theological context they become understandable if not excusable.

What emerges positively from the pool of MacDonald's sexuality is a tendency towards saintly androgyny. Margaret Elginbrod receives the best part of her feminine nature from her father and not her mother (while Euphra 'was not in the least effeminate herself'[62]) and MacDonald's otherworldly children — Diamond in *At the Back of the North Wind*, and the boy Clare Skymer in *A Rough Shaking* — both have names that are neither male nor female as they walk the thin edge between this world and the next, combining in their characters aspects of the human and the divine. Anodos in *Phantastes* also has a name that is neither male nor female as he sets out on a search for wholeness that is representative of all humanity. Negatively speaking all that the Victorian mind was suppressing bubbles up through dreams, reaching out to coil round the unsuspecting hero or heroine. A haunting indeed. A nightmare realized.

MacDonald's 'visionary' works are concerned with ultimate reality — that is, forms of spiritual truth, not the everyday realism of the conventional novel. MacDonald found that such spiritual concerns were often best dressed in the archetypal forms of the fairy tale and many of his novels can be read in this way. He often had to pinch himself to remind himself what he was writing. In *Alec Forbes of Howglen* he suddenly remarked: 'But I forget that I am telling a story and not writing a fairy tale.'[63] This is a fake apology, for in many ways MacDonald *was* writing a fairy tale and this tendency in his writing was noticed even by some of his contemporaries.

MacDonald has been criticized for setting cardboard cut-outs of saints and villains on his stage — the Margaret Elginbrods and Lord Rothies of unconvincing melodrama — but seen as characters from a fairy tale, or as fragments of the human psyche, they assume an interest which otherwise the reader would overlook. Allusions to fairy tales creep into many of MacDonald's novels. A description of Robert Falconer for example states that:

> 'His heart beat like that of the prince in the fairy-tale, when he comes to the door of the Sleeping Beauty.'[64]

Juliet Meredith in *Paul Faber, Surgeon* is described as a princess among goblins, though it is the Polwarths, the dwarfs, who are the real spiritual royalty. The novel even contains a flood, thus strengthening the allusions to *The Princess and the Goblin* and showing how fairy tale themes seep through into the novels and underlie the pretence of everyday life. Like all good fairy tales, the novels have happy endings which become credible only if they are read as fairy tales. In the world of Faerie a bad man can become good, a peasant can become a lord and a poor man can marry a lady. MacDonald's claim is that Faerie is the real world, while this one is but a pale shadow of the other. When he remarked in *David Elginbrod* 'What a strange thing the association of ideas is!' he probably did not realize how profoundly he was speaking.

There is little development in MacDonald's prose writing, but in the later novels, romance appears to take over reality. *Sir Gibbie, Donal Grant, Castle Warlock* and *The Flight of the Shadow* are pure romance compared with the portraits of Rothieden and Glamerton where romance and reality jostle side by side. G.K. Chesterton noticed that *Malcolm* was *The Princess and the Goblin* cast into novel form while Sir Gibbie, a young dumb orphan, acts like an elemental sprite or brownie, becoming a figure of pure mythology.

The world of romance which MacDonald found in books as much as in hills and fir trees invades every corner of his novels. His books are not only interspersed with dreams, but also with ballads and poems. His novels can be seen as ballads and courtly romances written out in prose. There was a precedent for such writing to be found in Walter Scott and MacDonald may well have read Scott's essay *On the Supernatural in Fictitious Composition*. Hogg, too, combined elements of Scottish folk tales and myths in his books and these elements held a twofold attraction for MacDonald. First, they enabled him to reach back into the world of his childhood to the traditions he had been cut off from by life in the city. In the Huntly of MacDonald's boyhood there were still kelpies lingering in rock pools, ghosts out haunting at night in Greenhaugh and Kinnoir, local witches who possessed the power to change themselves into hares, and the Horseman's Word[65] who held Cain to be their master and who practised raising the devil in the form of a horse. The world of *Tam o' Shanter* was not so far removed and grim ballads such as *The Twa Corbies* and *The Wife of Usher's Well* were deep-seated in the Scottish soul. Margaret Oliphant too set about trying to revitalize Scottish legends in her supernatural *Tales of the Seen and Unseen* but in MacDonald the ancestral voices spoke very loudly:

> 'In each present personal being we have the whole past of our generation enclosed, to be redeveloped with endless difference in each individuality. Hence perhaps it comes that, every now and then, into our consciousnesses float strange odours of feeling, strange tones as of by-gone affections, strange glimmers as of forgotten truths, strange mental sensations of indescribable sort and texture. Friends, I should be a terror to myself, did I not believe that wherever my dim consciousness may come to itself, God is there.'[66]

The other attraction of romance was to uphold the Christian courtly virtues based rather on the French and English medieval traditions. King Arthur was perceived as a Christ-like figure by the Victorians, and his knights could be linked with the apostles, so the chivalric code could be seen as essentially Christian. Tennyson's *Idylls* with their picture of courtly society worm-eaten from within was a salutary reminder to the Victorians of their precarious plight regarding faith and security. MacDonald's heroes are knights, therefore, of a Christian order, standing against the money-grubbing spirit of corrupt commercialism and the other evils spawned by the age.

In the context of the ballad tradition Sir Gibbie, Malcolm and Richard Lestrange ending up as noblemen becomes more acceptable as the fairy tale connection between ancestry and goodness is made over and over again. MacDonald was obsessed with ancestry. In MacDonald's eyes good forebears go a long way to determining good character and his heroes and heroines are measured against a Darwinian sliding scale of moral integrity. They either climb nearer the angels or descend towards the beasts. MacDonald described the insipid and rather corrupt Lady Anne in *There and Back* as:

> 'An age-long process of degeneration had been going on in her race, and she was the result: she was well born and well bred for feeling nothing.[67]

Money is the great corrupter and MacDonald approves of the unlikely combination of impoverished nobility such as Cosmo in *Castle Warlock*, the Macruadhs in *What's Mine's Mine*, and Wilfrid Cumbermede in *Wilfrid Cumbermede*. The ancestral home exercises an age-old pull and so Duncan Campbell in *The Portent* returns to 'the possession of my forefathers', the clan Macruadh return to Scotland from Canada in *What's Mine's Mine* to buy back their land, and Walter Colman, realizing the error of his ways after a seedy literary life in London, stumbles homeward through a snowstorm in the aptly named *Home Again* to renew his strength and his judgement behind his father's plough. Mac-Donald may well have felt some guilt at leaving his birthplace coupled with some longing to settle back there which is why many of his characters return to their roots. MacDonald often introduced elements of his own ancestry into his novels. Mrs Falconer's name is plucked from MacDonald's own family tree, and the sword in *Wilfrid Cumbermede* hails back to a story that was passed down MacDonald's own family. The two leaders of the clan Macruadh, Alister and Ian, also have names that have some connection with MacDonald's family.

In addition to MacDonald's interest in ancestry, his fastidious morality and excessive reverence for women can all be seen as part of the courtly ethic. Paul Faber worries for instance that Juliet Meredith might be offended to find a strange man's blood flowing through her veins after he has given her a transfusion of his own: 'a horror seized him at the presumptuousness of the liberty he had taken'; while Alec Forbes shows a similar hesitation in dissecting a beautiful female corpse. This concern with the details of chivalry climaxes in *St George and St Michael*, MacDonald's only historical novel, set against the background of the English Civil War — a war in which no one is killed, and indeed, there is hardly so much as a bruise in the whole book. The most important moral difficulty is when Dorothy Vaughan conceals a message from Richard Heywood which she is trying to smuggle to the King's lines. He is a Roundhead while she is a Royalist and they are both cousins and lovers. They finally marry — after her confession, of course.

Poetry, not prose, is the traditional medium of romance, and poems are scattered liberally throughout all the novels. Most MacDonald heroes write their own poetry, once again showing the importance of the imagination at work, and the unconscious working itself into a text. The equation which MacDonald makes is that true knights are also true poets and Hugh Sutherland, Thomas Wingfold, Donal Grant and many others go about producing sonnets and ballads at the drop of a hat. The novels are in turn filled with the traditional poetry of the Bible, Shakespeare, Dante and Spenser, enhancing the characters' pretensions to grandeur and chivalry. Florimel, for example, is a name taken from Spenser,

Euphrasia from Milton, and Barbara Wylder is compared to Words-worth's *Lucy*. Juliet Meredith finds reading *Othello* a painful experience, but her disappearance and 'resurrection' along with the discovery of Faber's lost child contain echoes of *The Winter's Tale* and their final reunion means that she is at last fit to play her part of Juliet to Faber's Romeo. In *St George and St Michael* the very names of the characters — Heywood, Herbert and Vaughan — all bear some poetical allusion and indeed the poet Henry Vaughan himself makes an appearance. Mary St John in *Robert Falconer* is a composite of the virgin and the apostle of love, a fit name for her character, while MacDonald in *Mary Marston* went as far as to engineer a marriage between Mary and Joseph in Mary Marston and Joseph Jasper. Their names are emblems, signs, pointing towards the text, acting as guides to the message contained within them.

Events follow the pattern of names. Most striking is MacDonald's repeated use of the Prodigal Son as a model and his many resurrections. Francis Gordon is raised from a tomb-like cave in *Heather and Snow*, Walter Colman and Annie Anderson are revived from the snow, Paul Faber finds his wife again and, most strikingly, Isy in *Salted with Fire* returns to life after sinking into a cataleptic state for two weeks, to reclaim her lover, a young fornicating minister of the church, James Blatherwick, who is first seen symbolically near a peacock, and her child whom she has previously lost on the moor. The three are united in a new holy family transformed from death to life in spiritual as well as physical terms with the past set firmly behind them.

Yet, like Tennyson, MacDonald felt some anxiety about the code he was preaching. In *The Princess and Curdie* the town Gwyntystorm collapses after Irene and Curdie (the ideal chivalric couple) are no longer there to rule, its foundations mined through by greed and gain. Similarly in *St George and St Michael* Raglan Castle is finally deserted and is left as a monument to an age that has passed away never to return.

But if the ruins of Raglan and Gwyntystorm are potent images of Victorian society crumbling into dust, it should also be remembered that in MacDonald the disinherited do inherit. Sir Gibbie, Malcolm, and Richard Lestrange gain their rights and finally resurrection does succeed destruction. MacDonald was optimistic and pessimistic by degrees. After lingering over the shell of Raglan he went on to write: 'But this era too will pass, and truth come forth in forms new and more lovely still.'[68]

MacDonald's chivalric hopes are eschatological as well as nostalgic:

'Every age is born with an ideal; but instead of beholding that ideal in the future where it lies, it throws it into the past. Hence the lapse of the nation must appear tremendous, even when she is making her best progress.'[69]

In the end MacDonald tried to look forward as well as back, beyond the rot to an age where what was best in the past would come again in the future, pulling mankind on to better days.

If MacDonald's novels appear divided — between Scottish and English, Gothic and Romance, real and fairy-tale — it is because he lived in a divided age and was trying to reconcile his own divided consciousness. In the end, it is impossible to separate MacDonald's work out into neat categories, and his novels show this best. Just as everything Midas touched turned to gold, so everything MacDonald touched turned to MacDonald. His entire *oeuvre* represents a psychological continuum of his own psyche, meshing together novel, poetry, romance, fairy tale and theology. Even if he deserves some merit as a passable mid-Victorian Scottish novelist or as a theological storyteller, his greatest achievement is as a novelist of the unconscious, giving expression to the inner workings of the mind and grasping at a dimension of human experience which has been largely ignored or else rejected as indescribable.

CHAPTER TWENTY-ONE
John Ruskin

No matter where the MacDonalds lived, their house was always filled with noise, music, children, visitors, relatives and friends. Many were attracted to them by their informality, warmth, and charm and the unusual mixture of Christianity, bohemianism and discipline which characterized their peculiar family life. At the centre of it all loomed MacDonald, with his flowing coal-black beard, reading poetry, writing, lecturing and coughing, giving time to anyone who came to his door.

One person in the midst of all this throng, who found herself warmly drawn to the MacDonalds, was an Irish woman called Maria Price La Touche, wife of the banker and landowner John La Touche, who lived at Harristown House, Harristown, in Co. Kildare, an imposing Georgian mansion set in the midst of a spacious and beautiful estate. The La Touches had three children: Emily, Rose and Percy. Young Rose, whom her mother thought the most artistically gifted of all her children, was despatched to MacDonald's course of lectures on Shakespeare in February 1863. She was a studious girl, intense, pious and ethereal, with a talent for drawing, a thin, waifish elf, prone to mysterious bouts of 'brain sickness' which sometimes seriously disturbed the timbre of her mind.

Mrs La Touche in contrast was a healthy, full-blooded and generous woman. She loathed the isolation of life in Ireland where the only interest was balls and hunting, describing it as 'living in Boeotia', and instead preferred to soak herself in the literary and artistic climate of London where the family would come every year to spend the winter. Charming and sociable, her friends thought her witty and prized her letters. She treated the MacDonald children with affection and quickly settled on intimate terms with Louisa calling her 'Mother Brown-bird' and writing:

'Indeed I won't be half friends with you — tho' that would be much better than not being friends with you at all.'[1]

Mrs La Touche was friendly with John Ruskin the art critic, a man whom MacDonald admired, and she was anxious for her two literary friends to meet. Ruskin had just returned from Talloires where he had fled to escape the pounding by the critics of his economic articles recently published in *Fraser's Magazine* and later to appear as *Munera Pulveris*. Consequently Maria La Touche wrote to George MacDonald:

> 'Will you be so kind as to send a card for your course of lectures to John Ruskin Esqr — Denmark Hill, Camberwell, S — He is a friend of mine, and I found him here on my return today — on hearing of your lectures he immediately expressed a wish to accompany us for the future and begged me to ask you for a card — I am sure you know his works and I think you would like to know him, perhaps you will let me introduce him to you next Monday. I cannot tell you how much my daughter and I enjoyed ourselves at your house this afternoon...'[2]

MacDonald must have felt honoured to be meeting Ruskin at last for he was one of the giants of nineteenth-century Victorian Britain and his influence pervaded many areas of contemporary life. This was because he was something of a polymath, and he felt profoundly that every area of life was related to every other. Life as an entity was indivisible, and he had no time for rich people who enjoyed art one minute but treated their workers badly the next. His goal in life was to make people *see* and he accomplished this first of all through his art criticism. Ruskin's first major publication was *Modern Painters* (Volume I) published in 1843 when he was only twenty-four. In it he championed Turner, whose reputation had been languishing, as the greatest of living English painters, a true artist who used the given classical traditions and transformed them through the power of his remarkable imagination.[3] But above all Ruskin claimed that Turner was true to nature and this was the keystone of his genius.

One of Ruskin's many gifts was an ability to perceive and absorb the essence of an object — a painting, a building, a mountain or a plant — and then set down a luxuriant description of it in intoxicating prose, guiding the reader line by line to look at the object as he did, and so enter into something of what he saw as its absolute truth. Turning to buildings, Ruskin proclaimed that the highest artistic expression in architecture was the Gothic and in *The Stones of Venice* he lamented the decline into the morally inferior Renaissance style of craftsmanship. The Gothic was supreme because it left room for the individual workman to contribute something of his own self-expression to the building, and at the same time its imperfection showed a restlessness of spirit, a longing for change and to become perfect, that was indicative of growth and hence life. The perfection of Renaissance architecture was to Ruskin a still-birth, a horror, a falling away. Largely due to Ruskin's influence, there was a new upsurge of Gothic building. It was no accident that when MacDonald first came to London with his family in 1859 he chose a Victorian Gothic house to set up home in — an emblem which accorded with his own imagination.

Ruskin moved from art to nature, seeing the world as God's book which he had the privilege of interpreting, and at the same time moved from art of society, claiming that the freedom of the craftsmen who had built the great Gothic cathedrals of Europe was denied the everyday man in contemporary England. Nature was, after all, disappearing under the relentless steam-roller of the industrial revolution. Valleys were capped by railway bridges, clouds of soot fouled the air and chimney stacks spoiled once-lovely views.

Ruskin shuddered at these horrors, and at the bad conditions in the factories, still prevalent despite the recent reform acts, and was moved to protest against them. He did so in the *Cornhill Magazine* in 1860 from August to November with four essays on social and economic conditions. Asking the question 'What is wealth?' he rejected the current notion that wealth was only accumulated riches and hit out against the philosophies of Adam Smith and Jeremy Bentham who had reduced the relationships between employer and employee to a mere contractual question of money. Instead Ruskin claimed that 'there is no wealth but life' and that it was the quality of life enjoyed by its people that made a nation great and not the amount of money jingling in its coffers. The most important thing that the workers were denied, in Ruskin's eyes, was neither food nor cash, but education, the key to a better standard of living.

These essays, a statement of the social views to which he was to become inceasingly committed, earned Ruskin nothing but scorn from the critics who universally dismissed him as a cracked amateur. When the essays were published in book form as *Unto this Last* in 1862 it took ten years to sell a thousand copies, though their ideas have since touched British society deeply at many levels.[4]

MacDonald had much in common with Ruskin — a love of nature, a touch of mysticism, the rejection of Calvinism, and a Scottish heritage. Both Ruskin's parents were Scottish, cousins who had married after a long engagement lasting nine years while Ruskin's father worked to discharge some family debts, and he always retained the temper of 'my old Scotch shepherd Puritanism'. But his parents also exercised a hold over him and made demands of him that were extreme, to say the least, and he paid a high price for their affection. Like Hannah, Margaret Ruskin had determined to dedicate her child to the Lord. He was to become a bishop at least, and his education was directed towards this end.

The Ruskins' 'regular and sweetly selfish manner of living' distanced them from both friends and relations. Margaret Ruskin, with her strong sense of class-consciousness, either considered people too good for them or else not good enough, and so it was under her iron regime that Ruskin grew up, not mixing with many boys or girls, into a sensitive young man with sandy hair and wistful blue eyes, wearing a battered brown frock-coat with a velvet collar, and a distinguished blue neckcloth. He saw the world around him from the eyrie of Denmark Hill, Camberwell, where he lived with his parents, much as he did gazing on the treasures in an art gallery. The girls he met were paintings sprung to life, and when he married the prettiest of them, the dazzling Euphemia Chalmers Gray, in 1847, the marriage was a disaster. In 1854 she left Ruskin for the painter Millais.

For a woman to leave her husband was an unusual occurrence in 1854. It was generally thought that it was best to make the most of a bad lot, and Effie's lot seemed better than most — a considerate, cultivated and sensitive husband. But she had been trapped, as if in a museum, and she was spirited enough to escape. She brought a suit against Ruskin against which he made no protest, and after a thorough medical inspection was declared to be 'virgo intacta' and the marriage was annulled.

Rumour burned. Effie's departure was the biggest scandal since Lady Byron had left her husband forty years previously, and all the talk that season was of Ruskin's marriage and the Crimean War. Ruskin retreated to the seclusion of his parents' home and remained there for another twenty years until his mother died aged ninety. In a curious way, perhaps partly through his dedication to contemplating art, Ruskin had become 'disembodied'. What was beautiful in art was simply too threatening in life. Perhaps Effie's bolt was a relief for both of them.

Fate, however, was to deal Ruskin a raw hand. Soon after losing his wife he lost his faith. Like many Victorians he found himself labouring under the crushing weight of duty. In 1858 the crash came. In the Palazzo dell'Accademia in Florence Ruskin had gazed on the glory of Veronese's *The Queen of Sheba before Solomon*. Making his way to a small protestant chapel, he heard a sermon in which the preacher condemned the Catholic hordes outside to hell, while the twenty-four scattered individuals in the wooden pews were destined for bliss. This was too much. Worn out by doubt and despair, his mind confused by the latest findings of geology, and repulsed by the narrowness of the preaching, he found himself finally 'unconverted'.

In the same year that he abandoned his childhood faith he met a child, Rose La Touche, who was to have disastrous consequences on his life.

Mrs La Touche was in search of a drawing teacher for her girls, and though Ruskin tried to fob her off with William Ward, a student from the Working Men's College, she insisted that only he would do.

Soon Ruskin became a regular visitor at the La Touches home and they all fell into chattering intimacy, christening one another with saccharine nicknames. Rosie labelled Ruskin 'St Crumpet', later changed by his more polite friends to 'St Chrysostom'. Emily, Rose's sister, was called 'Wisie' and Maria La Touche heralded as 'Lacerta' in order 'to signify that she had the grace and wisdom of the serpent, without its poison'.[5]

It was a happy, golden time, and continued so for a few years.[6] John La Touche, Rose's father, seemed partial enough to Ruskin who regarded the Irishman as 'a staunch evangelical of the old school'. He had recently succumbed to the preaching of Spurgeon, the famous Baptist clergyman, and was baptized by him at the Metropolitan Tabernacle some time during 1863. Maria La Touche never became reconciled to her husband's new faith. She preferred Anglicanism and at the same time looked out for tempers that matched hers. With two such lively and sensitive conversationalists as Ruskin and MacDonald it was natural that she should desire them to become friends. Besides, she was anxious about Ruskin's loss of faith and heavy despondency and hoped that MacDonald's open mind and sympathetic spirit might win him back into the fold:

> 'Nothing will ever get *me* right, save getting *him* right — for somehow if he were holding on to a straw and I to a plank — I must leave my plank to catch at *his* straw. Still I don't care what becomes of me as long as anyhow he can be brought to some sort of happiness and life.'[7]

It has been suggested that Maria La Touche was to some degree infatuated with Ruskin and believed that his attentions to her family were in some way directed towards her, but Greville MacDonald stated in *Reminiscences of a Specialist* that 'My parents never thought her feelings for him were in any way irregular' and she may have been simply generous, innocent and blind to the fact that Ruskin was becoming increasingly attracted to her younger daughter. There was, after all, thirty years age difference between them. She wrote to George MacDonald:

> 'I don't think anyone can help him or understand him as well as you can. You will talk to him, and let him talk — about his pet Rosie if he pleases. You will like Denmark Hill and the beautiful things there — and you and he will always be fast friends. It is quite my strongest wish.'[8]

And she was right. Ruskin and MacDonald took to each other and remained very firm friends, firmer perhaps than Maria La Touche might have wished. When Ruskin met MacDonald he was at a particularly vulnerable point in his life. Both his wife and his faith were gone and his relationship with his parents was strained. His friendship with Rossetti was on the wane, and he felt that he had missed out as a geologist and as a lover. He hungered for affection and then, through the agency of the beautiful and restless Georgina Cowper, shortly after the death of his father in March 1864, he turned to spiritualism for some assurance. She, like MacDonald, was to be a 'tutelary power' in the events that were to buffet him. He had glimpsed her many years before in Rome where he had gazed on her as: '...the kind of beauty which I had only hitherto dreamed of as possible, but never yet seen living...'

Both MacDonald and Ruskin shared an interesting taste in aristocratic women. Ruskin had the Ladies Waterford and Trevelyan for company — artistic and humanitarian, childless and unavailable, who responded to him; and MacDonald, for his part, had deep friendships with Lady Byron and Lady Caroline Charteris, both of whom were charitable and loving towards him. Ruskin and MacDonald shared Maria La Touche and Georgina Cowper, also artistic, religious and socially-aware ladies, and both of whom played important roles in their lives. Georgina Cowper, the daughter of Admiral Tollemache, had married William Cowper, nephew of Lord Melbourne and stepson of Lord Palmerston, in 1848. They became Cowper-Temple in 1869 on receiving the Temple estates, and then Lord and Lady Mount-Temple in 1880 when he received a baronetcy. While she was restless, turning to mediums, quack utopian figures and vegetarianism for salvation, he had a quiet and enduring faith and made a solid career as a statesman, bringing about some interesting and lasting reforms. He also secured F.D. Maurice his post at the Vere Street Chapel, and, among his other more notable achievements, saved Epping Forest for the people, put flowers in the London parks, worked to found the Royal Society for the Prevention of Cruelty to Animals, and ensured Bible reading in all schools after the Education Act of 1871. They were an attractive and sympathetic couple, modest in their habits, abstaining from blood sports and strong drink.

By the time they introduced Ruskin to his first seance at Mrs Gregory's (home of the widow of the chemist Gregory whom MacDonald had once wished to work under) they had already attended more than thirty. Ruskin warned Georgina Cowper that, 'You will find me a fatal Non Conductor' though the manifestations proved interesting enough for him to repeat the experiment. Some aspects of the seances worried him however and he reported to Mrs Cowper that: 'I had a long talk with Carlyle yesterday. He says Spiritualism is real witchcraft, and quite wrong.'[9]

Certainly Daniel Dunglass Home, the famous spiritualist whose seances they attended, was to be hounded out of Rome for sorcery. Like many people Ruskin was also irritated by the banality of the spirit messages and hoped for some interesting communication:

> 'I meant to ask next time, for the spirit of Paul Veronese, and see whether it, if it comes, can hold a pencil more than an inch long.'[10]

But Paul Veronese was held up and could not appear. Ruskin's first phase of involvement with spiritualism lasted until 1868 when he warned Georgina Cowper: 'If the Testament is true, I have no doubt that it is your duty at once to abstain from all these things...to receive what you *have* seen of them as an awful sign of the now active presence of the fiend among us, —' and he abjured her to '...have done with mediums.'[11] So it was that Ruskin slipped away from table-rapping for a while. But spiritualism was burgeoning. Elizabeth Barrett Browning (who had died in 1861) had been convinced by it, and the Pre-Raphaelites performed various psychic experiments. The Howitts — Mary (who had translated Hans Christian Andersen's fairy tales into English) and her husband William, author of the *History of the Supernatural* in 1863 — forsook their Quakerism for Spiritualism. MacDonald stood on the sidelines watching, convinced of the supernatural, but not convinced that the dead would want to communicate in this way. Yet it is hard to see how he could have escaped the intense interest in psychic activity, as so many of his friends were reading books on the subject and attending seances. Annie Munro, for example, sister of the sculptor and godmother to MacDonald's son, Robert Falconer, claimed that she had second sight, and even Maria La Touche was fascinated, if cautious, regarding the subject.

When Rose fell ill in the autumn of 1863, Mrs La Touche wrote to the MacDonalds and claimed that there were what the doctors called 'psychical phenomena' associated with her ailment. These were 'a sort of clairvoyance both of spiritual and earthly things, which was startling.' Mrs La Touche insisted that Rose knew what would happen to her beforehand and Rose herself said that she was 'guided' in everything:

> 'The doctors were perfectly amazed and actually yielded against their judgement in allowing her to follow this "guidance" which never once erred.'

Rose became weaker and more emaciated until at the end of four weeks:

> 'Then came the most wonderful change. From a state of weakness so great that she could not sit up in bed, she suddenly after one night's sleep awoke perfectly strong in body, but with an infant's mind, an

infant's playfulness, and an entire oblivion of all acquired knowledge and of every person and thing not known to her eleven years ago.'[12]

Gradually she grew out of this state and returned to normal, but evidently she was in some deep way 'touched'.

The La Touches and the MacDonalds continued their affectionate correspondence and meetings. Rose felt at home with her 'brothers and sisters' and once back in Ireland Mrs La Touche would send MacDonald scraps of Rose's poetry for scrutiny. Brimming with emotion she wrote to Louisa:

'I can't tell you how often I have thought, with a feeling of grateful love that you would hardly understand, of the many hours of real happiness you have given me — *all* of you including each child. . . They are the best and in every way the nicest children I know and I love them for not being shy with me as all my neighbour's children are. . .'[13]

Soon after the first meeting with Ruskin, Mrs La Touche was arranging another, and they fixed on going to Ruskin's lecture at the Royal Institution on 5 June. After that Ruskin and the MacDonalds began to cannon letters to one another, sending invitations and literary criticism each other's way. Ruskin wrote to MacDonald at the end of June:

'I hope to get over to tea to-morrow — only — and we are to be by ourselves — you must keep the 'kettle' — which I hope you are too great a poet to have discarded — hot till 7 for I can't get over sooner.

David E. is full of noble things and with beautiful little sentences. I can't read it for it is sad to me — all novels are — but I should like Euphie if I *were* to read it, to be worried to death when she died. I don't care about Margaret a bit. Besides, I being in Hugh's pleasantest state of 'awake in his coffin' — only care for observation on the clay which I can scratch through the chinks in the lid — and hate to hear of grass and flowers — except fossil.

It's all nonsense about Everybody turning good. No one ever turns good who isn't.'[14]

Ruskin soon responded to MacDonald's invitation and invited the whole family and Annie Munro out for a Monday lunch to Denmark Hill with strawberries in the garden. He also persisted with *David Elginbrod* and found:

'I have been reading *David* bit by bit — *falling* into it, and I like it so much, now I've got to Harry's education. It is *so* good and right. Do you know — that about his stepping on the diamonds of the carpet is precisely what I did when I was a boy — only it used to be on steps of stairs, and I used to jump over three or two or one and wonder whether God cared how many I missed. Did you find that out for yourself?'

And so it was that they quickly struck up a close emotional and literary companionship. Ruskin was probably yearning for a friend — someone who would not point the long finger of evangelicalism at him, and MacDonald appeared at the right moment. Ruskin found MacDonald comforting and assuring even if he felt that he had set himself beyond the pale as far as religion was concerned. He admired MacDonald's work, praising his novels, and enjoying *Within and Without*: 'It is very grand and good. I enjoyed it so much.' MacDonald even passed the acid test of Margaret Ruskin's approval — perhaps his being Scottish helped — and she too enjoyed his books.

Ruskin did have doubts about MacDonald's fairy story *The Light Princess*, though. Ruskin's only sortie into Faerie had been a tale called *The King of the Golden River* which he had written for Effie Gray when she was still a very young girl. Although a powerful fable written in the tradition of the Grimm brothers, it differs enormously from the temper of MacDonald's work. Ruskin did not like the tinge of eroticism he found in MacDonald's story for young children:

'I have been lingering over the Light Princess, trying to analyze the various qualities of mind you show in it. I am certain that it will not do for the public in its present form: — owing first, to some of your virtues; — that you see too deeply into things to be able to laugh nicely — you cannot laugh in any exuberant or infectious manner — and the parts which are intended to be laughable are weak. Secondly, it is too long and there is a curious mixture of tempers in it — of which we will talk — it wants the severest compression. Then lastly, it is too amorous throughout — and to some temperaments would be quite mischievous — You are too pure-minded yourself to feel this — but I assure you the swimming scenes and love scenes would be to many children seriously harmful — Not that they would have to be cut out — but to be done in a simpler and less telling way. We will chat over this. Pardon my positive way of stating these things — it is my inferiority to you in many noble things which enables *me* to feel them and prevents you.'[15]

Much of the criticism in this letter hits the mark. MacDonald does feel too deeply to 'laugh nicely' and that is a persistent feature of his work. And there *is* a 'curious mixture of tempers' in *The Light Princess* though the 'amorousness' is a bonus and hardly harmful. If MacDonald did listen to Ruskin's criticism on this subject, he did not heed him, but took perhaps a silent revenge. The following year when *Adela Cathcart* was published, Ruskin wrote to MacDonald in mock-fury:

'You *did* make me into Mrs Cathcart — She says the very things I said about the fairy tale. It's the only time she's right in the whole book, you turned me into her, first — and then invented all the wrongs to choke up my poor little right with. I never knew anything so horrid.'[16]

In many ways Ruskin made himself useful to MacDonald. After old Mr Ruskin died in March 1864 he was heir to a large fortune — £120,000 plus £10,000 in property and pictures — and spent the rest of his life giving a lot of it away. It was with some of that money that he bought three houses in the ironically-named Paradise Place for Octavia Hill to begin her work in improving tenements. He often sent MacDonald sums of money and was irritated when MacDonald did not tell him when he was in need: 'I hope the enclosed may be in time to be of some use — if you want any more tell me directly, or I'll be angry next time I find it out.'[17] Greville MacDonald remembered Ruskin's many visits to their home and recalled that:

'In 1866 Ruskin lent my father a sum of money. A few months later it was returned, but Ruskin refused it, saying he did not need it, and that my father must accept it as a gift. Again my father writes claiming the necessity of his own conscience. But Ruskin, having ascertained that my mother and sisters were in need of a new piano, insists upon giving one to my eldest sister and so gets his way.'[18]

He also gave MacDonald a copy of *Modern Painters* in its original green morocco binding.

When he went abroad in the autumn of 1863 he wrote to the Mac-Donalds from Baden saying: 'This is only to say I'm grateful to you for loving me — and that I hope to see more of your kind faces, yours and your wife's than I did last year.'[19] Though his sky was cloudy — 'I'm so puzzled with everything — and so dead to everything' — meeting the MacDonalds had been a bright spot in a gloomy year and he looked to their friendship to stand him in good stead during the rougher time to come.

CHAPTER TWENTY-TWO
Abroad

During 1863, the bulk of work weighed heavily upon MacDonald. He was working at Bedford College, giving lectures in his own home, writing stray journalism, and trying to turn out novels. After *David Elginbrod*, *Adela Cathcart* appeared, half composed of pieces he had written and published before in the *Monthly Christian Spectator*. As soon as this book had been corrected and bundled off to the printers, he began work on *Alec Forbes of Howglen*, another visit to his Scottish childhood. It was little wonder that he longed to escape back to the hills and rushing rivers of Huntly. He smarted at being cooped up in the city with its noise and crowds and clattering carriages, but there was nothing to remedy the situation as London was the only place where MacDonald could support his family adequately, and even then precariously. There were breaks, however. Soon after the move to Earles Terrace MacDonald took some of the children to the Sharmans, Louisa's cousins at Wellingborough, where they were able to roam the country and breathe fresh air.

Then autumn broke over London, and the MacDonalds settled down for a long winter. But in January 1864 MacDonald was soon off lecturing again, first of all to Manchester when he saw the Scotts, but found that 'not many people — somewhere over a hundred' came to listen to him. Then he moved on to Liverpool and stayed with Helen and Alex Powell. He returned to Earles Terrace in time to witness Louisa giving birth to another son, named Maurice after F. D. Maurice. The venerable man was happy to stand as godfather to the new baby, and MacDonald also approached John Ruskin to be the other. Ruskin however felt that he was past such Christian frills and refused.

The pregnancy left Louisa feeling weak, compensated only by the fact that the baby 'sleeps all day', and in April the family decided to separate for a while. Louisa took some of the children down to Hastings to refresh herself by the sea, and MacDonald stayed at Earles Terrace trying to write and lecture and at the same time cope with Grace, Winnie, Bob and Mary. Even with the children clambering all over him he managed at least one outing to see Shakespeare's *Henry IV*. Louisa sat with Lily in the evenings, listening to the soft wash of the waves outside, making a smoking-cap of blue and gold for William Matheson's birthday. 'This lazy life doesn't seem right somehow,' she murmured, but she was hardly protesting as the sojourn in Hastings was the first rest she had had for a very long time. When she had recovered her strength she and MacDonald managed a trip north to Oban, taking the boat on up to Inverness and stopping off on the way to Huntly to see Munro the sculptor's parents.

Their trip was only a brief respite until London swallowed them again, and as the months passed, it was clear that MacDonald needed a rest, though there was none to be had as he had so many commitments. In the summer of 1865 however it proved finally possible for MacDonald to lay his pen aside and journey abroad, the first time he had done so since his trip to Algiers nine years previously. His original plan was to join A. J. Scott's family, who were travelling up the Rhone to Les Plans near Bex, but Ruskin intervened. He had been travelling on the continent since his early boyhood and had a well-worn path that he recommended to all his friends. He was also tart with MacDonald on the question of money:

> 'The main thing is, you are *not* to disturb yourself about money, as long as I am to the fore. The second is — that you must go as straight as you can to *Berne* not Geneva. Geneva is now one wilderness of accursed gambling and jewellers shops — mixed up with cafes and stonemason's yards.[1]

Thus it was that towards the end of July Louisa retreated to her father at Elm Lodge in Hampstead with the children, and MacDonald set off with William Matheson and another friend for Antwerp in Belgium. The railway had opened up Europe to the tourist, much to Ruskin's disgust, but it meant that MacDonald and his two friends could travel speedily from place to place. Though he was plagued throughout the holiday with intense heat, asthma, lumbago, toothache and sleeplessness, he wrote ravishing reports of his journeys to Louisa. MacDonald had always had a passion for stairs, heights, spires and mountains — 'God's own towers' he had dubbed them — and he was delighted with the lofty spire of Antwerp Cathedral when he caught sight of it rising above the city. He insisted on their all climbing it, as he did every spire that they came across on their travels:

> '. . . God be praised for that spire. I *would* go up though my head ached and I seemed worn out. 616 steps, 410 feet! . . . Oh, how I should delight to build a cathedral-tower if nothing else. *God be praised*! was all I could say — as the arabs say when they see a beautiful woman.'[2]

It was little wonder that they were worn out after their twenty-one hour journey, but after two days in Antwerp to recover their wits they felt able to press on to Cologne. MacDonald found the heat dreadful in the German city. It was 'not greatly to our taste — the smells are as bad as Coleridge says.' That night he tossed and turned in bed, sleepless in the midst of a violent thunderstorm broken only by a tremendous peal of bells that lasted all through the night. He was tired again when they set off sight-seeing early the next day. He was grumpy about the German beer which had garlic in it and complained that, 'I can't get on with my German. I can't keep French out of it.' The Catholic cathedral itself, grand and imposing, with its majestic crimson-robed clergy, was sadly disappointing:

> 'The cathedral is very fine outside from one point of view. But the inside though very beautiful and very graceful greatly lacks mystery to me. I was disappointed and sorry to be forced to confess it.'

Leaving Cologne behind, they threaded their way on to Basle, via Weissenburg, a town in Alsace, and stopped off in Strasbourg, graceful and evocative with its Germanic timbered houses:

> 'And here again we found a glory of a city. I never saw anything to compare it, except the old town of Edinburgh, and that is squalid and vile — this rich and ancient and glorious — rather smelly, of course, like the other.'

Gradually they came within sight of Schaffhausen, a place Ruskin had insisted on their visiting. A medieval town with a castle, Schaffhausen sits by the impassable falls of the Rhine and always served as an ancient crossing point of the river. Old, beautiful, it attracted many Romantic painters and Turner had sketched the Falls many years before. MacDonald found his romantic spirit in short supply, however, as his back flared up into pain:

> 'Last night I could only bear the sheet over me and slept so all night, and there was a change towards morning and there was no watchful woman beside me to cover me up (crippled with lumbago). I go about like an old man, and ashamed of being stared at.'

But the pain slowly subsided, and they left Schaffhausen behind, moving on to Thun where the town was decorated for the annual *Fest*. Bunting fluttered in the streets and the locals sat out on benches drinking wine and beer. There were singing competitions and prizes.

MacDonald's goal, however, was the Alps, where he was awaiting a breathtaking experience. Slowly they travelled to Interlaken and thence to Lauterbrunnen, where they climbed to the edge of a precipice, and moved along its dizzying height till they came to the dolls-village of Mürren, a collection of sharp-eaved chalets on the side of a steep slope. The village faces the grandeur of the Jungfrau and the Eiger; and MacDonald waited impatiently for the veil of mist to rend in order to see this earthly revelation of the divine:

> 'Yet I am not sure whether amidst the lovely chaos of shifting clouds I have seen the highest peak of the Jungfrau. It is utterly useless to try to describe it. . . .'

The Alps feature largely in MacDonald's novel *Wilfrid Cumbermede* written in 1872, in which an alpine holiday is described, and the opening of *The Princess and Curdie*, with its grand evocation of the mountain, may owe something to MacDonald's journey through Switzerland. But it is left to Robert Falconer to make obeisance to the divine as revealed through the dazzling white peaks:

> 'He fell upon his knees, bowed down in the birth of a great hope, held up his hands towards heaven, and cried, Lord Christ, give me thy peace.'[3]

Ruskin too wrote of his first sight of the Alps and he realized that Rousseau and Scott had enabled him to perceive a beauty that had remained undistinguished for generations. MacDonald, partaking of the same tradition as Ruskin, gazed on the mountains in the way that he did, and they forced him to worship.

In the best of biblical traditions MacDonald and his two friends had to come down from the mountain and, once more in Lauterbrunnen, decided to press on to Gründewald. Gründewald was the furthest point of the trip for MacDonald and his friends, and after that it was time to zig-zag back across Europe to Louisa who was waiting patiently in London. After the scenic magnificence of Switzerland it is not hard to imagine how MacDonald felt about returning to London at the height of summer. But suddenly there seemed a chance of escape — back north to Scotland. W. E. Aytoun,[4] the well-known poet and contributor to *Blackwoods Magazine*, had died, and the Chair of Rhetoric and *Belles Lettres* (Literature) at Edinburgh fell vacant. This was the sort of chance MacDonald had been waiting for, and why he had been dallying for so long with the Ladies' College in Bedford Square. He immediately threw himself into drumming up testimonials and arranging his application for the post, though he must have known that he had only a hairsbreadth chance of success. The dangerous heterodoxy contained in *David Elgin-brod* stood against him, and letters of support from the pagan Ruskin and the heretic Maurice were as much a hindrance as a help in some eyes. MacDonald wrote anxiously to Mrs Scott in Manchester, asking if her husband, who was recovering from a serious illness, would pen some support for him:

> 'I write in great haste to save a post which is now of great consequence to me. My testimonials are just going to press, and they will be very incomplete without one from him whose opinions I value most. Would he not be able to let me have one without too much fatigue? . . . My friends think I have a good chance, but I don't think I shall get it, for Dr Hanna, Dallas, Masson, Dr Daniel Wilson and three or four others are applying.'[5]

Scott thought that his signature would not do MacDonald any good, however, and MacDonald began counting up his influential friends, wondering if Kingsley, Carlyle and Ruskin would help him.

In the event he marshalled a glittering array of intellects to testify for him: Dean Stanley, Erasmus Darwin (whom he knew through Bedford College), Lord Houghton, John Stuart Blackie, Norman MacLeod, Charles Kingsley, Dean Plumptre of King's College, London, his old friend Henry Crabb Robinson, and of course Maurice and Ruskin. Most of them praised him to the skies. John Stuart Blackie[6] wrote:

> 'I have seldom read a poem which left on my mind so strong an impression, not of genius only, but of something much better, of wisdom, as Mr MacDonald's *Within and Without*.'[7]

In his testimonial Ruskin wrote:

> 'I am always glad to hear you lecture myself, and if I had a son, I would rather he took lessons in literary taste under you than under any person I know.'[8]

The testimonials were printed and submitted on 4 September to the Home Secretary as the position was to be awarded by the Crown. MacDonald waited worriedly, but his time was taken up with Louisa, who gave birth to her tenth child, another son, on 25 September. They named him Bernard Powell and for a while were concerned, as he showed signs of whooping cough, but he pulled safely through. Mrs La Touche was his proud godmother.

But MacDonald was not successful in his candidature for the Chair at Edinburgh, and the prospect of money, tenure and respectability slipped out of his grasp. Louisa was half-disappointed, but glad not to be leaving her friends, and grateful that MacDonald's weak lungs would not have to endure the harsh Edinburgh winters. The post went to David Masson, a friend of MacDonald's, who had written to him apologetically, advising him that he too was applying for the Chair. Masson was actually the worthier candidate, a sound academic whose several-volume biography of Milton was much admired during the nineteenth century. If MacDonald was disappointed, he did not show it, but one thing was certain, he never applied for an academic post again.

CHAPTER TWENTY-THREE
On and Back

New Year 1866 opened with a sad blow. When he heard in January that A. J. Scott had died at Veyteaux in Switzerland MacDonald suddenly felt that a light had gone out of the world. Scott's legacy was to be seen in the people whom he had influenced and his work at Owens College, and his friends held him in enormously high esteem. He was barely over sixty when he died, and he had nurtured MacDonald through some of his most difficult times, helping him to find teaching and strengthening his faith when he had felt an outcast from church and family. MacDonald wrote to Mrs Scott, who remained a close friend, with his customary depth of comfort at these times:

> 'My very dear Friend,
> May I come near you now just to let you know that my heart is with you? What else can I say? The best comfort is what you know better than I do — the Will of God, and the next best, that he who has left us was the best and greatest of our time. . .'[1]

That year *Annals of a Quiet Neighbourhood* was running in the *Sunday Magazine*, and, looking around for a new subject, MacDonald turned back to an old one — his boyhood. The character of Robert Falconer had already appeared in the final third of *David Elginbrod* and in the unpublished *Seekers and Finders*. MacDonald was anxious to mould his hero further and give him a whole history, and so he furnished Falconer's boyhood with his own. After a family holiday at Kingswear in July, MacDonald returned to the 'mystic signs' of his childhood once again. He stayed at The Farm during August, watched over by his Uncle James, who kindly helped alleviate his asthma. He had no idea that MacDonald was about to paint so much of real life into his fiction.

With a writer's eye MacDonald combed the town and went out riding up past the Ba' Hill which rose behind The Farm. Below him the little granite town lay peacefully in the broken ring of hills that surrounded it. He reported to Louisa that, 'I think I have got good for my book.' His friend Robert Troup was still there with his growing family, and he and MacDonald spent much time together. He was invited to preach at the Missionar Kirk without any of the misgivings on the part of the congregation that had been evident eleven years previously and he gave a free Wednesday evening lecture to all who would come on the subject of *Macbeth*. Now, as an author, he was a noted figure in Huntly as he strode across the Square, in the pelting August rain, past the 'stannin' stanes' dressed in his Inverness Cape. He was in his forties, full in his prime, a striking figure.

Having put Huntly into a book — *Alec Forbes of Howglen* — MacDonald's friends and family were eager to see what he would do next. They little suspected that he would cross the bounds of decency by grafting wholesale people they knew into *Robert Falconer*.

The Huntly visit was a success, and while MacDonald was working on his new novel in London, he took on more lecturing duties, this time at King's College in the Strand. As usual he needed the money, though he may have been becoming disenchanted with his work at Bedford College even at this stage, as the atmosphere of the place had changed following the death of its founder in April 1866. King's College, founded in 1828, was a specifically Christian foundation. Entry was not restricted to Anglicans, however, though the staff were Anglican, and so Nonconformists were able to attend courses. The college was concerned about its orthodoxy, still smarting after the ejection of F. D. Maurice on the grounds of his heresy ten years previously.[2] As well as its daytime courses, the college performed pioneer work in instituting evening classes, which led to a diploma at the end of a course lasting several years, and it was to this department that MacDonald attached himself after the departure of Henry Morley for the rival University College.

The college authorities at King's were at first satisfied as to MacDonald's orthodoxy — Dean Plumptre had seen him receiving communion at the Vere Street Chapel in true Anglican conformity — but then worrying reports reached his ears about MacDonald's other religious activities. He warned MacDonald on 1 December 1866:

'The fact of your having preached at an Independent Chapel has become known here and people are talking of it . . . Pray don't turn this place into an *unquiet* neighbourhood.'[3]

The last thing anyone wanted was for the college's reputation to be battered again. In his own defence MacDonald sent a letter to the Principal, Dr Jelf, outlining his reasons for preaching in a variety of churches, and this was read out to him by Dean Plumptre. 'The letter really moved him to a glow of sympathy,' reported the Dean encouragingly, and

MacDonald's eloquence in stating that his message was one of reconciliation and brotherhood quietened the Principal's fears. Dr Jelf was happy
for MacDonald to remain at the college and preach where he liked
provided that he did not publicly broadcast his connection with King's
College. This was an undertaking MacDonald was willing to make, and
he remained at King's until the end of the session in March 1868, when he
was succeeded by the scholarly John Wesley Hales, fresh from Christ's
Cambridge.

The crisis at King's was minor, however, compared with the cracks and
strains that had emerged between Ruskin and the La Touches. Mac-
Donald was alarmed at the agony Ruskin wrote into his letters, and by
his erratic mental state. He was assailed by sudden fits of giddiness, his
mind was plunged into cloud so that he could not think straight, and
sometimes his eyes misted over to the extent that he could not even draw.
He had already confessed his increasing preoccupation with the young
Rose La Touche before MacDonald's departure for Switzerland in July
1865:

> 'Mind you're not to mind saying you love me, because of these
> tiresome things — though I can't love anybody, except my mouse pet
> in Ireland who nibbles me to the very sick death with weariness to see
> her.'

In reply to MacDonald's questioning response, Ruskin wrote again of
Rose five days later:

> 'She's the only living thing in the world — since my white dog died —
> that I care for — and I very nearly died myself, when she got too old to
> be made a pet of any more — which was infinitely ridiculous — but I
> never had any right people to care for — and one can't get on with
> stones only — unless one shuts oneself right up at the great St.
> Bernard. I tried that plan too — last year — but it was too late — and I
> only disgusted myself with the mountains — I've got over the worst of
> it, now — and the stones will do, after this, I hope.'[4]

Worried, MacDonald confessed some of his doubts about Ruskin to
Louisa, but he believed that God had the matter in hand and hoped for a
change in his friend's state of mind:

> 'Perhaps he may have a miracle shown him or such a sight as doubting
> Thomas had, but will have to go without the praise of those that don't
> need such sights. Still there is great praise to the hopeless man who will
> yet do his duty.'[5]

MacDonald reckoned without the force of Ruskin's personality, however, or the depth of his agony. After bottling up his emotions for so long, Ruskin saw Rose La Touche again after a gap of three years on 10 December 1865. Unable to contain himself any longer, he determined that she should be his. He encouraged friendship between the Cowpers and the La Touches in the hope that he could insinuate himself apparently innocently beside Rose, but on her birthday, in February 1866, he blurted out his feelings and asked her to marry him. Her parents were horrified, and took Rose back to Ireland in March, enforcing an absolute separation between her and Ruskin. Mrs La Touche, who had been reluctant to sever relations with Ruskin, was finally forced to act. Distraught, Ruskin poured out his heart to Georgina Cowper in a long series of letters in which he bared his soul to her:

'The love of her is a religion to me — It wastes and parches me like the old enthusiasms of the wild anchorites — I do not know how long I can bear it without dying.'[6]

Mrs La Touche, formerly an affectionate friend, now loomed in Ruskin's mind as a monster and he could never forgive her for depriving him of her daughter. She had become 'the very ashes of what she used to be to me'. The graceful serpent had shown her fangs.

In the midst of this turmoil, Rose was divided at the thought of becoming Ruskin's wife. She cautioned him to wait three years until she was of age, but in the intervening time she wavered uncertainly. Certainly, the idea did not fill her with disgust as it did her mother, and she was fondly attached to Ruskin in a girlish, playful way. Ruskin begged Georgina Cowper to go to Harristown to intercede on his behalf, but Mrs Cowper was reluctant, unwilling to prejudice her friendship with the La Touches, and rush in where angels should fear to tread. In the end she did go, after some gentle probing which resulted in a letter from Rose:

'I cannot say more than I have said to St C — that in three years (if we are both alive, and I believe we will be), God helping me I will give him his answer.'[7]

With this flicker of encouragement from the girl, the Cowpers did go over to Ireland, and as a result of their visit a few tentative dinner parties were arranged with Ruskin present the next time they were in London. But it was to no avail. Then news came that Rose had a mysterious lover, and Ruskin's world crumbled for a time, until she sent him a rose the following summer which he took as a sign that this relationship had ended.

Mrs La Touche never mentioned the whole subject to the Mac-
Donalds, and kept up her friendship with them as best she could, visiting
them when she was in London, and writing familiarly of Rose's measles
contracted at a party for poor people hosted by Georgina Cowper in
February 1867. Ruskin, despite his frustration, was still active; *The
Crown of Wild Olive*, *The Ethics of the Dust*, and *Time and Tide* all
appeared in 1866 and 1867 and even with his own workload and problems weighing him down, he was not blind to the fatigue and suffering
of the people round about him.

It was clear by 1867 that Octavia Hill was exhausted. In her work at
Paradise Place her aim was not only to provide, but also to educate, and
she spent endless hours with her tenants, and on the properties —
cleaning things again and again, and always repairing things. Though her
tenants formed the main slice of her work, she drew no salary for
attending to them, but lived off what she earned from teaching at the
family school, in nearby Nottingham Place, staffed by her mother and
her sisters. She was desperately in need of a holiday and, partly at
Ruskin's suggestion, was delighted to join the MacDonalds on their jaunt
to Bude in North Devon. Devon was not quite Scotland, but the secluded
coastline and quiet village were a respite from the hungry city. The family
carried their luggage down to two cottages 'at the end of the quay, close
to old Sir Thomas Acland's cottage built almost into the rocks'. The
family was now complete as the last baby, a boy, named George MacKay
after his great-uncle at Banff, had been born earlier in the year on 23
January.

MacDonald delighted in the rocks and the scenery and began busying
himself on *The Seaboard Parish*, which he set in the magical Devon
landscape. *Dealings with the Fairies*, illustrated by Arthur Hughes, had
appeared, and MacDonald's first volume of *Unspoken Sermons* was hot
off the press.

For Greville, it was the happiest of childhood holidays, not least
because his father found time to lay his book to one side and join in their
romps and games on the beach:

> 'The breakwater was our joy, especially at high tides when the south-
> west wind brought furious, white-maned sea-horses scrambling over
> the sea-wall into the haven. My father, happy as his boys in dodging
> these drenching smotherers, would, with Maurice and Bernard, ages
> three and two, one under each arm, race across it to the Chapel-rock,
> and sometimes half up to his knees in the foamy water.'[8]

Octavia Hill, dowdy yet majestic, and still weak, was appalled at

Greville's ignorance and the teaching instinct was too strong in her for even her illness to quench:

> 'Every morning she took me out alone with her on to the Chapel Rock at the end of the breakwater, our delightful solitude shared only by the gulls and the Latin Grammar, which, so long my enemy, she soon taught me at least to respect. Nor did she have much difficulty. Her personality overruled all adverse suggestive influences, and I went back to school finely grounded in my Latin, my stupidity no more insuperable.'[9]

There were outings to Tintagel Castle close by, seat of Arthurian romance, and as they climbed to the top of the ruin it seemed as if they were breathing a different world, broken into only by occasional letters from London. One arrived from Ruskin:

> 'I am very anxious about Miss Hill . . . I can't put things into polite form just now — but what expense she is to you, I should like to replace to you as far as her illness has increased it — and I should be glad if she could stay with you and near you — under present circumstances till you return to town . . .'[10]

On their return from Bude in September, the MacDonalds found that they had at last outgrown Earles Terrace, and moved again, to Hammersmith, to a large late-Georgian house called The Retreat. Hammersmith was quieter than Kensington, and the Upper Mall, stretching by the river, had a village atmosphere that pleased the family.

The house was huge, with a rather austere front, but behind it the children could lose themselves in the large orchard and vegetable garden. Inside there were three garrets perched at the very top of the house, and a long drawing-room facing the river which MacDonald claimed as his study:

> 'His friend, the artist Cottier, who some years later attained much the same position in New York as William Morris in London, so far as his influence in decorative art was concerned, adorned the room for him in a sort of barbaric splendour: crimson-flock wallpaper with black fleurs-de-lis stencilled over, a dark blue ceiling with scattered stars in silver and gold, and a silver crescent moon, and specially designed brass-ball wall-brackets and chandeliers for the gas.'[11]

In his book-lined refuge MacDonald struggled with his latest novel, *Guild Court*, set in the heart of commercial London.

He needed to finish the book quickly as Christmas was fast approaching and, straight after the family celebrations were over, he and Louisa were going north to Scotland where MacDonald had a demanding lecture tour already arranged. Leaving Lilia in charge of the children and the finances, the steam train whistled them out of King's Cross, more or less as their Christmas pudding was still being digested, and Louisa watched entranced as the flat English landscape grew more rugged the nearer they drew to the border.

Aberdeen was cold when they arrived, and Louisa shivered as she stepped off the train, which stood steaming in the station. They were to be guests of MacDonald's old friend Geddes, now Professor Geddes, who welcomed them warmly, and took them to his grand Aberdeen home. MacDonald's first appearance on the lecture platform was a success and he spoke magnificently: 'There was a famous attendance at the lecture last night with an ovation at the last. . .' wrote Louisa to Lilia.[12]

The couple travelled over to Huntly soon after, the first time Louisa had ever seen the town in the depths of winter — greyer than ever and the hills powdered with snow. She stayed at The Farm while MacDonald went further up the railway line to lecture at Keith, one stop away, and then over to Banff, raw with the January winds that blew off the sea. At that time MacDonald was involved in numerous journeys as he was sitting for his portrait in Aberdeen.[13] The painter was a young man in his twenties, with a gaunt El Greco face and straggly beard, named George Reid. He took a month to complete the canvas — a powerful, mystical representation of MacDonald — much like a strange nineteenth century image of Christ.

When Reid had finished with him, MacDonald and Louisa went down to Glasgow where the crowd that came to hear him preach was so large that as many as piled into the church had to be sent away disappointed. He was famous at last. From Glasgow they went to Dundee and then on down to Edinburgh. Shortly after his return to London, he received an exciting letter from Geddes:

> 'I have the pleasure also of announcing that today the Senatus without dissentient voice accorded to you the degree of LLD, the highest literary distinction they have it in their power to confer.'[14]

This honorary degree for 'high literary eminence as a poet and author' ensured MacDonald's place in the Aberdeen University Hall of Fame, and was a flattering way of rewarding one of their past students for his achievements. For MacDonald, it was a long-sought after mark of recognition — not the award itself so much — but the acknowledgement of his status as a man of letters, a poet, a novelist — and a theologian.

CHAPTER TWENTY-FOUR

God our Father and Mother — MacDonald's Theology

Many personal histories in the nineteenth century are tales of emancipation, but the laying aside of childhood things (and more often than not childhood faith) posed problems for the Victorians that were difficult to solve. Cutting the umbilical cord with the past could too easily set one adrift in the present, and a substitute had to be found for the aching gap that was left. Ruskin toyed with spiritualism and devoted himself to social improvement; George Eliot embraced ethics and Feuerbachian philosophy; while Hardy wrote and rewrote the places of his childhood, picturing an ever-darkening landscape. MacDonald kept his faith, though it underwent (that most nineteenth century of terms) an evolution.

At odds with those around him, MacDonald plummeted into a depression during his university years from which it took an anxious time of effort and searching to emerge. By the time he had arrived in London he had already steeped himself in the romantic poets, and was beginning to read the Bible according to their light. He wrote to his father:

'One of my greatest difficulties in consenting to think of religion was that I thought I should have to give up my beautiful thoughts and love for the things God has made...'[1]

Discovering that this need not be so, MacDonald turned to his Bible with relief, and blew the dust off the systems and stringencies that had cluttered his head as a child:

'I love my bible more — I am always finding out something new in it — I seem to have had everything to learn over again from the beginning — All my teaching in youth seems useless to me — I must get it all from the bible again.'[2]

When MacDonald entered Highbury Theological College he found his teachers eager to imprison him in the old rather than allow him to explore the new, and he became bored and dissatisfied with his studies. There were compensations in his friends James and Greville Matheson, however, and in two individuals who cast a spell over him — Caleb Morris and A. J. Scott. Scott was, at this time, a professor at University College, London, while Caleb Morris was approaching the end of his celebrated twenty-year career as minister of Fetter Lane Chapel, begun in 1829. Morris was a Welshman and a mystic, and the students he gathered round him were passionately devoted to him. Among their number was William Hale White, better known as Mark Rutherford, whose famous *Autobiography* was published in 1881.

Both Hale White and MacDonald used poetry to set their theological agendas at a time when poetry and theology seemed somehow inseparable. Coleridge had fused together aesthetics, philosophy and theology in such a way as to bring living water to the young men parched by the dry rationalist theories of the Enlightenment, and Wordsworth, for his part, had taught the Victorians how to feel. So strongly was Wordsworth a touchstone for the Victorians in their experience of the world that Matthew Arnold wrote on the poet's death in 1850:

'Others will strengthen us to bear —
But who, ah who, will make us feel.'

If the eighteenth century had viewed the universe as a rather elegantly designed building, with all its parts in their proper places and order reigning throughout, Coleridge turned to images of organic growth, where the soul was forever developing and grasping after spiritual truth. His scattered writings are evidence of a mind in progress, and his ideas were, at the time, either dismissed as the blubberings of a crank, or an incoherent prophet, or were received as a revelation. Coleridge's message was that poets were prophets, divine metaphysicians who mediated revelation to mankind, and that this was done through a symbolic writing which pointed up the relation of man to the supernatural through nature. Coleridge affirmed that there was a transcendent element in nature which found a living response in the heart of every man whether he was a believer or not. Such a response was an emotional one, made with the heart, to symbolic truth as presented through nature, and involved the total person, as opposed to a mere assent of the will to propositions or sentences. Christianity was more than a series of doctrines therefore — it was a personal revelation, independent of churches and with strong social implications.

From his early days, Coleridge's mind had been accustomed to the vastness of nature. As a boy he had gazed up at the flickering constellations displayed above him, and as a man he continued to believe that the Whole was a living unity, rooted and grounded in God. Coleridge's vision of man was as a being who is becoming, a being who creates, and meaning was discerned through right perception. Perception therefore became a creative act of the mind, culminating in the idea of the symbol as a mediator of truth.

Coleridge's poems — *Christabel, Kubla Khan*, and above all *The Rime of the Ancient Mariner* — employ such a symbolic mode in that they are visionary glimpses of a whole of which the reader sees and experiences only a part. *The Rime of the Ancient Mariner* is puzzling, disturbing and tantalizing, containing several different levels of meaning.

Coleridge's own quest, in part like the Ancient Mariner's, was to make sense out of apparently disparate experiences, resolving them through what he called Polar Logic into a higher synthesis where unity could be attained. His was the old problem of the One and the Many — how can God be immanent and transcendent, in everything and yet beyond everything at the same time? Coleridge's answer was that this was possible *poetically* as two things apparently contradictory, even opposite, could be simultaneously true. John Stuart Mill put some of Coleridge's ideas in a nutshell, claiming two differing orders of truth: scientific truth and poetic truth, and this proved a starting-point for many of the Broad Church theologians, among them, MacDonald, who were anxious to stress the poetic over the literal in any case. Many of Coleridge's ideas were also absorbed by Wordsworth into his poetry and he in turn introduced them into the bloodstream of his readers — among them an avid MacDonald. Reading *Tintern Abbey* for the first time must have been like throwing open the windows to greet the spring after a long dreary winter:

'...And I have felt
A presence that disturbs me with the joy
Of elevated thoughts; a sense sublime
Of something far more deeply interfused
Whose dwelling is the light of setting suns,
And the round ocean and the living air,
And the blue sky, and in the mind of man:
A motion and a spirit, that impels
All thinking things, all objects of all thought,
And rolls through all things.'

Behind Coleridge's thought stood an array of German thinkers, many of whom MacDonald also read: Schelling, the Schlegels, Fichte (whose idealism MacDonald was particularly attracted to), Kant, and Schleiermacher, whose notions of religious experience MacDonald found very attractive. Then, of course, there was Novalis, who was to MacDonald much as Virgil was to Dante in *The Divine Comedy*. Novalis's poetic philosophy was one MacDonald revelled in, and he found that it fitted his own mind exactly. 'We are closer to things invisible than to things visible,' wrote Novalis, and his belief that the heart was the key to the world and life itself, and that all men and women were on a journey Homeward, had the right mixture of comfort and transcendence for MacDonald's restless and uneasy spirit. Novalis also exalted the poet as a priest and philosopher, holding that poetry 'represents what cannot be represented', and saw poetry as expressing a fundamental relationship with this world and the next that somehow the Enlightenment had missed.

If Coleridge acted as a prism through which these German ideas were filtered, the other great 'Germaniser' of the time was Thomas Carlyle, whose blustering broadsides were delivered against increasing materialism and unbelief through books such as *Sartor Resartus* and *Past and Present*. His was a religious temperament severed from religion, but he nevertheless stressed faith as against unbelief, and emphasized the reality of the invisible. His great philosophical enemies were Hume and Voltaire who, in his eyes, had reduced the spirit to mechanical electrics. The world, according to Carlyle, was the vesture of God, matter of thought, and the transient of the eternal. Carlyle's message, delivered with the force of a prophet from his home in Cheyne Row in London, found many adherents in the 1840s and 50s when MacDonald's ideas were still fluid and forming and he won for himself many disciples during that time.

Carlyle's ideas had considerable impact on the church, and Coleridge's ideas were channelled into the ecclesiastical community through MacDonald's mentor F.D. Maurice, whose *Kingdom of Christ*, published in 1842, propounded much of Coleridge's own 'organic' philosophy. Unity was the keynote — and most particularly that men and women were children of God and part of his family simply by dint of being born, and not through any special experience or merit attained during their earthly lives. Maurice's influence on MacDonald cannot be stressed too strongly. MacDonald's son was named after the great man, and where Maurice led with his theological light, MacDonald followed.[3] Maurice, like Coleridge (and MacDonald), looked back to the Cambridge Platonists, to Plato himself and to Plotinus, as the well-spring of much of his thinking, stopping off on the way to consult the mystics Swedenborg and Boehme.

Though Maurice was one of the most influential churchmen of the nineteenth century, he was only one of a fascinating nest of thinkers who overlapped and influenced one another to an extraordinary degree. These men hoped for a new reformation — that the winds of change would blow across Britain and revitalize the church. Many of these thinkers were Scottish, and the most notable among them was Thomas Erskine of Linlathen,[4] a quiet, saintly man, who held court on his large estate in Scotland to some of the finest minds of his day: Thomas Carlyle, Charles Kingsley, Augustus and Julius Hare, F. W. Robertson of Brighton and, of course, Maurice all made the pilgrimage north to talk with this kindly mystic. MacDonald met him in 1865. Erskine, like Maurice, turned to Kant, Schleiermacher and the writings of William Law for inspiration, and rejected the sterner decrees of Calvinism. He believed that the character of man ought to be conformed with the character of God and that this was the aim of Christianity. He repudiated a God of rewards and punishments, emphasizing that such a view led only to increased selfishness in the heart of the individual Christian focussing on what could be obtained from God. Instead he focussed on the character of God as Love — Universal Love.

Erskine met A.J. Scott, MacDonald's other great mentor, in Edinburgh in 1828. Scott, with his mixture of Owenite Socialism, Scottish background, and romantic theology had worked for a while as assistant to the celebrated Edward Irving at the National Scotch Church in London. He had been the church's missionary to the poor, and so had come into contact with the dreadful conditions prevailing in many parts of London at that time. The services on Sunday, however, were far from the slums. Irving, a dazzling orator, packed his church with many of the famous people of his day — Hazlitt, Coleridge, Jeremy Bentham, who all turned up to listen to the young man's lengthy sermons.[5]

Irving knew Carlyle well, and another of these men's friends was Norman Macleod[6] who became editor of *Good Words* in 1860, in which MacDonald had *Guild Court* serialized. Interestingly, Macleod made a trip to the Holy Land with MacDonald's friend and publisher Strahan in 1864, publishing an account of the journey as *Eastward* in 1866.

Erskine, Scott, Maurice and the others had more than a tinge of mysticism in their theology, struggled with the problem of evil, adhered to a form of Christian Socialism, and had an outlook that was fundamentally romantic. With the exception of Maurice they were all Scottish, and though all their theologies overlap and are by no means identical, if their emphasis were to be summed up, it would be this: the rediscovery of the Father.

MacDonald's immediate theological inheritance was through Wordsworth, Coleridge, Maurice and German theology, but north-east Scotland where MacDonald grew up has a strong mystical tradition of its own of which MacDonald must have known something.[7]

MacDonald's own theology was expressed through everything he wrote — his novels, his poetry and his fantasy writing, but he did write five purely theological works. These were three volumes of *Unspoken Sermons* published in 1867, 1885, and 1889 and dedicated to Louisa; *The Miracles of Our Lord* in 1870, dedicated to F. D. Maurice; and Mac-Donald's final volume of sermons, *The Hope of the Gospel* published in 1892. MacDonald's writings are shot through with ideas culled from Maurice, Erskine, Scott, F. W. Robertson,[8] Coleridge and German theologians, but these men's writings should be seen acting on him rather as a dye on cloth — colours merge — echoes of other hues are visible — but the final mix, the colour, is MacDonald's own.

MacDonald found a place in the Broad Church, becoming a lay member of the Church of England through the lure of F. D. Maurice. In Anglicanism MacDonald found a greater individual freedom than in any other Christian tradition. Not only could he think as he pleased, but he could drink, smoke, play cards, dance and go to the theatre without being criticized.[9] Like Maurice and A. J. Scott, MacDonald eschewed any defined theological system:

'I will send out no theory of mine to rouse afresh little whirlwinds of dialogistic dust mixed with dirt and straws and holy words, hiding the master in talk about him.'[10]

Maurice and Scott used words like the brushstrokes of an artist, and their lack of system was dismissed by many as a lack of coherence. They were both notoriously difficult speakers to understand, and many found their phrases as tangible as dissolving oils, or else simply beyond them. Yet to their followers they were prophets, and both had suffered over the Universalist issue as MacDonald had. Like them, MacDonald was quick to detach himself from popular opinion: 'I am as indifferent to a reputation for orthodoxy as I despise the championship of novelty.'[11] MacDonald's theology, like that of those who influenced him, celebrated the rediscovery of God as Father, and sought to encourage an intuitive response to God and Christ through quickening his readers' spirits in their reading of the Bible and their perception of nature. Theology for MacDonald was a washing down of the doors of perception. First to go was the martinet God of the Calvinists:

'They yield the idea of the Ancient of Days, "the glad creator" and put in its stead a miserable, puritanical martinet of a God, caring not for righteousness, but for his rights; not for the eternal purities, but the goodly properties. The prophets of such a God take all the glow, all the hope, all the colour, all the worth, out of life on earth, and offer you instead what they call eternal bliss — a pale, tearless hell.'[12]

Instead, insisted MacDonald, God was Father, like the Father of the Prodigal Son, welcoming his wayward children Home. The approach to God, either through the Bible or through nature, was without obstacles, as the whole of creation had its origin in him. Men and women were born out of the heart of God, not *ex nihilo* as traditionally held by the church, and thus MacDonald aligned himself with the Neo-Platonic theories of Plotinus and Origen.[13]

Being born out of God, in MacDonald's eyes, affirmed God as Father, more than just a Maker, and meant that everyone, whether they realized it or not, was on a road leading back to him. He was Home. These ideas came close to the 'Logos' theology of Justin Martyr, the earliest of the Church Fathers. This theology appropriated earlier figures such as Socrates as 'Christians before Christ'.[14] Such an outlook had several important repercussions for MacDonald's theology. The first was that Justin's Logos let him off the hook as far as conversion was concerned. The workings of grace in a person's life was the sign that all anxious Calvinists looked for — otherwise they were doomed to hell. But MacDonald believed that people were either responding to God or turning away from him — good or bad, they were part of a continuum with him and so there was no absolute need for the turning-point of a conversion, though MacDonald did believe in conversion and his novels contain many of them. Barbara Wylder in *There and Back*, however:

'. . . was one who, so far as human eyes could see, had never required conversion. She had but to go on, recognise, and do. She turned to the light by a holy will as well as holy instinct.'[15]

Such a figure of response corresponded with the Coleridgean one of organic growth, instead of describing spiritual awakening as a sudden discontinuity with the past.[16] The soul instead was like a young plant, reaching out after the light that enlightened every man. And the light illuminated every man, whether Christian, Hindu, Buddhist, Muslim or atheist. F.D. Maurice gave two sets of lectures in 1845 and 1846 called *Christianity and the Religions of the World*, and they achieved considerable popularity when published in book form. Maurice asserted Justin Martyr's philosophy of the Logos, though he singled out Christianity, Judaism and Islam as having more of a divine initiative than other religions.[17] MacDonald adopted this same outlook, and went to great lengths in *Robert Falconer* to point out that Dr Anderson's good Brahmin friend would find a place in heaven, and he was equally firm in *Paul Faber, Surgeon* in declaring that he preferred a good atheist to a bad Christian:

'It is better to be an atheist who does the will of God, than a so-called Christian who does not. The atheist will not be dismissed because he said *Lord, Lord* and did not obey.'[18]

MacDonald was trying to prick an audience who were smug in their doctrine, but weak in works. Light in every man meant, consequently, social responsibility towards every man as every man was a brother.

Light in the world meant that the Bible, though the main channel through which God revealed his character and will, was not the only way of learning about him. MacDonald's involvement in the education of working men and women was one symptom of the break-up of the old classical education systems which had prevailed in schools and universities for centuries. Women and working men turned to English literature, not to the Latin and Greek classics, and the idea that there was something of God's truth reverberating through the world could mean that literature outside of the Bible was in some profound way Christian. Reading was seen as a road to moral improvement. This kind of education prided itself on improving the quality of people's lives, not just the number of facts in their heads, and thus MacDonald, through encouraging people to enjoy literature, and through his own novels and poetry, was spreading the Word and bringing about the rule of the Kingdom of Heaven on earth. The Bible, though crucial, no longer had the monopoly on revelation, and MacDonald went on to maintain that in fact it was Christ, not the Bible, who was God's revelation to man, and that one had to read the Bible in order to respond to Christ. Reading the Bible therefore, became a means to an end, rather than an end in itself. Ranald Bannerman asks his father:

'"But aren't we to read the Bible, father?"
"Yes, if it's in order to obey it. To read the Bible thinking to please God by the mere reading of it, is to think like a heathen." '[19]

Reading the Bible, however, was plagued with problems throughout the nineteenth century. Strauss' *Leben Jesu*, translated into English by the twenty-seven-year-old George Eliot in 1851, ushered in cold, rational criticism from Germany, and began straightway to dissect the miracles of Jesus and many of the Old Testament texts. What had hitherto been regarded as fact was suddenly demoted to myth. Fact had become fairy story. On top of that, the nineteenth-century man or woman had already received several severe shocks to the system. Up until the 1820s many people accepted, at least unconsciously, the time-scale calculated by Archbishop Ussher, that the world had been created in six days some time in 4004 BC. More than that, each part of the creation was seen as having its place in the Great Chain of Being, which ascended from the lowest of the animals up to the highest of the angels with man as the midpoint, the fulcrum between the animal and the divine. Suddenly, dinosaurs, dug up out of the earth and pieced together, took on the monstrous shape of nightmares, and it was claimed that they were not hundreds, but millions of years old. Fossils, too, revealed plants and animals undreamed of, that had no place in the neatly charted Chain of Being. So it was that somewhere between the 1820s and the 1840s, Geology, which was the most important science of that time, convinced the public that the world was millions of years old and could not possibly have been created in six days, and that there could have been no such thing as Noah and a universal flood.[20]

These findings were closely followed by the German critical onslaught from 1850 onwards, and when in 1859 Darwin published his *Origin of Species*, it was clear that a watershed had been reached, for here was a book that seemed to flatly contradict everything that was in Genesis. The early 1860s saw much confusion in church circles over the subject of biblical historicity, but by 1871 evolution had largely won the day. MacDonald's attitude to this ferment revealed itself in a number of ways. As a poet he believed that the Bible enshrined a poetic truth, somehow immune from scientific facts and theories, though, like Maurice, he held that a strong historical element in theology was vital. Science was the husk; religion was the kernel. The Bible was a signpost to Christ:

'Sad, indeed, would the whole matter be, if the Bible had told us *everything* God meant us to believe. But herein is the Bible itself greatly wronged. It nowhere lays claim to be regarded as *the* Word, *the* Way, *the* Truth. The Bible leads us to Jesus, the inexhaustible, the ever-unfolding Revelation of God. It is Christ "in whom are hid all the treasures of wisdom and knowledge", not the Bible, save as leading to him.'[21]

The ideal was that Christ should be perfected in every person, and when that work was completed, then the Bible could be thrown away. As a mirror reflects an image, so it also contains an image, and this was the figure MacDonald used when illustrating how a Christian should harbour the spirit of Christ:

> 'Our mirroring of Christ, then, is one with the presence of his spirit in us. The idea, you see, is not the reflection, the radiating of the light of Christ on others, though that were a figure lawful enough; but the taking into, and having in us, him working to the changing of us.'[22]

MacDonald maintained that the Bible was certainly true, whether strictly historical in places or not, as it was part of God's revelation to the world of himself, and he could declare with confidence:

> 'I care not whether the book of Job be a history or a poem. I think it is both — I do not care how much relatively of each . . . I would gladly throw out the part of Elihu as an interpolation.'[23]

He was more careful, however in scrutinizing the words of Jesus. While he accepted that the Apostle John may have put some of his own sentiments into Jesus' mouth, he denied firmly that there was anything in the Gospels which contradicted the character of Christ as revealed there, and so, according to this logic, all the sayings of Jesus were authentic as faithfully recorded by the Apostles and transcribed by the Gospel writers. Nevertheless MacDonald entered cheerfully into another debate that was raging at the time. With the wealth of Greek manuscripts then becoming available, it became clear that the King James version of the Bible of 1611 contained many mistakes which needed rectifying. In 1853 Hort and Westcott, two Cambridge men, agreed to work together to produce a revised text of the Greek New Testament, and this was finally published after a long and bitter struggle in 1881. MacDonald had studied Greek from boyhood, and must have begun reading the New Testament in Greek either at Highbury or earlier. Comparing versions and commenting on different Greek texts was a pursuit he enjoyed. In the *Unspoken Sermons* (Second Series) he wrote, in his sermon 'The Way', for example:

> 'The reading of both the Sinaitic and the Vatican manuscript, the oldest two we have, that preferred, I am glad to see, by both Westcott and Tischendorf, though not by Tregelles or the Revisers, is, "Children, how hard is it to enter into the Kingdom of God!"'[24]

For MacDonald, removing flaws from the New Testament texts was like removing fine scratches from a lens.[25] The fewer the mistakes, the more clearly could God's character be revealed. Science, on the other hand, busied itself with facts and not with meanings. Meaning could only be discerned by a creative act of perception, aided by the Spirit of God working from within:

> 'To know a primrose is a higher thing than to know all the botany of it — just as to know Christ is an infinitely higher thing than to know all theology, all that is said about his person, or babbled about his work...[26]

MacDonald, like Charles Kingsley, had had a scientific training, and his mind was not closed to the latest discoveries, but his separation of truth into scientific truth and poetic truth, or the husk and the heart, enabled him to remain undisturbed by Darwinism or by the geological column. In fact, many of the German romantics had adhered to evolutionary theories of moral and spiritual development. Man, for them, was not a fixed point in the universe, but was in the process of changing, and so evolution, a theory containing aspects of progress and growth, was one which MacDonald could adapt to his own ends. In *The Elect Lady*, for example, Andrew Ingram praises the fine form of a horse:

> '"God makes beautiful horses," returned Andrew: "whether he takes the one way or the other to make them, I am sure he takes the right way."'[27]

MacDonald believed that the animals were all perched on different rungs of the evolutionary ladder and interlocked with one another through service and sacrifice. In *The Golden Key*, the puzzling episode in which the winged fish leads Mossy and Tangle through the wood to the woman's cottage, only to jump into a pot on arrival and be eaten by the children, becomes a further mystery when the woman opens the lid of the pot and a creature like an angel flies out. What MacDonald was stressing here is that it is through submission and sacrifice that one climbs the evolutionary scale — that through dying one is made alive. It is no coincidence, of course, that the fish is a Christian symbol.

At any rate, MacDonald had no difficulty in believing that God took many millions of years to bring about man, his only creature with a will capable of conforming to God's own:

> 'I imagine, I say, the difficulty of such creation so great, that for it God must begin inconceivably far back in the infinitesimal regions of beginnings — not to say before anything in the least resembling man, but eternal miles beyond the last farthest-pushed discovery in *protoplasm* — to set in motion that division from himself which in its

grand result should be individuality, consciousness, choice, and conscious choice — choice at last pure, being the choice of the right, the true, the divinely harmonious.'[28]

Evolution, for MacDonald, was clearly not only a physical, but a moral question. The goblins in *The Princess and the Goblin* flee underground to degenerate not just physically, but morally, with the passing of the generations, and Curdie too, at the beginning of *The Princess and Curdie* is slowly losing his sense of wonder in the world and descending to the commonplace.[29] One is either responding to the light, or turning away from it, but to turn away from it means to turn away from the meaning of the world itself, which is God. MacDonald's last word on science was:

'. . . science will never find the face of God; while those who reach his heart, those who, like Dante, are returning thither where they are, will find also the spring-head of his Science. Analysis is well, as death is well; analysis is death, not life. It discovers a little of the way God walks to his ends, but in so doing it forgets and leaves the end itself behind. I do not say the man of science does so, but the very process of his work is such a leaving of God's ends behind. . . God's science in the flower exists for the existence of the flower in its relation to his children.'[30]

MacDonald was eager to stress both relation and revelation. God was not just a Trinity of Father, Son and Holy Spirit, but of Father, Mother and Child. As Father, he held the world in profound relation to himself, having created it out of himself. As this was so, to escape entirely from God's influence would be to cease to exist. There was nowhere one could go to flee God, and no one in whom God's spirit was not active. Such a Neo-Platonic doctrine could, by extension, lead to pantheism, where the different forms of creation are only as different as the hair and fingernails of a single body, and theologians had also traditionally shied away from claiming any divinity for mankind. The counter to this was that Christ himself had declared, 'Ye are Gods' in the Gospel of John, and in any case, at the heart of the relationship between God and his creation, MacDonald sought to stress the divine in the human and the human in the divine. The Elginbrod epitaph was central to MacDonald's grasp of God's character:

'Here lie I, Martin Elginbrodde:
Hae mercy o' my soul, Lord God;
As I wad do, were I Lord God,
And ye were Martin Elginbrodde.'[31]

Many of MacDonald's contemporaries found these lines shocking. To them they either sweetened God or dethroned him. If the charge were to be laid to MacDonald that the epitaph humanized God, then he would agree, as man is made in the image of God and God must therefore have a character that is recognizably human, only more so, as he is God:

> 'I suspect that a great part of our irreligion springs from our disbelief in the humanity of God. There lie endless undiscovered treasures of grace.'[32]

As a Father, God is far from the petulant king of the Calvinists, or the God of the Philosophers. He is neither impassible, nor immovable. He can change his mind, just as his creatures can change theirs, as Christ changed his at Cana when he gave in to his mother and proceeded to turn the water into wine. He is, above all, a God who reveals himself, calling his children Home:

> 'God hides nothing. His very work from the beginning is *revelation* — a casting aside of veil after veil, a showing unto men of truth after truth. On and on, from fact to fact divine he advances, until at length in his son Jesus, he unveils his very face.'[33]

God reveals himself through his creation, but supremely through Christ, the obedient God.

MacDonald's important sermon in *Unspoken Sermons* (First Series), 'The Child in the Midst', expresses the linking of God, Christ and Man in the symbol of the Child. As children of God, we must become like children in order to inherit the Kingdom of Heaven. It is the heart of a child alone who can find faith, and when Jesus set a child in the midst of his disciples, he did so to reveal something very profound concerning the character of God:

> 'God is represented in Jesus, for that God is like Jesus: Jesus is represented in the child, for that Jesus is like the child. Therefore God is represented in the child, for that he is like the child. God is child-like. In the true vision of this fact lies the receiving of God in the child... Our Lord became flesh, but did not *become* man. He took on him the form of man: he was man already. He could never have been a child if he would ever have ceased to be a child, for in him the transient found nothing. Childhood belongs to the divine nature.'[34]

God is a child. Christ is a child. In the child is reflected something of the truth of the Godhead. This casts MacDonald's writing about children and his portrayal of them into a different light. Both Clare Skymer in *A*

Rough Shaking, and Diamond in *At the Back of the North Wind* become types of Christ, sufferers and redeemers, acting out God's plan in the world, helping bring his creation back to him.

Christ was more than just a cosmic symbol to MacDonald, however; he was a real person who ate and drank and walked the earth, and with whom MacDonald believed he had a relationship. Nowhere is this clearer than in *The Miracles of Our Lord*, which, though it portrays the first-century world as one of flowing robes, open-toed sandals and stained-glass piety, was an honest attempt by MacDonald to connect emotionally with his material, and bring the biblical characters to life for his audience. He elaborated the Bible stories, bringing in the impatience of Jairus, waiting for Christ to heal the woman with the issue of blood, while his own daughter lay at home dying, for example, and scrutinizing the sorrow of Martha and Mary weeping for their dead brother Lazarus. By projecting himself psychologically into these characters, MacDonald sometimes arrived at some surprising conclusions, such as that Lazarus was unwillingly dragged from the tomb to comfort his sisters in their unbelief, and that Christ wept, not with them out of mourning, but at them for their lack of faith:

> 'He would do his best for them — for the sisters — not for Lazarus! It was hard on Lazarus to be called back into the winding-sheet of the body, a sacrifice to their faithlessness, but it should be done. Lazarus should suffer for his sisters!'[35]

Christ's story was one of outward devotion to men and women, and inward devotion to his Father in Heaven. MacDonald believed that he was, in all points, a man:

> 'That he did not in this world know everything, is plain from his own words, and from signs as well: I should scorn to imagine that ignorance touching his Godhead could be hurt by what enhances his devotion. It enhances in my eyes the idea of his Godhead.'[36]

Christ's supernatural power was something that MacDonald did not doubt. He held firmly to the literal truth of the miracles, though he acknowledged that:

> 'Either the miracles are fact, or I lose — not my faith in this man — but certain outward signs of truth which these very signs have aided me to discover and understand and see in themselves.'[37]

MacDonald believed with John that the miracles were signs of God's power, but he insisted that Christ had no love of display, and that these actions were performed only for the benefit of the sick, hungry and frightened whom Jesus helped. The miracles in themselves were not an integral part of Christ's message.

MacDonald also reacted against viewing the miracles as violations of the natural laws governing the universe. Instead, he preferred to see these actions of Christ as evidences of a higher law of love. Perhaps the miracles appeared to many as violations of the natural order, but in fact they were not. Following F. W. Robertson's assertions,[38] MacDonald wrote that:

> 'We know so little of law that we cannot certainly say what would be an infringement of this or that law. That which at first sight appears as such, may be but the operating of a higher law which rightly dominates the other.'[39]

MacDonald continually insisted that the heart of Jesus was obedience. He had lived to keep laws, not break them, and MacDonald claimed that the miracles Christ performed were flashes of what the Father was busy doing all the time. God healed, though slowly — or drew water from the soil into grapes and caused wine to ferment, but slowly. Speeded up, the miracles revealed the nature of God, showing in an instant what would normally take God years to accomplish. The most important miracle of all, however, was the miracle of the empty tomb. Christ rose bodily and this truth is an assurance that there is a life to come. On this, MacDonald did not yield one inch:

> 'If Christ be risen, then is the grave of humanity itself empty. We have risen with him, and death has henceforth no dominion over us. Of every dead man and woman it may be said: He — she — is not here, but is risen and gone before us. Ever since the Lord lay down in the tomb, and behold it was but a couch whence he arose refreshed, we may say of every brother: He is not dead but sleepeth. He too is alive and shall arise from his sleep.'[40]

Sin and death were concepts that MacDonald had a hard struggle with. He followed Plato in thinking that evil was, to a large extent, a result of deprivation and not depravation. Man erred because he did not see the truth clearly, and to have a clear vision of God would mean that man would be so overwhelmed by his love, that all wrongdoing would be immediately set aside. Seeing right was the beginning of acting right, and Christ was the clearest picture of God given to humankind. There were certain doctrines concerning Christ that MacDonald repudiated strongly, notably the doctrine of penal substitution. This held that Christ was punished as a wrongdoer for the sins of the human race in order that God could reclaim the souls of the lost. MacDonald called it:

'...a mean, nauseous invention, false and productive of falsehood...It is the meagre, misshapen offspring of the legalism of a poverty-stricken mechanical fancy, unlighted by a gleam of the divine imagination.'[41]

MacDonald felt very deeply on this topic:

'Better the reformers had kept their belief in a purgatory, and parted with what is called vicarious sacrifice!'[42]

Instead MacDonald insisted that Christ had come to save people from their sins, and not from the punishment of their sins. The wrath of God was not the problem, but the disease of sin itself:

'Christ died to save us, not from suffering, but from ourselves; not from injustice, far less from justice, but from being unjust.'[43]

MacDonald's doctrine of man affirmed that the aim of Christianity was to enable a progressive Christ-ening to take place in order that God's idea of each man and woman should be finally realized:

'The truth of every man, I say, is the perfected Christ in him. As Christ is the blossom of humanity, so the blossom of every man is the Christ perfected in him. The vital force of humanity working in him is Christ; he is the root — the generator and perfecter of his individuality.'[44]

What stops this process from taking place is the Self, the evil shadow that destroys true perception, like the shadow in *Phantastes*, and sets man on the slippery slope down the moral evolutionary scale in the direction of the beasts.

MacDonald graphically illustrated this in *The Princess and Curdie* where Curdie is given the power by Princess Irene's great-great-grand-mother to feel the beast under the skin of everyone he touches. Some have hoofs or claws — one is a snake — while his own mother, under her rough hands, has the hands of a princess. The Self is the only true death and encourages the worship of Mammon. It deforms and twists, marring the image of God in man. The only way off this downward road is through obedience. For obedience is the most important response that a man or woman can make to God's love:

'...the highest creation of which man is capable is to will the will of the Father. That *has* an element of the purely creative, and then is man likest God.'[45]

If, however, a man or woman does *not* want to obey and conform to the will of the Father, then God, in his love, will send down his consuming fire to burn the evil out of them:[46]

> 'The wrath will consume what they *call* themselves; so that the selves God made shall appear, coming out with tenfold consciousness of being, and bringing with them all that made the blessedness of the life the men tried to lead without God. They will know that now first are they fully themselves.'[47]

Much of what appears as evil — suffering, illness, distress and misfortune — can, in fact, be shapes of good, sent to bring the sinner back to God:

> 'All pains, indeed, and all sorrows, all demons, yea, and all sins themselves, under the suffering care of the highest minister, are but the ministers of truth and righteousness.'[48]

MacDonald was stern on the subject of sin: 'All sin is unpardonable. There is no compromise to be made with it,'[49] but evil itself is a no-thing, a discord, which will eventually be brought into harmony with God when the whole of creation is reunited in him. Hell, for many Victorians, was the ultimate deterrent, and they worried as they saw the doctrine crumble, for without such a sanction, mere anarchy might be loosed upon the world. For MacDonald, however, the very worst of hells is not a place of punishment, but a place of purification:

> '. . . the outer darkness is the most dreadful form of the consuming fire — the fire without light — the darkness visible, the black. . . But at length, O God, wilt thou not cast Death and Hell into the lakes of fire — even into thine own consuming self? Death shall then die everlastingly . . .'[50]

MacDonald did believe that no one would be coerced into going to heaven, and held that a real repentance was necessary in order to gain entry there. In *Lilith*, Lilith lying in the House of Mara is entered by a worm that crawls out of the cottage fire and into her breast. At that moment the true state of her soul is revealed to her, and she begins to sweat and shudder. There begins a long and agonized struggle towards the point at which Lilith finally repents, and the land can flow with water once more. There was no other way forward. A person had to be scrubbed clean before they were fit to be admitted to God's presence:

> 'If they fail, and choose the evil, he will take yet harder measures with them. If at last it should prove possible for a created being to see good and evil as they are, and choose the evil, then, and only then, there

would, I presume, be nothing left for God but to set his foot upon him and crush him, as we crush a noxious insect. But God is deeper in us than our own life; yea, God's life is the very centre and creative cause of that life which we call *ours*; therefore is the life in us stronger than the Death, in as much as the creating Good is stronger than the created Evil.'[51]

MacDonald was open to the possibility that some people might see the good for what it was, and still choose the bad, but he did not really believe it.[52]

One consequence of MacDonald's doctrine of evil was that the border-line between this world and the next narrowed until it became almost invisible. The saving work begun in this life could be carried on in the next world, just as well as in this. Death, as Schiller said, could not be an evil as it was universal — on the contrary, it was a very big adventure: 'People talk about death as the gosling might about life before it chips its egg.'[53] In *Mary Marston*, when Tom Helmer dies, MacDonald commented:

'For my part, I think he was taken away to have a little more of that care and nursing, which neither his mother nor his wife had been woman enough to give the great baby.'[54]

MacDonald saw the boundary between life and death as simply dividing two different countries:

'For I suspect the next world will more plainly be a going on with this than most people think — only it will be much better for some, and much worse for others, as the Lord has taught us in the parable of the rich man and the beggar.'[55]

To be with God was bliss, but first one had to be made sinless. At the same time, heaven would be a grand reunion, where people, given new bodies out of the ruins of the old, would be recognizably themselves:[56]

'Do you not see that he is as continually restoring as taking away — that every bereavement is a restoration — that when you are weeping with void arms, others, who love as well as you, are clasping in ecstasy of reunion.'[57]

If God is Home, then, as pilgrims on their way Home, men and women can never find this world a natural resting-place:

'This world looks to us the natural and simple one, and so it is — absolutely fitted to our need and education. But there is that in us which is not at home in this world, which I believe holds secret relations with every star, or perhaps rather, with that in the heart of God whence issued every star, diverse in kind and character as in colour and place and motion and light. To that in us, this world is so far strange and unnatural and unfitting, and we need a yet homelier home. Yea, no home at last will do, but the home of God's heart.'[58]

For their passage through this world, MacDonald called on his readers to implement a humane Christianity in everyday life — a practical out-working of love and service. He did not approve of a fierce evangelism that attempted to frighten people into the Kingdom of God: 'To let their light shine, not to force on them their interpretations of God's designs, is the duty of Christians towards their fellows.'[59] He despised those who visited the poorer areas of the city with a loaf of bread in one hand and a bundle of tracts in the other, such as the 'combative Bible reader' who visits the enfeebled De Fleuri household in *Robert Falconer*. It was not doctrine that was needed, MacDonald complained, but doing good — for that was contagious, and would encourage others to do good, and so help them onto the road back to God.

With God himself, prayer could be as natural, even more natural, than talking to the person beside you. MacDonald cast off all set forms of prayer and long involved phrases, as was often the custom. So, when Clare Skymer in *A Rough Shaking* begins to pray, he does so naturally:

'And now he prayed the right kind of prayer; that is, his prayers were real prayers; he asked for what he wanted. To say prayers asking God for things we do not care about is to mock him.'[60]

Whether an answer was forthcoming or not, one thing MacDonald was convinced of was that God listens, though his response may not come in the form of the request:

'...but a God that would grant every request of every man or every company of men would be an evil God — that is no God, but a demon. That God should hang in the thought-atmosphere like a windmill, waiting till men enough should combine and send out prayer in sufficient force to turn his outspread arms, is an idea too absurd. God waits to be gracious, not to be tempted.'[61]

MacDonald did try to live as he believed. During much of his time in Manchester he exasperated his family by acting like one of the 'lilies of the field', believing that God would provide for him, and refusing to settle into any secure occupation. Once established at The Retreat, MacDonald's doors were thrown open to all kinds of people, to come and enjoy the family celebrations, or to stay awhile if need be. Greville MacDonald remembered:

'Anyhow, there was always someone to be taken in and befriended. One was an Oxford graduate, who came begging in rags and remained with us many weeks; but when at last my father found employment for his great abilities on the staff of a London newspaper, he decamped and was no more seen. Then another drunkard was adopted for reformation, and his fiancée was made welcome to help the cure. He married and had more than one child, I believe, before he succumbed to a shattered constitution.'[62]

MacDonald was also tireless in helping new and young authors, often petitioning the Royal Literary Fund on their behalf, and in addition giving out of the moth-eaten family purse all that he could to help others. Following the Bible maxim that the left hand must not know what the right is doing, much of his generosity remained hidden, and was only displayed in the imaginative entertainments laid on for the variety of people who came to their home — concerts, garden parties, and plays staged by Louisa.

There was always a mix of people at these gatherings at The Retreat, and, as a member of the Church of England, MacDonald remained in touch with both rich and poor. It must be said, however, that Vere Street gave him the company of the rich and aristocratic. His friend, the novelist Margaret Oliphant, moved during her lifetime from a background of Nonconformism to the rarified peak of the High Church, sending her sons to Eton to be educated. MacDonald never became such a firm member of the Establishment, though he did abjure the philistinism of the shop-keeping Dissenters, as did William Hale White. Both Mr Snale in Mark Rutherford's *Autobiography* and the Appleditches in *David Elginbrod* are recognizably the same type. They could easily be related, and both are treated with disgust and snobbery by writers who had suffered at the hands of that mentality in their younger days. MacDonald did not follow Mrs Gaskell and George Eliot in giving a sympathetic portrayal of Dissenters in his novels, not at least until he drew Walter Drake in *Thomas Wingfold, Curate* and even he had been hounded out of his church. All MacDonald's clergyman heroes were Anglicans, though in *Annals of a Quiet Neighbourhood* Walton establishes good relations with the local Dissenting Minister and this is portrayed as a wholesome ecumenical move.

In his own life, MacDonald continued to preach at and pack Dissenting Chapels, and occasionally even agreed to preach for the Unitarians, provided he was allowed to maintain his own doctrine of the Trinity. After he began to make money from his books, MacDonald never accepted any money for his preaching, but filled pulpits gladly and for free. People would flock to hear him, cramming the galleries and squeezing into the pews. When he ascended into the pulpit, a hush would fall on the assembled congregation. He never wore a gown or a dog collar, but would stand, with his beard flowing to his chest, like an Old Testament prophet, the diamond pin in his tie glinting as the sunlight fell through the glass windows of the church. Dramatically and arrestingly, he would begin to preach.

MacDonald's religion was tinged with both mysticism and magic. Mysticism involves knowing God intuitively through the senses without the need of words as a mediator.[63] And it involves the soul seeking a union with God — a union of substances in fact. Thomas Erskine of Linlathen used a picture of pools joining to illustrate this:

'The love of God which gave Christ, is the immense ocean of the water of life, and men's souls are ponds dug upon the shore, connected each of them, in virtue of Christ's work, with that ocean, by a sluice. Unbelief is the blocking up of that sluice; belief is the allowing the water to flow in, so that the pond becomes one with the ocean, and man becomes partaker of the divine nature, and has one life with the Father and the Son.'[64]

MacDonald believed in a union in which the individuality was retained, rather as Jacob Boehme had, whose flash of insight in the reflection of the sun from a bronze bowl caused him to see into the heart of all things. Such insight was what MacDonald thirsted for, and so he taught that Faerie is all around, if only people will open their eyes to see it:

'. . . I suspect we shall find some day that the loss of the human paradise consists chiefly in the closing of the human eyes; that at least far more of it than people think remains about us still, only we are so filled with foolish desires and evil cares, that we cannot see or hear, cannot even smell or taste the pleasant things round about us.'

There was also magic mixed in with the mystery. MacDonald was drawn to studying the New Testament Apocrypha, for example, translated by M. R. James, the famous ghost story writer, and in *The Vicar's Daughter* Marion Clare reads a portion of *The First Gospel of the Infancy of Jesus Christ* to her assembly. She does this merely to show how different it is from the authentic gospels, but nevertheless, it indulged MacDonald's taste for the esoteric. He read widely in the Kabbalah, and, like many of his friends, pored over Swedenborg. One of his friends from early days was Garth Wilkinson, the famous Swedenborgian doctor and homoeopath, who treated MacDonald on occasion, and gave him an introduction to the Leigh-Smiths when he and Louisa and Mary went to Algiers in 1856.[65] The Mount-Temples were also intrigued by Swedenborg, and MacDonald may well have attended the lecture given in London in 1848 on Swedenborg by Ralph Waldo Emerson, whose own pantheistic soul held some attraction for MacDonald. In *The Golden Key*, the so-called 'Old Men' whom Mossy and Tangle meet on their journey, grow ever younger, until the oldest man of all is no more than a baby. They are growing successively younger, because in growing older they are moving closer to the source of Life. This touch in the story is a direct reference to Swedenborg, who had declared that the angels were growing ever younger for just this reason. Angels and demons were no problem for MacDonald. He believed in them wholeheartedly as they were presented in the Bible, and at the same time he had more than a passing interest in Spiritualism.[66]

Magic and mystery — and the practice of love. In his own family life, MacDonald felt that his own fatherhood had to be a reflection of God's Fatherhood, and he looked back to his own father as someone who had taught him that, '...fatherhood is at the great world's core.'[67] He did have some problems with his own children, however. For one thing he failed to teach them properly. Though he thought that they should be more interested in Dido and Aeneas than in declensions, his lessons were never successful, and it was left to other adults to pick up the pieces. He was a strict disciplinarian but thawed more to his daughters than to his sons, as he far preferred little girls to little boys. Indeed, as MacDonald and Louisa dressed their children according to Pre-Raphaelite fashion, it could almost be said that they dressed their boys as girls — to their chagrin and torment, as Greville found out when he attended school. Yet MacDonald joined in his children's games and took part in their tableaux, and when questioned on spiritual matters he could be patient indeed. In reply to a question from Mary on love, he wrote a long letter from Dovedale where he was staying at that time:

'Love is the best thing; the love of God is the higher thing; we cannot *be* right until we love God, therefore we cannot *do* right — I mean thoroughly right — until we love God. But God knows this better than we do, and he is always teaching us to love him.'[68]

But for all his talk about love, MacDonald had been starved of physical affection as a boy, and it may have been that he found it difficult to be tender, especially with his sons. In a poignant passage in *Weighed and Wanting*, describing the gruff Mr Raymount, MacDonald may have been giving some insight into his own character:

'His father was always kind to him, but betwixt him and his boys he had let grow a sort of hard skin. He had not come so near to them as to the feminine portion of his family — shrank indeed from close relations with their spirits, thoughts, or intents. It arose, I imagine, from an excess of the masculine element in his nature. Even when as merest children they came to be kissed before going to bed, he did not like the contact of their faces with his.'[69]

Louisa, too, had failed in her role as romantic pupil during their courtship, by not understanding the books MacDonald had given her to read and then immediately succumbing to depression, but their marriage was a rock for both of them. Despite MacDonald's highflown romantic philosophy, he and Louisa were devoted to one another in an affectionate, commonsense way, rather than boiling with passion as Charles Kingsley and his wife Fanny. They shared one mind on most subjects, and Louisa never lost the feeling that she was lucky to have married George, and that her life had turned out more interesting than any of her sisters. Their clan of children was a delight, and never a distress. Both MacDonald and Louisa came from large families, and MacDonald had been brought up in a house where two families had lived as one. With their own children, they both felt cheated at having to stop at eleven. It was 'the wrong side of a dozen', and Louisa wrote cheerfully to MacDonald:

'I'm sure it doesn't matter about having so many children — after all, you can't do what you ought for two so you may as well have eleven or twelve for that matter.'[70]

Louisa was quite capable of calling MacDonald 'Our Head' or 'Our Master'[71] and he sat at the head of his family like a patriarch. Yet in many ways he was also liberal, even feminist. The Leigh-Smiths, whom he had met in Algiers, and remained in touch with, were among the most enlightened on the matter of women's rights for their day. Barbara Leigh-Smith and her friend, Bessie Parkes (also at Algiers), were allowed to travel round Europe unchaperoned, and when Barbara came of age, her father allowed her an independent income as if she were a boy.[72] She and Bessie Parkes campaigned for a change in the law regarding a woman's right to property, and 'the Ladies of Langham Place' formed a nucleus from which the later feminist cause sprang. Barbara Leigh-Smith also helped Emily Davies found Girton College in Cambridge.

MacDonald knew many such women, who were fighting to better the lot of their sisters, especially through his long connection with Bedford College, and he saw how many women were relegated to the hearth or to loveless marriages. He addressed himself to the question of the women's demands in *The Seaboard Parish*:

> 'And here I may remark in regard to one of the vexed questions of the day — the rights of women — that what women demand it is not for men to withhold. It is not their business to lay down the law for women. That women must lay down for themselves. I confess that, although I must herein seem to many of my readers old-fashioned and conservative, I should not like to see any woman I cared much for either in parliament or in an anatomical class-room; but on the other hand I feel that women must be left free to settle that matter. If it is not good, good women will find it out and recoil from it. If it is good, then God give them good speed. One thing they *have* a right to — a far wider and more valuable education than they have been in the way of receiving. When the mothers are well taught the generations will grow in knowledge at a four-fold rate.'[73]

He wrote this in 1868. By 1871 he had, as had F. D. Maurice, changed his mind on the suitability of a medical education for women. Perhaps meeting Elizabeth Garrett Anderson, the first woman doctor, through his friends, the Russell Gurneys, helped convince him. He signed a letter along with Florence Nightingale, James Balfour and Charles Darwin, and wrote to Louisa Stevenson, who was arranging the petition that:

> 'You are heartily at liberty to use my name as desired in connection with your efforts for rendering possible the medical education of women...'[74]

There was, however, a disparity between some of MacDonald's precepts and his practices. Though he advocated a better education for women, none of his own daughters attended any higher institute of learning, except Irene who was a pupil at the Slade School of Art. MacDonald's half-sister Louie was, at MacDonald's encouragement, a student at Bedford College for a time, but it seems that MacDonald needed his own daughters to help run the family enterprise. Equally, though he attacked the double standard and held up Jessie Hewson's illegitimate baby in *Robert Falconer* as a blessing from the Lord, in the same novel, Robert Falconer is outraged that Shargar hopes to marry Mysie Lindsay, whom he believes has fallen prey to Lord Rothie. This, in fact, is not the case, and the couple wed happily, but MacDonald unfortunately made himself out willing to save fallen women, provided they did not become part of the family.

One subject MacDonald said nothing on was women's suffrage. Probably he did not see the need for it. His association with Octavia Hill may even have prejudiced him against the question. With middle-class women having fewer children and more servants, there was time for them to devote themselves to good causes, and in addition, a surplus of women meant that there was an army of spinsters ready to be recruited for charitable work. Octavia Hill picked and trained her troops with care, and worried that political equality with men would see her workforce vanish into fruitless areas of political wrangling. The political ideas of women's equality stemmed from the Enlightenment through the writings of Mary Wollstonecraft, and in the nineteenth century were propagated largely by the Unitarians. MacDonald did not interest himself in political systems of any kind, and though he thought that women ought to be well-educated (if only to become better mothers), and reviled the marriage market, his view of woman remained fundamentally romantic. In *Mary Marston* Godfrey Wardour is blind because:

'He did not know that in a woman's love there is more of the specially divine element than in a man's — namely, the original, the unmeditated.'[75]

At the same time, MacDonald's Christianity asserted patriarchy and submission, even if it was mutual submission. His two women narrators, Ethelwyn Walton in *The Vicar's Daughter*, and Belorba Day in *The Flight of the Shadow*, see themselves only in relation to their menfolk, and voice the opinions held by their men. MacDonald commented in *The Vicar's Daughter*:

'...notwithstanding this, I venture the sweeping assertion that every woman is not as good as every man, and that it is not necessary to the dignity of a wife that she should assert even equality with her husband. Let *him* assert her equality or superiority if he will; but were it a fact, it would be a poor one for her to assert, seeing her glory is her husband. To seek the chief place is especially unfitting the marriage feast.'[76]

These lines should come as no surprise from a novelist whose tales celebrate courtly knights and their ladies, and whose theology emphasized complete submission to the divine will. To stand on one's rights could be no more than selfishness, almost an act of rebellion. It was through dying to one's desires that one gained the Kingdom of Heaven.

MacDonald also held woman in a kind of mystical awe, an erotic angel, mediating her influence through nature, who aroused man's senses and turned him back to God.[77] Yet the God she revealed was not only Father, but Mother, or rather Grandmother, that is, Grand Mother. Ordinary mothers receive short shrift in MacDonald's writings: Mrs Appleditch in

David Elginbrod, Mrs Worboise in *Guild Court*, Mrs Gordon in *Heather and Snow*, Mrs Cathcart in *Adela Cathcart*, Lady Cairnedge in *The Flight of the Shadow* and Lady Malice in *Mary Marston* are all unnatural, eaten through with ambition or twisted in some way. Of Lady Malice, MacDonald wrote: 'There is no language yet the word invented to fit the vileness of such mothers,'[78] and it is telling that Margaret Elginbrod receives her femininity, not from her mother, but from her father. MacDonald's devouring vampire-woman, exemplified above all in Lilith, the most unnatural of mothers, haunted him all his life. She was a devil he shrank from. The great-great-grandmother in *The Princess and the Goblin* and *The Princess and Curdie*, however, is a face of God, welcoming, loving and motherly. She baptizes Irene in a bath of stars, reveals herself at will, and guides the children where they need to go. Linked with the moon, she is the poetic, mystic, hidden face of God — a motherly nurse and not a power-wielding triumphant king. She is the left hand, as the Father is the right. In *Adela Cathcart*, MacDonald called God 'Him who is Father and Mother both in one' and 'father and mother and home.'[79] Picturing God as mother stemmed back to the Elginbrod epitaph, for generally mothers are seen as being kinder to their children (representing grace) than their well-principled fathers (representing law). Mrs Falconer, praying for her son whom she now believes to be in Hell, pleads with God:

> 'O Lord! I *canna* say thy will be done. But dinna lay't to my chairge; for gin ye was a mother yersel, ye wadna pit him there.'[80]

Robert Falconer is a novel about a quest for a father, but the God revealed throughout the book is the motherly God whom Mrs Falconer's Calvinist conscience cannot accept exists. Many of MacDonald's stories are such quests, and Fatherhood was an important concept for Mac-Donald, but the Prodigal Son's father with his arms outstretched, and the great-great-grandmother, are twin faces of the same loving God Mac-Donald wants his readers to believe in. This God's kingdom rule was primarily over the individual, and so MacDonald did not worry too much about the larger political questions of his time. He stood in the tradition of Christian Socialism along with Maurice and Kingsley,[81] but was probably at heart the kind of aristocratic old Tory that Ruskin was. He certainly believed in bettering the lot of ordinary people, and hoped that the quality of their lives would be transformed, but he did not link this into any political transformation such as the Webbs or Karl Marx sought. Any political thoughts he had were directed towards charitable work. MacDonald hated the charity organizations which made people dependent on their handouts. Such pauperization was demeaning. He believed in freedom and that meant people becoming responsible for themselves, and being educated to take control over their own lives. His blueprint for work among the poor is to be found in *Robert Falconer* where:

> 'By degrees, without any laws or regulations, a little company was gathered, not of ladies and gentlemen, but of men and women, who aided each other, and without once meeting as a whole, laboured no the less as one body in the work of the Lord, bound in one by bonds that had nothing to do with cobweb committee meetings or public dinners, chairmen or wineflushed subscriptions. They worked like the leaven of which the Lord spoke.'[82]

The Lord spoke to individuals. These individuals worked with other individuals, and this was how the Kingdom of Heaven was brought about on earth. MacDonald's vision of a society without greed or selfishness or ambition is described in 'A Shop in Heaven' in *Thomas Wingfold, Curate*, where everyone takes what they want and gives freely in return, bartering their goods and gifts. It is a spiritualized version of the doomed New Harmony Community which Robert Owen set up in America, but MacDonald was careful to build his shops in heaven and not on earth.

On the larger political issues, MacDonald remained silent, at least in print, though he favoured the reinvasion of Ireland when trouble flared up there in the 1880s. He felt, however, that politics was outside the sphere of the church. In 1893 he wrote to his cousin James at The Farm in a somewhat irritated tone:

> 'I too have been for some time greatly dissatisfied with the Congregationalists, as they seem to be trying more and more to save the world from the outside by politics, and not by the rule of the Kingdom in the individual heart.[83]

By this time, Maurice's type of Christian Socialism had become a thing of the past, and a new, aggressive, secular Socialism had come to the fore. MacDonald, for his part, turned from outward to inward rule. If he flinched at political movements gaining strength which dislodged his hopes for a Utopian Christianity, his evergreen message remained that society should be composed of men and women loving God and doing good to their neighbour, responding to their inward light and obeying Christ's teaching, and seeking always to move nearer the source of Life, to God, our Father and Mother, who is our Home.

CHAPTER TWENTY-FIVE
The Retreat

Moving to The Retreat meant that the MacDonalds had at last found a house big enough for them all to fit into. For meals, with the scramble of eleven children, Louisa simply set out a table of cold meats and cheeses on the first floor, and members of the family could cut and come as they liked. There was only one servant, parked in the cavernous cellars under the street level, and these were too damp to be inhabited.

It was often foggy by the river, and as the level of the water would drop to reveal thick, foul-smelling black mud, the MacDonalds continued to worry about their health. In addition to that, the autumn leaves in the garden swirled and dampened into a swamp so that the family kept themselves dry on the upper floors of the house, spending their evenings by gaslight.

Visitors came in abundance, and none more so than on Oxford/Cambridge boat race days, when the children would act as servants and lay out tea on the lawn for the guests. There was a colourful mixture of East End accents and Pre-Raphaelite poise, with the occasional canon or dean stirred in, at these events. The Russell Gurneys, Cowper-Temples, Burne-Joneses, Arthur Hughses, and many others, all came to enjoy the day out. Whatever the food was like, there was no doubt that the main attraction of the day was the play — even more so than the race:

'The coachhouse was converted into a theatre with a gas-lit stage, and the loose boxes served as green-room — though a cow for a time had lived in one and supplied the family with milk, daily drawn and watered by the gardener, whose eyes were so blue that the honest cow got all the blame for the milk's poverty, and he was forgiven. There we acted our plays; and friends came from afar, if only to see Lilia Scott MacDonald play Lady Macbeth to her father in the title rôle. She was in close friendship with Kate Terry, the first and greatest of that gifted family, but who had left the stage and become Mrs Arthur Lewis in, I think, 1868.[1] Phelps, the tragedian, came once, and was so profoundly impressed that he talked to my father of her gift as marvellous and

264

vowed to one of us not many years ago, "If your sister had gone on the stage, *So-and-so* would have had no career."[2]

The first of all these entertainments, with its performance of *Beauty and the Beast*, was so chaotic, that poor Ruskin went home without having had anything proper to eat. MacDonald wrote apologetically to him afterwards:

> 'My wife and I are troubled in our minds that in our anxiety to entertain the poor people, we neglected to make proper provision for our other guests. I believe you went home half dead with unfed fatigue. It was our first attempt, and we shall do better next time, I hope. We ought to have had one room in the house provided with refreshments, but everything was sacrificed to the one end, which I hope was at least partially gained...'[3]

As the children grew more proficient in music, they would travel out to perform for Octavia Hill's tenants in a decorated entertainment room, converted out of a basement in Barrett's Court. Here the children would act or sing. Grace would play Beethoven on her piano, and Greville would scratch on his violin. Their speciality was Carols at Christmas time, punctuated by MacDonald's dramatic renderings of specially composed nativity verses.

Though Lilia was generally the star of the show, and charming as an amateur actress, her parents would have thrown up their hands in horror at the thought of her going on the stage. She did harbour dreams of treading the boards, and possessed a well-thumbed collection of actors' and actresses' portraits. MacDonald and Louisa had been warned off a theatrical career for their daughter, however, by the American actress, Miss Cushman,[4] whom they had met at Bude in 1867, and Kate Lewis too had hinted darkly at immorality behind the painted scenes. So Lilia was restricted to playing opposite her father, as she was restricted in so many ways. Despite her talent, which was so often remarked on, she never rose above playing the role of Christiana in *Pilgrim's Progress*, and her other interests, too, had scarcely room to breathe. She was forced by circumstances to be a second mother to her large family, as well as to be a good hostess to all the guests who came to stay. In the spare time she had, she wrote down stories of her own in a big book, but these never saw the light of day, and, a voracious reader, she knew most of Shakespeare intimately by the time she was eleven. A few years later, when she pined to be more useful, and go and help Octavia Hill with her social work, she realized all too quickly that her first duty was to her parents, who relied on her too heavily to let her go. Yet she rarely complained, and suffered all Louisa's cajoling patiently and submissively. If she had been a boy, however, there is little doubt that she would have probably gone to either Oxford or Cambridge and made a career for herself.

That autumn the family scattered to various places. Lilia was unwell in October and November and went down to Hastings with Mary and Irene for a healing breath of sea-air. Louisa stayed at The Retreat with the younger children, while MacDonald, after an earlier visit in April to Mrs Scott's at Manchester, sortied out to lecture once again, this time in Nottingham, Lancaster and Liverpool, where he stayed with Helen and Alex Powell. Without Louisa he grew reflective, and sad thoughts flitted through his brain:

> 'I feel very lonely without you tonight. I saw you, or at least something white for some time after you could not see me. It was like death, for gradually the mouth of the tunnel grew small, and then the smoke by degrees filled it to the very bottom and then it grew quite dark.'[5]

Perhaps MacDonald was more sunk into himself than usual, as revising *Robert Falconer* had taken its toll, forcing him to consider the moral and social issues all around him in London that cried out for some answer. He felt helpless to effect any serious change, and at the same time was aware that a writer's life was basically a selfish one. He wrote to Louisa:

> 'I have been anxious — for the first time in my life about the future of our country, and the kind of days on which our children will fall; but it is only for moral considerations. I feel I must do something for it and them for my poor part. . .'[6]

At the same time he was still perplexed about his rôle. Even with half a dozen novels under his belt, plus all his short stories, fairy stories and poetry, MacDonald was unsure as to where his true talents lay:

> '. . .for I don't know yet what especially God made me for. I have done very little if anything that is first rate and feel as if I could do a good many things I have not tried yet. . .'[7]

Whatever the case, *Robert Falconer* was fairly well received as a novel, and its dangerously unorthodox sentiments caused ripples of alarm in sound evangelical households. Louisa joined her daughters at Hastings in November and stayed with them at White Rock Place. Walking into a shop, she found herself the centre of a controversy:

> 'I went into Diplock's to get some pens just now and he called me into the corner of his room and asked me if it was true that you absolutely denied eternal punishment and the Incarnation of Christ in *Robert Falconer*. He said he had all your other books in his library but a lady

had come to him in great distress begging him not to say that because of those two things you utterly denied — He has sold a good many *Unspoken Sermons* — I told him I did not think he would find anything worse in *R.F.* than in those sermons.'[8]

These words must have come as some crumbs of comfort to MacDonald in his uncertainty. When his temper turned, however, he could be fearsome indeed, and soul-searching gave way to searing temper:

'I had to — baby this evening. He is a stubborn little fellow. I sent him home with his hands tied behind him with a flannel. He is so often troublesome. Irene had a bad time of it something I fear with him and the bigger boys; but we shall soon get things right now.'[9]

On another occasion he threw some flowers one son had picked for his mother onto the fire to punish him for being naughty. Despite all his preachings against the glowering Calvinist God, MacDonald could sometimes appear like one himself.

That December the family gathered for Christmas, as usual, and then almost immediately MacDonald started out on his most strenuous lecture tour to date. He was to travel round Scotland, speaking at twenty-eight different places in five weeks. It was a hard task, especially at the time of year when his lungs were at their most vulnerable to attack. Sure enough, an hour's train journey out of Glasgow, on 6 January, he saw a streak of red on his handkerchief, and problems followed with bronchitis and asthma. Despite these setbacks, MacDonald was still able to address 1,200 people at Dunfermline on 12 January, but to be on the safe side, Louisa joined him at Dumfries on 17 January and helped nurse him through the rest of the trip.

No sooner was MacDonald home, than he set off again on another round of lectures — this time from Birmingham, and moving on to Ilkley, Bradford and Hull. While he was at Ilkley, he underwent a course of treatment for his troublesome eczema, at the Ilkley Hydropathic, but to no avail. Besides, he hardly lived the life of an invalid there, writing, visiting, and preaching to anyone who would have him. He continued to stretch his health to its limit, and while Greville was suffering dolefully from mumps, MacDonald had another ten days in bed with congestion of the lungs. He needed another rest from 'children and bricks and omnibuses' and planned to go with Louisa to Switzerland during the summer, when an invitation came from John Stevenson, a Glasgow merchant, to join him on his yacht *The Blue Bell* and sail to Norway. It had always been one of MacDonald's ambitions to go to sea, and the thought of the smell of salt in his nostrils excited him. In June 1869 therefore, Lilia and Grace travelled up to Glasgow, to stay with the Campbells at Tullicheiven

Castle in Dumbartonshire, and MacDonald joined them for a few days on his way to the boat. It was a sumptuous yacht of 120 tons, schooner-rigged, with a crew of twelve besides a steward and a cook. The party comprised of the Rev. Dr Buchanan of Glasgow, the Rev. Laughton, and the Rev. W. Ker, all hale and hearty Scotsmen with a good sense of humour. They met on 10 June at Weymss Bay, and took the steamer to Largs where they boarded ship and weighed anchor at noon. MacDonald took to his new companions, and to the freedom of the boat, and a slight twinge of pain from his knee could do nothing to dull his spirits:

> 'While we sat at breakfast, we got under way, and so smooth was it that we could tell by no motion that we had moved a yard.'[10]

Unfortunately, MacDonald had a shivering-fit that night, a sure sign that something was wrong, and his knee began to swell uncomfortably. With each passing hour it grew more and more painful until he was in agony. When the boat docked at Lerwick, a doctor was brought on board who prescribed poultices and administered leeches to bring some relief.[11] Confined to his bed, without window or porthole, there was nothing MacDonald could do except write letters and listen to the creaks and bumps of the ship as it moved through the water. There was nothing to read, 'but that awful *Vanity Fair.*' Unable to move his leg for the pain, MacDonald was given a cabin with a skylight on 15 June, but lingered alone, in a twilight world, fortified only by Liebig's beef tea. Every day his knee grew worse. On the 21st, approaching Oslo, MacDonald wrote:

> '. . . It was a week last night since I took to bed and have seen neither sea nor sky since. Sometimes I have thought I *must* come home to you — but it would be an awful undertaking, with a leg which I can't draw up in bed, and no one to take care of me. . . If I only were on the way home to you! It seems likely Mr Stevenson will bring the yacht up the Thames — up to London — and then you can come and take me home — and that will be joyful. . .'[12]

MacDonald had to forego the pleasure of glimpsing the midnight sun or a single aurora. His only illumination was the blue that poured through the skylight above his head as he lay in the cabin. At Trondheim, a serious Norwegian doctor probed the knee, and recommended wine and nourishing food. There was an alarming abscess, and a large basinful of matter was collected after it was lanced. By chance, a steamer, *The Norway*, was due to set sail for the Tyne, and MacDonald decided to return with her to England. The skylight of his cabin was removed, and he was hoisted up through it and carried to a stateroom aboard the steamer. On arriving at Newcastle, he wrote to Louisa from the Station Hotel there:

'Oh, I have gone through some of the folds of the shadow of death since I saw you, but the light has never ceased to shine...'[13]

It had been three weeks since he had left home.

Alex Stevenson fetched a wheelchair, and rushed to MacDonald's side, refusing to allow him to pay a single penny for any travel arrangements. At King's Cross the following day, Louisa was waiting anxiously on the station platform, and her heart leapt into her mouth at the sight of the shrunken figure propped up with pillows in a wheelchair, his voice barely more than a croak. When Greville saw his father being carried up to his bedroom he thought that he was dead. But though MacDonald may have hankered after the next world, his grip on this life was tenacious, and soon he was hobbling round the garden on crutches and working once more translating his beloved Novalis. He was sent off to Derbyshire to recover fully, and when he was back on his feet, work continued to pour in.

Strahan offered MacDonald the editorship of *Good Words for the Young* at a salary of £600 a year, and MacDonald snapped it up. *At the Back of the North Wind* had just finished a serial run in the magazine from November 1868 to October 1869. It was a quality monthly, with contributions from the Howitts, Henry Kingsley and W.S. Gilbert (of Gilbert and Sullivan fame). Full of poems, stories and adventures, it was lavishly illustrated with atmospheric line drawings by Hughes and others, and in it MacDonald found a niche for the kind of writing he had had to bury away after the failure of *Phantastes*. After *At the Back of the North Wind*, *Ranald Bannerman's Boyhood* ran from November 1869 to October 1870, with *The Princess and the Goblin* following swift on its heels from November 1870 to June 1871. As was so often the case, MacDonald was bewildered by the quality of what he was writing:

'I know it is as good work of the kind as I can do and I think will be the most complete thing I have done. However I shall drop that sort if people do not care for it. Perhaps I could find a market for that kind of talent in America — I shouldn't wonder.'[14]

Good Words for the Young began well, but then numbers slumped and Strahan became worried:

'I have had a bit of bad news. The Magazine, which went up in the beginning of the volume, has fallen very much since. Strahan thinks it is because there is too much of what he calls the fairy element.'[15]

MacDonald continued editing the magazine for a third and fourth year, in 1871 and 1872, but he finally relinquished command and the publication changed its name to *Good Things*.[16]

In January 1870 MacDonald and Louisa paid their first visit to Broadlands which the Cowpers (now Cowper-Temples) had recently acquired. It was to be the first of many stays there, a splendid mansion set by a lake from which one could see the Isle of Wight on a clear day. The family was also spending more time down by the coast at Hastings — in Caroline House in April, moving to Reculver Cottages in May, and then returning in July to stay at Montpellier. That April, MacDonald's aunts from Australia paid a visit to London, the sisters of MacIntosh MacKay. MacDonald thought that he was by now far too High Church for them to accept his offer of accommodation, and so he was proved right. His regard for his uncle, however, had never diminished, even though the keen-minded Gaelic scholar had found his nephew's ventures into literature rather disagreeable, and close to blasphemy. Aided by Matthew Arnold, MacDonald spent some of 1871 trying to secure a Civil List pension for MacKay, but the old man died before the scheme could come to anything.

In April 1870, old Mr Powell began to fail. He had still ridden horseback at eighty-six, as full of energy as ever, but finally he lay bedridden, waiting to join his wife who had departed so many years before. He was aged ninety. Louisa sat by his bedside, waiting, and reported to Lilia:

> 'I saw Grandpapa last night — I don't know whether he knew me but I was alone with him for quite half an hour. Mary and Papa both saw him too and the doctor thought he would live a day or two longer.'[17]

It was not to be, however. Ann, who was tending her father's bedside, called Carrie, while she went to make a cup of tea, and as Carrie sat down beside him, he gave two gentle sighs and breathed no more.

It seemed that Mr Powell had hardly been laid to rest when Alex Powell fell seriously ill. Helen watched her husband patiently in Liverpool. He was operated on, but there was never much hope, and he died in September 1870. MacDonald travelled up to Liverpool, to the funeral, and comforted Helen, who later sent him some of her husband's things:

> 'Though our much-loved friend has vanished over the hill, we are walking up the same path after him. It is only in God that any two can really meet and be one. When he dwells in us, and we in him, there can be no more separation. Death will then be powerless over us.'[18]

The only bright spot in these gloomy months was that Louisa finally found her way into print. Her *Chamber Dramas for Children* was published by Strahan with a frontispiece by Arthur Hughes, and contained most of the pieces she had adapted for the family theatricals.

In January 1871 the family abandoned The Retreat entirely, leaving it to the mice and the spiders, and nestled for the winter at Hastings. The year had opened with the sudden and shocking news of the death of the sculptor Munro: he had been plagued by bad lungs for many years, and had finally been forced to exile himself in Cannes for most of each year, where he had built himself a house and a studio. He was slightly younger than MacDonald, and after the agony of *The Blue Bell*, MacDonald must have felt still fragile, at least in body.

In May the MacDonalds found a more permanent fixture in Hastings when they rented Halloway House, a narrow red-brick house on the Old London Road, scarce seeming large enough for the whole family. The study was papered, painted and decorated with stars by the girls, and from now on began a division of time between London and Hastings as there were increasing doubts as to the wisdom of living so damply near the Thames. A box and two hampers arrived, along with a sofa, ottoman, trestles and table — all dredged out of The Retreat to furnish the new home. It poured all day. Sometimes Louisa would cream off some of the children and take them down to the sea-side, leaving MacDonald more peace and time to write in London:

> 'I have been hard at work all day, and only for the last little while able to work with comfort. It was a great pull in the morning, for I was still very tired and uncomfortable. I almost fear going for the joining — it knocks me up so, but I daresay if I don't work my way, it won't hurt me much.'[19]

MacDonald was lucky with the arrival of William Carey Davies, who acted as his secretary, keeping the family accounts straight, and proof-reading for him, especially the troublesome manuscripts that had to be turned from magazine serials into three-volume novels. He became the family's unsung hero.

That summer, MacDonald's *Works of Fancy and Imagination* came out in ten small volumes, summing up all the poetry, fairy stories and short stories he had published thus far, including *Phantastes* and *The Portent*.

That autumn, George and Louisa managed another trip abroad. After their original plan to go to the passion play at Oberammergau fell through, they spent some time in Holland instead, taking Lilia with them, and travelling with their artist friend George Reid. They were introduced to Joseph Israels in Amsterdam, who gave MacDonald a sketch entitled *Farewell!* showing a woman with a baby in her arms looking out to sea at a distant fishing boat.[20]

Letters continued to flow in to The Retreat — some abusive, some desperate. Often they were from young ladies who complained of being 'misunderstood'. MacDonald answered these patiently, but paid especially careful attention to young poets who sought his help, and spent time giving detailed replies to their entreaties.

January 1872 saw the family ensconced at Halloway House in Hastings once again, where Lilia resolved to sit upright for a whole year in the hope that it might become a habit. The family's musical tastes were enhanced by an evening out at a recital given by Madame Schumann in February, whose extraordinary piano playing was by then a legend.

But April was the cruellest month, however, bringing an ashenfaced Strahan to their door at Hastings on 1 April to announce the death of F.D. Maurice. Maurice had been ill for several weeks, and the end had not been unexpected, but the news was, nevertheless, shaking. Young Maurice's godfather, such an old friend, was finally gone. In his last years, Maurice had resigned from Vere Street, owing to ill health, and had become chaplain at St. Edward's Church, Cambridge. Reviled so often in life, he was almost sainted at the point of death, and received glowing obituaries. MacDonald attended the funeral, where the congregation joined in singing Maurice's favourite hymn, *Abide with me*. MacDonald, for one, was sure that he would see his friend again.

The family acted at Edgbaston in the spring, charming the old ladies who had gathered to watch them, and raising £42 for a convalescent home. Then, in May, with the editorship of *Good Words for the Young* off his hands, MacDonald took a train north with Maurice, his favourite son, to Huntly and Cullen, to begin work on another Scottish novel. This one was to be set by the sea. The proofs of *The Vicar's Daughter* still needed correcting, and they weighed heavily on MacDonald. He finished them hurriedly on the train.[21] He and Maurice stayed at The Farm, and drove out to Cullen where they stayed at the Seafield Arms Hotel. MacDonald questioned the local inhabitants, and tried to soak up the ambience and history of the little village. One day they visited Dunottar Castle, which MacDonald thought looked much like Tintagel. It was huge, and looked gaunt and gloomy, wreathed in storm cloud.

MacDonald and Maurice returned to London via Liverpool and Leicester in time to help give a performance of *Blue Beard* and a garden party for Octavia Hill's tenants. It was now May, but April had brought a pressing concern before MacDonald, a letter from someone MacDonald had not heard from for a long time — a young lady who most certainly did feel misunderstood, and whose troubled spirits were more than she could bear. Rose La Touche was about to open a fresh chapter in all their lives.

CHAPTER TWENTY-SIX
St George and the Rose

The tangle of Ruskin's relationship with Rose La Touche had been growing steadily worse, and he was bitter against Maria La Touche — whom he described as 'a horror of iniquity' — and against God:

'As far as I can see or have known anything of the Deity, He makes noble and beneficent laws, which if one keeps — it is fairly probable — not by any means certain — that one won't come to any terrific mischief, — but if one doesn't — there's but one word for you. Fire is on the whole pleasantly warm — If you choose to burn your fingers in it — and then go to God for "comfort" He only laughs at you and says "What did you do it for? I told you you had better not." . . . Now — if it were possible for me to go to my Father in a direct personal way (which it is not) the very first thing I should say to him would be — "What have you been teasing me like this for? — Were there *no* toys in the cupboard, you could have shown me, — but the one I can't have?"'[1]

The last is a grim reference to his mother's habit of rationing his toys when he was young. He felt that God had dangled Rose in front of him as a promise of salvation, and then snatched her away — now he was Tantalus and Prometheus bound in one — and it was religion that separated them. John La Touche's Calvinism, Maria La Touche's evangelicalism, and Rose's own fastidious blend of social conscience and biblical intensity had cut him off and left him in outer darkness. Adding insult to injury, Percy La Touche, Rose's brother, became engaged for a short time to Ruskin's cousin, Joan Agnew, only to break off the relationship soon afterwards.[2] Ruskin saw the hand of Maria La Touche in this affair, and became even more virulent about her. Percy was only a young, scatter-brained sportsman, however, and his mother had her own problems in handling him. Distressed at Ruskin's attitude, Maria La Touche wrote to Georgina Cowper:

'She knows that I *never* thought my boy worthy of her, and *he* knows how bitterly ashamed of him I have been, and how grieved, both at what he did and at the way he did it. All I ever said or wrote to Joan was said and written in sincerest affection.'[3]

Events took a turn for the worse in 1868, when Ruskin and Joan Agnew sailed over to Dublin, where Ruskin was to lecture on *The Mystery of Life and Its Arts*. He was eager to see Rose, but on arrival found a note from her waiting for him declaring: 'I am forbidden by my father and mother, to write to you or receive a letter.' As a small consolation, she had included two rose leaves as symbols of her continuing affection for him. The La Touches had become increasingly worried that the influences of Rose's friends, such as the Cowpers and the MacDonalds, might sway the young girl towards Ruskin and away from them. There was a rift in the air. Ruskin had already written a dark and troubled letter to MacDonald in March:

'Will you pardon my asking you what are your relations with Mrs La Touche — and if they are beneficial to you — or could without much loss, be broken off?. . . Be that as it may; the conditions between Miss La Touche and me have now reached nearly to the darkness of the story of the Bride of Lammermuir — the mother got her, after she had stayed staunch and true for these last two years — at last into her power, through, as far as I can trace, the influence of an evangelical friend on Rose: — and the child gave me up — the mother wrote lie after lie about her for some time after that to my cousin — but at last, in the vilest and cruellest way, abandoned my cousin also — and I know from other sources that Rose is suffering, and I cannot reach her.'[4]

This letter put MacDonald into a quandary, for how could he be asked to choose between two friends close enough to be considered as godparents for his children? Before he could possibly support Ruskin in his suit for Rose, there were several issues he was anxious to have clear in his own mind first of all. MacDonald put his questions to Ruskin in private, though he later passed on some of the details of their conversation to Greville:

'My father, moreover, before he would be party to the courtship of Rose La Touche in opposition to her parents' approval, put certain questions concerning his early marriage; and he told me all the particulars.
   "Was it true you were incapable?" my father asked pointblank. Ruskin laughed merrily and denied it unconditionally.

"Then why," pursued my father, "did you not defend yourself?"

"Do you think, if she wanted to be rid of me, I would put any obstacle in her way? I never loved Euphie before I married her; but I hoped I might and ought to, if only for her beauty." Then he proceeded to explain his deplorable foolishness; how over-persuaded by his parents, he proposed to a girl whom he only admired. Curiously ignorant, he presumed that the necessary love would follow the marriage, as he had been assured it would."[5]

Ruskin made a similar confession to his friend, George Allen, and certainly, the story passed down the MacDonald family was that Ruskin was an innocent, who had had charges trumped up against him.

Convinced by his friend's protestations, MacDonald took Ruskin's part, and laid aside his warm friendship with Maria La Touche, with a certain amount of pain on both sides. The root of MacDonald's conviction must have been strong, for in anyone's eyes it would have been a strange match — the middle-aged bachelor and the young unpredictable girl. Such marriages were not uncommon in the Victorian era — older men often married younger women — but they were not favoured in literature as MacDonald's own description of Hesper and Lord Redmain's marriage in *Mary Marston* bears witness. Perhaps images of romantic lovers floated through MacDonald's mind — Romeo and Juliet, Dante and Beatrice — or Novalis and the short-lived Sophie Von Kühn. It was true that Ruskin was a kindly man, even a great one, and that Rose showed flashes of affection towards him in turn. But it was equally true that both of them were disturbed to a degree that would probably have rendered marriage impossible, even if all the daunting obstacles had been overcome and Rose's parents had given way. The indelible shadow on Ruskin's character was, however, the scandal of his marriage to Effie. He had, after all, been proved impotent in public, and even though he protested otherwise to MacDonald, his sexual capabilities must remain in doubt. He had never laid a finger on any woman in his life, and unlike many Victorian men, had not sought solace in the arms of the prostitutes who thronged London at that period. The only sexual activity that had tortured Ruskin's delicate conscience was guilt over masturbation — something he confessed to Georgina Cowper-Temple — but hardly proof of his ability to have sexual intercourse.

The curtains closed further when, in 1868, Maria La Touche consulted a solicitor over Ruskin's affairs. Unfortunately she was wrongly advised, as she was told that if Ruskin were to marry again and father children, this would void the divorce decree. His second marriage would be illegal therefore, as he would still be technically married to Effie, and all his ensuing children would be illegitimate. Ruskin's own solicitor, however, confirmed that it would be impossible to impeach the decree, and told Ruskin on 21 July 1871 that, 'For all practical purposes, you are free to marry again,' and William Cowper-Temple was of the same mind.

Maria La Touche finally wrote to Effie Millais to ask her about Ruskin's true capabilities, and received an expected answer. Effie had fought hard to regain respectability, and did not want her character thrown into doubt if Ruskin successfully remarried and produced children. At the same time, she *had* suffered, and told Maria La Touche in no uncertain terms that Ruskin was only capable of extending sympathy to women through art, and that he was quite incapable of making any woman happy. Her final toll of the bell was, ominously, 'He is quite unnatural.'

Maria La Touche decided to end the relationship between Rose and Ruskin for ever, then and there, and it is not surprising that a mother should wish to protect her impressionable daughter from the advances of an impotent, middle-aged man. Family life had been further shaken in the La Touche household with the death of Emily on 1 June 1868, returning home from Mauritius with her husband Bernard Ward, the fourth son of Lord Bangor, whom she had married in 1865, and her young child. Now Rose was a solitary girl, and the sole object of her mother's attentions. She was shown Effie's letter and was severely shaken by it, though she maintained strongly that Ruskin's influence over her had never been a harmful one. In despair, Ruskin wrote to Georgina Cowper: 'You know, without doubt, by this time that all is over — and perhaps you will not read this note.'6

Wounded and battered, Ruskin wandered abroad, restless and haunted by the 'paradisical walks with Rosie' which he could not shake out of his mind. Rose, for her part, was squeezed between her parents and Ruskin, with no one else to turn to. Isolated in Ireland, she had no friends or companions to call her own, and her mother soon forced her to sever her correspondence with Georgina Cowper and Joan Agnew, who had continued writing to her. But more than that, she herself was disturbed, and her mental state divided her in two.

Once Lily Armstrong, a friend of Ruskin's, went to visit Rose in a nursing home where she was recovering from one of her mysterious illnesses, and was horrified to find her strapped to the bed. In a way, it was the story of *Alice* gone wrong. Like Dodgson, Ruskin had many friendships with little girls, and spent much time at Winnington Hall, a school for girls, where he would retreat to give occasional lessons. As for Dodgson, young girls represented to Ruskin a kind of Eden, a purity, a freedom, which was somehow liberating from the straitjacket of normal adult intercourse. He was determined to worship his image of the child in Rose. She was a saint, 'though a cruel one', and Rose somehow took upon herself this image, starving herself and veering towards anorexia, perhaps in an attempt to deny her own femininity, and remain in the form of a quaint, fairy child. She seemed petrified at the thought of sexual love.

Locked together, they could be neither together, nor apart, and the cycle of misery began once more when Ruskin met Rose by accident at the Royal Academy on 7 January 1870. At first she tried to break away from him to look at the pictures, but then she remained to talk to him. He offered her the letter of engagement she had given him, which he kept between golden plates next to his breast, but she refused it, not understanding what he wanted. That March, before he was due to go off to Italy and Switzerland on another expedition, she wrote to him, 'I love you — still and always' and he informed MacDonald from Denmark Hill:

'You have every right to know that the great darkness has ended for me. R. has come back to me — and nothing now can take her from me — in heart — though if fate will have it so I may never see her — but she is mine — now. No one must know this however — as it would cause her infinite grief and pain with her people — but she is in peace now — and I also — which is much. It is all too late — all vain and full of shadows. But not full of *bitterness* any more. . .'[7]

Despite this emotional battering, Ruskin continued productive in other areas of his life. He sat on numerous committees dealing with social issues such as unemployment, trades unions and strikes. He pursued a couple of hare-brained schemes, opening at one point *Mr Ruskin's Tea-Shop* in London which came to nothing, but more importantly he was appointed Slade Professor of Art in Oxford in 1869 and this gave him an important platform from which to voice his opinions. Then in 1871 he began *Fors Clavigera* (which lasted until 1884), and was a series of monthly letters to working men, while in that same year he sank his utopian hopes into the founding of the Guild of St George. Finally his mother died, also in 1871, and the old family home was broken up.

Rose herself remained in melancholy exile in Ireland, publishing a little volume of verses in 1870 entitled *Clouds and Night*:

'I, in those years have learned that life is sad.
Sad to heart-breaking did we walk alone.
I, who have lost much which I never had,

Yet which in ignorance I held mine own,
Would leave that clouded past, its good and bad,
Within his hands to whom all things are known.'[8]

Ruskin had continued his desperate pleas to MacDonald, as he felt that one by one his friends had fallen away, until only MacDonald and the Cowpers remained faithful. On 14 March 1870 he wrote to MacDonald:

'You must not act just now — when it is time — I will tell you — and then — you must act merely as you choose on the fact that one of your friends says another is his murdress — and that that other says he lies. You can have no more evidence on either side. I am not going to bring *this* case into court — whatever I may do with my flints...'[9]

When Rose's letter to MacDonald tumbled out of the sky in April 1872, it was a desperate bid for advice. She had read MacDonald's books and felt that he would understand her problem. It was so long since she had seen him last that she began:

'I wonder if you remember me at all... Do you think God ever puts us in positions where we cannot do his will...?'

She was tired out by the loneliness of life in Ireland, and the pressure of the unspoken matters between herself and her parents. She wanted to be useful, and help alleviate the misery she saw around her, and was racked with guilt at seeing young peasant babies fed only on bread and water, while she went home to feast on strawberries and cream:

'I have nothing in the world to do from day to day but what I like. All my parents want from me is that I should be well and happy... For my daily life is simply hour after hour of spare time, bringing neither occupation, work or amusement except that I make for myself... I feel like a child tired out after a long lonely holiday.'[10]

MacDonald was convinced that Rose was not quite in her right mind, and first of all sent his reply to be vetted by Georgina Cowper-Temple before sending it on to Rose. Almost a month later, on 14 May, she replied:

'... let me write to you freely choosing you as a friend and adviser, because I cannot help trusting both yr kindness and wisdom...'

She wrote painfully — 'I shall not believe I shall marry,' she declared, and ended her letter with a lament:

'If it could have been so that I might have kept the friend who has brought such pain and suffering and torture and division among so many hearts — if there had never been anything but friendship between us how much might have been spared. But now all that cannot be gone over again . . .'[11]

In July Rose came over to England and stayed with an aunt in Tunbridge Wells whom Ruskin had written to a couple of years earlier 'with absolute openness' hoping that this aunt would speak to Rose on his behalf. The aunt showed Rose Ruskin's letters and she was shocked. She wrote to MacDonald:

'In his own writing I have what in almost all particulars corresponds to the statements in the letters you read and I do not and cannot disbelieve one of them. I have his own account of it written two years ago — not to me. And nothing can make that darkness light in me.

He thinks because he has loved me strongly, and has enormous perceptions and love of what is good and what is beautiful, and has been given many good gifts by God, that this overweighs transgression against God's laws . . . it utterly overpowers me with the ghastliness of it all.'[12]

Rose asked MacDonald to send a letter to Ruskin which she had written, but he kept it, believing it too damaging to give to his friend:

'I will not judge or condemn you. But I *must* turn away from you. Can you wonder, you who know what I have had to know, that my nature recoils from you?

Your love to me, all your great perceptions of whatsoever things are good and lovely, your gifts — all that God has given you — these cannot expiate, but to my deep sorrow intensify and darken, your sins against God's law.'[13]

Rose planned to go to Broadlands, but was diverted by William Cowper-Temple to their home in Curzon Street instead, and from there she came to stay at The Retreat. For Rose, the roomy house lived up to its name, as she slumped into the red velvet armchair in MacDonald's study, and took in 'draughts of peace and kindness' from George and Louisa. At home with all the MacDonald brothers and sisters, she felt like a lost fledgling who had found her nest. There were suppers and breakfasts and rows on the river. In the evening, Greville would play wistful German *Lieder* for her on his violin, and she would stare outside at the noiseless river, trying to recapture a sense of peace. It was here that George and Louisa finally persuaded Rose to see Ruskin once again, to try and patch together two people who had made each other so unhappy. Ruskin was, at this time, in Venice with his cousin Joan and her husband, Arthur

Severn, a friend called Mrs Hilliard and her daughter, and an artist he had employed to make sketches. He was busy looking at paintings by Botticelli and Carpaccio, and writing notes on the Cavalli Monuments at Verona for the Arundel Society. MacDonald wrote to him, but Ruskin was irritated and bitter in his reply. He agreed to meet Rose at Genoa, provided that George and Louisa took her there, but MacDonald sent a telegram which arrived at 6a.m. on the morning of 5 July saying, 'We dare move no further.' Rose's parents were agitating for her return to Ireland and a trip to Italy was out of the question. Ruskin at once put pen to paper:

'Kindly set down without fail, (by return of post if you can) in the plainest English you know — the precise things R. says of me — or has heard say of me. I am weary of justifying myself — and if I do so once more — it will not be for this woman's sake who has killed me with her want of plain justice to the truest love ever woman threw away — but for the sake of many others who now need me. But I am a little surprised at your letter. Have I then *no* friends but you — whose opinion is worth anything to R. — was there no one who could have been listened to but you only...?'[14]

He finished, '...write instantly — and speak plainly and *utterly*...' After another letter, Ruskin relented, and wrote to MacDonald on 12 July:

'I am coming home, now in haste — but not for my own sake — nor, perhaps, much for any one else's. Whatever good can come now, is too late, except peace — which I hope to get or give, at last.'

Rose had returned to her aunt's at Tunbridge Wells and was troubled and confused. She feared that the MacDonalds had persuaded Ruskin to return from Italy against his will, and burst out: 'I am truly at my wits end,' but arranged to meet them at the Cowper-Temples' house in Curzon Street at 3 o'clock on 16 July to find out what plans had been made. After having the situation explained to her, Rose returned for a short period to Harristown and then came back to England to meet Ruskin at The Retreat some time at the beginning of August, a few days after his return on 27 July. All anguish, recrimination and fear dissolved, and there followed 'three days of heaven'. Greville MacDonald recalled:

'It is these days that bring back to me the great man and the fragile girl, as if in living presence. I recall clearly Ruskin's grandeur of face, his searching blue eyes, and his adorable smile — his ultramarine cravat also! Supreme was my joy in the grip of his hand, or in running to bring him a cab. I remember the frail Rose, so amazingly thin yet with such high colour and her great eyes, with the tenderest of smiles possessing so readily her exquisite lips. I was astonished at her being alive, seeing that, I well remember, her dinner once consisted of three green peas, and, the very next day, of one strawberry and half an Osborne biscuit! She was too frail to sit at table, of course. But Ruskin would be left alone with her either in the drawing-room or in the study.'[15]

There she would lie on the sofa, and she and Ruskin would murmur to one another as he stroked her hand. A few days later, Rose travelled to Broadlands to stay with the Cowper-Temples, and summoned Ruskin, who spent another day by her side. He accompanied her back to London on the train, and made a drawing for her, and when she travelled up to Preston to stay with the Leycesters, some relatives of Georgina Cowper-Temple, on her way back to Ireland, she begged Ruskin to join her, and he had the pleasure of standing with her at church, and holding her prayer book for her. With grateful thanks, Ruskin sent a letter to MacDonald on 11 August:

'I thought, before I saw her, that she could never undo the evil she had done — but she brought me back into life, and put the past away as if it had not been — with the first full look of her eyes. What she has done now, she has no power to help — it is natural — human pain, and not deadly — but think what it was to have her taught daily horror of me — for years and years — in silence. I had prepared myself to hear that she was dead — and had died in indignation with me. I know now that she is ill — but she is at peace with me, and I may help to save her.'[16]

But, as so often in the past, Ruskin's precarious happiness was not to last. At Coniston in September, just before he was about to move into his new home at Brantwood, he received his letter to her unopened, as he stood in front of the church door. Once more he was plunged into anguish, and that night, he wrote in his diary the words of Jesus on the cross: 'It is finished.'[17] He told MacDonald:

'No friend could have behaved more cruelly than she has done to me: but she is mad and it is an experience for me of what "possession" means, which I could not have had otherwise, nor have I just cause to be angry with her, but only to be grieved for us both and angry enough with the people who have driven her to this...'

He sent MacDonald a cheque for a hundred pounds to defray his expenses in caring for Rose, and instructed him:

'Would you kindly write to her saying nothing more than that you are requested to direct her to send the drawing I gave her (in the railway carriage up from Broadlands) back to me, carefully packed, as I made it for Oxford, not for her . . .'[18]

Ruskin was miserable and grieved indeed. He took possession of Brantwood on 13 September, and gave his Oxford lectures, later printed as *Ariadne Florentina*, in November and December.

Back in the twilight world of Ireland, Rose began her long descent into incurable illness. She pencilled a note from her sickbed to Louisa, who had sent her a photograph of the family as a memento:

'I send you all my blessing and some — much love out of the very depths of my heart. I shall see you all again some day. Meantime you know there is a twelfth child somewhere not wholly out of reach of the Mother bird's wing . . .'[19]

But that was still not the end. Rose wrote some of 'the loveliest letters' to Ruskin once again, in the autumn of 1874, but by the December of that year, the last vestiges of sanity were gone. She was only twenty-six. A trip to England to bolster her health failed, and one night in London she was raving to the extent that Ruskin was the only one who could comfort her. She lay with her head in his arms, and recited *Jesus, Lover of My Soul*, before dropping back exhausted on to the pillow. Ruskin announced in *Fors* in January 1875 that, 'the woman I hoped would have been my wife is dying . . .' and wrote to MacDonald:

'But poor Rose is entirely broken like her lover — and what good there may be for either must be where Heaven is but I don't know that much of the Universe or of Time.'[20]

It was the last time that Ruskin saw her. She died on 26 May 1875, before even her parents could reach her, in Ireland, and was interred in the La Touche mausoleum after services at St. Patrick's Church in Dublin. Ruskin informed Carlyle on 4 June, with a characteristically sweet melancholy:

'I was away into the meadows, to see buttercup and clover and bean blossom, when the news came that the little story of my wild rose was ended, and the hawthorn blossoms this year would fall over her . . .'[21]

MacDonald, who was staying at Great Tangley Manor near Guildford, wrote to Ruskin consolingly:

'. . . But the Psyche is aloft, and her wings are broad and white, and the world of flowers is under her, and the sea of sunny air is around her, and the empty chrysalis — what of that?

Now we are all Psyches half awake, who see the universe in great measure only by reflection from the dull coffin-lid over us. But I hope, I hope, I hope infinitely. And ever the longer I live and try to live, and think, and long to love perfectly, I see the scheme of things grow more orderly and more intelligible, and am more and more convinced that all is on the way to be well with a wellness to which there was no other road than just this whereon we are walking...

For Rose, is there anything fitting but gladness? The growing weight is gone; the gravestone heaved from off her; the fight with that which was and yet was not herself is over. It may be she haunts you now with ministrations. Anyhow the living God does. Richter says it is only in God that two souls can meet. I am sure it is true.'[22]

Ruskin thanked MacDonald for his affection, and replied to him from Oxford, where he was staying:

'I have fought *no* good fight — except — that the little fight I have made is from narrow vantage ground. For you know — so far as *I* can see — or feel or understand — she is only gone where the hawthorn blossoms go...'[23]

Rose's death marked Ruskin deeply, and he was still obsessive about her, confusing her at times with Beatrice, or St Ursula, the Gothic saint who had betrothed herself to a heathen prince, on pledge of his baptism and a delay of three years while she went on a pilgrimage to the Holy Land. Gradually Ruskin slipped back into spiritualism, eager to find Rose beckoning to him from the other world. MacDonald, for his part, had already written his feelings about Rose and Ruskin into his novel *Wilfrid Cumbermede,* published in 1872. It is an agonized tale of madness and estrangement, waiting for a final reconciliation. All such hopes were to be dashed in the girl's death.

A few months after Rose's death, in December 1875, both Ruskin and MacDonald were staying at Broadlands where they met a society medium called Mrs Ainsworth. Annie Munro, the sculptor's sister, was then working at Broadlands as governess to the Cowper-Temples' adopted daughter:

'There is a Mrs Ainsworth here. I don't take to her much, but Ruskin is very interested in her. She sees spirits, and Annie, though she feels to her as I do, thinks her quite honest. She has seen and described, without having ever seen her, Rose whispering to Mr Ruskin. He is convinced...'[24]

Ruskin's confusion deepened further, until St Ursula, Beatrice and Rose merged into a single iconic figure. Then, one night in February 1878, Ruskin had a vivid dream. He was standing in a church... dressed as a bridegroom...and Rose was coming to greet him. Out of his mind, he wrote to MacDonald the following day:

> 'We've got married after all after all — but such a surprise — Tell the Brown mother — and Lily.
>
> — *Bruno's* out of his wits with joy...I'm in an awful hurry such a lot of things to do —
>
> —I've just got this down before breakfast — the fourth letter. Ever your lovingest
>
> John Ruskin — Oh — Willie — Willie — He's pleased too, George dear.'[25]

MacDonald wrote to Joan Severn at once, informing her of Ruskin's condition. He was found on 23 February in a state of collapse, and it took several months for him to recover. The doctors said that his fit had been caused by overwork and worry.

After that, Ruskin lived half-in, half-out of madness, plagued by nightmares in which he feared the Evil One would come and snatch him away, and gradually he and MacDonald went their separate ways. Ruskin came back into the fold of the church after an experience in 1882 when, at La Fontaine, the birthplace of St Bernard, he fell on his knees and spent a long while in prayer. He emerged as a 'Catholic Christian' and, though he carried on with *Fors*, and wrote *Praeterita*, he spent more and more of a hermit life up in the Lakes. He and MacDonald and Maria La Touche had a number of tentative reunions in the 1880s, about ten years after Rose's death, and though they met as friends, with affection and some regret, the shadow of the dead girl lay forever between them.[26]

CHAPTER TWENTY-SEVEN
America

New ways of providing for his family never ceased to impress themselves on MacDonald. He was in increasing demand as a speaker and lecturer, roving over much of the British Isles for several months a year, on exhausting, punishing trips, and the idea was suggested to him that he might like to make a similar trip to America and try out his talent there. MacDonald's writing had had a very warm reception in America, and he had welcomed several American admirers to The Retreat. His books sold over the Atlantic by their thousands, but as no proper copyright law existed at that time between Britain and America, he had never seen a cent of American money. Grievously, many of his books had been pirated, circulated in cheap editions, with the Scots rubbed out and English words put in their place. This upset MacDonald deeply, much more than the loss of any money, but was evidence of his popularity, and he believed that a successful lecture tour would give the family finances a boost that they sorely needed. Accordingly, before the end of 1871, he had contracted himself to Messrs Redpath[1] and Fall of Boston, a notable lecture bureau, for a tour of six to eight months the following winter. He wrote to Richard Watson Gilder, assistant editor of *Scribner's Monthly Magazine*, a devotee of MacDonald's writing, and soon to be a firm friend:

> 'But I thank you heartily for your kind words, and am now able to say that I hope next autumn to see you face to face, for I have now written to Messrs Redpath and Fall of Boston, putting myself in their hands.'[2]

One of the main conditions of their agreement was that MacDonald should not lecture more than five nights a week, and that his fee should be £30 a lecture. This was much more than his usual five guineas, but less than his true worth — yet, as he refused to send the American agents any press cuttings or testimonials, there was no thought of trying to coax any more money out of his hosts. Though sailing to America was a big adventure for MacDonald, such lecture tours were very popular at that time. It was a way of seeing the famous writers whose books were devoured in the magazines month by month. Both Dickens and Thackeray had preceded MacDonald to America with noticeable success, and he was hoping for something similar.

The months running up to his departure were busy ones for the family. MacDonald was lecturing, and in London the difficulties between Ruskin and Rose La Touche reached their sad climax. In July, Norman Macleod, the editor of *Good Words*, died, but an even more painful bereavement was the death of Greville Matheson on 6 September. He had been the earliest and closest of MacDonald's friends, almost a brother to him, and MacDonald described him as, 'the man whose literary judgement and sympathy I prized beyond that of the world beside.' Matheson had faded slightly in his last years, shy of the crowds of people who came to The Retreat, and his illness finally shut him off from the world. Despite his literary leanings, he had remained a bank clerk, dutifully supporting his large family. MacDonald was on the point of delaying his departure to America to remain by his friend, and stayed with him, along with William Matheson, until the very end.

The MacDonalds felt very strongly that Louisa should travel with George, for company and in case of illness, and they also decided to take Greville with them. Lilia and Mary, now aged twenty and nineteen respectively, were to be left in charge of the family, tutored by a beleaguered governess, Miss Bishop, and slowly they moved in stages down to Halloway House, Hastings, where they remained for most of the winter.

After packing and rearranging and endless farewells, the great day finally dawned. Loaded up with presents — ginger from Aunt Flora, and grapes from William Matheson — George, Louisa and Greville boarded the Cunard liner, the SS *Malta*, and set sail for the New World. Louisa had laid in store a selection of her daughters' best dresses to wear on appropriate occasions, for as she was so slightly built, she could still slip into them easily. MacDonald was wrapped in fur against the cold that ruffled his shaggy locks, and Greville gazed up at the flocks of seagulls flapping round the mast of the huge ship. Britain receded as the nose of the vessel surged through the Irish Sea. Down below, their cabins were comfortable, but the lurch of the sea had an immediate effect, and all three of them were violently sick, growing greener with each day that passed. By the time they arrived at Queenstown in Ireland on 20 September, they were already lying groaning on their beds, refusing all food. Entry into the open Atlantic only unleashed a Pandora's box of further terrors, and both George and Louisa were so sick that they could not even undress to clamber into bed properly. Louisa remained confined to her cabin throughout the voyage writing stoically, '...the time moves slowly in the nausea of sickness.' The noises about her only jarred her head into throbbing pain as she squirmed under the blankets. Greville was sprightly by comparison, up and exploring the ship, and even MacDonald managed to stagger to the Captain's table and down a meal. He was soon dubbed 'The Professor' by all aboard, and was well enough to give a dramatic reading at a benefit concert for the *Seaman's Society*, though Louisa did not stir.

Whatever their pains, the crossing must have been relatively smooth, as it was accomplished in only twelve days, and they arrived in Boston on 30 September, two days before their planned date of arrival. A welcome was hurriedly arranged, and they were greeted by General Sherwin and James Redpath, before being ushered to the home of James T. Fields[3] in Charles Street, where they were to stay while MacDonald remained in the city. Fields was a great literary man, and had an astounding collection of autographs and memorabilia. His home was a centre for many of the famous people of the day. On arrival there, the MacDonalds were lodged in the top floor of his house, in a Morris-patterned room with old furniture, and with access to Fields' library, which contained many first editions and old manuscripts. There they could secure some privacy for themselves, adjusting after their long trip. MacDonald was able to have plenty of rest, while Louisa read him to sleep, '...for the more he sleeps *you* know the better,' she wrote to her children at home.

Boston itself, with its brownstone houses and crooked streets, the most European of all American cities, was lapped up by the MacDonalds, who loved this first taste of the New World, which was yet so like the old.

After her arduous voyage, however, Louisa was so thin that she could hardly keep her rings on her fingers, but American hospitality demanded that they meet hosts of people and attend numerous receptions, and she had little time to recover. In the midst of sightseeing, teas and parties, the business arrangements made so far were revealed. There was a list of forty engagements stretching up till Christmas, with many more to be added. Redpath, eager and efficient and driving, was keen for MacDonald to lecture as much as possible, but was not sure how to gauge his probable success:

'...but Mr Redpath says that Papa's popularity goes very much in strata — very much, I think as it does at home — Those who care for him care very much — others can't endure his writings. So they can't tell till they try whether he will take.'[4]

The first lecture was due to take place on 9 October at the Union Hall,

Cambridgeport, but before that MacDonald and Louisa were whisked round most of the New England literary society. On the whole they were pleased with the Americans, who had such charming manners, generosity and courtesy, but they could not abide their eating habits. After a large and varied breakfast in the morning, the main meal of the day came at 3p.m. and then there was nothing except wafer-thin biscuits and tea until the following morning. Swiftly, MacDonald, Louisa and Greville became adept at smuggling food back to their rooms to break the long fast through the evenings. They found the Fields good hosts, if a little enthusiastic. Fields himself was a Unitarian and a humourist. He kept them all entertained with endless funny stories, so that Greville wrote to Lilia, 'Do you know we hardly do anything but laugh here.' Though the Fields were good about turning album and autograph collectors away without letting MacDonald see them, Louisa could find them a little overwhelming:

'I find it difficult enough to keep engagements off for him — there are so many kind people who want to see Papa — and the Fields forget sometimes and make engagements for us without asking us when they are their friends. I have however had to make myself very disagreeable and break up some excursions into the country or Papa would not be fit for his lecture on Wednesday.'[5]

But they were pampered, and whatever Boston was, it was fun. Greville wrote to Winifred:

'We first dined at one of the hotels... and then we saw a romantic sensational melo-dramatic, rather good drama — all about gipsies stealing little boys, sliding panels, murders, and everybody and everything turn out to be somebody and something else. It lasted four hours! Is not that tremendous?'[6]

If MacDonald did not move in the very highest circles at home, he was introduced to all the New England literati almost at one go. Unfortunately, the first person they were intfoduced to was Harriet Beecher Stowe,[7] author of the phenomenal *Uncle Tom's Cabin*. One of her recent books, *Lady Byron Vindicated*, had put into print confidences which Lady Byron had made to Harriet Beecher Stowe while she was still alive. MacDonald and Louisa had seen this publication as a slur on Lady Byron's memory, and were reluctant to be effusive towards Harriet Stowe despite her fame:

'Did you hear that the very first person we saw in Mr Fields' house was Mrs Stowe! It was hard lines to be introduced to her and have to shake hands with her before one had time to draw one's breath in the new country.'

Still, Louisa conceded, '. . . she is rather fun — but her voice and Yankee tones are to me horrid.'[8]

Gathering followed gathering, and Louisa continued to pull dress after dress out of her ample trunks. She reported back to Lilia all the details of each occasion she could:

> 'We had such a full day yesterday! Emerson, his wife and daughter came to lunch. After lunch we went to see Longfellow. He showed us his rooms and his pictures and we saw one of his daughters. His house was Washington's head quarters — a hundred years old — which here is as wonderful as a three hundreder would be with us. Then in the evening we went to a severe tea — and an elegant one — at the house of Mrs Lowell's sister (*He* is in England just now). She is a very interesting person. . .'[9]

They attended a reception for Miss Cushman,[10] the American actress whom they had met at Bude, and travelled out to Manchester, to the Fields' summer home, to taste the country and view the glory of the New England Fall. Back in Boston there were more parties. Louisa descended the staircase in her black silk with white lace to greet the new admirers who pressed round her and her husband, trying to fake interest as the same questions were asked over and over again: *'What are the differences you find between our two countries? How long do you plan to remain? Is this your only boy or do you — no — really? — do you have a photograph of them all? I must say you don't look — and Mr MacDonald bears his years wonderfully. I was expecting a younger man, but — the Fall, oh, the colours are much paler than usual this year. Do you like Boston? Well, it's so English, of course. . .'*

And, naturally, they met Oliver Wendell Holmes,[11] the 'poet laureate' of Boston, and uncrowned king of literary society:

> 'Did I tell you of the reception on Saturday night here? Such a roomful of people. Mrs Whitney and her daughter and Wendell Holmes were the most interesting people in the room. There were two people from England friends of Mrs Craik's but I did not speak to them. Mr Alger and wife and daughter, and Mr and Mrs Rufus Ellis — the marmalade lady — and her daughters and two other Unitarian clergymen, and the Governor of Boston and his daughter — They had invited us to their country house.'[12]

If Louisa felt a little ill at ease in meeting new people, and broke down on occasion with her customary headaches, she was soon comforted by the arrival of their old friends, the Russell Gurneys. Gurney had been appointed as British representative on the Commission to settle land claims arising out of the Civil War, and they had arrived in America a few weeks before the MacDonalds and were staying in Washington. They had travelled over to Boston in time to hear MacDonald's first lecture, which was on Burns.

That Wednesday night, fifteen hundred people crammed the Union Hall at Cambridgeport to listen to MacDonald. Longfellow was there, and Fields, as well as many other critics and literary people. The crowd was hushed as MacDonald mounted the podium, carrying only a small volume of Burns in his right hand. As ever, he looked the part of a poet. He was wearing a black dress-coat and white necktie, glasses balanced on the end of his nose, and was sporting a prominent gold watch chain and fine rings.[13] He leant on the desk as if it were a pulpit cushion and began — his Scots voice pouring out over the heads of his listeners — and from the start his homely, frank and earnest manner won his audience over. He told them plainly that this was the first time he had ever lectured on Burns, and began by stressing that though people often spoke of poets as if they were different from other men, this was, in fact, quite a mistake. Each and every person had in him what Burns had, and it was this that made them understand and feel all that a poet such as Burns wrote: 'Between the giver and the receiver the same feelings must exist.' Burns' passion for the lower animals was one of his strongest characteristics, and his sympathy for all living things led him to write poems on subjects that were a closed book to the Edinburgh sophisticates, and went even as far as feeling some compassion for the devil himself. He was a natural man of the soil, and though he drank (it was true), he did so only for the company and not for the drink. When Burns died, his books were ranged in order and his accounts settled — two marks of character which showed that he could not possibly have been a drunkard. MacDonald went on to illustrate his theme with readings from *The Daisy* and *My Nannie's Awa'* which were powerful in their effect. As usual, MacDonald spoke without notes, and with some hesitation, but this served only to heighten the dramatic effect of his speaking — or perhaps preaching would be a better word, for as with everything, MacDonald gave a moral twist to his message, uplifting and encouraging his audience in the ways of God, and it was this combination of naivety and clarity which gripped all those who heard him. What he said was not nearly as important as how he said it. As one newspaper reported, 'In the others we have known the force of great minds, but in him the glow of a great soul.'

After speaking for over a hundred minutes, MacDonald descended from the podium to thunderous applause, and dropped, exhausted and perspiring, into a chair in the reception room. James Fields rushed up to him and clasped him by the hand, his eyes full of tears, saying that there had been nothing like it since Dickens, and Redpath followed, angrily snarling, '...Why didn't you *say* you could do this sort of thing? We'd have got 300 dollars a lecture for you! Guess the Lyceums all over the United States'll think they've *done* Redpath and Fall, sure! You make me sick! Yes, *Sir*.'[14]

Relations with Redpath remained strained, and he and MacDonald often rubbed each other up the wrong way. While Redpath was eager to cram in as many lectures as possible, Louisa was worried that MacDonald's health would break, as it often did, and on the tour lectures that had been long advertised had to be cancelled. Aside from that, MacDonald would insist on preaching for nothing, giving people a free glimpse of him, and this offended Redpath's money-making instincts as well as adding an unnecessary strain to MacDonald's health. Redpath could not understand MacDonald's infuriating otherworldliness, while MacDonald in turn had no hard head for business matters, and was not sympathetic towards Redpath's tribulations in trying to organize him. Greville wrote to Lilia about the row over his father's preaching:

'Mr Redpath was in an awful way about it...and Mother says he gave her a scolding such as she has not had since she was twelve years old, just because he is afraid he will break down, you know.'

Louisa referred to MacDonald as a dancing bear, and to Redpath as the keeper holding the chain, forcing him to perform all over the East Coast.

After some favourable notices in the press, MacDonald repeated his Burns lecture at the Boston Lyceum to an audience of three thousand, and he was well and truly launched. Louisa wrote excitedly to her children at home:

'It was a time of great excitement — there were two thousand eight hundred and fifty ticket holders besides a few that got in as friends. Such a hall! far bigger than St James Hall with two balconies all round it. They say Papa was heard in every corner of it. Was it not delightful for me? There I sat between Mr and Mrs Russell Gurney — one of the "proudest moments of my house"! and to sit there with them and see all those earnest eager faces listening — almost breathlessly sometimes (we sat on the platform where we *could* see) was a sight I shan't soon forget.'[15]

As a true romantic, the cornerstones of MacDonald's literary consciousness were Shakespeare, Dante and Milton. MacDonald did not lecture on Dante in America, but his repertory did include *Hamlet, Tom Hood*, the *Lyrics of Tennyson, King Lear, Macbeth* and *Milton*. But by far his most popular subject was Burns, on whom he lectured over forty times, and was to lecture on many times more in the future, though never in England. MacDonald's second most popular topic was *Hamlet* and, holding up the Dane as an exemplar of all the Christian virtues, he would fastidiously elucidate the moral drift of the play.

After his initial success at Boston, MacDonald, Louisa and Greville moved to New York to stay at the house of Dr J.G. Holland, the editor of *Scribner's* magazine. Thirty miles from the city, Richard Watson Gilder came eagerly to greet them. He was aged about thirty with sallow, clear-cut features, coal black eyes, and an impetuous boy-like manner. He soon attached himself to George and Louisa as a self-styled son, and they cherished his support on all their travels. MacDonald was not due to speak in New York until 18 November, but he attended some receptions there, before the little party took a train further to Philadelphia. There they were met at the station by Lippincot,[16] the famous publisher, in a carriage of rich golden brown satin — only one of his six carriages. They were whisked at once to his magnificent mansion built of Italian and Pennsylvanian marble. 'Grosvenor Square's almost cottages to it,' gasped Louisa, and gulped as she stepped inside. It was from this magnificent edifice that MacDonald travelled to speak at the Philadelphia Opera House where three thousand people turned out to hear him. The lecture took place on Monday 21 October. MacDonald was nervous at the rows of people waiting to hear him, but he spoke successfully. At the end of the lecture, however, he found that he could not walk off the stage, as the curtain had come down, and made his exit with an athletic leap into a stage-box to hearty cheers from the audience.

From this moment on, travelling began in earnest. Often the Mac-Donalds would visit four or five towns in a week, either moving from place to place heading towards some major destination where they could have a brief rest, or else basing themselves in a large town, and darting to the smaller places round about. After leaving Philadelphia, they found themselves in Worcester, Massachusetts on 24 October, and by the 28th had arrived in Amesbury with the purpose of visiting John Greenleaf Whittier, the well-known Quaker poet.[17] After so many hours on trains,

Louisa wrote: 'We have been travelling everyday and I am sick of the cars (the railroads) and the motion of travelling is still in my head.' At Whittier's home, the MacDonalds were struck by the poet's quaint Quaker 'thees and thous' and his simple, gentle manner. Two nieces kept house for him and there was a baby besides. Whittier had been kind enough to write to the local press before MacDonald's visit, urging all to come and hear him. Louisa gave a pleasant sketch of the man and his surroundings:

> 'Mr Whittier's house is a sweet, country-like cottage, wooden and low. We dined in the room that the roadside door opens on. Then through that was the little sacred study of one of the sweetest, most dignified, loving, humble and gentle of men. After the lecture, some of the Scotchmen made Papa a present of Whittier's poems. In the morning Mr Whittier said that "Friend George must not be the only one to have presents," and he gave me his latest volume. He is a most lovable, holy man, but full of fire and enjoyment of all things good. He is very wide in his beliefs.'[18]

After this first sortie out on the tracks, the MacDonalds returned haltingly to Boston. At Providence, Rhode Island, they stayed with the Ellises whom they had previously met at The Retreat, but Louisa was glad to be settled back in Charles Street, for they had been to four towns that week: Amesbury, Providence, Lowell and Dover — and somehow she felt more at home in Boston and nearer her children than in the other American cities they had visited. MacDonald lectured at the Boston Lyceum once again, this time on *Tom Hood*, and a reception was planned for them on 9 November. Louisa steeled herself for the usual battery of questions that she now answered as if by clockwork. Many invitations to preach came from the Unitarians, though the Episcopalians and Congregationalists were slower to respond, but by the ninth, MacDonald's exertions had taken their toll. He was confined to bed with a bad gumboil and threats of a bronchitic attack. He could scarcely open his mouth and was bloodspitting. Louisa had tripped, fallen and lamed herself in her bedroom, so both of them were feeling sorry for themselves. As MacDonald tossed and turned in bed, Louisa met the crowd gathered in Fields' salon, when suddenly news came that there was a fire. The whole heart of Boston had gone up in flames. The hungry fire licked down street after street, and for a while it was feared that even Charles Street would be affected. Smoke and sparks filled the air. Timbers cracked and fell. Louisa and Greville watched the glow of the flames from the Charles Street windows, and Fields set to work packing valuables in case they should have to evacuate. Luckily they were safe. After a troubled night, in which Greville walked round the streets with Fields, the morning dawned to reveal a hundred acres of central Boston reduced to ashes. Twisted hulks of buildings jutted out of mounds of mouldering ash. The banks and insurance companies were in chaos. Nobody knew what was happening. Many of the people the MacDonalds had just met believed themselves ruined, and relief began coming in to help those homeless left only clutching a few bags or a pramload of belongings rescued from their houses. Greville poked round the ruins, awed at the scenes of desolation he encountered. The fire had lasted from 7.30p.m. on the Saturday evening until 2p.m. the following Sunday afternoon. Greville wrote to Winifred: '...a hundred cares worth millions — are now lying in burning masses and smoke, and not worth a cent.'[19]

As it turned out, people were not as ruined as they thought, but the ensuing chaos and grief was terrible, and a *dea ex machina* was provided in the person of Mrs Cunningham of Milton, eight miles away, who swooped down on the Fields' house and removed the MacDonalds from the city. She became a good friend and protectress to the MacDonalds, shielding them and providing them with an oasis in their travels. But soon it was time to move on, and lecture succeeded lecture until at Scotch Plains, New Jersey, MacDonald had his first bad attack of lung problems. Luckily his host, Dr Abram Coles, was a medical man, and he helped MacDonald through. Louisa described him as:

'...Such a delightful man is our host. He fetched us from Jersey City, and at once Papa and I saw the most wonderful resemblance in his walk, his hurried hesitating manner to whom do you think? F.D.M. the Good! He carried our bags for us from the cars. Then we talked with him, his eyes, his mouth, but most of all his manner and the dearest, loveliest, most humorous little laugh so wonderfully like him.'[20]

When MacDonald had regained some strength, they travelled to Washington, where MacDonald arrived muffled in a fur coat with a handkerchief tied across his mouth. By now he was feeling the first pangs of winter, and they seared his lungs. The Russell Gurneys met them and held a reception for them on 24 November. Already it had become clear that 'He *can* not do *all* he had intended' and Louisa wrote dolefully to Lilia: '...they pay him so little compared with his audiences, but then of course they did not know *how* he would take.' The MacDonalds had now to face the grim reality that they would not be as awash with dollars as they had initially hoped. Social life, however, continued effervescent, and at the Gurneys' reception in Washington, politicians were thick on the ground.

At Washington, still not fully recovered from his earlier attack, Mac-Donald's health broke down completely. He was assailed by bronchitis, and a number of lectures had to be cancelled. It was a serious set-back, and Louisa wrote worriedly to Lilia:

'. . . I never saw him more prostrate, except, of course, at the time of the Manchester illness. It is very serious this attack for him — we do not know yet whether he will be able to lecture again at all, and if he does he can scarcely make up all he has lost before the close of the lecture season. But if he can but get what will cover the debts that trouble him I do not think we ought to mind about more. . . I wrote letters enough yesterday to put off lectures this side of Christmas to the value of £300. . . But the Life is more than meat or money, and if you get Papa back alive and well we shall not mind that he could not make so many dollars as he intended.'[21]

The MacDonalds were very fortunate in having the Gurneys on hand to help them. They could have easily been stuck in a hotel in some town where no one knew them. Tended by Louisa, MacDonald clawed his way back to health with his usual resilience, and after Abram Coles came specially to see him, he began to mend in earnest. Finally he was well enough to travel in a Pullman car to Elmira, New York, where they stayed at the home of Mark Twain's mother-in-law, Mrs Langdon, 'revelling in lapsury's luck'. MacDonald became very friendly with Mark Twain, and they saw each other several times during MacDonald's visit. They even discussed collaborating on a novel together to defeat the copyright laws, but this project came to nothing. Back in England, Lilia's twenty-first birthday was due on 4 January, and MacDonald sent her a long letter on 22 December, full of affection and promise:

'But may you have as many happy birthdays in this world as will make you ready for a happier series of them afterwards, the first of which birthdays will be the one we call the day of death down here. But there is a better grander birthday than that which we may have every day — every hour that we turn away from ourselves to the living love that makes us love, and so are born again. And I think all these last birthdays will be summed up in one transcendent birthday far off it may be, but surely to come — the moment when we know in ourselves that we are one with God, and are living by his life, and have neither thought nor wish but his. . .'[22]

He sent her a poem, composed a few days previously in a railway carriage on his way to Buffalo, and reminded her that seven times three were mystical numbers for the Jews and other eastern religions, and so, 'May all the good of the unknown be yours, my child.'

On Christmas Eve, MacDonald, Louisa and Greville took a train once more, this time from Elmira to Jersey City, but the journey was slow, and they were halted frequently 'by great snowdrifts in the cuttings'. The stoves in the carriages would not burn properly, and the temperature fell. Three hours late, MacDonald stepped out into the thick snow, exhausted and hungry, but there was no one to meet them as they had crossed by the wrong ferry to the wrong depot. Luckily their hotel was not many yards away, but once in the freezing air, MacDonald's asthma worsened, and it looked as though he might stiffen in the cruel night stillness:

'...He stood gasping in the street holding on to Greville's arm, tears rolling down his cheeks as if he would die then and there — and could not move for whole minutes, though it was only across the road he had to go to get to our inn. But the thermometer was five degrees below zero, and he said afterwards the air felt like strong acid cutting up his lungs. It was agony for him, and it was agony to see him...'[23]

Richard Watson Gilder had left his own Christmas party and gone to meet them. Realizing there had been a blunder, he arrived at their hotel and was able to help. The following morning, MacDonald was well enough to go and stay with Gilder's mother at Newark, New York. It was there that the trio spent Christmas, and MacDonald rested, but the New Year found them pressing on to Orange, New Jersey, where they stayed with the Rev. George Bacon who had seen them six or seven years previously at Vere Street. It was a cold, bleak day when they arrived. The snow was lying thick on the ground, and the wind blew it about in heavy drifts. The whole landscape had frozen, encasing the clothes lines, chimneys, trees and telegraph poles in crystal, and bringing down branches under the weight of the ice. The sky was pale clear, setting off the burning setting of a red sun. At George Bacon's, one of the first things MacDonald did for the New Year was to send some money to Lilia — £400, mainly to pay back debts and loans, but leaving £100 for her own use:

'...but my work has been so interrupted by my illness that I cannot well send you more just yet. I am not going to do much for a month. But the snow is now melting away under a steady thaw, and I hope to be better...'[24]

He commissioned Lilia to give 5/- to the girls, and 2/6d to all the boys to buy New Year presents with. Louisa had given MacDonald a splendid sealskin cap, and Greville a beaver one to keep out the cold and give them both a distinguished air. MacDonald, turning back to the business in hand, summoned enough strength to preach for Bacon on 5 January, standing among pots of arum lilies on the platform to deliver his message, 'One thing is needful.' Chimes called in the congregation from a fair distance, and the service was simple and straightforward, enhanced by the beautiful organ playing.

After MacDonald's long illness, Louisa was keen for them to settle for a while, and at the risk of offending their friends insisted on 'ganging our ain gait'. She travelled to New York and found lodgings for a fortnight where she, MacDonald and Greville could be completely by themselves. This was an idyllic retreat where the days passed slowly and sweetly, and Greville MacDonald remembered:

'...Dr Holland's daughters, Miss Maria Oakley...would entrance us with droll and pathetic stories of Irish life; R.W. Gilder, Miss Helena de Kay, whom he married in 1874, and his sisters, flocked to our bohemian *ménage*. The impromptu lunches, fetched from pastrycooks' and ice-cream stores, the English teas, were happy indeed; and not least in enjoyment of his brief respite was my father. We saw Edwin Booth play *Hamlet*, Sothern *Dundreary*, Wallack and Miss Cushman in *Guy Mannering*, heard Rubinstein's recitals, and the Jubilee Singers. We usually dined at a hotel on 4th Avenue, in the same block — never once at Delmonico's! Near at hand Miss Oakley and Miss de Kay shared a studio at the top of a Broadway house, greatly to their parents' dismay. But they painted delightfully; and I, being only a callow youth, with Richard W. Gilder ten years my senior, whom I chaperoned, were the only males ever admitted. The two ladies painted my portrait in oils — 'The Music of the Future' it was called.'[25]

This respite over, MacDonald was soon travelling again, and they went up to Princeton to lecture at the theological college there on *Macbeth*. They stayed the night at a Presbyterian minister's house:

'Papa gave such a glorious lecture on *Macbeth*. He is improving so wonderfully in dramatic power. It is lovely. He really sent us all into the cold shivers last night over the Ghost scene and the sleep walking scenes! He gets so eager and strong on what he has to say that it pours out with great flashes of eloquence that astonish even me. All the divines and young men, 500 students, listened to him last night. Imagine *Macbeth* in a Presbyterian Church! This is quite the hot bed of the old Theology too, and yet they came out to hear him! And this old Dr McCosh *asked Papa to preach*!'[26]

One arrangement that had been made long before MacDonald had even set foot on the shores of America was that he should address the Burns Society in New York at their annual Burns Supper on 24 January:

'He accepted, and asked whether these Scots in New York followed the custom set by the Caledonian Society in London — of appearing at the annual dinner in full dress kilt. The reply was that it was *de rigeur* for those who were Highlanders to wear their native costume. So my father of course took his kilt with him — even sword, dirk and skian dubh. And to Delmonico's on January 24th he went in his MacDonald tartans — and was the only guest not in black swallow-tails and white tie! He was greeted with rapturous delight, and being the guest of the evening, had opportunity, in responding to the toast 'Scottish Literature,' for explanation and apology, and for vowing vengeance on his most particular friend who had so misled him!'[27]

But from this spectacular highspot they had to press on soon afterwards, planning to stop at Williamsport for the night, and then travel further to Harrisburg or Pittsburg. It should have been only a three-hour journey, but the snow was deep, and as there were no Palace cars to be had, the MacDonalds had to travel in a carriage reeking of tobacco smoke, and sat surrounded by rough-looking men. Within forty minutes of their goal, the train jolted to a halt, and a man passing through the cars informed them that there was a wreck in front on the line and they would probably be stuck there the whole night. They huddled close. Fires went out and lamps dimmed. Finally, at half past two in the morning, their hope no more than a flicker, the train moved once again, but only two miles, as the locomotive of the passenger train in front of them had frozen solid. They were forced to stay there the whole of the night until they were freed from their coop the following morning at nine. But their troubles were not yet over. At Harrisburg they had no time to fetch their luggage, which had MacDonald's coat and lecture books in it, and the next stage of their journey to Pittsburg took seventeen hours instead of the scheduled eleven:

'. . . it was the *coldest* night known this winter! They couldn't keep the cars warm. Poor Papa — oh! if you had seen him at seven o'clock this morning you would have all cried. The conductor was very good to us, and had us into his little room where was a stove all to itself — he made up the stove and saved Papa's life — but not till he had been severely sick did his breathing get any better. When we arrived and came out into the cold air, it all came on again, and seemed as if he would suffocate. When we gave our names at the hotel the man, when I told him how ill Papa was, turned someone out of a room to give us a better one...'[28]

Travelling, however, was not always as tough as this, though the steaks served up at many of the American hotels they stayed at were. MacDonald often passed from place to place on a diet of milk and eggs, while Louisa ate as many vegetables as she could. The further west they moved, the worse the reviews it seemed, and the dreary hotel existence took over. No one was much interested, and their spirits flagged. To while away their many hours travelling, they would play whist, either with a dummy, or a three-handed game devised by MacDonald. Sometimes they would write verses in competition to send back to the others at home, who were still snug at Halloway House in Hastings.

From Pittsburg they travelled to Dayton, Ohio, Columbus, Ohio, and from there moved to Cincinnati where they were welcomed by Mac-Donald's cousins, the Spences. The family did not live in much grandeur, but after so many hotels it was good to have a real home to stay in. MacDonald, however, found himself orating in an indifferent climate:

'The lectures were not a success numerically considered, and the papers were more disagreeable than anywhere, I think...'[29]

Their stay at Delaware was the nadir of the whole trip, as they were stuck in a third- or fourth-rate hotel with only a 'feeble youth' to meet them:

'The chamber towels are precisely like our knife-cloths at home, one for Papa and one for me. Unruly infants at table and idiotic-looking damsels staring their eyes out of their sockets at us, as if we had just escaped from Barnum's menageries. Did you hear all His show was burned up? The poor elephants, lions, two camels, roasted to death.'[30]

There was still snow on the ground, and they were often delayed by derailed trucks which had shot off the line ahead of them:

'I am on the sofa after having scoured myself and garments from the thick black of Pittsburg and cars. Pittsburg for blackness and darkness beats Manchester hollow. We left it yesterday morning at nine o'clock and were travelling all day — except when we were stopping. It was 12.30 before a ramshackle omnibus ejected us into this hotel — glad enough to escape from the coarseness and oaths of the men in the car, not to mention over again that daily trial to our commonest feelings of cleanliness and the fitness of things — their habit of ejecting streams of tobacco-juice all around you. The longer the journey the harder they spit; and the demon-like noises that precede the operation are quite as trying as the sight of the brown puddles all across the floor when you have to walk down the car and take your seat. Don't we need pity?'[31]

Indiana was their next stop, where Louisa was proud to see that hung over the front of the Court House was a blue banner with silver letters proclaiming, '*George MacDonald, England, Eminent Scotch Orator* subject *Robert Burns.*' Though the banner fluttered welcomingly, no one invited them for a meal, and they were left to their own devices to pass a short night at a hotel. After the lecture, they rose very early the next morning, while the moon was still sparkling on the snow, and in the deep dark before dawn, caught a train. Three hours later at 8.30a.m, they came to a junction, where there was only a shed, and they were told to wait there until 11.30a.m. Sending Greville on ahead as a scout, he returned with the news that there was a little hotel nearby, and they left in search of it, leaving the tobacco-chewing Americans spitting round the stove, just as MacDonald was showing the first signs of asthma. At the 'toylike' family hotel, they found a paradise, and were waited on by the owner and his son, and his wife cooked them breakfast. Greville read his parents to sleep with a book picked out of the hotel parlour, and they had three pleasant hours of oblivion until it was time to take the train further to Altoona in Pennsylvania. 'Papa and I are both very much dilapidated,' wrote Louisa, but gradually they wound their way back east, back to friends and acclaim. They stayed with Dr Holland, the editor of *Scribner's Magazine*, in New York as MacDonald was to lecture there on Burns on 25 February, and by 5 March they were settled once again at Mrs Cunningham's at Milton, after travelling through Burlington and Vermont. MacDonald was ill again, but recovered by 9 March, though he had to give up five lectures for it. They decided that the best thing to do was to extend their stay and try to make up for some of the places MacDonald had missed owing to illness — especially Chicago which he had had to bypass in the December. Mrs Cunningham was once again a very considerate hostess:

'Mrs Cunningham drove Greville and me out in the wee-est little sleigh and, turning a curve, over we went on to a high bank of snow — I first, and we were so fastened in that there we lay. I could not move, and if the horse had persisted in going on, my arm would have been torn out of the socket; but he was very good and only dragged us a few steps. Greville extricated himself and went to the horse's head and we were soon picked out of the snow; and shaking it off with our laughter, we were soon packed in again and went smoothly enough for the rest of the day . . .'[32]

During the second week in March they visited Boston once again, calling at Mrs Payne's, the sister of Oliver Wendell Holmes. From Boston, Redpath and Fall directed the MacDonalds back to New York, where they were pleased to see Richard Watson Gilder, Maria Oakley, George Bacon, and Dr Holland's daughters. Then they had a stiff journey north, to Buffalo and up to Niagara, entering Canada and lecturing on Burns at Toronto on 1 April. With the image of the falling water still in her mind, Louisa wrote to Lilia:

> 'Niagara was our greatest and only treat of the kind since we came. The standing on the top of that Terrapin Tower and feeling borne up and away from everything and seeing those mighty waves rolling and dashing beneath us, brought the idea of infinity and majesty more *intent* upon me than anything in my life — anything material, I mean, that I ever saw. I felt as if I might be, and behold yet not be, of the earth or on it. I imagine I knew more certainly then than ever before what it would be to have a spiritual body and belong to Creation — not merely to this little earth-bit of it. . .'[33]

Standing on the brink of the Falls, all three of them knew that the worst was now behind them. It was spring, and it seemed as if the date on which they would cross the Atlantic back to their family was hurtling towards them:

> 'Monday, Hamilton, Canada — shall like to be in our own dominions. Tues. April 1st, Toronto, Can. Wed., Ann Arbor Mich — where the Spences' mother lives. Friday, Chicago, Ill., about 900 miles from New York. . .April 23rd, Montreal; April 26th, Boston! Then to New York, and Hurray! a few more lectures and on the 24th May the torture of the sea, and then my Heaven if we get to our Haven. . .'[34]

At Chicago they were entertained by the Rev. Robert Laird Collier, a well-known Unitarian preacher. He was a widower with four children, whose wife had died only the previous September. MacDonald lectured on Burns and *Macbeth* at the Chicago Halls, to good audiences, before travelling to Ann Arbor, where they met Mrs Spence, mother of the Spences at Cincinnati, and a cousin of MacDonald's grandfather. They were able to talk over old times and places, with Mrs Spence telling MacDonald many things about Huntly that even he did not know. That Sunday, MacDonald preached very powerfully in one of the local churches:

> 'All the other places in the town, except the Episcopalians, shut their churches that their ministers and their congregations might have the

opportunity of hearing him. If ever, dear, he was truly eloquent, it was tonight; if ever he was speaking the truth as if by the power of the Spirit within him, it was tonight. I hung on every word as an utterance of the voice of the Father speaking through him... The effect was tremendous, the listening was silence itself. He was so overcome afterwards that I was afraid for him — and he has to lecture tomorrow...'[35]

It was at the Royal Hotel, Hamilton, in Canada, that MacDonald had a tiff with a waiter who had asked him to remove his hat. MacDonald crimsoned and threatened to leave, causing a fuss in the restaurant. Fortunately the manager was on hand to smooth things over. They went back to Chicago and then travelled via Detroit to Montreal, where they arrived late in the evening. MacDonald spoke on Burns once again the following Monday, and from there they descended to Massachusetts and Vermont, making a farewell visit to Boston with a benefit matinée lecture. James Fields hosted a farewell dinner party for them with Emerson, Oliver Wendell Holmes, Sothern the actor, and Dr Bellows to say goodbye to the intrepid trio, and there was a further surprise recalled by Greville MacDonald:

'A most generous and understanding thing was done at that time by friends in Boston. Inaugurated by Mrs Whitney, author of the then celebrated *Gayworthys*, they presented what they called a 'Copyright Testimonial' to my father, raising over $1500 in recognition, by a few among the tens of thousands indebted to him, of the fact that his books in America had brought him practically no remuneration. I do not think any of the piratical publishers contributed to the fund; but at least two items were of $500 each.'[36]

They moved for the last time, and their final days in America were spent at Dr J.G. Holland's house on Park Avenue in New York. There were a number of farewell dinners and receptions, and Greville remembered with astonishment:

'A deputation of deacons from a church on Fifth Avenue waited upon my father to ascertain whether he would accept its pastorate at a stipend of $20,000 per annum.'[37]

Without hesitating, MacDonald turned down their offer. Money had never been a lure for him, and homesickness was surging through his blood. As their last days ran out like grains of sand through the neck of an hourglass, MacDonald and Louisa must have reflected that though they had had a marvellous, if at times difficult, experience, their financial hopes had not been fulfilled. Though MacDonald had given his pen a rest, apart from publishing *The Haunted House* in *Scribner's* magazine, and tinkering with Novalis, he went home with only about one thousand pounds in his pocket, a sum he could have easily earned at home. To supplement his bare purse, fifty of his American friends collaborated in organizing a farewell lecture at the Association Hall in New York on Thursday 22 May at 8p.m. Their handbill read:

> 'Learning with regret that you are soon to return to England, we approach you with the hearty request that, before you leave New York, you favor the great multitude of your friends in the city with the opportunity to hear your voice once more in public, on some literary theme agreeable to yourself. We cannot willingly part with one whom we not only admire as an author, but love as a teacher and friend, without, in some practical way, expressing to him our earnest and affectionate good will.'

Tickets were priced at $1.00 and $1.50 in order to bring in a substantial sum, and many of his friends turned out in force to hear him for the last time, including Mark Twain, Richard Watson Gilder, Dr Abram Coles and Dr Holland. Every seat was taken, and the corners of the hall were full. William Cullen Bryant presided, and Dr Bellows bid him farewell on behalf of his American admirers. The subject asked for was *Hamlet*. After Dr Bellows sat down, as so often before, MacDonald mounted the podium and began to speak without notes. His voice rose over the audience:

> 'I have been a student of Shakespeare for many years, and I need not say — at least to those who have also been students of him — that the more I read and the more I think, the more I find out. He is a soil in which you may furrow and find endless roots and flowers that seem to act of themselves... He never gave a single form of human life the cold shoulder... I find that his stories are of no value to him except as they set forth the truths of human nature...the whole main question is: "What sort of a man was this Hamlet? Can we understand him...?" ...when we do not understand we yet feel that we touch the man. We feel that he is of our kind. We are aware that he is not only a type of the human race, but a type of the humanity in each individual; that it is the play of a something come to us all that is there depicted. We perceive a man in perplexity, and yet compelled to act...'

At the end of his address, MacDonald turned to his audience, and gave his final words to America:

'For the kindness I have received in America I am very grateful. We came to you loving and knowing that we should love yet more, and instead of being disappointed, with our hearts larger for the thoughts of so many more friends than we had before, and if word of mine could be of any value, the love between the countries will surely be at least a little strengthened by the report of your goodness which in honesty we are compelled to carry back with us . . . I trust and hope that we in England and you in America, who have the same blood, and the same language, and the same literature, the same Shakespeare, not to speak of the same Bible — whatever our little bickerings be — will only be the better friends for any word that compels us to explain what we mean to each other.'[38]

So saying, he finished, and climbed down from the platform to thunderous applause, where the audience swarmed round him to shake him by the hand.

With tears, emotion and farewells, the MacDonalds boarded the *Calabria* on 24 May and set sail across the Atlantic. June brought sight of Britain looming on the horizon once more, and on the sixth of that month they were finally in the arms of their family once again, on terra firma.

CHAPTER TWENTY-EIGHT

In the Folds of Faerie — Fantasy Novels

Despite a stimulating eight months on the other side of the Atlantic, MacDonald's American experiences never found their way into print, and his later years in Italy were to be expressed in only the first few introductory pages of *A Rough Shaking*, published in 1891. Though Arundel, Bude and London are all described in MacDonald's novels, it is Scotland and Huntly that are most lovingly set down, and it is clear that this is so because they were the places associated with his childhood. Childhood is an elusive thing, and the need to maintain such an image of childhood in himself was strong in MacDonald as his obsessive and constant revisiting of Huntly with all his childhood haunts suggests. He became almost one of his own ghosts, haunting the places of his past.

MacDonald's keen interest in his own ancestry and his Scottish blood was a symptom of his desire to maintain a link with his Scottish heritage. Cut off from his family and his roots in the throbbing metropolis of London, MacDonald felt the need to find a point of integration for his split identity as country boy from Scotland and English city dweller: he did so in his creation of the image of the child. His reading of Wordsworth would have encouraged him to the view that 'The child is father to the man' — an apparent paradox which becomes true if the child is seen somehow as the man's precursor, dwelling in an Eden from which the adult has been expelled. Separated from his rural past, MacDonald must have looked back to his boyhood days as almost existing in a foreign time and place. They had become a fairy-tale, and yet he realized the need to enter imaginatively into his childhood experiences in order to retain a complete identity.[1]

In realizing within himself the spiritual image of the child, he grew more childlike and hence nearer to God. Childhood, for MacDonald, was an important symbol in theological terms as well as emotional and poetic, as he stated so clearly in his *Unspoken Sermon*, 'The Child in the Midst'. As far as MacDonald was concerned, everyone had to become like a little child before they could enter the Kingdom of Heaven, and so, though he found fame as a children's writer, he was not writing for the childish, but for the childlike, as he commented in his essay 'The Fantastic Imagination':

> 'For my part, I do not write for children, but for the childlike, whether of five, or fifty, or seventy-five.'[2]

MacDonald's intention to write for the childlike, and not just for children, marks him off from many other nineteenth-century children's writers. Much of their work was marked and marred by their didacticism and too many of their books were turned out tailor-made for the confines of the schoolroom and the nursery. MacDonald was concerned to teach — but not to give lessons; he was interested in development, and not in restraint.

MacDonald's books were published in the second half of the nineteenth century at a time when children's literature had undergone many changes. Children were now viewed in a different light than they had been earlier; moreover, it was now possible to earn money by writing children's fiction, though it was not a very honourable profession. As a genre children's literature was not established until the 1780s. This was still the Age of Enlightenment and reason held sway: good was rewarded, evil was punished, and the virtues of punctuality, diligence, obedience and industry offered models of what children were supposed to be. Out of the wealth of books that rolled off the Georgian presses, three retained a strong influence until well into the nineteenth century. These were: Mrs Barbauld's *Evenings at Home* (1792–96), Thomas Day's *Sandford and Merton* (1783–89), and Mrs Trimmer's *Fabulous Histories*, later known as *The Robins* (1786), the only one of these books that MacDonald read as a boy. He recalled reading it with delight. Mrs Trimmer wielded a hefty influence in the public domain as a moral guardian and her word was law in many quarters. A writer who enjoyed equal, if not even greater, authority was Maria Edgeworth — she attained some fame as a minor novelist, but her *Moral Tales* and *Practical Education* held sway in many middle-class households. She had a markedly secular approach to her task, and believed in conquering all problems by reason. Any hint of irrationality was firmly excluded, and so magic and fairy-tales were frowned upon. Mrs Trimmer, too, censured fairy-tales in *The Guardian of Education*, pronouncing them:

> '...only fit to fill the heads of children with confused notions of wonderful and supernatural events.'[3]

In the minds of these Georgian writers, then, the image of the child was one of an unkempt garden flourishing with vices which had to be pruned and checked. As a result of this, the books were austere and eschewed all frivolity, and fairy-tales had no place in this scheme of things. To the strict guardians of children's souls they were seen not only as frivolous and irrational, but, even worse, plainly immoral. *Puss in Boots* or *Sleeping Beauty* appeared to have little advice to offer, and there were no worthwhile lessons to be drawn from *Cinderella*. In addition, the unpredictable power of the imagination expressed in fairy-tales was a threatening force that had to be quashed within the well-defined rational order.

By the middle of the nineteenth century, however, the situation was beginning to change. The first collection of fairy-tales in English was published by Benjamin Tabart under the title *Popular Fairy Tales* in 1818, but far more important was the first appearance in 1823 of some of Grimm's fairy-tales, illustrated by George Cruickshank in a sugared edition with many of the bloodcurdling portions cut out. They were an overnight success. Then in 1846, Mary Howitt, herself a successful children's writer, translated ten of Hans Christian Andersen's tales under the title *Wonderful Stories for Children*. Andersen made a triumphant tour of England during the following year and was seen off from Ramsgate pier by Dickens himself. At last fairy-tales were beginning to establish themselves. Progress was slow, but after 1840 the literary fairy-tale — as opposed to rewritten versions of traditional tales — began to make its appearance and with increased leisure time and the acceptance of the novel as entertainment for adults, it became grudgingly accepted that children could have their fun too.

As the novel gained ground, many adult writers such as Mary Howitt, Harriet Martineau, Dinah Mulock, Norman Macleod, Charles Kingsley — and George MacDonald — tried their hand at writing for children. Many of them had a serious religious intent even in their adult fiction and, perhaps with *Pilgrim's Progress* somewhere in the backs of their minds, they began to realize that the allegorical and symbolic elements contained within the fairy-tale could be used for a religious purpose to teach moral lessons to children. A great weakness of the fairy-tales of this period is that many of the writers were so intent on putting the adult point of view, that children had little freedom to sift the meaning of the story for themselves. Dinah Mulock's story *The Little Lame Prince* (1875), for example, strikes a note nowhere to be found in MacDonald. Her tale tells of Prince Dolor, who is dropped accidentally by his nurse as a child, and so remains lame throughout the whole of his life. He is a saintly, Christ-like figure, a little like Diamond in MacDonald's *At the*

Back of the North Wind. Dinah Mulock was a close friend of MacDonald's, and it may well have been that her fairy-writing was strongly influenced by his. Her morality, however, was different:

> 'The sense of *the inevitable*, as grown-up people call it — that we cannot have things as we want them to be, but as they are, and that we must learn to bear them and make the best of them — this lesson, which everybody has to learn soon or late — came, alas! sadly soon, to the poor boy.'[4]

But the fairy-tale world is one in which wishes are realized. The 'inevitable', in the way Dinah Mulock conceives it, is foreign to its borders. For, if fairy-tales are about anything, they are about transformation. It is the failure of the Victorian moralists to see this that caused their tales to be so dull and constricting.

And so even after fairy-tales had achieved a toehold in the nursery, several difficulties lingered. Gillian Avery writes:

> 'They pondered chiefly over two problems, whether children who read fairy tales would ever learn to distinguish between truth and fiction, and whether it was not an iniquitous waste of time to study the kingdoms of fairyland instead of learning the latitude and longitude of Otatieite, and the main products of Peru.'[5]

Facts appeared worryingly opposed to imagination, and magic at odds with morality. Even Dinah Mulock in her preface to *The Fairy Book* in 1863 was careful to say: 'The tender young heart is often reached as soon by the imagination as by the intellect: and without attempting any direct appeal to either reason or conscience, the Editor of this Collection has been especially careful that it should contain nothing which could really harm a child.'

Fairy-tales could sometimes be seen as a dangerous keg of gunpowder about to go off, and they had to be contained in some way. George Cruickshank, who had illustrated the first edition of Grimm's tales in 1823, rewrote some fairy-tales introducing contemporary cautions on temperance and the like, and was soundly taken to task by Dickens. In 'Frauds on the Fairies', Dickens acknowledged the power of fairy-tales for moral good:

> 'Forebearance, courtesy, consideration for the poor and aged, kind treatment of animals, the love of nature, abhorrence of tyranny and brute force — many such good things have been first nourished in the child's heart by this powerful aid.'[6]

From a writer who included many fairy-tale elements in his own novels, perhaps these sentiments are not surprising, but his words were refreshing and new for their time, and he went on to give a hilarious parody of Cruickshank, on the story of *Cinderella*:

> 'Once upon a time, a rich man and his wife were the parents of a lovely daughter. She was a beautiful child, and became, at her own desire, a member of the Juvenile Bands of Hope when she was only four years of age. . .'[7]

Dickens finished his article by declaring:

> 'The world is much with us, early and late. Leave this precious old escape from it alone.'[8]

It was precisely this escape that the moralizing adult voice could not allow. It had to intrude everywhere, instructing the child how to behave at every juncture. Escape to another world was out of the question — there was only this world, and duty and obedience were the set means of living in it, in order to gain a smooth entry to the next.

Fairy-tales were meant to entertain as well as instruct, but purely entertaining books for children only finally reached the nursery with the publication of *Alice's Adventures in Wonderland* in 1865, though Edward Lear's first *Book of Nonsense* had been published, with much acclaim, in 1846. Dodgson's 'amoral' work remains the outstanding children's book of the nineteenth century, written in part as a protest against the didacticism of the children's writing of the day. Dodgson was concerned to give children something to read without pointing an evangelical finger at them, and Wonderland provided the escape that everyone was waiting for. Many such books followed, and as the century progressed, so the adult view of the child continued to shift, and by the 1880s and 1890s children had become over-sentimentalized, either turned into sinless miniature prophets evangelizing their elders, or presented as visions of arcadian sweetness simply beyond belief. Dodgson's own *Sylvie and Bruno* suffers from this, as does MacDonald's protrayal of the Little Ones in *Lilith*.[9] Such a view was a complete about-turn from Mrs Trimmer's ilk and the fulcrum was perhaps *Alice's Adventures in Wonderland*, though Dodgson's book probably marked rather than caused the shift. MacDonald's writing swings to neither pole and his fairy-writing for children is probably the most significant in the English language as he is one of the very few British writers to write lasting fairy-tales and his imaginative power even today stands unrivalled.

It would be tempting to suggest that MacDonald's success was due to the fact that he understood children better than most of his contemporaries — after all, he had eleven of his own — but this does not appear to have been the case. Dodgson and Lear were far more at home with children than MacDonald ever was, and his preface to *Dealings with the Fairies* (1867) stated:

'My Children,
   You know that I do not tell you stories as some papas do. Therefore, I give you a book of stories. You have read them all before except the last...'[10]

This suggests that these stories were not told first to his own children as one might have supposed. In fact, MacDonald had a very grown-up vision of the purpose of fairy-tales, but they had to be floated on to the children's market as there was nowhere else for them to go. He slipped some in, rather unsuccessfully, to *Adela Cathcart* in 1864, for which the critics rapped his knuckles, and the commercial failure of *Phantastes* in 1858 persuaded MacDonald's main energies away from fantastic writing. He did publish a few scattered fairy-tales in the early 1860s which were collected in *Dealings with the Fairies* in 1867 and reissued with much of MacDonald's other work (including *Phantastes*) in the ten-volume set *Works of Fancy and Imagination* in 1871. Fairy-writing remained a negligible part of MacDonald's output, however, until he took up the editorship of *Good Words for the Young* in 1869 which gave him a children's outlet for the kind of writing that he did best. It was almost by accident therefore that *Ranald Bannerman's Boyhood*, *At the Back of the North Wind* and *The Princess and the Goblin* came to be written.

MacDonald's own fairy-writing shows a merging of three distinct trends: the first springs from the romantic thought that was so close to his own heart and expressed itself in everything he wrote. But the mainspring of MacDonald's own romantic theory was to turn the inside outside and in so doing to convey spiritual truth. Earlier in the century there had been a debate between the romantics and the rationalists as to whether it was legitimate to invent creatures of the imagination — such as centaurs or fauns — which did not really exist, but as the analogy of poet as creator gained ground during the nineteenth century, the situation changed, as M.H. Abrams in *The Mirror and the Lamp* comments:

'Thus by the mid-century, what had once been a purely rhetorical figure had become an act of creation, the result of a mental process having its analogue in God's peopling of this world, of which, naturally, the effect on the reader is a sublime astonishment and enlargement of the soul. As a result, poetic personification, together with the fairy way of writing, was elevated to the highest achievement of poetic imagination.'[11]

With this divine dispensation to invent, Spenser at his back, and Dante's *Divine Comedy* to show how moral states could be powerfully realized in strong, visual images, MacDonald naturally turned to fairy-writing as the best means of expressing his intent. More than that, he thoroughly enjoyed fairy-tales. He was a firm admirer of the Grimm brothers and Hans Christian Andersen, and even of Perrault, whose rather cynical and worldly-wise slant he might well have found distasteful. In his own fairy stories MacDonald drew on the literary sources offered to him and did not delve very deeply into local Scottish lore. Kelpies and brownies remain asleep in their rock pools, though the toeless feet of the goblins in *The Princess and Goblin* are a traditional feature, while 'The Carasoyn' has a strong atmosphere of Border minstrelsy. The harsh local history of Huntly, which included warlocks, ghosts and ruined castles, remained part of MacDonald's adult novel world. Most of MacDonald's fairy-tales have a strong Germanic influence, though *The Light Princess* has pleasing echoes of Perrault, and indeed the third trend found in MacDonald's fairy-writing is German romanticism.

If fairies were relegated to the nursery in Britain, this was not at all true in Germany where Hoffmann, Novalis, Tieck and De la Motte Fouqué turned out fantasies for adults. Theirs was a writing which concentrated on spiritual values and differing states of consciousness — in Hoffmann's case bringing the reader to the very edge of madness itself. These writers acknowledged the powerful inner world and the importance of the human spirit. They drew their inspiration from occult writers and ultimately from Hegel. There was simply no place for such writing within the context of the domestic Victorian novel, heir as it was to the British empirical tradition—at least, not overtly. But German romanticism ran deeply in MacDonald's blood, and the fluidity of Hoffmann's prose, for example in 'The Mines of Falun' where the melancholy Elis Fröbom wavers between waking and dreaming, resembles many passages in MacDonald's own writing.[12]

MacDonald felt a similar split within himself, though he thought that his vital spiritual vision ought to serve to transfigure the commonplace. Indeed the whole Victorian mind itself was split, though it did not realize it. The strange fairy paintings of J.A. Fitzgerald, for example, showing colourful dream scenes issuing out of the minds of sleeping individuals, or the canvases of Richard Dadd who actually went mad, bear testimony to an inner world that was crying out for recognition. There was no place for a British Hoffmann, however, and MacDonald's stories went out under the guise of 'children's writing'. MacDonald's fairy-tales were dear to him and keep cropping up in different publications throughout his career.[13] The MacDonald family theatricals included many renditions of fairy tales such as 'Cinderella', 'Beauty and the Beast', and 'Bluebeard' and sometimes MacDonald , tiring of lecturing, would read a fairy-tale to his audience and on occasion even advertised such readings. Clearly fairy-tales had an important role to play in his life, and his imagination naturally shaped itself in their direction. Such a tendency can also be seen in his manuscripts. While he laboured over the novels, correcting and recorrecting many times, his children's work is much freer from heavy corrections and obviously flowed from his pen with greater ease.

The fairy-tale, when all is said and done, is a deceptive form: for all its apparent simplicity there are very few people who have successfully written lasting fairy-tales. Even today children are reared on Perrault, Hans Christian Andersen and Grimm. There is an elusive quality about a good fairy-tale which marks it off from imitations. MacDonald counted among his friends many writers who attempted some fairy-tales, including Thackeray, Ruskin, Dinah Mulock, Norman Macleod and Charles Kingsley, but of these only Kingsley's *The Water Babies*, Ruskin's 'King of the Golden River' and Thackeray's *The Rose and the Ring* are regularly reprinted.[14] The German poet Schiller wrote:

> 'Deeper meaning resides in the fairy tales told to me in my childhood than in the truth that is taught by life.'

MacDonald, in fact, had a very coherent idea of what a fairy-tale was, and what it should be. In "The Fantastic Imagination" he wrote:

> 'Everyone, however, who feels the story, will read its meaning after his own nature and development: one man will read one meaning in it, another will read another . . . But indeed your children are not likely to trouble you about the meaning. They find what they are capable of finding, and more would be too much.'[15]

This essay, printed first as the preface to an American edition of *The Light Princess and Other Fairy Tales* in 1893 and later incorporated into *A Dish of Orts*, was the first and only treatise in the nineteenth century on the writing of fairy-tales. MacDonald's intention was to bring to consciousness something which had until then remained firmly in the unconscious — that is, fantasy writing. In some ways, MacDonald would have agreed with Bruno Bettelheim. In *The Uses of Enchantment* Bettelheim makes the point, for instance, that in Hindu medicine, fairy stories are used to overcome an emotional disturbance. In MacDonald's second novel, *Adela Cathcart*, fairy-tales are put to precisely that use. Adela Cathcart is ill with a wasting ailment and the innovative Dr Armstrong devises a homoeopathic cure for her: a reading club is devised and stories — mainly fairy stories, including 'The Light Princess', 'The Shadows' and 'The Giant's Heart' — are read aloud night after night until the girl is better and able to make her own fairy-tale ending by marrying the doctor. It was no coincidence that the novel was dedicated to Rutherford Russell, himself a distinguished homoeopathic doctor and friend of MacDonald's.

Having established the therapeutic quality of fairy-tales, the progress of his characters from immaturity to maturity in the tales is distinct. In 'The Light Princess', for example, the princess has to regain her gravity, in every sense of the word, while in 'The Wise Woman' the wise woman herself, intent on improving the character of the spoiled Princess Rosamond admonishes her with:

> ' "Nobody can be a real princess — do not imagine you have yet been anything more than a mock one — until she is a princess over herself, that is, until, when she finds herself unwilling to do the thing that is right, she makes herself do it." '[16]

And the theme of rebirth is never far distant. In 'The Golden Key', when the fish that has led Tangle through the wood hops into the grandmother's pot, she reassures the girl that:

> ' "In Fairyland," resumed the lady, as they sat down to the table, "the ambition of the animals is to be eaten by the people, for that is their highest end in that condition. But they are not therefore destroyed. Out of that pot comes something more than the dead fish, you will see." '[17]

The woman lifts the lid of the pot and a creature like a young winged angel flies out, reborn through its willing sacrifice into a higher form of life. What this means is hard to pin down precisely — it is an event to puzzle over — but MacDonald happily invited an imaginative participation in the meaning of his stories. Such openness is a marked difference from the intrusive adult voices intent on laying down the law in the Victorian nursery.

MacDonald's strength was that he allowed children to think for themselves while reading his tales, and at the same time fed them symbols which would help them to master their inner experiences. He did fall into line with other Victorian writers on many issues — but usually with a difference. In stressing obedience, for example, MacDonald did not see this as an end in itself, nor did he ever threaten children with eternal punishment — rather he saw obedience as opening the door to further spiritual development. Obedience was not merely to please God, or one's parents, but to bring about growth. Similarly, in his tales punishment is always a form of purification and evil usually turns to good in the end. MacDonald never exposes children to the grotesque just for the sake of it, and never promises them an evil fate if they are not good. Unlikely as the conclusion of 'The Cruel Painter' seems, with Teufelsbürst's sudden conversion from an evil maniac to a kindly grandfather, his end is the necessary one, in MacDonald's eyes, so that all will turn good. Instead of expunging the fantastic and the bizarre, MacDonald delighted in it, and his fairy-tales draw on many traditional motifs. 'The Giant's Heart' has shades of *Jack and the Beanstalk*; christenings go wrong in 'Little Daylight' and 'The Light Princess' as they do in 'Sleeping Beauty'; Anodos's room in *Phantastes* is named like Beauty's in 'Beauty and the Beast' and it seems characteristic of MacDonald's vision that when Irene trips up the stairs in *The Princess and the Goblin* and hears a spinning wheel, she opens the door to find, not a cruel fairy, but a grandmother to protect her and watch over her. Though evil and cruelty exist in MacDonald's tales, his view of the world is ultimately benevolent.

For MacDonald, a fairy-tale was a special kind of construct which enabled him to express his particular view of life. In the strange and symbolic 'Letter to American Boys' published in 1878, MacDonald showed how a fairy-tale might begin:

> 'There was once a wise man to whom was granted the power to send forth his thoughts in shapes that other people could see. And as he walked abroad in the world, he came upon some whom his wisdom might serve.'

Using this as a basic model, MacDonald went on to write in *The Fantastic Imagination* of the two most important considerations in creating a fairy world:

> 'His world once invented, the highest law that comes next into play is, that there shall be harmony between the laws by which the new world has begun to exist; and in the process of his creation, the inventor must hold by those laws. The moment he forgets one of them, he makes the story, by its own postulates, incredible. To be able to live in a moment in an imagined world, we must see the laws of its existence obeyed. Those broken, we fall out of it.'[18]

Though physical laws could be changed for the purposes of storytelling, and indeed the introduction of magic into a fairy-tale necessitated this, MacDonald insisted that moral laws were universal and immutable:

'In the moral world it is different: there a man may clothe in new forms, and for this employ his imagination freely, but he must invent nothing. He may not, for any purpose, turn its laws upside down. He must not meddle with the relations of live souls. The laws of the spirit of man must hold, alike in this world and in any world he may invent... In physical things a man may invent; in moral things he must obey — and take their laws with him into his invented world as well.'[19]

This statement is a blueprint for MacDonald's use of the fairy-tale. What he did was to take the traditional form and restructure it, giving it a moral vision, without killing it. That is perhaps his greatest legacy to children's literature as a whole and his vision, through time, has become the accepted one.

In dealing with the fairy-tale form MacDonald was struggling to bring unconscious material — the stuff of fantasy — to consciousness, and he was always aware that the action of the fairy story on the reader was something that could not be scientifically measured. In *The Fantastic Imagination* he only offered definitions of the fairy-tale by analogy, likening it to a sonata and writing:

'Let fairytale of mine go for a firefly that now flashes, now is dark, but may flash again. Caught in a hand which does not love its kind, it will turn to an insignificant, ugly thing, that can neither flash nor fly.

The best way with music, I imagine, is not to bring the forces of our intellect to bear upon it, but to be still and let it work on that part of us for whose sake it exists.'[20]

MacDonald is a curious writer in that the sum of his work is greater than its individual parts. While he is one of the most potent writers of fairy-tales in the English language, perhaps the greatest of all, his individual tales are often clumsy and very uneven. Head and shoulders above the rest stand 'The Light Princess' and 'The Golden Key' while the others have much to make the reader wrinkle his brow. 'The Giant's Heart', for example, paints an uncomfortable picture of a giant who gorges himself on vegetable-like children, and who is finally outwitted by the embarrassingly named Tricksy-Wee and her younger brother Buffy-Bob. With the aid of some spiders (imported from *Heinrich von Ofterdingen*) the children manage to steal the giant's heart and destroy him by dropping poisonous spider-juice on it to torture him, and then at the last minute Buffy-Bob finishes off the job with his knife:

'But Buffy-Bob was too quick for Thunder-thump. He sprang to the heart, and buried his knife in it, up to the hilt. A fountain of blood spouted from it; and with a dreadful groan the giant fell dead at the feet of little Tricksy-Wee, who could not help being sorry for him, after all.'[21]

Perhaps it is the cynicism of the children, their lack of compassion, and their readiness to break their word which makes this story such uncomfortable reading. The violence is too excessive and the different elements of the tale do not cohere. MacDonald had an eye for what made a story work and what did not, though he could not always explain it. Early in March 1861 he wrote to Louisa:

'I read Ulf and several other stories, they are all translations and very bad ones. But as stories they just want the one central spot of red — the wonderful thing which whether in a fairy story or a world, or a human being is the life depth — whether of truth or humour or pathos — the eye to the face of it — the thing that shows the unshowable.'[22]

Whatever that 'one central spot of red' is, it seems missing from 'The Giant's Heart'.

Another problematic tale is 'The Cruel Painter', a Hoffmannesque piece set in Prague. A young student called Karl von Wolkenlicht is infatuated with Lilith, the beautiful but cold daughter of an evil painter called Teufelsbürst. Teufelsbürst's greatest delight is to depict gross suffering in the context of indifferent beauty. It is a tale of cruelty and mock vampirism, whimpering out in a rather pathetic joke, but the descriptions of the paintings themselves are horrific:

'He had represented poor Wolkenlicht as just beginning to recover from a trance, while a group of surgeons, unaware of the signs of returning life, were absorbed in a minute dissection of one of the limbs. At an open door he had painted Lilith passing, with her face buried in a bunch of sweet peas.'[23]

Similar cruelty is found in an early draft of 'The History of Photogen and Nycteris,' though it was later excised: the witch Watho 'who desired to know everything', slits open a pregnant woman while she is asleep in order to peer at the workings of the growing embryo. Such uncoverings of the dark side of the psyche, adapted from German romanticism, reveal an unexpected element of violence in MacDonald's imagination. If fantasy brings to the surface areas of the mind normally repressed, then it is a salutary reminder that even in a man as humane as MacDonald such elements have a powerful existence. They remind us of our own shadowy sides.

Another side of MacDonald's fairy writing is to be found in the appropriately named 'The Light Princess', the most humorous of all

MacDonald's stories. It tells of a young girl who is enchanted at her christening so that she loses her sense of gravity — that is, she floats about and cannot take anything seriously. The only time she regains her weight is when she falls into the nearby lake and, true to form, a handsome prince arrives to find her swimming and falls in love with her. She shows no interest in him however, until, through the machinations of the evil Fairy Makemnoit, the level of the lake begins to subside, and the prince offers to sacrifice himself as a plughole, the only way to save the lake, and the princess, who is wasting away. This is a startling image combining elements of Christ's own sacrifice with sexual union. At the last minute she saves him, regains her weight, and they live happily ever after. The tale follows the princess from light-headed immaturity to maturity in regaining her gravity and sacrificing her own nature to save the prince's life. It also includes the traditional 'fairy' christening with kings and queens and wicked fairies. Some critics have read it as a parable involving menstruation. It is certainly a tale in which sexuality plays an important role. The swimming scenes are so overtly erotic that Ruskin took MacDonald to task over them — though MacDonald did not heed his friend's advice. As fairy-tales became more and more a popular diet for children, so the passions were expunged from them, but MacDonald reintroduced them. 'The Light Princess' is very erotic in places, while in *The Princess and the Goblin* Irene and Curdie are both obviously attracted to one another, though still young children, and the first book ends with a kiss, while *The Princess and Curdie* shows their marriage.

MacDonald believed in a wholesome integration of feeling, while Ruskin was not so sure. He wrote back to MacDonald:

> 'Only one word about that question of the passions. I wholly feel with you that the harm done by ignoring them has been fearful. But I think they ought to be approached in a graver and grander manner — that fairy tales — and everything calculated for readers under 14 or 15, should be wholly free to every sexual thought — that afterwards passion should be given in serious and glorious truth — as the great law and sanctification of all bodily life — I can't quite define the manner — I only know as a boy, that Romeo and Juliet and Corregio never did me harm — but French novels and pictures did. There is much to be thought out — and *tried* out before we can talk with any probability of useful result on this matter — nevertheless — but I shall so like to have a talk with you about it when you come back.'[24]

MacDonald, however, was determined to go his own way and did not snip out any of the erotic elements in his stories. Perhaps he was enlightened enough to realize that the sexual element never can be fully repressed.

The other tale which ranks with 'The Light Princess' is 'The Golden Key' (1867), an original tale that stands outside the mainstream of the fairy tradition. Though it contains many elements common in MacDonald, such as the wise grandmother, the wood, and the children living on the borders of Fairyland, it is more of a mystic parable, akin to 'The Parable of the Singer' in *Within and Without* or the symbolic tale embedded in 'A Letter to American Boys'. Mossy and Tangle, two children who stumble into Fairyland, are led by a marvellous 'air-fish' to the cottage of the wise woman, who allows the children to call her 'Grandmother'. After eating the fish, Tangle finds that all her senses are heightened, for Fairyland is a place of perception, where the marvellous lies hidden in the mundane. At the very beginning of his tale, MacDonald tells us:

> 'Things that look real in this country look very thin indeed in
> Fairyland, while some of the things that here cannot stand still for a
> moment, will not move there.'[25]

Mossy, the boy, finds a golden key, and together with Tangle, is sent out on a journey by the wise woman to find the keyhole and with it 'the country whence the shadows fall'. When Tangle is reluctant to leave the wise woman's cottage, she is warned:

> 'You must go with him, Tangle. I am sorry to lose you, but it will be
> the best thing for you. Even the fishes, you see, have to go into the pot,
> and then out into the dark.'[26]

On their journey the children grow old until their hair is streaked with grey, and they finally lose each other. The story then follows Tangle's journey down to the heart of the earth and her three encounters with the elemental Old Men of the Sea, Earth and Fire. The Old Man of the Sea gives her a bath of water from which she is renewed to continue her journey to find the Old Man of the Earth; he points her on her way to the Old Man of the Fire, the oldest man of all, who is yet no more than a baby. It is here that MacDonald's symbolic writing comes into its own, and anticipates fully what he was to achieve thirty years later in *Lilith*. The visual images of the tale are indelibly powerful:

> 'Then the Old Man of the Earth stooped over the floor of the cave,
> raised a huge stone from it, and left it leaning. It disclosed a great hole
> that went plumb-down.
> "This is the way," he said.

"But there are no stairs."

"You must throw yourself in. There is no other way."

She turned and looked him full in the face — stood so for a whole minute, as she thought: it was a whole year — then threw herself headlong into the hole.'[27]

Tangle arrives in the secret heart of the earth and finds the Old Man of the Fire:

'He went on busily, tirelessly, playing his solitary game, without looking up, or seeming to know that there was a stranger in his deep-withdrawn cell. Diligently as a lace-maker shifts her bobbins, he shifted and arranged his balls. Flashes of meaning would now pass from them to Tangle, and now again all would be not merely obscure, but utterly dark.'[28]

The Old Man of the Fire hatches a serpent out of an egg for Tangle which leads her to find Mossy. Finally reunited they find the keyhole in the rainbow:

'He took his key. It turned in the lock to the sounds of Aeolian music. A door opened upon slow hinges, and disclosed a winding stair within.'[29]

At last they are able to ascend slowly to the country whence the shadows fall. There is nothing irrational or extraneous about the events of 'The Golden Key', though its symbolism is complex and puzzling. In it, MacDonald passes far beyond ordinary morality — he is offering a myth to live by. It is the reader's task to realize that myth within him or herself.

Though MacDonald's longer books for children are often different from his fairy-tales in style and tone, he never abandoned the underlying mechanism of fairy-tales and indeed they lie at the base of all his fiction, including his novels. MacDonald's recipe for a story was formed according to his view of the world, and the world's story was for him one big fairy story. As he wrote in *Mary Marston*:

'For nobody can make a story without somebody wicked to set things wrong in it, and then all the work lies in setting them right again, and as soon as they are set right, then the story stops.'[30]

MacDonald's longer stories for children fall into two groups of three. On the one hand are the less well-known *Ranald Bannerman's Boyhood*, *A Rough Shaking* and *Gutta Percha Willie*. These are 'realistic' stories and counterbalance MacDonald's more famous fantasies — *At the Back of the*

North Wind, The Princess and the Goblin and *The Princess and Curdie.*
Ranald Bannerman's Boyhood is another account of MacDonald's boyhood experiences, cast into English, while *Gutta Percha Willie* is a slight
tale about a boy with a marvellous engineering skill who discovers a
healing stream and builds a spa for the poor and disabled.

A Rough Shaking is perhaps the least satisfactory of these three
stories: the boy Clare Skymer, orphaned by an earthquake, journeys
through the tribulations of life until he is finally reunited with his
father. St Clare was the female counterpart of St Francis, and the
book opens with the narrator marvelling at the adult Clare's
St Francis-like relationship with his animals. The problem with the
book is that MacDonald piles misfortune after misfortune on to his
young hero, who comes smiling patiently through each catastrophe.
The degree of cruelty he undergoes is disturbing: after being rescued
from the ruins of the earthquake, he is fostered by a parson and his
wife who later die; on their deaths he is forthwith rejected by his
crabbed aunt, and taken in by a farmer and his wife who also reject
him. Finally forced to tramp the open roads, Clare is bruised, beaten,
kicked and mistreated for the rest of the book. At one point he
rescues an abandoned baby whose feet are gnawed by rats. With a
few other boys he sets up home in an abandoned house until he is
arrested and the baby taken away from him. The story continues
until Clare's final abduction when he is stowed on a ship by his
enemies. Miraculously, it turns out that his father is the captain of
the ship. MacDonald has a clear purpose in writing the story:

> 'The chief difference between Clare's history and that of most
> others was, that his began at the unusual end. Clare began with
> loving everybody; and most people take a long time to grow to
> that.'[31]

Clare Skymer is another version of Diamond, saintly and Christ-like,
but as in the old story of Patient Griselda, the need for psychological
truth distorts MacDonald's tale and the result is an unease in the
reader which MacDonald did not intend. Clare Skymer appears, not
so much as a laudable figure, but as someone in need of psychiatric
help. While Diamond is largely the stuff of fairy-tale and can be
accepted on those terms, Clare Skymer's adventures are presented
realistically, and though his life is one long fairy-tale of adversity
until the miraculous end, it jars because MacDonald has mixed his
worlds to no good purpose quite unlike his triumph in *At the Back
of the North Wind.*

MacDonald's fantasy works, on the other hand, have achieved a lasting place on children's bookshelves. Like his fairy-tales they deal with transformation and plumb the workings of inner reality. The leap from fairy-tale to fantasy is a short one, moving from a traditional to a personal structure, but retaining the deeper purpose. MacDonald's fantasy writing is an act of reclaiming those areas of the psyche long repressed by rationalism and coded out of recognition in 'realistic' fiction. Trying to define the fantasy mode is as elusive a task as pinning a single meaning to any of the symbols MacDonald employs in his work. But fantasy can be seen as the 'night side' complement to the 'day side' rationality of the realistic novel. It is the novel's shadow, its shimmering shadowy reflection. As the 'night side' is largely a dream-world, so figures and forms slip and slide into one another and meaning itself becomes fluid and elusive. The day-time concrete familiarity dissolves in the fantasy world, uncovering another kind of 'truth' which normally remains hidden, laying the psyche, with all its confusions and contradictions, bare to inspection.

Through his fantasy MacDonald wished to transform his readers' relationship with the world. In one sense *At the Back of the North Wind* sets out to do just this. As in MacDonald's novels, it is full of dreams and poems — for example, Nanny's dream of the man in the moon, and Diamond's strange landscape of left-handed cherub boys. Carrying his love of horses to an extreme, MacDonald names his young hero Diamond, after his father's horse, and pictures him sleeping above the stable. The story is about Diamond's night-time adventures with North Wind, who appears to the boy in the guise of a beautiful woman, and tells how Diamond got to the back of the North Wind and returned. It is a sprawling, loosely-written book and Diamond emerges as a stained-glass Victorian emblem of perfection. The only other book it resembles is Charles Kingsley's *Water Babies*, published earlier in 1863.

While it is true that Kingsley and MacDonald share some interesting features in their work — such as Tom's purgatorial cleansing from grimy chimney sweep to clean water baby; the embracing female figure of Mother Carey, a little like Irene's great-great-grandmother; and an interest in devolution in the tale of the hapless Doasyoulikes — Kingsley's aim is to make Tom grow into a fine English gentleman and his outlook is too contemporary for MacDonald, even though Tom's cleansing is to make him fit for the kingdom of heaven. Both took F.D. Maurice as their master, and both were heavily influenced by Dante, so there is a similarity of outlook, but MacDonald is much more metaphysical than Kingsley. Kingsley is happy with allegory and the terms of marine biology; *At the*

Back of the North Wind by contrast contains complex theological ideas, many of them drawn from Dante.

The book begins with MacDonald's claim that:

> 'I have been asked to tell you about the back of the North Wind. An old Greek writer mentions a people who lived there, and were so comfortable that they could not bear it any longer, and drowned themselves. My story is not the same as his. I do not think Herodotus had got the right account of the place. I am going to tell you how it fared with a boy who went there.'[32]

Herodotus and his Hyperboreans apart, the country at the back of the North Wind resembles Dante's account of the Earthly Paradise in the *Purgatorio* (Cantos 28–33) as does Diamond's first sight of the land rising sheer as a peak out of the ocean. This is exactly Dante's account of Purgatory as a mountain rising out of the water on the other side of the world from Jerusalem and which he and his guide, Virgil, begin to ascend. When Diamond finally arrives at the back of the North Wind, MacDonald comments:

> 'The Italian, then, informs us that he had to enter that country through a fire so hot that he would have thrown himself into boiling glass to cool himself. This was not Diamond's experience, but then Durante — that was the name of the Italian, and it means Lasting, for his books will last as long as there are enough men in the world worthy of having them — Durante was an elderly man, and Diamond was a little boy, and so their experiences must be a little different. The peasant girl, on the other hand, fell fast asleep in a wood, and woke in the same country.'[33]

MacDonald altered Dante's name to uncover some of the meaning that the poet held for him. The name Durante signifies eternity, and is fitting for one who was, to MacDonald, the poet of poets and unrivalled in his moral and spiritual vision. The peasant girl he refers to comes from James Hogg's poem *The Queen's Wake* (1813) in which Kilmeny, a young peasant girl, falls asleep and into a dream world greater than the reality — a familiar fate for MacDonald's characters. Both Dante and Kilmeny are thus pioneering explorers in a realm to which MacDonald is about to introduce his child readers. Giving Dante to children may seem a fruitless task, but, as *At the Back of the North Wind* was the most popular of all his children's books, MacDonald must have, at least in part, succeeded.

The book has a double story, alternating between the daily city life of the London streets and Diamond's night-time adventures with North

Wind. At first Diamond undergoes the usual MacDonald confusion as to whether he is asleep or awake:

> 'He began to wonder whether he was in a dream or not. It was important to determine this; "for," thought Diamond, "if I am in a dream, I am safe in my bed, and I needn't cry."'[34]

Soon convinced that he is really awake, Diamond flies off with North Wind into the night and begins observing her at her work. She has some curious qualities. Like the great-great-grandmother in *The Princess and Curdie* books, North Wind has the protean ability to change shape, often according to the moral state of those who encounter her. One of the first things she does is to frighten a gin-swigging nurse away from her bottle by assuming the shape of a wolf. Explaining her action to Diamond, she says:

> '"I had to make myself look like a bad thing before she could see me — If I had put on any other shape than a wolf's she would not have seen me, for that is what is growing to be her own shape inside of her."'[35]

This is a theme which MacDonald picked up more powerfully later in *The Princess and Curdie* (1883). North Wind thus reveals herself as primarily a theological instrument using apparent evil to bring about good. It is clear that her morality is different from that of the everyday world when she tells Diamond: '"We call your father a gentleman in our house..."' Shortly after the incident with the nurse, Diamond sets off with North Wind once more, but she leaves him at a church in order to go and sink a ship. Diamond is a little alarmed at this, but North Wind comforts him with:

> '"No; I could not be cruel if I would. I can do nothing cruel, although I often do what looks like cruel to those who do not know what I really am doing."'[36]

In a roundabout way the story shows good coming out of evil in the sinking of the ship. First, it brings Diamond's old neighbour Mr Coleman to bankruptcy:

> 'So North Wind had to look after Mr Coleman, and try to make an honest man of him. So she sank the ship which was his last venture, and he was what himself and his wife and the world called ruined.'[37]

Apart from this attempt to make Mr Coleman grow honest, it seems that his former wealth has proved a barrier between his daughter and her poor lover, whom she believes has drowned with the ship. When he returns and is guided (with a few helpful puffs from North Wind) back to Miss Coleman, the two are reunited and marry, and at last the course of true love runs smooth. The moral lesson is an old one of MacDonald's — that good will come out of evil and, in fact, evil is just another shape of good. Given that this tenet is central to MacDonald's thinking, he did not hedge the difficulties in his portrayal of a storm and a sinking with loss of life. When Diamond asks the question 'Why?' even North Wind herself can only answer that she is 'obeying orders'.

The longer Diamond spends with North Wind the more unearthly he becomes, until his mother begins to worry about his health and a trip is arranged to stay with an aunt at Sandwich. It is while he is staying there that Diamond asks North Wind if he can travel to the country at her back, and she agrees, though she warns him that the journey is a long and difficult one. Lifting Diamond up, she first deposits him on a German ship sailing to the North Pole, and from there Diamond sails further into the Arctic on an iceberg. Finally, after many days, he catches sight of the peak rising sheer out of the water, and sees North Wind sitting feeble and wan on the threshold of the country he wishes to enter. He must first of all pass through her:

> 'Diamond walked towards her instantly. When he reached her knees, he put out his hand to lay it on her, but nothing was there save an intense cold. He walked on. Then all grew white about him; and the cold stung him like fire. He walked on still, groping through the whiteness. It thickened about him. At last, it got into his heart, and he lost all sense. I would say that he fainted — only whereas in common faints all grows black about you, he felt swallowed up in whiteness. It was when he reached North Wind's heart that he fainted and fell. But as he fell, he rolled over the threshold.'[38]

Having taken Diamond to the country at the back of the North Wind, MacDonald had problems in describing it: 'I have now come to the most difficult part of my story. And why? Because I do not know enough about it.'[39]

It is a strange place where there is no sun, only a rayless light, and where the flowers have no strong colour. Only the singing river provides any sound — a sound not heard with the ears. There are few other people there, but when they look at each other they understand everything. When Diamond climbs a tree he can see the whole land unrolled beneath him like a map. One day, after he has decided to go home, he realizes that it really has turned into a map and he walks across it back to the threshold of the country where he finds North Wind still waiting for him. Diamond feels that he has been gone for a hundred years, but North Wind tells him that he has been away only seven days. She picks him up in her arms and Diamond falls asleep, only to wake up in bed in Sandwich. His mother bursts into tears, and with a start the reader learns that the boy has been seriously ill and is only now recovering. From the moment Diamond returns to the real world and leaves his sick bed he has two intentions: one is to return to the country at the back of the North Wind; and the other is to do good. Diamond's experience at North Wind's back has 'touched' or 'sainted' him, as though he has been let in on some of the secrets of existence, and after being at the back of the North Wind he realizes that he need never be afraid of anything ever again.

When Diamond's family tumble on hard times, and his father is forced to become a cabman, and then falls ill, Diamond takes his place and is soon a feature of the London streets. He sings strange songs to his baby sister, helps rehabilitate a drunken neighbour, and rescues the street-sweeper, Nanny, and her friend Cripple Jim from destitution. Both Nanny and Jim have little time for Diamond, thinking that he is simple, and calling him 'God's baby', but Mr Raymond, their benefactor, who is also a poet, believes in him: '"I suspect the child's a genius," said the poet to himself, "and that's what makes people think him silly."'[40] Diamond *is* silly, but only, according to MacDonald, in the old, true sense of being blessed.

To many modern readers Diamond is a prig, a cardboard saint without an ounce of real blood in his veins. They find him sentimental. But MacDonald was in no doubt as to Diamond's true nature. When the narrator of the story meets Diamond, he writes:

'It seemed to me, somehow, as if little Diamond possessed the secret of life, and was himself what he was so ready to think the lowest living thing — an angel of God with something special to say or do. A gush of reverence came over me, and with a single *good night*, I turned and left him in his nest.'[41]

Such children are, in Victorian fiction, ready for heaven and too good to live, and Diamond is no exception. But, as is always the case with MacDonald, dying for Diamond is like going home — a happy, peaceful event without tears, and just before he does so he learns that the country at the back of the North Wind which he first visited was only a pale imitation of the real country where he is now headed. It is only towards the end of the book that North Wind reveals herself as the lovable face of Death:

'"People call me by dreadful names, and think they know all about me. But they don't. Sometimes they call me Bad Fortune, sometimes Evil Chance, sometimes Ruin; and they have another name for me which they think the most dreadful of all..."'[42]

Self-indulgent and sentimental though *At the Back of the North Wind* may be, MacDonald's skill in translating complex theological ideas into language fit for children is impressive, and the haunting figure of North Wind remains compelling long after the reader has laid the book to one side.

Diamond was actually no mere figment of MacDonald's imagination, but was based squarely on his ill-fated son Maurice, MacDonald's favourite son. MacDonald held high hopes that he would enter the church and even become a bishop. Sadly this was not to be. The boy makes another appearance as the equally saintly Mark Raymount in *Weighed and Wanting* published in 1882. Maurice, however, was not the only one of MacDonald's children to find his way into print. As in many families, the MacDonalds had nicknames for all their children. Maurice had the fairy nickname of *Bogie*, Lilia's was *Goosie*, and Irene's was — *Goblin*.

The Princess and the Goblin is often reckoned as MacDonald's master-piece for children, and is certainly the most straightforwardly written of all his books. The book itself is a deceptively simple story of a motherless princess called Irene who is growing up alone, attended by servants, in a half castle, half house, half-way up a mountain. Unknown to her, the goblins who live under the mountain are hatching a plot to tunnel through to the house and abduct her, intending to marry her off to their Crown Prince Harelip. Their plot is foiled, however, by Curdie, a miner's son, and the princess's great-great-grandmother, who lives at the top of the house unbeknown to anyone except Irene, who discovers her one day. What makes the book special is the way in which everything is charged with a mysterious symbolism. The whole book falls under the spell of Irene's great-great-grandmother — as indeed does the reader.

Climbing a stair one day when she is bored, Princess Irene finds a mysterious woman spinning in the moonlight, an activity only indulged in on moonlit nights when the moon is shining on her wheel. The wheel, then, is a symbol of cosmic creativity, associated with the moon, and suggesting female wholeness. The great-great-grandmother figure herself is further associated with the moon in that she can wax and wane, appearing young or old at will, yet she only appears at night. In *The Princess and Curdie* she appears under the chapter heading 'Mistress of the Silver Moon'. Her room is itself a picture of the night sky, for the walls are painted blue with stars (a little like MacDonald's own study at The Retreat), and she has a silvery lamp which shines like the moon and can guide lost travellers when she wants it to, though it is not often that anyone catches sight of it. She lives in the midst of a swarm of white pigeons and feeds off their eggs, and in her room she also has a fire:

> 'Then Irene looked again, and saw that what she had taken for a huge bouquet of red roses on a low stand against the wall, was in fact a fire which burned in the shapes of the loveliest and reddest roses, glowing gorgeously between the heads and wings of two cherubs of shining silver.'[43]

The rose has long been a mystic symbol in the Western tradition, and the two cherubs only add to the suggestion that this is a holy fire. Equally, the white pigeons, so like doves, are messengers or angels, symbols of peace, while the fire and the moon suggest both purity and virginity.[44] There is something purgatorial and purificatory about the grandmother, as well as comforting, as she appears in the guise of an older female, all-encompassing and protective relative. At one point the grandmother cleanses Irene, giving her a bath, as a form of baptism, for, as the young girl comes out of it, she finds: 'When she stood up on the floor, she felt as if she had been made over again.'[45]

The grandmother is too mysterious to be a purely allegorical figure, though she shows many faces. One of the times Irene visits her she notices:

> 'There was the moonlight streaming in at the window, and in the middle of the moonlight sat the old lady in her black dress with the white lace, and her silvery hair mingling with the moonlight, so that you could not have told which was which.'[46]

The woman reveals that she is hundreds of years old, but there is nothing feeble about her. Her name is Irene too, and she chides her young great-great-granddaughter with:

> '— but it *is* so silly of people to fancy that old age means crookedness and witheredness and feebleness and sticks and spectacles and rheumatism and forgetfulness! It is so silly! Old age has nothing whatever to do with all that. The right old age means strength and beauty and mirth and courage and clear eyes and strong painless limbs.'[47]

Like North Wind, Irene's great-great-grandmother exists, to some extent, in the eye of the beholder. Irene finds her because her grandmother wants her to, but sees her only because she herself is perceptive enough to do so. As the old lady tells the princess:

> 'Besides, nobody could find the room except I pleased. Besides again — I will tell you a secret — if that light were to go out, you would fancy yourself lying in a bare garret, on a heap of old straw, and would not see one of the pleasant things round about you all the time.'[48]

And so, when Irene finally takes Curdie to see her great-great-grandmother, he can see nothing at all and is hurt that Irene is poking fun at him:

> '"I see a tub, and a heap of musty straw, and a withered apple, and a ray of sunlight coming through a hole in the middle of the roof, and shining on your head, and making all the place look a curious dusky brown."'[49]

Irene, then, is more spiritually advanced than Curdie, which is why she can see her grandmother and Curdie cannot. And whereas the goblins, who long ago scurried underground, have degenerated both physically and morally (though they have increased in craftiness — of all sorts), Irene's grandmother represents a higher form of existence. Physical and geographical position reflects moral and spiritual purity: Irene has to climb a stair to reach her grandmother and she lives at the top of the house. Curdie, who spends most of his time under the ground, cannot see her, and in *The Princess and the Goblin* encounters her only once in a dream when she comes to heal his wounds. It could be said that the tripartite structure of grandmother, princess and goblins suggests spirit, mind and body. Certainly within the story there is a decided move from immaturity to maturity: up until the beginning of the story Irene has led a totally sheltered life, unaware even of the goblins' existence, but through her adventures she gains courage — rescuing Curdie from being trapped behind a rock, for example, and leading him out of the mountain — all at her grandmother's instigation. The book ends with her first erotic kiss, showing her approach to the threshold of womanhood.

In many ways the story fuses romance and Christian symbolism. For instance, the biblical references are overt when Curdie announces, 'I'm Peter's son,'[50] and later we are told that his family cottage is built on a rock so that the flood does not destroy it. On the other hand, the world presented is an ideal one of medieval romance, as realized through the figure of the king, Irene's father (drawn by Arthur Hughes to look like MacDonald) who is the epitome of *largesse*:

> '... but he moved from place to place, that all his people might know him. Wherever he journeyed, he kept a constant look out for the ablest

and best men to put into office; and wherever he found himself mistaken, and those he had appointed incapable or unjust, he removed them at once.'[51]

MacDonald was a vigorous adherent of the nineteenth-century cult of medievalism, a protest against the materialism of his day. He saw enshrined in medievalism all the virtues which he felt necessary to build a truly Christian society. All these virtues are embedded in the world of *The Princess and the Goblin* and epitomized in the figure of the king. It is easy to see how repulsed MacDonald had been by the *laissez-faire* ethics of selfishness and material gain.

The world of the book, however, is a fairy world, where there is room for the marvellous and the unexpected. Irene's grandmother gives her the gift of a ball of thread attached to a ring:

> '"It is spider-webs — of a particular kind. My pigeons bring it me from over the great sea. There is only one forest where the spiders live who make this particular kind — the finest and strongest of any."'[52]

Irene's grandmother tells her that if she is in danger she must put the ring under her pillow and follow the thread where it leads her. At one point it leads her to rescue Curdie; at another, during the goblin attack, it leads her to Curdie's mother who looks after her until the goblins have been defeated. The thread guides Irene under her grandmother's watchfulness and, though pregnant with meaning, more is never explained. Again, such a presentation is a mark of MacDonald's strength as a story-teller.

In contrast to the awesome figure of the grandmother, the goblins are burlesque caricatures, like misshapen overgrown children, even though they do have a sinister side — they cannot stand music and their feet are particularly vulnerable to attack. They are ugly and selfish and partly defeated by getting drunk as they sup up the wine in the castle cellar. Their plans come to nothing, and the book ends with a cleansing flood that washes away the last trace of the goblins, leaving Irene ready to go back to the city with her father.

Crossing over into *The Princess and Curdie* is like entering into another country. If *At the Back of the North Wind* is the most moving, and *The Princess and the Goblin* the most poised, then *The Princess and Curdie* is the most powerful of all MacDonald's books for children. It was published in 1883, eleven years after *The Princess and the Goblin* first appeared in book form. While *The Princess and the Goblin* is, in many ways, a straightforward story for children, in *The Princess and Curdie* MacDonald asks his readers to wrestle with many difficult ideas.

In *The Princess and Curdie*, the medieval world of *The Princess and the*

Goblin is under severe attack from the commercial greed and selfishness of the city dwellers of Gwyntystorm. The king himself is sick, symbolic of the country's moral disease, and Curdie's task is to go out and rescue him. Curdie himself, at the beginning of the book, however, is not in any moral state to perform such a task:

> 'Still, he was becoming more and more a miner, and less and less a man of the upper world where the wind blew. On his way to and from the mine he took less and less notice of bees and butterflies, moths and dragonflies, the flowers and the brooks and the clouds. He was gradually changing into a commonplace man.'[53]

After shooting one of the great-great-grandmother's pigeons, Curdie at last comes face to face with her. He marvels at her moon:

> '"But there's no moon outside," said Curdie.
> "Ah! but you're inside now," said the voice.'[54]

In this book the old Princess Irene reveals her darker shapes, a little like North Wind, and her cosmic power is more in evidence. The second time Curdie comes to visit her he is taken aback:

> 'Curdie opened the door — but, to his astonishment, saw no room there. Could he have opened a wrong door? There was the great sky, and the stars, and beneath he could see nothing — only the darkness! But what was that in the sky, straight in front of him? A great wheel of fire, turning and turning, and flashing out blue lights.'[55]

It is the old lady's spinning wheel, which has gained in power and majesty. Curdie associates it with his childhood and his mother, and remembers how he used to learn songs from it, while old Princess Irene uses the wheel to spin wisdom and illumination into the young miner in order to bring him to knowledge and repentance over the unjust shooting of her bird. The grandmother's task is twofold. She is eager to help the king and sends Curdie out as her messenger. But he does not go unarmed. She gives him a precious gift. After plunging his hands into her stinging fire of roses, Curdie gains the ability to determine the state of men's souls by being able to feel what beast they are becoming. As the grandmother explains:

> '"Just so two people may be at the same spot in manners and behaviour, and yet one may be getting better and the other worse, which is just the greatest of all differences that could possibly exist between them."'[56]

As men degenerate morally, so they grow more like beasts, and the old princess goes on to say:

'Now here is what the rose fire has done for you: it has made your hands so knowing and wise, it has brought your real hands so near the outside of your flesh gloves, that you will henceforth be able to know at once the hand of a man who is growing into a beast; nay, more — you will at once feel the foot of the beast he is growing, just as if there were no glove made like a man's hand between you and it.'[57]

Armed with this gift and given a worthy companion in the form of Lina, a hideous but loyal animal, Curdie sets out for Gwyntystorm to prove himself and save the king. The second intention of the old princess is her secret hope that Curdie himself should one day become king. Royalty disguised as peasantry is one of MacDonald's favourite recurring themes, and at last his favourite fairy-tale ending for the heroes in his novels finds its way into a real fairy tale. The old Princess Irene tells Curdie's father:

'"...you, Peter, and your wife both have the blood of the royal family in your veins. I have been trying to cultivate your family tree, every branch of which is known to me, and I expect Curdie to turn out a blossom on it."'[58]

After his journey, Curdie arrives in Gwyntystorm to find the city ravaged by greed. He says sadly to his companion:

'"Lina," he said, "the people keep their gates open, but their houses and their hearts shut."'[59]

In Gwyntystorm the daily philosophy is now every man for himself. The only person who is willing to take in Curdie is a poor old woman and her grandchild, and the following morning, Curdie is clapped in jail. He escapes into the palace to find it in complete disorder and filled with corrupt servants. Gradually, he finds his way to the king's chamber where a graver and older Irene is tending her sick father. Curdie quickly realizes that the king is the victim of a plot to enfeeble him so that his closest advisers can take over the kingdom and rule in his stead. Their chief henchman is the insidious Dr Kelman (Kill Man) whose soul, Curdie divines, is turning into a snake, slippery and evil. The doctor is slowly drugging the king to death. Through giving him good wine and honest bread behind the doctor's back, in a version of the eucharist, the king is brought back to health, aided finally by Irene's great-great-grandmother who purifies him in a fire of roses. It seems the king has long been worried about the moral state of his people, as he informs Curdie:

'The King told him that for some years, ever since his queen's death, he had been losing heart over the wickedness of his people. He had tried hard to make them good, but they got worse and worse. Evil teachers, unknown to him, had crept into the schools; there was a general decay of truth and right principle at least in the city; and as that set an example to the nation, it must spread.'[60]

After due warning, the palace is purged by a band of 'uglies' — an array of phantasmagoric creatures whom Lina fetches to rout the servants and cleanse the city. Even the false preacher in the temple who is haranguing his congregation with a discourse on utilitarian ethics is cast down from his pulpit and dumped in the ruins of a rotting library. Finally the king is well enough to lead his army into battle against a neighbouring invading force, but they are saved by the grandmother and her army of pigeons who drive away the intruders. Thus the day is saved, the city is saved, and the king is saved. He goes back to teach his subjects goodness with a rod of iron.

Years later Irene and Curdie marry and become king and queen. While they rule Gwyntystorm flourishes but they have no children, and a greedy king succeeds them. Eventually, one unsuspecting day, Gwyntystorm collapses, its foundations mined through by the greed of the people seeking the gold that is buried there. This end is a salutary warning that goodness is not hereditary and must be fought for in every generation. Perhaps MacDonald hoped that the future lay with his child readers taking his lesson to heart.[61]

The Princess and Curdie, along with *At the Back of the North Wind* and *The Princess and the Goblin*, will probably have a lasting place in the canon of children's literature. They take children seriously and do not underestimate their ability to cope with difficult existential, moral and metaphysical problems. At the same time they allow children some free rein to participate imaginatively in the stories. Though most nineteenth-century children's writing has a serious and moral purpose, MacDonald's innate imaginative power has given his stories a lasting power, and it is an irrefutable testimony to his mastery as a story-teller and creator of powerful images that children continue to turn to him today.

CHAPTER TWENTY-NINE

Home Again

Greville MacDonald remembered the years 1873 and 1874, spent mainly at The Retreat, as amongst the happiest that the family ever enjoyed. The children were glad to have their parents back again from America, after being separated from them for the greater part of a year, and they thronged MacDonald, Louisa and Greville with long embraces on their safe return. Perhaps life had been a little humdrum and narrow under Lilia's tutelage at Halloway House, Hastings, where the unwilling boys had suffered under 'the frail dominion of a daily governess' — Miss Bishop, who wore a chignon and a bustle and taught them assiduously and boringly out of Magnell's *Questions*.

MacDonald's health had been severely worn down by his long trip, and it was a while before he ventured out lecturing again. But he was soon under pressure to pick up his pen and continue novel-writing and he locked himself away daily into his study to work. Back in London, the American experience did not fade merely into a distant dream, for he and Louisa were good at picking up friends, and they continued relationships with many of the people whom they had met in the States. First on their list was Richard Watson Gilder, who had become almost a substitute son to them, but there was also a slow trickle of other friends who made their way to The Retreat. Greville MacDonald remembered:

'Laird Collier and his two sons; Mrs Whitney with her deaf husband and her daughter; Mark Twain; Mary Mapes Dodge, author of *The Silver Skates*, with her son; and Antoinette Sterling, attended by her lover and future husband, paid us longer or shorter, single or frequent visits.'[1]

Mark Twain came eagerly up to the front door of The Retreat, only to find the house empty. 'And out of eleven children,' he complained, 'we couldn't scare up even one!'[2] Excited by America, and pleased by his reception there, MacDonald had it in his mind to return, and wrote to James Fields in 1874:

'Best thanks for your most kind letter. I have given up the thought of visiting America this coming winter, but if I find they want me, I think it very likely I shall venture again next year... I know it is a risk for me to try the lecturing again; but I mean to manage better next time...'[3]

As it turned out, the next time never came. MacDonald made several false starts on trips back over the Atlantic during the next few years, but they all came to nothing, and he never left Europe again. His trip there had been, in some ways, a mixed blessing, for his popularity had encouraged the adverse reaction of increased piracy of his novels, and as a result his own income slumped.

Fortunately, his own writing at home was making money. *Malcolm* proved lucrative, and was serialized very successfully in the *Glasgow Herald*. This type of serialization in a newspaper was an experiment that worked admirably. There was a run on *The Glasgow Herald*, with customers queuing up to ask only for 'Makim', and the same arrangement was repeated, equally successfully, with *Malcolm's* sequel, *The Marquis of Lossie*. MacDonald found the whole business of writing *Malcolm* very draining, however, and wrote to a friend of his early in 1874:

'I have only just got through the printing of the second volume of my story *Malcolm*, and the third is only partly written. I cannot tell how it is that I have been so long over this book. I never was so long over one before.'[4]

MacDonald's fears were groundless. *Malcolm* proved one of his most readable and exciting novels, and was popular with the public. After the effort he put into this novel, he was ill again in the winter of 1873, but somehow he maintained his output unchecked. As well as working on *Malcolm*, *Gutta Percha Willie* ran through the final year of *Good Words for the Young*, and appeared in book form in 1873. *St George and St Michael*, MacDonald's historical novel, appeared serialized in the *Graphic* during the same year, while MacDonald finished *The Wise Woman* in 1874, the year that also saw the publication of *England's Antiphon*.

After battling through the weary winter, MacDonald was delighted when, on 24 January 1874, his second daughter, Mary, announced her engagement to Edward Hughes, Arthur Hughes' nephew.[5] It was a sure sign that his family was growing up and he congratulated the couple heartily. Edward Hughes was a minor but distinguished painter in his own right. Later in his life he became Holman Hunt's assistant and, when

Hunt's sight failed, finished for him the third version of *The Light of the World*, which now hangs in St Paul's Cathedral in London. Ted Hughes had long been adopted into the MacDonald family as yet another son, often accompanying his uncle on visits, and helping out by painting scenery for the amateur theatricals in the coal-house. He confessed to having been in love with Mary for eight years — since the age of fourteen, 'with that sure steady hope of some day winning her.' The Retreat echoed with surprise at the happy announcement, for the news had come suddenly. Mary's old friend, 'Uncle' Dodgson, hearing of her happiness, wrote to her a little wistfully:

'They say that, when people marry, they generally find it best to drop all their *former* friends, and begin again with a new set. Is it a *universal* rule, I wonder? And does it include *very* old friends as well as new ones?'

Dodgson's affection for his young friend had not dimmed, and he was astonished at how quickly she had grown. He wished that she would be:

'. . . truly happy in your marriage and in all your future life is the hope and prayer of your loving Uncle. C.L. Dodgson.'[6]

With the initial excitement of Mary's engagement past, the year moved quietly as the family flitted to and from The Retreat in Hammersmith and Halloway House in Hastings. In London Irene and Winifred were packed off to Durham House, a day school for girls in Chelsea, while Greville worked hard at his books, intent on entering King's College in London to study medicine. Towards the end of the year MacDonald went to lecture in Liverpool, Bradford, and Leicester, while at home, Ronald, the roughest of the boys, broke his leg. His parents bore him off to Halloway House, where the family snuggled for the winter, and once more MacDonald took to his bed — a result of overwork and bad weather. To lift him out of the doldrums of bad health, Louisa rented Great Tangley Manor between Guildford and Wonersh for six months, in the spring of 1875. It was an oak-beamed farmhouse, built in 1582. MacDonald was excited at the prospect of staying in a house that had been built when Shakespeare was a boy, and, in addition, it meant he could go riding every day on the nearby Blackheath. Louisa had decided that the best cure for MacDonald's faltering health was a horse, so she invested in one, using some of the money her father had left her as a legacy. Her plan worked. MacDonald rode joyfully, day after day, and as his health improved so new stories buzzed in his head. His only cause for complaint was that he and Louisa could not often be together, as the family was divided between Halloway House and Guildford. Besides, Mary was feeling off-colour, and had to remain by the sea. MacDonald made sure, however, that some of the family were at The Retreat for the annual party on the Oxford/Cambridge Boat Race day. He was delighted when, in the midst of the throng, the Poet Laureate turned up unannounced:

> 'Tennyson came here uninvited to the boat race and was with us two or three hours. He seemed delighted with my little library, which he did not think a little one: there seemed so many books he had never seen... What do you think he borrowed? A splendid copy of the Gaelic Ossian which I bought at Uncle's sale, that he might read the prose Latin translation which seems to be a literal one. He had never believed Ossian was a reality, but seemed a good deal more ready to believe in him when he had read a few lines with which he was delighted.'[7]

Unfortunately, just as MacDonald's health and spirits were rising, so Mary was sinking. Always robust, to the distress of her family she contracted scarlet fever and began to lose weight rapidly. Despite careful nursing and fresh sea air, she continued listless and wan and it was clear that her illness was not of the usual round of coughs and sicknesses. Her parents were concerned and watched as she worsened throughout the summer until, with the autumn fall of leaves, came haemorrhage, and tuberculosis settled in her lungs. MacDonald watched on helplessly as Mary slowly faded away. He spent a lot of time with her, taking her for drives, and writing wistful scraps of poetry for his 'Elfie'. Ted Hughes was dazed and stricken by the worrying change in his fiancée's health, and to compound his anguish, his own father suddenly became terminally ill. At first the MacDonalds thought that the cause of Mary's ill-health was The Retreat, with its attendant problems of damp, and they decided to move away for a while, perhaps even give up the house for good. A little sadly they locked up the doors and windows, leaving only River Villa inhabited by the Miss Cobdens.[8] In seeking a healthy refuge for Mary the MacDonalds lighted on Bournemouth, at that time a fashion-able resort for those afflicted with lung trouble, and they took on a house surrounded by pine trees which they named *Corage*, perhaps to give them courage in their difficulties. The title was taken from the anagram MacDonald had made out of his own name and used on his book-plate — *Corage! God mend al!* At one point George and Louisa were doubtful if Mary would pull through the winter, but the move seemed to help her. As it was, Mary survived into 1876, and MacDonald worked steadily, polishing the translations he had worked on for so many years, and at last seeing his labours come to fruition in *Exotics*, his first volume of translations to be commercially published. He wrote to Richard Watson Gilder:

'I send you by this same post a little book I have just published. I have spent an immense amount of labour on the translations, distributed over seven and twenty years...'[9]

With *Exotics* out of the way, MacDonald immediately began work on his annotated edition of *Hamlet*, which was not published until 1885. MacDonald was happily settled at Boscombe, attending Mary and delving deep into Petrarch and Goethe, but at the same time he had to tout for lectures in order to fill his pockets. That March, Louisa's sister Carrie died and no doubt they looked at Mary and wondered how long it would be before she followed. In 1876 MacDonald attended for the first time one of the Cowper-Temples' religious conferences at Broadlands. These had begun in 1874 and were to continue until 1888, the year of William Cowper-Temple's death. They were ecumenical gatherings and aimed to bring together Christians of all persuasions and backgrounds. Anglicans, Baptists, Methodists, Quakers and French Protestants — all converged on Broadlands for a few days of spiritual renewal. They sat at the feet of some of the most celebrated Christian speakers of the day, from both sides of the Atlantic, including, for example, Bishop Wilberforce of Oxford — and George MacDonald. The conferences were intellectual and serious and perhaps slightly esoteric. On arrival, each participant at the conference was given a set of written intructions, informing them among other things to:

'Avoid all conversation that may divert your mind from the object of the meeting. Avoid particularly all controversy. If any differ with you, pray with them.'

These gatherings were meant to be a time of contemplation and listening to God. Many of the meetings were held outdoors, under the arms of a grove of beech trees, the motherly, protective presences of *Phantastes*. To those who came, it seemed that they were worshipping in a natural 'church' where even the flowers and grass held a message for them. The aims of these meetings were to encourage a conformity to the likeness of Christ, and an indwelling of his Holy Spirit. It was not long before MacDonald became a regular presence at the conferences, as Georgina Cowper-Temple remembered in her privately circulated *Memorials*:

'At several meetings, Dr George MacDonald seemed to be entrusted for us with special messages, not poetic alone, as his cannot fail to be, but, above all, eminently practical, in for ever pressing upon his hearers the fact that willingness to do the will of the Father leads to knowledge of his doctrine; and as the tender filial communings of his mind with God were revealed, we recognized that we also of the nineteenth century had our George Herbert.'[10]

In 1877 MacDonald took Mary with him to Broadlands, and they all prayed for her under the beech trees. That same year Greville had realized his ambition and was at last studying medicine at King's College, while Irene was attending the Slade School of Art. At King's, Greville met up with Edward Troup, the son of MacDonald's old friend, Robert Troup, and his cousin Margaret MacDonald. In April Edward began the arduous task of tutoring the younger boys at The Retreat, and trying to instil in them, among other things, Greek. While Edward battled with declensions and the lack of interest of his young charges, MacDonald was battling with severer problems that gathered over his head like storm-clouds. As usual, his health was fitful, interrupting his work, and consequently affecting the family's income. To make matters worse, Mac-Donald's friend and publisher Strahan had separated from his partners, and could not offer MacDonald the prices for his books that he had become accustomed to. Strahan went as far as rejecting MacDonald's recently finished *Paul Faber, Surgeon* as not being suitable for his newly-established journal *The Day of Rest*, and gave him only £400 for the three-volume edition — less than half of his previous prices. MacDonald was helpless and crestfallen. He needed more money, not less, as there was the burden of Mary's health to think of.

Louisa was troubled at her husband's anguish and decided to take matters into her own hands. She devised on her own a startling scheme for bringing about an increase in the family's finances — she would put her children on the stage. She reckoned that the family had charmed friends and charity audiences for long enough, and determined to cull some income from their acting. As can be imagined, many of the MacDonalds' friends were appalled, as acting was hardly a respectable occupation. More than that, it was demeaning for a novelist's children to be exhibited in this way — and a religious novelist's at that. But Louisa was adamant and soon the girls were designing Morrisy curtains and sewing costumes. If the family did lose a few friends through treading the boards, most of their intimates stuck closely by them and supported their performances.

At first Louisa mounted her old production of *The Tetterbys*, but the family became best known for their adaptation of the second part of

Pilgrim's Progress, starring Lilia as Christiana. The first performance of this piece took place on 8 March 1877 at Christchurch in Hampshire — on the twenty-sixth wedding anniversary of MacDonald and Louisa.[11] Appearances at Bournemouth and Romsey soon followed, and they were launched. MacDonald himself joined in the performances for the first time in June at Grosvenor House where Princess Louise was amongst the audience. He played Greatheart, a part previously taken by Ronald, but which was soon stamped as MacDonald's own. So it was that the novelist, poet and preacher, in his middle years, also became an actor. The literary world was bemused. As the years passed, so the family became dominated by their play, to the extent of calling each other by the names of the characters whom they acted, as indeed did many of their close friends. There was no doubt that the family apart from Lilia had little talent, but somehow the curious spectacle of an entire family acting with such sincerity, and including so many children, was one that drew the crowds, and at the end of their short season, Louisa did have some money to put into her purse.

By now, Mary's health was such that the doctor recommended a winter abroad. Faced with the prospect of yet another difficult move, or their daughter's death, the MacDonalds decided to take Mary to the balmier climate of the Riviera where the gentler weather might do her good. Such a decision meant a huge undertaking. Louisa had to travel overland with an invalid, accompanied by trunkfuls of personal belongings, find a house, and contend with a new language. The MacDonalds truly began to feel that they were indeed pilgrims. Louisa did not quail. At the end of September 1877, while the weather was still warm, she, Lilia, Mary, Irene and Ronald set off as a little band on the long journey across the channel and down through France to the Mediterranean coast. Their destination was Menton close to the Italian border, a town surrounded by hills near Monte Carlo and Nice. From there, strung out along the Ligurian coast, to Genoa in Italy and beyond, there were resorts bustling with British people who suffered from lung complaints. On arrival, therefore, they found a large expatriate community with whom they could fraternize, and were lucky to have friends on hand who could speak the language for them. The Riviera was an adventure, the land of romance, and under its gentle skies Louisa and the others began moving up and down the coast house-hunting.

MacDonald was left with the younger boys at The Retreat, with Grace and Winifred to keep house for him. He was locked in his study for most of the time, but in October had to retreat to his bed with a little bleeding from the lungs and an affected liver.

Yet though he lay sick in bed without his wife, he was not forgotten. Ellen Gurney came to visit, bringing grapes and an armful of flowers, while Georgina Cowper-Temple insisted on his moving over to her house in Stanhope Street where he could be properly looked after. By then Winifred and the others had all abandoned The Retreat, which was in the process of being dismantled, and there were boxes, clothes and piles of books everywhere. They had exchanged The Retreat for Corage at Boscombe, where MacDonald limped down to join them. As well as his physical ailments, money troubles were still pressing him hard and he was gloomy. He was keen to join Louisa and the others in Italy for Christmas, but it did not seem possible that he and the others could get away. Even after *Paul Faber, Surgeon* was sold and his debts paid, he was down to his last £50. He prayed, and two marvellous things happened. First of all, Georgina Cowper-Temple arrived, smiling, and presented him with a cheque for £200 from her and her husband. If that was not enough he then received the astonishing news that he was to be awarded a Civil List pension of £100 a year 'for services to literature'. MacDonald was stunned. This was a compliment indeed. *The Times* announced the news on Tuesday 15 November, and MacDonald wrote excitedly to Louisa, telling her of the letter he had just received:

'It is from Lord Beaconsfield's secretary, telling me that the queen has given me £100 a year. Isn't it nice? The letter shall follow. Mrs Temple *thinks* it is the Princess Alice's doing. She herself knows nothing about it.'[12]

In her own way, the queen was a warm admirer of MacDonald's. It became known that she gave a copy of *Robert Falconer* to each of her grandsons.[13] Now at last it was possible for MacDonald and the others to cross the channel and the whole family could be united for Christmas. But, as winter thickened and the bright prospect of reunion approached, MacDonald warned Louisa:

'Dear, we cannot keep Mary if her Father wants her, but we can trust him and go on.'[14]

MacDonald had seen too many of his relatives die to be anything other than realistic about Mary's chances of survival. Though he urged Louisa to trust, such trust was difficult when the way was so dark.

Before they all left, MacDonald went to stay with the Cowper-Temples at Broadlands and then went on to Southampton. From there he endured a rough crossing to Le Havre where he began the next part of his journey to join his family. Louisa, Lilia and the others had been busy, and had rented a house called Palazzo Cattaneo at Nervi, just outside Genoa. The house was quite a climb up a hill, but it meant that the family had privacy, and the view from their summit was marvellous. There were orange trees all the way down to the Mediterranean, with its sparkling, milky blue water and the Palazzo itself was a veritable palace of brick floors and marble staircases. Lilia and Ronald went to meet MacDonald, tired after his trip, at Genoa and brought him proudly to their new home. After they had all greeted one another, they made MacDonald close his eyes, and led him to a surprise. He wrote afterwards to Georgina Cowper-Temple, his 'great-great princess grandmother':

> '. . . there I was looking into a little cold chapel through a latticed opening — with a marble altar in front and the madonna upon it, while one of them played *Abide with me* on a harmonium behind. It is such a lovely idea to have a little core of rest in the heart of the house — a chamber opening into the infinite. . .'

Looking eagerly round the rooms and marvelling at the space, he confessed:

> 'I could play the prince in this house very comfortably, and I know my wife would keep it always full.'[15]

Climbing up to Mary's bedroom, he found her weak, but cheerful. As she lay in bed, family life fell silently into place round about her. She complained laughingly:

> 'I feel just like a badly cut nine-pin, when I try to stand up, I tumble over before the ball touches me.'[16]

So it was that the MacDonald family spent their first Christmas abroad, and all together. But in the midst of the carols, games and revelry, MacDonald and Louisa could not but help a few anxious glances at Mary, and as her condition worsened, so their doubts about the future deepened.

CHAPTER THIRTY
Pilgrims

The MacDonalds spent the whole of 1878 in Italy, so MacDonald was able to slough off his lecturing for a while and concentrate solely on his writing. Louisa mounted *Pilgrim's Progress* at Genoa in January and March, while, at Nervi, Mary lingered by a thread. Ted Hughes arrived early in January to visit her, while in February Octavia Hill came to stay, accompanied by her friend Harriet Yorke. Octavia Hill was tired out and her doctor had ordered her to Europe to rest. Worse than that, Ruskin, who had been becoming increasingly unstable, had blasted her on the pages of *Fors Clavigera*, to her profound distress. Such hostile criticism from someone she had always looked up to as a model and a protector had affected her very adversely, and she needed a clean break away from her demanding duties in London. She was tired, but appreciative of the MacDonalds' care and was soon on her way south to visit other cities in Italy. Meanwhile, Mary had been growing weaker and weaker until MacDonald remarked that there was 'nothing on her bones', and at last on 27 April, she died. She was only twenty-four and had been engaged for over four years. Ted Hughes had come the moment the family had sensed danger, and saw her before she died. Tragically, the white silk that was to have been her wedding dress became her pall.

Louisa was numbed, for death had come so often to her door to take her husband, and yet each time he had been spared. Now it was her daughter instead who was gone, and with all the days and months of solid nursing at an end, her hands lay idle and she was tormented at being parted from her child. Death had always worn a more fearsome aspect for Louisa than for MacDonald. It seemed impossible to console her, and MacDonald wrote a poem in an effort to communicate:

'To tell thee that our blessed child
Is watching thee from somewhere nigh,
Mourns with thee when thy agony grows wild,
Sits sometimes by thy bed while slow the hours go by,
Were but to mock thy weary pain

With pleasant fancies of a half-held creed,
To gather up and offer thee again
What thou hadst cast away as nothing to thy need.'[1]

After Mary had been buried, in one sense the family's reason for staying in Italy had come to an end. Louisa noticed, however, that MacDonald's own health had improved enormously and, as he was also working so well, the family decided to continue their sojourn abroad. The weather was good, and the romantic landscape of orange trees wafting against the blue sea was soothing. MacDonald could go for long walks down on the beach, or else take a boat out with his sons. Life was much slower, more leisurely, than it ever had been in London with its disagreeable soot and clamour. Perched on their hill, the family enjoyed seclusion and rest, and MacDonald was able to spend far more time with his children than formerly. When the tenancy of Palazzo Cattaneo was up in May 1878, the family moved further along the coast to the huge Villa Barrata at Porto Fino, overlooking the bay of the town and across to Rapallo. It was:

'. . . about a third of the way between Genoa and Spezzia, its station being Sta. Margherita, three miles along a good road closed at both ends, so the journey was done by row-boat.'[2]

MacDonald was entranced by the scenery, and thought it the most beautiful place he had ever lived in.

But scarcely had they settled there when the sudden news came that Russell Gurney had died. MacDonald wrote to his widow, Ellen:

'Be sure of this, the grandest thing in England, the justice of her
administration of the laws, is a purer, grander thing yet, because
Russell Gurney has had a share in it. And the Lord who loves justice as
his own being will know how many cities to set him over.'[3]

Gurney showed his admiration for MacDonald by leaving him £500, which went far to clear off his accumulating debts. As far as his own work was concerned, *Paul Faber, Surgeon* was ready to come out in the autumn, while he had half-finished *Sir Gibbie*, soon to be serialized in the *Glasgow Weekly Mail* starting in September. While the boys messed with boats and the girls sunned themselves, Greville came out from England, fleeing the confines of King's, and remarked on his father's good health. As a sad contrast, however, Louisa had sunk into a bath chair under the strain of the months since Mary's death. But, despite the all-pervasive ache caused by their sister's passing, it was a happy summer.

The good effect of the Italian weather on MacDonald's health was not lost on Louisa, and she determined that he should spend a few more winters abroad — and, as usual, she got her own way. Besides, life was much cheaper in Italy than it was in London, as well as more pleasant, and as 1878 slipped into 1879, MacDonald told his friend, William Cowper-Temple:

'What a mercy our coming here has been. We have lived on so much less — and I made not half my usual amount last year. Had we been in England — I was going to say I should have been in despair, but then it would have been managed differently for us.'[4]

The Retreat was at last off their hands. After a few preliminary investigations by Dante Rossetti, William Morris took it and renamed it Kelmscott House. But the Italian sun was also to cast deep shadows. As winter turned to spring, so young Maurice's face grew longer and paler, and then in February 1879 he succumbed to pneumonia, and died in the short space of eighteen days. Maurice had always been a delicate and thoughtful boy, but at the same time a strong swimmer and diver. He had been fitfully ill all through the winter, but had been nursed until his cough vanished — but then, a few days afterwards, he had haemorrhaged violently in the middle of the night. Louisa rushed to his bedside and ended up tending him for ten nights and days till the end of his illness. He scarcely ever complained, but gave a weak smile, like a watery sun breaking through the clouds. Finally, he murmured to Ronald that '. . . I have to remember that God is with me', and repeated it to himself two or three times before giving a little short sigh and ceasing to breathe. While Mary's withdrawal from the family had been slow and extended over several years, Maurice's death was sudden and brutal, like the unexpected fall of an axe. The double blow of having two of her children taken from her within a year was almost more than Louisa could bear, while MacDonald wrote to his stepmother in Aberdeen:

'Neither Louisa nor I knew much about death till those two were taken from us within the year — and now we know its terror and its comfort.'[5]

Under MacDonald's shining optimism there was always an ingrained seam of the darkest pessimism, and doubts and despair hung about him. Now he only saw through a glass darkly — and the glass was very dark. MacDonald turned in on himself and brooded anxiously on his dead children. They began to appear, ghost-like, in his verses. In the *Diary of an Old Soul*, for instance, he wrote for 4 January:

'Death, like high faith levelling, lifteth all.
When I awake, my daughter and my son,
Grown sister and brother, in my arms shall fall,
Tenfold my girl and boy . . .'

To add more pain to their loss, it was difficult to secure a burial place for
Maurice, as he was not a Roman Catholic, and they had to tussle to find a
suitable plot of land to bury their boy. What was more, the burial had to
take place swiftly, and so the ceremony was performed at night, under
the light of the moon. Ronald and Bob carried the coffin, and the English
chaplain from Nervi, Mr Woodroffe, came over to read the service. Bob
held a lantern for him to read by in the eerie gloom. They all watched as
the coffin was put into the ground. Lilia told her friend Nellie Matheson:

'. . . we buried the dear body by moonlight the day after he left it. How
soon has the silk for Mary's wedding dress become a second time a
pall. It is a beautiful family possession full of promise — it gleamed so
white in the moonlight. We put on it this time the crimson cross of
Greatheart's tabard . . .'[6]

The myth of Maurice took a deep hold of the MacDonald family after the
boy's death. In his father's eyes Maurice had been the son destined for
great things — the one who never achieved the career in the church that
MacDonald had so longed for him. He was the family's own Diamond,
petted by Lilia and Grace and beloved of Greville. When the boy
disappeared, his aura remained, but with the death of Maurice, Mac-
Donald's hopes for all his sons seemed to vanish. Years later, Ronald
wrote to Greville, remembering an occasion after Maurice's death with
some bitterness:

'A few days after came Father's birthday, when he summoned all his
sons at hand, I, Bob, Bernard, McKay, to his study; we trouped in . . .
Then he gave a homily, the gist of which was that none of us four could
hope ever to become as good as our sisters. I silently wondered how he
knew that? He went on to say that I had been rude to my mother, and
added that I had already begun to do harm (I can't remember the
phrase precisely) to Maurice before he died. I do or say anything to
lower Maurice! Impossible.'[7]

Putting the dark month of March behind them, the MacDonalds
welcomed Richard Watson Gilder and his wife Helena to stay with them.
Gilder had recently had a breakdown and was very exhausted, but found
being with the MacDonalds a tonic. He and Helena left their baby,
Rodman, in the strong arms of Louisa who had now recovered while they

went on wandering alone to Pisa and Rome. Meanwhile, the MacDonalds decided that it was about time they returned to England. They returned there for the summer months, but had to stage *Pilgrim's Progress* in order to pay for their travelling expenses. Louisa hired halls all over London and took the players as far afield as Malvern, Cheltenham, Nottingham, and Leicester. MacDonald wrote merrily to his American friend, James Fields:

> 'We are now, as you may have heard, turned into a sort of company of acting strollers — I mean strolling actors — and have a good reception and tolerable results. We have really hardly tried the country yet though people seem a good deal interested in our attempt.'[8]

MacDonald began lecturing again on 28 May, while the family had fun, playing to appreciative audiences, and enjoying the attention given them. They were soon experts at hanging the curtains and striking up on the piano in the oddest places. Often MacDonald would sit in the wings, in his spangled costume, maniacally correcting proofs while the children tripped out one by one to play their roles. Greville regarded the whole operation with some trepidation. He thought the acting interfered too much with schoolwork and routine life, and did not enjoy seeing his brothers and sisters sporting themselves on stage.

But if Greville felt some anxiety about the family flaunting themselves in costume, MacDonald came to reverence the activity as a kind of holy mission. One of the company's staunchest supporters was Charles Dodgson. A disadvantage of the move to Italy had been an uncoupling of friendships with people at home, and Dodgson wrote to Lilia in June 1879:

> 'I have been living for a very long time in the belief that you were all in Italy, and only learned the fact of your being in England, a few days ago, from Miss Willets, step-daughter of Professor Legge (our Chinese professor). . .'[9]

When Dodgson finally called round on the MacDonalds, he was astonished to find that some of them were 'grown almost out of my recollection'. That summer and the following he attended several performances of *Pilgrim's Progress*, usually taking one of his child friends to accompany him. He hoped even to lure the little band of pilgrims to Oxford, but as no suitable venue could be found, the plan fell through. In his diary for 26 July 1879, he recorded:

> 'Lily appeared in all the pieces, and was the only one who could act.

Met Mr Clemens [Mark Twain], with whom I was pleased and interested...'

Mark Twain, for his part, was astonished at how shy and withdrawn Dodgson was — certainly in contrast with MacDonald's liveliness. Twain had fallen under MacDonald's spell in America, and the two men had become good friends, to the extent of musing if they could collaborate on a novel together to defeat their copyright problem. After the law had finally been changed, Twain wrote to MacDonald in 1882:

'A book of mine used to pay me nothing in England — pays me two to three thousand pounds now. I perceive, now after all these wasted years that an author ought always to be connected with a highway man.'[10]

Twain's children read their copy of *At the Back of the North Wind* until it wore out, and Twain himself was captivated by MacDonald's work to the extent that *Sir Gibbie* may have partly fuelled *Huckleberry Finn*, published six years after MacDonald's book in 1885. Certainly there are some striking parallels between the works.

The MacDonald family returned to Italy late in the summer, after Greville had finally qualified as a doctor. Strangely, the romance of that country was beginning to work on Lilia, who at last shuffled off the mantle of mother and put on that of lover. Her sole previous suitor had been William Matheson, Greville Matheson's brother, but as he was only ten years younger than her parents, she could never think of him as anything other than an 'uncle'. Among the rarefied expatriate circles in which they moved on the Ligurian coast, there was a young man named Charley Granet de la Rue. He was a thin, handsome man with a moustache and due to inherit a fortune from cigarettes. Lilia and he were quickly drawn to one another and her family became very fond of him — he even made a few wooden appearances in *Pilgrim's Progress*.[11] The couple announced their engagement in August 1879, but Lilia's happiness was to be short-lived. Though they were in love, the twin barriers of her acting and his money soon raised themselves. His family deplored Lilia's involvement with the stage and threatened to cut off his money. His aunt, who was holding the purse-strings, was especially virulent and Granet was brought round to her way of thinking. He urged Lilia to forsake the stage. All Lilia's education, however, had been based on the philosophy that it was better to be penniless and free, than rich and in chains, and, heartbroken, she felt she had to send him away. Ellen Gurney took her to Genoa to bid farewell to her lover, and in October 1880 the engagement was broken off. Louisa informed Richard Watson Gilder:

'Dear Lily, I don't know whether you heard that her lover turned
round and sided with his worldly old Aunt and cares more for her £SD
than for Lily's golden heart. Well, he has his reward doubtless and
Lily has her suffering — for she loved right nobly. But she bears too as
few can bear. Don't refer to it in writing the wound is too sensitive to
bear the least touch — even from loving hands.'[12]

While Lilia regained her freedom in one sense, she remained ever after
tied to her own family, and the prospect of matrimony never raised its
head again. MacDonald wrote out an account of his daughter's troubled
relationship in the story of Hester Raymount and Charles Vavasor in
Weighed and Wanting (1882).

As the year wore on, the MacDonalds were impatient to have their own
house, and in November and December 1879 Clarence Bicknell, a friend
of theirs, wrote, luring them further along the coast to another town,
quite near the French border, where he said there was a villa for sale.
George and Louisa thought that they had better have a look at it and
began making preparations for another trip to Italy and to have a look at
the place Bicknell had suggested. The name of this town was Bordighera.

CHAPTER THIRTY-ONE
Bordighera

January 1880 saw the cold weather biting into MacDonald at Boscombe in England. He and Louisa were looking forward to crossing over to Italy again in the hope of securing the house at Bordighera. But the constant moving was a wearying business, and MacDonald wrote to Georgina Cowper-Temple:

> 'I could say things with which I could comfort myself, but the things God says to you come in mostly at the back door, and what the others say, at the front.'[1]

Yet MacDonald was determined that faith should win out, even when the way ahead was clouded. To add to their huge family Louisa adopted another two children, as well as their mother, in 1881. The mother of Honey and Joan Desaint, an Englishwoman, had been deserted by her French husband. The two girls rapidly became part of the MacDonald household, while Louisa arranged for Gertrude, their mother, to go into the Firs Home at Bournemouth to rest. If Louisa had not swooped down on the girls when she did, then they would certainly have gone straight to the workhouse. While the English colony gossiped, Louisa felt duty bound to take them in.[2]

George and Louisa crossed the channel once more, and the spring of 1880 found them at last in Bordighera.[3] It was a gentle, sleepy resort, very Anglicized, situated on a hill that rose from the sparkling blue of the Mediterranean. White villas fringed with palm-trees looked dreamily out to sea, and the landscape abounded in oranges, olives, and rich, lush gardens. The Ligurian coast as a whole had the reputation for being healthy, and British people who could afford to winter there came in great numbers. The English population of Bordighera alone numbered several thousand, and had initially been inspired to settle there by Ruffini's novel *Doctor Antonio*, published in the 1850s.[4] This novel had painted an enticing picture of the Riviera (Nice and Cannes were not far away) and Bordighera in particular, and the English community began arriving there from the middle of the 1860s onwards. As is often the case, the English abroad tried to be as much like the English at home as possible. They formed the first tennis club in the whole of Italy in 1878 and founded a library. They built the Victoria Hall to hold concerts in and organized a great many entertainments, parties and picnics. Sorties along the coast to Nice or Cannes were frequent, and there were always visitors from England. But the spell of Bordighera lay in its climate — not too hot in summer, and not too cold in winter, and the English rested content with their drinks under the waving of the languid palms.

MacDonald was concerned to establish himself as a Christian presence within the English community and, finding that there was no Sunday evening service at the English church, wondered if he could arrange a weekly gathering in his own home — when he had one. It was only an idea. House-hunting, however, was not going well. MacDonald and Louisa found, to their consternation, that the Villa Patrick where they were staying was not for sale. MacDonald wrote with disgruntlement to Georgina Cowper-Temple:

> 'We should not have come here, had we not thought this villa was for sale. The owner has declined to part with it, and we feel sold instead...'5

They were there with Lilia, Grace and Ted Hughes, but soon had to return to England. They had booked the Steinway Hall in Lower Seymour Street in London for two days every week from the middle of May until the middle of July for the performing of *Pilgrim's Progress*. Before they left Bordighera, however, they decided to emulate the custom of the English community by building their own villa. This was a hard decision but was made possible from subscriptions and gifts from friends. They inspected the plot of land beside the English church where their home was to be raised.

That summer the Pilgrims travelled further than ever before, performing in Bradford, York, Leeds, Liverpool and Chester. And so it was that a new pattern of life gradually became established for the MacDonald family. The winters from October to May were to be spent in their new house at Bordighera, while the summers were spent touring with *Pilgrim's Progress* as MacDonald lectured. The company added *Polyeuctus* by Corneille and Shakespeare's *Macbeth* to their repertoire, but *Pilgrim's Progress* remained top of their list. The new division of the year worked well and benefited MacDonald's health. The only disadvantage to their itinerant way of life, and it was a major one, was that MacDonald's withdrawal from literary life in London left him more and more isolated, and the stimulating artistic friends of the 1860s and 1870s were exchanged for the rather prim inhabitants of Bordighera. MacDonald handed over his literary business to his friend A.P. Watt who began acting as his agent, while MacDonald simply sat in his study in Italy and wrote. In one sense he had found a welcome retreat, in another he had settled in a ghetto. In September, as the tour of *Pilgrim's Progress* made its way round the towns of England, disaster struck when Grace was suddenly taken ill. The hall was booked, and somehow they had to appear. As a desperate measure the family drafted in Octavia Hill, whose mother wrote to Octavia's sister:

'If you were to spend all your time from now till Christmas in guessing what Octavia was doing last Friday afternoon you would never guess aright. So I will tell you. She was acting to a Harrogate audience the part of Piety in the MacDonald's *Pilgrim's Progress*. On Thursday we had spent the day at Harewood, and on our return found Lily and Bob here waiting to ask if she would act for poor Grace, then lying seriously ill of haemorrhage at Ilkley. The rooms for the performance were engaged, and it seemed impossible to postpone. Octavia agreed and learned her part (eight pages) that night. I cannot tell you how beautiful she looked, and how lovely her voice sounded. It was *most* pathetic to see the MacDonalds so brave and energetic; but all so pale and feeling — full. Poor Mr Jamieson acted Mr Brisk. Mr MacDonald was so chivalrous and beautiful to his poor wife and to us, — forgot no tenderness to her, or politeness to Miss Yorke and me.'[6]

'Mr Jamieson' was, in fact, Kingsbury Jameson, a cousin of Ellen Gurney's, and fresh from Cambridge. He was about to enter the church and was to be attached to the English community in Bordighera as assistant chaplain. He and Grace soon became engaged, and were married the following April in Rome, where the family had to go in order for the ceremony to be legally and properly done.

Meanwhile, in Bordighera the house was taking shape. It was planted at the front with Scotch firs, and the massive building itself had four floors and a stucco tower. It stood almost back to back with the English church, and only a gate separated the MacDonalds' garden from the church grounds. The house was a gift from friends, a testimony to the esteem they had for MacDonald. Greville MacDonald wrote:

'In 1877 a plan had been organized for giving my parents a freehold house of their own, to which H.R.H. the Princess Alice of Hesse, the Earl and Countess of Ducie, Lord and Lady Darnley, the Cowper-Temples, Russell Gurneys, Lord Lawrence, the Charringtons,

Mathesons, the Baroness Paul Ralli, the Miss Hills, Mr and Mrs
C. Edmund Maurice, and a host of relatives and other friends, even old
servants, contributed. To this a further sum raised by mortgage was
added . . .'[7]

The most magnificent feature of the whole house was 'the Temple and
Gurney given hall', a massive room where the MacDonalds could mount
plays or hold religious services. It could seat two hundred people, or take
four hundred standing — and on occasion did so. The family were soon
steeped in black paint and different coloured stains as they decorated the
house and made it habitable, and soon they were all installed, along with
the Desaints, and rehearsing the first part of *Pilgrim's Progress*. It was not
long before the MacDonalds were firmly established as part of the
Bordighera community, and Casa Coraggio, as the house was named,
threw open its doors to all who wanted to enter there. Louisa quickly
became the church organist at All Saints, the English church, and the girls
helped out with the choir.

MacDonald's idea of having a Sunday evening gathering in his home
was one that actually came about, and these were soon a regular feature of
expatriate life in Bordighera. It was as if the vision he had had in
Manchester thirty years previously, of gathering people about him in the
little room in Renshaw Street, had finally been fulfilled.[8] As many as a
hundred people would crowd into the large salon, resplendent with
hangings and paintings and flowers, and at eight o'clock MacDonald
would emerge from a side door, often wearing a black skull-cap, and with
a book in his hand. He looked very much like a prophet now, for as he
had grown older, so his hair and beard had coloured snowy-white,
heightening his mystical and authoritative presence. Some of his followers
went as far as to call him 'the blessed St Mac'.[9]

These gatherings were held for a good many years and were supple-
mented by Wednesday afternoon *At Homes* at which MacDonald would
lecture on Shakespeare or Dante or some other literary topic. But in the
firelight and candlelight of the Sunday evenings, he would begin by
reading poetry, sometimes his own, often pieces by Herbert or Vaughan,
and would follow these up with a chapter, or part of a chapter, from the
Bible, commenting as he read. Then there would be a prayer, and a
hymn and an anthem, usually first rehearsed by the girls, and after that a
talk on a text or a special topic. MacDonald taught like an old philosopher or rabbi discoursing to his disciples: '. . . False prophets are not
necessarily false in doctrine but are those who *do* not as they preach. For
Christ told them to do as the Pharisees *told* them, but not as the Pharisees
did . . .' And, with his sure optimism, he lamented that the poets had
placed the Golden Age in the past, when, in fact, it was yet to be . . .

To teach in this way came close to fulfilling MacDonald's calling. He confessed to his cousin James in 1887:

> 'But when it pleases God that I stop writing stories I shall be glad, for I never *feel* that is my calling by nature, though it is, I hope, by a yet higher command.'[10]

MacDonald felt that his true calling was to impart the word of God, and this he did to all those who came to hear him. He was a compelling figure to those who sought him out, either in his booklined library, where he spent much of the day, sitting under a globe of the world, or to those who climbed the marble staircase at Casa Coraggio to hear him speak. Greville MacDonald vividly recalled:

> 'I have many vivid pictures of my father hung in the long gallery of my life. They glow in colour, and not one, whatever of reawakening of sorrows they may bring, would I turn to the wall. This, however, has a niche and illumination all its own: the old man with his white head and beard, his searching blue eyes, his crimson velvet cap, seated in low armchair by the fire, two candles on a little gate-legged table before him, the red glow of the olive logs occasionally breaking into flame and lighting up the green and red tiles, just as his words of fire leapt into flaming life and drove out the dark shadows from our souls. I recall no other light in the great room, and its contrast with the listeners so still and rapt. At last my father would, quite unexpectedly, rise and kneel, so that all, needy or critical, whatever their creed or hope, must feel their hearts opening out to God, for once perhaps if never again, like the red rose finding its freedom in the root-idea of the divine will. And then came a blessing, wonderful in its quiet, deeply penetrating, almost tremulous words, recalling the tones, still lingering in my heart from childhood's days, of Frederick Denison Maurice's benedictions; then a deep silence, and perhaps the organ softly rolling forth Handel's Largo from the far Jerusalem. Still and quiet even now, the guests would at last rise and go down the wide stone stair and out beneath the flashing stars of the huge Italian sky.'[11]

The family often used to take their plays along the coast, acting *Twelfth Night* in Cannes, for example, or else mounting productions in the great room at Casa Coraggio. Occasionally they would hold a dance there, and at Christmas there would be special festivities, carol singing, a Christmas tree, and *tableaux vivants*, based on Italian paintings. The MacDonalds did not regulate themselves according to the separatist rules of the English community, but invited in all and sundry — including the Italian locals and their children — which did not always please the

English who preferred to hold themselves aloof. Just like the old garden parties at The Retreat, rich and poor, old and young, English and Italian, all rubbed shoulders, and the family went even as far as holding a concert to help pay off the debts on the completion of the local Roman Catholic church. MacDonald's ecumenical spirit had a free rein, and he revelled in it. If the English gossiped about the unorthodox MacDonalds behind George and Louisa's backs, they still turned out in force every time there was an event at Casa Coraggio.

In the winter of 1883, Georgina Mount-Temple fell and injured the nerves in her spine. To speed her recovery, her husband took her to Bordighera for a rest where they rented a villa. She remembered:

> 'On Christmas Eve, we were dining in our little room looking on the olive wood, and we heard the sound of many voices, and looking out, lamps glimmered among the trees, and figures carrying lanterns and sheets of music. Who should they be but the dear MacDonald family visiting the houses of all the invalids in the place, to sing them carols and bring them the glad tidings of Christmas. The next day they had beautiful tableaux of the Annunciation, the Stable, the Angels, and the Shepherds, ending up with the San Sisto, in their wonderful room in the Coraggio, and they had invited the peasants to come and join this, for them novel representation of the event of the blessed Christmastide. That house, Coraggio, is the very heart of Bordighera, the rich core of it, always raying out to all around and gathering them to itself.'[12]

MacDonald's only interdict seemed to be that no one could come to Casa Coraggio who had so much as set a foot inside Monte Carlo. He claimed that he had seen too many lives twisted and destroyed by gambling to countenance it, though he enjoyed his evening game of whist. MacDonald's judgement was well in keeping with the moral tone of Bordighera, however, as it was far beneath the dignity of the English there to travel along the coast to play at roulette.

Though MacDonald had consciously planted himself on the Italian coast as a clan chief, and hoped that his family would always stay round about him, one by one his sons began to foray out into the world. Greville was already a doctor, and in 1882 Ronald went up to Trinity College, Oxford to read history where he soon made contact with Charles Dodgson, who invited him to dinner at Christ Church. At the same time, Bob entered the offices of J.J. Stevenson in London in order to train as an architect, along with his cousin Frank Troup. Earlier that year, on 17 March, Grace gave birth to a daughter — the MacDonalds' first grandchild — named Octavia Grace Jameson after Octavia Hill. Then in 1883 MacDonald's old stepmother made the long trip out to Bordighera, while Greville, who had qualified but not settled, tried unsuccessfully to set up a practice there. After this failed, he went to Florence in the April of the following year, along with Irene and MacKay — loved Florence — found no patients — and eventually returned to England where he built up a distinguished Harley Street practice as an ear, nose and throat specialist.

Death was never long idle in the MacDonald family, and Grace, whose lungs had been weak for a long time, died on 5 May 1884.[13] Suddenly little Octavia was motherless and sought solace in her grannie's arms. It seemed cruel to Louisa that the children, all of whom had grown safely past infancy, should be plucked while in the prime of adulthood. Kingsbury Jameson was a widower, and the family mourned. That summer there were no theatricals, and though MacDonald and Louisa travelled to England as usual, Irene and Lilia found themselves besieged at Bordighera by the outbreak of a cholera epidemic. People round about were burned out of their homes and there were some disturbing instances of violence, but luckily the epidemic did not reach as far as Bordighera.

MacDonald toured Scotland in August, visiting Huntly, and still speaking to large audiences. But he was almost sixty and beginning to feel old. The world that he had known was slowly slipping away, and he wrote to his friend, Margaret Roberts:

'The generation we are born into seems to us the original and everlasting generation, but how soon it begins to break up, until at length we find we could count our early friends on the fingers of a hand. I have but four blood relations of my generation left, one brother and three cousins. And we were a good many to begin with. It is all right. God made me with great hope, and I keep looking forward far more than backward. May He help you to look on at least as much as back.'[14]

Perhaps to make up for the lack of acting in 1884, the family went on tour with a vengeance in 1885, spending four months in Scotland, and playing in the most unlikely places, including St Andrews, Elie, Cupar, Crieff, Peebles, Dumfries and Greenock. They worked hard and made enough money to keep themselves, but there was little profit to show for their efforts. Louisa was exhausted by all the travelling, organizing, cajoling and marshalling she had done, and was eager to race back to the new organ awaiting her in Bordighera. MacDonald, for his part, lingered in London to mop up the last seven or eight lectures of his tour before setting out after her.

The following year, in 1885, Bernard went up to Christ's College, Cambridge to read law, and MacKay followed him the year after to study Natural Science at the same college. The boys had studied hard under Kingsbury Jameson, and now these fledglings were ready to leave the nest. Bob was still training, and now sharing rooms with Edward and Frank Troup. These boys depended, as did everyone else in the family, on MacDonald's slender income. It was like an inverted pyramid — fifteen people balanced on one. It was a heavy responsibility.

Life in Bordighera was normally a quiet and regular affair, but one still morning, at 5.30a.m. on 23 February 1887, there was a rumble and a crash. The ground shuddered as far away as Milan. An earthquake had struck.[15] Houses shook and fell to dust and the MacDonalds' own stucco tower was irreparably damaged. Louisa wrote to Anna Leigh-Smith, who was about to come to stay:

'An earthquake — yesterday morning, about six o'clock surprised us out of our beds. I remember some slight ones we had at Algiers, but I never knew the real terror of one before. The poor people have suffered the most — their houses came tumbling about their ears, some buried in the ruins. Our plaster cracked and ceilings and vases and jugs broken — but our walls so well built, stood firm. The only danger to us is from the stupid stucco tower that I dare say you remember vexed us so — George having ordered the tower to be of the same stone as the rest of the house. However it received such a shock yesterday that it will have to be taken down. Yesterday there was such a panic through the place that no one would do anything — besides it was Ash Wednesday, and no one would lift a finger to work. So the night was spent by all the poor, camping out and some terrified women from the cracked hotels would not accept any shelter and engaged carriages to sit in on the high road!

There is scarcely one hotel that has not had more or less damage. The ladies from the Angleterre were dressing and being dressed by their maids when scarcely light, out in the road and the whole of the colony were in the road or under the olives all day almost... We cannot help thinking perhaps it may put the drag on to the popularity of Bordighera which has threatening to become very unprecedented, I won't say fashionable — for that can never be, but the numbers of visitors here were on the increase, faster than we liked. Is it churlish to like it to keep quiet and sober minded...?'[16]

The earth tremors carried on for a few days afterwards, making the inhabitants of Bordighera gulp each time a new shake began. Greville MacDonald was told that:

'On the following morning, ie the 24th, my mother was in the English church close by sitting at the organ for a few moments' refreshment, when a second fierce earthquake occurred. "The whole bulk of the building began to shudder, just like the skin of a horse determined to be rid of a gad-fly;" and then such was the swaying and shaking that she felt sure it was going to collapse and bury them. My mother never failed the moment's need: she pulled out all her stops and played the Hallelujah Chorus.'[17]

All round Bordighera and in the outlying districts there were ruins everywhere, and the dust thrown up into the atmosphere caused the most magnificent sunsets for weeks. In his study MacDonald picked up the armfuls of books that had tumbled from the shelves, but in the whole house Louisa counted only 'one sad breakage' in the smashing of a 'Jameson pot'. But she put her domestic concerns aside as relief work was necessary — there were invalids rolled in blankets with umbrellas over their heads to tend and Louisa and the girls did what they could to help those who had been afflicted. The family contributed £100 to the Church Relief Fund for new clothing for the victims of the earthquake and fed some refugees at Casa Coraggio. The shock had left everyone edgy. MacDonald told his cousin James at The Farm:

'The earthquakes seem to be over now for a while, though it often seems as if one must be coming — a passing train, a cart, a foot overhead — anything raises the mental ghost of one, and makes you feel as if it might be on you in a moment.'[18]

Later that year Gertrude Desaint finally died,[19] and Ronald, who had been teaching at Clifton College, the boy's boarding school in Bristol, became engaged to Louise Virenda Blandy, an old drawing pupil of Ruskin's. He married her the following year on 7 July 1888. While the family were overjoyed at Ronald's good fortune, Greville did not fare so well when he announced his engagement a few months after Ronald's. He had fallen for the matron of the hospital he had been working at. The woman's name was Phoebe Winn, and the family were solidly opposed to her — perhaps because they felt she was 'only' a nurse — or that she had somehow trapped Greville in her clutches. More than that, she was fourteen years older than he was. Whatever the case, Greville was adamant that he wanted to marry her, but realized soon enough that broaching this subject with his parents was impossible. In March 1888 he announced to his mother from the safety of London that he was about to marry her, and despite a breathless dash from Italy on the part of Louisa and Lilia to prevent him, they arrived in England to find that the ceremony had already taken place. Deaf, awkward Greville — who was in many ways the most conventionally-minded of the family — proved himself in deed, if not in thought, the most unconventional of them all. MacDonald wrote resignedly to Louisa:

'I had your letter from Birmingham. Poor dear Greville and poor dear wife! What an experience for you to have to go through. It will be a wonder if you are not very ill after it. What a woman for any gentleman to marry! I wonder when and how it was settled for Saturday. I suppose they are really married! Well, this world and all its beginnings will pass on into something better.'[20]

It was a long time, however, before the family could bring themselves to refer to Greville's wife by her Christian name.

Then in 1889 Ronald decided to try his fortune in America. The family's reaction to his plans was mixed. Greville was against the idea as MacDonald, who was in London, told Louisa:

'I lunched with Greville yesterday... He is set against Ronald's going to Alabama. Mr Binney is dead against it too — bad climate and bad society.'[21]

As it turned out, MacDonald and Greville raised £500 apiece for Ronald to start him off, and he and his wife went out to Asheville in North Carolina, where Ronald became headmaster of an Episcopal school named Ravenscroft. Greville's disapproval extended to Bernard, who had desired, like his eldest sister, to become an actor. Greville persuaded him to set up as a teacher of elocution and voice production instead, and promised him a line of patients from his own surgery. These, however, failed to materialize, and Bernard was left to make his own way.

Ronald's school was not a notable success, and to add to his difficult lot, his wife died in 1890. In August of that year Lilia set out across the Atlantic to keep house for him, showing her usual mixture of doggedness and compassion. *Pilgrim's Progress* was finally laid to rest in 1889, as all the pilgrims had grown up and were going their own way. Only Irene and Winifred were left to keep their parents company at Bordighera as George and Louisa drifted from the parents' to the grandparents' generation. MacKay gained a third class degree in Natural Science from Cambridge and went to King's College, London in 1890 to follow his eldest brother in the study of medicine. In September that same year Bernard married Belinda Bird, the daughter of the Rev. J.W. Bird of

Foulsham, Norfolk, and MacDonald, who had endured a heavy lecturing load that summer, was glad to return to Bordighera for the winter. He was a little sad, perhaps, that its rooms were emptying, but apart from Irene and Winifred and Louisa, he had Honey and Joan, Desaint, and another young boy called Percy Harrat whom Louisa had taken in. Percy and Irene spent their days wandering along the coast painting, and watched the sun shimmer on the water. But there could be no doubt that MacDonald missed Lilia keenly, and at the beginning of 1891, while everyone else was at church, he sat down and wrote her a sad and searching birthday letter:

> 'I could say so much to you, and yet I am constantly surrounded by a cactus-hedge that seems to make adequate utterance impossible. It is so much easier to write romances where you cannot easily lie, than to say the commonest things where you may go wrong at any moment... Darling I wish you life eternal. I daresay the birthdays will still be sparks in its glory. May I one day see that mould in God out of which you came.'[22]

MacDonald's wistfulness was to turn to tears once again, for little Octavia Jameson began to sicken. Soon it was all too clear that her mother's disease had gripped her, and she became bed-ridden, scarcely being able to walk to the chair at the end of her room. One of her last acts was to send her grannie a hand-made Valentine and then, towards the end of February, she died. MacDonald wrote to Edmund Maurice, F.D. Maurice's son and Octavia Hill's brother-in-law:

> 'We are a house of mourning afresh at present, though by no means crushed, for we live and are saved by the sure hope of what is to come. Our little Octavia is gone to her mother. She was the young light of her grannie's eyes, but she takes comfort that our time is not, cannot be, so far away.'[23]

Even now, though not yet seventy, MacDonald had a sense of life drawing to a slow close before the awaited resurrection into new life. Perhaps he sensed instinctively that he was passing into his final chapter. His asthma had worsened considerably, and though he could lecture night after night, he could not walk far, and his memory at times went out of joint. He still smoked too much for Louisa's liking, but nothing she could do would induce him to give it up.

In the summer of 1891 he began his last long lecture tour. He had not lost his appeal, for just the previous October in Nottingham he had spoken to 1500 people at Nottingham — 'an audience almost foolishly enthusiastic' he had told Louisa. So, as usual, he packed his bags and took his Dante and, staying with Greville at Harley Street, he set off round the country for the last time. He even crossed the rough waters of the Irish Sea, lecturing in Belfast, and hoped for a sight of the Giant's Causeway. He had started for England before the rest of the family, owing to his engagements, and they were to follow on shortly. To his delight, Lilia was about to return from America. Ronald was in better health and had an elderly cousin now to act as housekeeper for him. Besides, Lilia had heard that a friend of hers, Eva Pym, was very sick with tuberculosis. Eva often spent the winters at Casa Coraggio, and Lilia wanted to come home to nurse her. As it turned out, Eva died terribly at Boulogne and, equally terribly, Lilia herself began to show signs of the disease. She went with the rest of her family to Stock Rectory, Billericay, which the MacDonalds had rented for their annual summer sojourn, but she was not well. MacDonald was absent for most of the time lecturing. He worried about his eldest daughter's health, and warned Louisa:

> 'I can't but think it would be better to have a doctor to Lily. There maybe something going on that will make you sorry you did not.'[24]

But MacDonald also had other things on his mind. He put his lecturing to one side and spent two weeks in Huntly at The Farm with his bachelor cousin James. All through the visit MacDonald acted as though he had come to touch his homeland for the last time. He and James travelled out to the Cabrach, the setting for *Castle Warlock*, a landscape filled with heather and deer, and he preached at both the Missionar Kirk and the Church of Scotland. The night he preached at the Church of Scotland the Congregationalists closed down their service, and from the pulpit it looked as if the whole of his native town had come to hear him preach. He was very moved by the occasion. He also made a final pilgrimage out to the lonely cemetery at Drumblade to look on where his relatives lay buried:

> 'I have just had it [Louisa's letter] on my return with James from the churchyard where the bodies of all my people are laid — a grassy place and very quiet, in the middle of undulatory fields and with bare hills all about. But I see the country more beautiful than I used to see it, for as a boy it did not much please me.
> "What is it all for?" I should constantly be saying with Tolstoi, but for the hope of the glory of God.'[25]

He and James made another pilgrimage, the five miles out to Ruthven where the ruined church still contains the bell that cried 'Come hame, come hame' to the fool in MacDonald's first published story *The Bell*, and later renamed *The Wow o' Rivven*. The ruin stands in a small silent churchyard, and at the foot of the wall lies John McBey, the fool of MacDonald's story, whom he must have known from his boyhood. Perhaps, standing there, MacDonald felt that the bell was ringing 'Come hame, come hame' for him. He told Louisa:

> 'I have been out for a few miles drive — to the old church of Ruthven, of which only the gable and belfry remain, with a beautiful old bell, looking quite new, though I think the date on it is 250 years ago, with the legend in Latin "Every kingdom against itself shall be laid waste." Right at the foot of the belfry the fool of my story is buried, with a gravestone set up by the people of Huntly telling about him, and how he thought that bell now above his body always said "Come hame, come hame." Close to him, in a place chosen by himself lies Dr Grant whose violin I bought. They are the only two lying there. I had never been there before. James made his man and another go up and take a rubbing of the legend on the bell. They could climb up the edge of the gable on the corbel-steps of it.'[26]

MacDonald finally left The Farm on 23 July and took a train down to King's Cross in London where Bob met him. He toured Scotland again in September, lecturing in Edinburgh and Glasgow, and meeting up with his friends the Geddeses and George Reid the painter and his wife in Aberdeen. Though he was fêted and applauded wherever he went, he could not shift the gnawing anxiety about Lilia's health, as she did not seem to be getting any better. Both he and Louisa grew fraught, and MacDonald's usual optimism wore thin:

> '... For Lily, it seems just the old story of ups and downs. But we must remember that we are only in a sort of passing vision here, and that the real life lies beyond us...'[27]

Strangely, MacDonald was convinced that the root cause of Lilia's illness was spiritual, and that some wilfulness or lack of confession on her part was preventing her from growing well. He complained to Louisa:

> 'I cannot help thinking if Lily would give herself up quite to him to whom she belongs, she would be at peace and then perhaps grow better... I do think Lily will be much better when she consciously gives in to the will of God...'[28]

But Lilia did not grow better, and the train journey back to Bordighera was a nightmare, with Lilia sitting stiffly upright and trying to show no signs of tiredness nor let any coughing pass her lips. Louisa was very distressed:

'...But oh! she did suffer! — and indeed all her life she has been an intensely suffering soul. Knowing all I do now of what unintentional agonies we have made our children suffer, all the while having a heart full of love and intended good will to them, I could not *dare*, of my own choice have over again such a lovely family as was given us to rear and teach and guide.'

MacDonald was held up lecturing in England into the first week of November:

'I got through well last night at Liverpool, feeling more master of my work than usual, though my memory was constantly aching like a naughty dog that would not keep to heel but was always ready to run away, when I was taken up with the thing I was at.'[29]

Just before he returned to Italy he visited William Matheson, Greville Matheson's brother, who had loved Lilia and who was lying gravely ill:

'I have been to see William — for the last time, I think I cannot doubt — in this world.'[30]

William Matheson died on the 21st, only two weeks later. MacDonald returned exhausted to Casa Coraggio after lecturing forty-eight times in fifty-eight days. He arrived home on 8 November and was grateful to see his family again, but his heart sank to see his weakened daughter propped up in a bath chair. Yet she was brave and cheerful and seemed even to recover a little, so much so that MacDonald resumed his Wednesday afternoon readings. But her recovery was short-lived. Lilia died in MacDonald's arms on Sunday 22 November, and was buried the following Wednesday on the 25th. She was thirty-nine. Louisa wrote to Greville who was in London:

'...Her beautiful body looked oh! so lovely — grand, gentle radiant almost though, more than all, peaceful... Father and Bob and Mr B— lifted her into La Cassa — plain wood with one long red cross and the flowers and wreaths and garlands seemed everlastingly numerous... It was in a drenching pouring rain that we put her lovely worn-out garment back to mother earth... Strange that W.J. Matheson should have been buried at the same hour!... We have been terribly dazed, dear; it was so sudden, awful for us, but for her, how blessed! — scarcely any distress, and just quietly saying, "I think I'm going, Mammy — to the others, you know, to join them." After one dead faint, she spoke as if she had seen Maimy; and then the quiet clasp of the hands saying, "If God wills"...But oh! my Greville, it's dreadfully hard to bear.'[31]

MacDonald's grief at his eldest daughter's death can scarcely be imagined. Lilia, whom the whole family had leaned on, God's Lily, a sign of his bounty, had been plucked away:

'When the coffin was carried into the church the congregation joined in the singing, "My God, my Father, while I stray." The tremulous, subdued voices showed how deeply everyone was mourning the loss of a cherished friend, that woman who, from her very childhood, had been a mother to old and young. Her father could hardly leave the grave: he came back twice after all the others had left, and it was with difficulty he was at last led away. The day was terribly wet: all nature was lamenting.'[32]

Lilia was laid to rest beside her sister Grace. Their twin graves are of a delicate Pre-Raphaelite design by Edward Hughes with their names etched upon them, and stand at the brow of the cemetery under some shady trees.

Lilia's death was the point at which MacDonald became truly an old man. His hold on life began to loosen and he felt almost that Lilia had gone to prepare a place for them and hoped that he and Louisa would not be long in following her. He wrote to his cousin Helen Powell:

'I think we feel — Louisa and I at least — as if we were getting ready to go. The world is very different since Lily went, and we shall be glad when our time comes to go after our children.'[33]

In that wistful letter of January 1891, when he had written to Lilia in Asheville while she was still with Ronald, MacDonald had said:

'. . . I still have *one* great poem in my mind, but it will never be written, I think, except we have a fortune left us, so that I need not write any more stories — of which I am beginning to be tired. If I do write one more of 3 vols., it will, I think be the last, but there are no signs of that one yet. I think Philip Sidney will be out in a month or two now, *There and Back* in about the same time.'[34]

There and Back was, in fact, MacDonald's last three-volume novel, and the 'great poem' was never written. But MacDonald did write one last great book. Startling and original, it returned to the world of *Phantastes* and he named it after a figure who had pursued him all his life — *Lilith*.

CHAPTER THIRTY-TWO

Lilith

Lilith is MacDonald's masterpiece. It was also his 'dark night of the soul', exposing the terrible struggle between light and shade that had battled in his consciousness since his earliest days. It is not an easy book to read and it took MacDonald five years from the time he first sat down to write it before it was published in its final form. As he withdrew daily into his study at Bordighera to write, so Louisa became perturbed at the dark disturbing words dripping from his pen, and thought that the book ought never to see the light of day.

In the end MacDonald's and Louisa's differences over the book came to a head and they asked Greville to arbitrate in their dispute. He sat down to read it and was so enthralled that he urged his father to carry on. That settled the dispute, though not Louisa's fears, for she was becoming increasingly worried about her husband's state of mind. *Lilith* seemed like madness to her, but MacDonald was convinced that the impulse to write it had come as a direct mandate from God, and his first draft was possessed of an unusual fluency. Greville MacDonald recorded:

'Its first writing is unlike anything else he ever did. It runs from page to page, with few breaks into new paragraphs, with little punctuation, with scarcely a word altered, and in a handwriting freer perhaps than most of his, yet with the same beautiful legibility. The mandate thus embodied in symbolic forms, over which he did not ponder, he then gave it more correct array: he rewrote it, allowing the typewriter its help, but adding his usual and profuse pen-emendations.'[1]

The first draft was 50,000 words long and ran without a break.[2] Its method of composition suggests that MacDonald was knowingly including a large amount of unconscious material, much of which he himself probably did not understand. This is true of all MacDonald's fantasy writing, but nowhere else did he make a claim to divine inspiration. Such a claim sets *Lilith* outside the normal categories of literature, showing that its intent was not merely to entertain or instruct, but to inspire and compel. If the book resembles any other literature then it is probably not scripture or the mystical writers, but Dante's *Divine Comedy* for which Dante also claimed divine inspiration, and to which *Lilith* is, in many ways, akin. *Lilith* was also written to influence the religious temper of the times, for the age when MacDonald's sentiments were daring had now long passed. Greville MacDonald claimed that:

> 'The book was written, I do think, in view of the increasingly easy tendencies in universalists, who, because they had now discarded everlasting retribution as a popular superstition, were dismissing hell-fire altogether, and with it the need for repentance as the way back into the Kingdom.'[3]

The dark troubled landscape of *Lilith* certainly does not express a doctrine of easy access into heaven. There the way home to God is terrifying and snare-ridden and there is no refuge from the relentless forces of the dream-world that MacDonald's hero enters.

Lilith was MacDonald's last major work; it stands at the opposite end of MacDonald's prolific output to *Phantastes*. After the failure of *Phantastes* in 1858, MacDonald's faerie strain ran through his short fairy-tales and longer children's books, lending an underlying coherence to his novels. But, forty years after *Phantastes*, it burst out with a vengeance in *Lilith*.[4] In many ways *Lilith* was the book MacDonald had been trying to write all his life, indeed had been writing all his life, and even after he had finished it he was excruciatingly aware of its shortcomings and inadequacies. Though she appears as a powerful and original conception of MacDonald's, the persona of Lilith herself has, in fact, a long and complex history, changing and reappearing in various works of literature throughout the nineteenth century, and forming and reforming throughout MacDonald's own work as well.

Originally Lilith was a character in Jewish mythology, probably based on an earlier Babylonian figure. The first account of the creation in Genesis '... in the image of God created he him, male and female created he them' was adapted in a cabbalistic retelling of the story in which Lilith was Adam's first wife, and like him created from the dust of the ground. Being created equally with Adam, she demanded equality, and refused to obey him in taking the subordinate position in sexual intercourse. Rebelling, she fled and took to killing babies, over whom she claimed power, and seducing sleeping young men. She herself gave birth to demons and spirits, a hundred of whom were to die each day as a punishment for her refusal to obey Adam. Later she became known as Sammael's (or Satan's) wife.[5] By the fourth century the commentator Hieronymos had noted that she was the Greek *Lamia*, and somewhere in later centuries she was conceived of as a vampire as well as a demon or succubus. There is scant biblical evidence to support her existence, though her legend was expanded and embroidered over many centuries.

Lilith had a changeable identity therefore and writers, finding little basis for her existence, found it possible to clothe her in many different guises. She makes an appearance on the Sistine Chapel roof, and Milton compares her to Sin in *Paradise Lost*. For the romantics, however, she was a siren, a fascinating and destructive seductress, surpassing Cleopatra, Salome or Circe — the supreme *femme fatale*.[6]

Lilith makes her first appearance in the nineteenth century in the first part of Goethe's *Faust*. There her appearance frightens even Mephistopheles who warns Faust against the lure of her magnificent hair. Shelley translated this scene into English, and Carlyle, who had read Goethe, made a passing reference to 'Lilis' in *Sartor Resartus*. But she became fully 'embodied' in 1864 when Dante Gabriel Rossetti painted her as *Lady Lilith*, combing out her long golden hair surrounded by roses and narcotic poppies.

MacDonald was much influenced by the Pre-Raphaelite painters, and their conception of Lilith, further embellished by Swinburne in his poem *Dolores* (1866), was in part the starting-point for his own use of the legend. But, for MacDonald, Lilith is more than just a character in one of his books — she provides a hermetic key to the understanding of all his work, for he was always dogged by this sinister figure. She appears explicitly for the first time in MacDonald's short tale 'The Cruel Painter', included in *Adela Cathcart* in 1864. Here Lilith is the daughter of the evil painter Teufelsbürst, who takes pleasure in portraying scenes of torture, including Lilith somewhere on the canvas as a cold, indifferent beauty. Though Lilith herself is actually a sweet and unassuming girl, her father's depiction of her highlights the romantic tension felt by the writers of the period between pain and beauty. Lilith's second appearance in MacDonald's work is not as a woman, but as the white mare in *Wilfrid Cumbermede* (1872). The horse, however, counter-balances the provocative Clara Coningham who appears as one of MacDonald's many temptresses. She is the real Lilith of the book, though in fact she is in bondage to her father, as the earlier Lilith had been to her cruel father, the painter. MacDonald originally intended the Lilith of *Lilith* to be similarly enslaved to the devil, but later reworked her as an independent and powerful figure so that she herself became the opposing force in the universe.

If Lilith's name occurs only twice in MacDonald's work before the publication of *Lilith* in 1895, there is nevertheless an occult moulding of her character throughout all his work, and a direct line can be traced from Euphra Cameron's wounded foot in *David Elginbrod* in 1863 to the dripping paw of the leopardess in *Lilith*. For Lilith is a whore and a witch, the negative of the Virgin and the maiden Beatrice — she is Euphra Cameron as opposed to Margaret Elginbrod. MacDonald's fatal women are often described in feline terms, and such metaphors are made concrete in, for example, *Home Again* where Molly dreams of a white cat lying across Walter Colman's face after he has fallen under the enchantment of Lady Lufa. MacDonald sometimes went even further, describing women as demons or vampires, as he described Lady Cairnedge in *The Flight of the Shadow*. In an earlier book, *Malcolm*, MacDonald described Mrs Stewart as a 'vampire demon' and Malcolm's meeting with her in a neglected library gives a foretaste of what he was later to write:

'A lady tall and slender, with a well-poised easy carriage, and a motion that suggested the lithe grace of a leopard. She greeted him with a bend of the head and a smile, which even in the twilight and her own shadow, showed a gleam of ivory.'[7]

Many of Lilith's attributes are to be found here, and MacDonald gathered together such preliminary sketches to sum up his last message to his generation.

Lilith was intended to be MacDonald's equivalent of *The Divine Comedy*, a visionary masterpiece to be presented to the end of the nineteenth century. Certainly MacDonald worked harder on his tale than anything he had done since *Within and Without* in 1855. No fewer than eight pre-publication drafts of *Lilith* exist, and the story underwent many mutations between the first drafts and the published book. In the first version the hero is called Mr Fane, and Mr Raven is called Mr Crow and Mr Rook before becoming Mr Raven. Lona,[8] Mara, and the skeletal Lord and Lady Cockayne are later additions, and the final version is, of course, much longer than MacDonald's original unbroken piece.

It is inevitable that comparisons with *Phantastes* should be made, and there are interesting parallels and similarities. Like *Phantastes*, *Lilith* is a quest, written in the first person, but instead of Anodos' pursuit of the marble woman, Vane pursues Lilith to her lair in Bulika. Whereas Anodos is pursuing his ideal, Vane is pursuing a *doppelgänger*. And just as Anodos spends twenty-one days in Fairyland to bring him to a symbolic maturity, so Vane loses his identity in order to regain a true knowledge of himself. At one point Mr Raven (Vane's interpreter in the dream-world of *Lilith*) challenges him with: 'What you call riddles are truths, and seem riddles because you are not true.' Vane must 'unriddle' himself into harmony therefore, in order to die that he might live. If Lilith herself is akin to any figure in *Phantastes*, then it is to the Alder-maiden who seduces both Anodos and Percival, while the shadow reappears in an even more terrible guise, blacker and more tangible than ever.

As a book, however, *Lilith* demonstrates several major advances over *Phantastes*. While Cosmo recognizes that 'all mirrors are magic mirrors', he is unable to pass through the glass to possess the beautiful woman he sees reflected there nightly. Vane, on the other hand, is able to pass through the mirror into the dream-world (as does Alice in *Through the Looking Glass*). It is as though some profound barrier in MacDonald's thinking has been overcome. In *Phantastes* Anodos is warned by the fairy being he meets that '. . . a man must not fall in love with his grandmother, you know,' while in *Lilith* Vane's bride Lona is described as a 'tender grandmother' and this wish is at last fulfilled.[9] While MacDonald's favourite saying from Novalis occurs in both books: 'Our life is no dream, but it should and will perhaps become one' — in *Phantastes* Anodos is returned to the everyday world, changed and hoping, but Vane's life really does become a dream and he is no longer sure where or how he exists. Both books are, in one sense, about maturity, but though they are both fantastic in form, they are different in nature. While *Phantastes* is a picaresque tale, light and associative, the brooding pages of *Lilith* have the dense structure of a novel.

Despite its novelistic form, *Lilith* is unlike anything else in prose that the nineteenth century produced. Though Rider Haggard experimented with facets of the anima in *She* and other books, they are quite different from MacDonald's work. One of MacDonald's struggles, which he admitted in 'The Fantastic Imagination', was to bring unconscious material to consciousness — *Lilith* represents the attempt to do so. The only two writers who could possibly invite comparison are Blake and Dante, and MacDonald felt an affinity with both of them. He certainly knew some of Blake's poetry, though Greville MacDonald claimed that he never studied any of Blake's longer prophetic books in detail. He did use one of Blake's drawings for his book-plate, however, showing a wizened old man leaning on a stick and entering his tomb, only to rise renewed and reborn above. The image of the soul hatching into bliss is a recurrent one in MacDonald and his whole hope was pinned on resurrection. MacDonald was strongly drawn to other aspects of Blake's art. Greville

MacDonald recalled:

> 'For as long as I can remember there hung in my father's study four of
> Blake's illustrations to Blair's *Grave* — the good man dead on his
> tomb-like bed, the bad man fiercely escaping with evil spirits, the Spirit
> of Man with the candle of the Lord searching all the Grave's inward
> parts, and the old man driven — the North Wind blowing where it
> listeth — into his tomb, to find himself reborn into the fulness of
> youth, with head uplifted to the risen sun...'[10]

Greville MacDonald felt that the image of the cemetery was drawn from
Blake.

More important than Blake, however, was Dante, and *Lilith* owes
much to his visions. The Bad Burrow, for instance, where the monsters
crawl out of the earth, resembles the eighth circle of Dante's hell, while the
dead souls are strewn on the moor like the petals of the white rose of
heaven, Dante's conception of the heavenly dwellers.[11] Lord and Lady
Cockayne who have been condemned to live together as skeletons, until
their love begins to regenerate them, are an example of the Dantean
notion of *contrapasso* in which the punishment is set to fit the crime, and
the leopard for Dante is a symbol of sensuality, a fitting figure for Lilith.
The very end of MacDonald's book with its ascent to heaven is a blend of
the book of Revelation and the *Paradiso* and includes several explicit
references to Dante.[12] MacDonald's intention to make *Lilith* like *The
Divine Comedy* is thus very clear.

As in all MacDonald's fantasy, *Lilith* is decidedly not allegorical and even
the allusions to other works of literature, including the Bible, do not help
much in determining its final meaning. It is MacDonald's final exploration
of the unconscious, which he began in *Phantastes*, and which he continued
in his novels, which he turned inside out to lay bare the processes of the
psyche. What is immediately evident about *Lilith* is that it is deadly
serious and aimed at an adult audience. The book begins with Mac-
Donald's very last visit to a library and tells how the symbolically named
Mr Vane passes through a mirror into a dream-world where he must
learn to die in order that he might live. The dream-world is occult,
peppered with biblical and classical allusions and remains beyond Vane's
(and the reader's) grasp. Mr Vane is so called to give the impression that
he is spiritually empty and the book explores his humbling and his journey
to self-knowledge. Like Anodos, Vane is an Everyman figure and Mac-
Donald expects his readers to identify themselves with Vane and so
become heroes of their own tale.

Vane is an orphan, as are so many of MacDonald's heroes, but significantly he knows nothing of his ancestry.

In fact the only ancestor Vane can refer to, Sir Upward, was given over to the study of the occult, and his portrait presides over his descendant's solitary porings in the library. What Vane does not realize is that the thoughts in his head are about to be given concrete reality, and idle rumination is about to be transformed into desperate struggle:

'I was constantly seeing, and on the outlook to see, strange analogies, not only between the facts of different sciences of the same order, or between physical and metaphysical facts, but between physical hypotheses and suggestions glimmering out of the metaphysical dreams into which I was in the habit of falling. I was at the same time much given to a premature indulgence of the impulse to turn hypothesis into theory. Of my mental peculiarities there is no occasion to say more.'[13]

What MacDonald was here outlining is an alchemical correspondence between the things of the spirit and the things of matter, highlighted in Swedenborg's theory of correspondences which MacDonald had studied. Vane's thoughts serve as a prologue to what he will find in the dream-world for, following what he takes to be a shadow, he climbs to the attic of his house and finds, not a great-great-grandmother spinning, but a mirror through which he passes into another world:

'I saw before me a wild country, broken and heathy. Desolate hills of no great height, but somehow of strange appearance, occupied the middle distance; along the horizon stretched the tops of a far-off mountain range; nearest me lay a tract of moorland flat and melancholy.'[14]

This wild, almost Scottish landscape is the beginning of the dream-world and the start of Vane's journey. In travelling through the mirror, Vane emerges into a world that is the mirror-image of this world, the complement and opposite of everyday reality. It is the world of the left hand, the occult and the irrational, normally repressed and hidden by the right hand, rational and determined conscious world. St Paul wrote in his first letter to the Corinthians that now we see 'through a glass darkly', that is, 'in enigmate' — in an enigma. The world that Vane stumbles into *is* an enigma, for it is a world of things without names,[15] where the mental and physical laws are different, though the moral remain the same.[16] This world exists 'in the region of the seven dimensions' on the planet Uranus, where the double worlds of *At the Back of the North Wind* are super-imposed on each other. As Mr Raven recites in a poem to Vane at one point:

'Ah, the two worlds! so strangely are they one,
And yet so measurelessly wide apart!'[17]

Mr Raven is the librarian of Vane's library, who appears as a man from the back and a raven from the front. He becomes Vane's interpreter, explaining his faults and reappearing at points through the book to comment on the action. He tells Vane, for example, that two objects can exist in the same place at the same time, and says:

'That tree stands on the hearth of your kitchen, and grows nearly straight up its chimney... If you could but hear the music! Those great long heads of wild hyacinth are inside the piano, among the strings of it, and give that peculiar sweetness to her playing — Pardon me: I forgot your deafness!'[18]

These different dimensions overlap as, in the dream-world, space is a psychical rather than a physical entity, similar to Swedenborg's conception of it. Swedenborg claimed to speak with spirits and roam through several dimensions, convinced that thoughts and ideas in this world could have bodily existence in another. This is profoundly true of Vane's dream-world where the landscape and narrative are driven by his own imaginings:

'"If I know nothing of my own garret," I thought, "what is there to secure me against my own brain? Can I tell what is even now generating? — what thought it may present me the next moment, the next month, or a year away? What is at the heart of my brain? What is behind my *think*? Am I there at all? — Who, what am I?"'[19]

When Vane enters the dream-world he perceives:

'A single thing would sometimes seem to be and mean many things, with an uncertain identity at the heart of them, which kept constantly altering their look... Even to one who knew the region better than myself, I should have no assurance of transmitting the reality of my experience in it. While without a doubt, for instance, that I was actually regarding a scene of activity, I might be, at the same moment, in my consciousness aware that I was perusing a metaphysical argument.'[20]

This is true of all that Vane encounters, and of his very position in space.

He asks Mr Raven:

> '"Oblige me by telling me where I am."
> "That is impossible. You know nothing about whereness. The only
> way to come to know where you are is to begin to make yourself at
> home."'[21]

And later Vane laments:

> 'But what mattered *where* while *everywhere* was the same as *nowhere*!
> I had not yet, by doing something in it, made *anywhere* into a place! I
> was not yet alive; I was only dreaming I lived! I was but a
> consciousness with an outlook!'[22]

Vane also experiences difficulty in translating his adventures into words:

> 'I begin indeed to fear that I have undertaken an impossibility,
> undertaken to tell what I cannot tell because no speech at my command
> will fit the forms in my mind.'[23]

A world without words cannot be described, but has to be suggested,
however inadequately. The reader sees it therefore 'through a glass
darkly'. In fantasy, there is a difficulty in using a word to refer to a thing
because that thing at any moment might change its shape or nature: the
fantasy world, not contained within the rational, is fluid and unsystematic.
Books are made up of words and a library made up of books. MacDonald's
explorations are concerned, therefore, with the nature of the word, and
mankind's relation to and perception of reality. MacDonald held a
profound reverence for books themselves, and books for him were
portals to other worlds. It is therefore fitting that Vane's adventures
begin in a library.

The world Vane enters is, paradoxically, contained within a book
(*Lilith*), but Vane, who has formerly dedicated himself to study, now
begins to hunger for experience and companionship. Here he complains
that '...my soul was athirst for a human presence...' and books have
become a dead thing:

> 'I felt as if the treasure of the universe were giving itself to me — put
> out my hand, and had it. But the instant I took it, its lights went out; all
> was dark as pitch; a dead book with boards outspread lay cold and
> heavy in my hand. I threw it in the air — only to hear it fall among the
> heather.'[24]

Vane is unable to understand the world he has entered at all: 'All in this world seem to love mystery!' he exclaims at one point, but the reason for his being there is made clear from the moment of his arrival, as Mr Raven tells him:

> 'But indeed the business of the universe is to make such a fool of you that you will know yourself for one, and so begin to be wise.'[25]

This is the old Christian paradox that the Kingdom of Heaven is to be given to those who are childlike and simple, but Vane's pride prevents him from seeing it. At the same time, the hidden meaning of the world is beautifully revealed in Mr Raven's action of tugging a worm out of the earth and tossing it into the air where it sprouts wings and becomes a gorgeous butterfly.

The Greek word *psyche* encompasses both the idea of butterfly and of soul, while the raven is a symbol of death. Through death, MacDonald shows that the dead are reborn to a new life, and this is in miniature what Mr Raven, who turns out to be Adam, intends for Vane. He takes Vane to his cottage where he and Eve give him a eucharistic meal of bread and wine, before leading him down to a chamber where countless people are lying asleep on couches under white sheets. They urge Vane to sleep, but he refuses and flees the chamber, only to find himself back in the library. Vane is puzzled by his experience, and later finds a manuscript written by his father telling of the other world. Excited by this discovery, Vane decides to return to the House of Death and ask Mr Raven if he can now sleep. He returns to the dream-world through the mirror, which gains a greater hold on him each time he enters it, but Mr Raven denies his request. Having rejected the shorter way to bliss, Vane must begin a long journey from the Bad Burrow, equivalent to Dante's Hell, up to Paradise — he must pass from nightmare to dream.

It is while he is in the Bad Burrow that Vane learns his first lesson:

> 'Then first I knew what an awful thing it was to be awake in the universe: I *was*, and could not help it!'[26]

In this place the very foliage takes on frightening shapes, animals hatch out of the ground, and Vane's worst nightmares are realized:

> 'With that, a step or two from me, the head of a worm began to come slowly out of the earth, as big as that of a polar bear and much resembling it, with a white mane to its red neck. The drawing wriggles with which its huge length extricated itself were horrible, yet I dared not turn my eyes from them.'[27]

Here Vane catches his first sight of Lilith, wrapped in mist, and watches as her body divides into bats and serpents.[28] Later he sees her make an appearance at a gruesome battle between phantoms and skeletons. It is then that Vane notices that the land is without water — it is a Waste Land needing renewal, again a picture of Vane himself, though he can hear water running underground, symbolic of his own unconscious.[29]

After this first terrible night, Vane wakes to discover the Little Ones or Lovers, children whom he befriends and who befriend him. They are unusual in that they have no memory or knowledge, but yet possess immense wisdom.[30] After asking many questions, Vane learns that they are found in the wood as babies, and grow only a little, but once they show signs of greed or selfishness then they change into stupid giants called the Bags who can no longer even see the children. The eldest of them, a girl called Lona who acts as their mother, tells Vane: 'The giants have lost themselves, Peony says, and that is why they never smile.'[31] The children are primal, Wordsworthian embodiments of the imagination, but Vane is acute enough to guess that their growth has been somehow hindered. Like the land, they too need water, and he decides to make it his mission to help them. He is rueful about the shocking transition from Lover to Bag:

> '"They call it growing-up in my world!" I said to myself. "If only she would teach me to grow the other way, and become a Little One! Shall I ever be able to laugh like them?"'[32]

Vane sets out once more on his journeying, passing the night this time at the House of Mara, the daughter of Adam and Eve, before continuing the following day.[33] It is there that he discovers the corpse of Lilith whom he tries to revivify in an attempt to gain some human company. The sexual and necrophiliac aspects of his endeavours are very explicit:

> 'I crept into the heap of leaves, got as close to her as I could, and took her in my arms. I had not much heat left in me, but what I had I would share with her! Thus I spent what remained of the night, sleepless, and longing for the sun. Her cold seemed to radiate into me, but no heat to pass from me to her.'[34]

Vane lies with the body for seven days and nights, and as it shows no signs of decay, he divines that there must still be some life left in her. For a time he lives in a cave, making clothes for the dead woman and steeping her in a hot stream, the only water he has found in the whole land. The cave could be seen as an extension of Vane's mind, and the

corpse the sexual principle within himself which he nurtures only to
have it attempt to enslave him. For after three months Lilith revives, but
she repels Vane scornfully, disgusted at his ministrations to her. He
realizes then that she is not good, but he is fascinated by her, and
follows her like an abandoned child following his mother. She, in turn,
sucks his blood, linking eroticism and vampirism as powerfully as Le
Fanu had done in his *Carmilla*:

> 'She drew down my face to hers, and her lips clung to my cheek. A
> sting of pain shot somewhere through me, and pulsed. I could not stir a
> hair's breadth. Gradually the pain ceased. A slumberous weariness, a
> dreamy pleasure stole over me, and then I knew nothing.'[35]

Vane's attempt to possess Lilith has failed, but his failure is not only a
physical, but also a psychical one, for Lilith in her varied guises as
leopard, cat, vampire, leech, princess and woman are all attempts by Vane
(and MacDonald) to comprehend her in a single mental image, which
proves impossible.

Vane travels on to Bulika, Lilith's city, and on his way meets a fugitive
mother who tells him that:

> 'There is an old prophecy that a child will be the death of her. That is
> why she will listen to no offer of marriage, they say.'[36]

Lilith's child is, in fact, Lona, and her refusal to accept the prophecy is a
refusal to accept that she is bound by the laws of the universe and submit
to a power greater than herself. Lona is a threat to Lilith's conception of
herself, and so must be crushed, just as the wicked stepmother is intent
on crushing Snow White in the fairy-tale and devouring her lungs and
liver.

Bulika, where Lilith rules, is a fallen city, an evil Gwyntystorm, like
Babylon, and a negative version of the city of Zion. Here the people have
grubbed up precious jewels from the earth and live on their riches,
disdaining to work. They are hostile to strangers, and have been lured
away from their former pastoral existence by Lilith's wheedling. They
think themselves rich, but they are, in fact, slaves. On his journey Vane is
puzzled to encounter two leopardesses, one white and one mottled. The
white leopardess helps him. She is an emanation of Mara, and good, while
the mottled leopardess is an emanation of Lilith, and bad. At first Vane is
not sure what to think when he comes face to face with the white
leopardess:

> '...she might be treacherous too, but if I turned from every show of

love lest it should be feigned, how was I ever to find the real love which must be somewhere in every world?'[37]

Vane goes to Lilith's palace and encounters the princess herself who appears to him in a dazzling show of beauty:

'All at once, a radiant form stood in the centre of the darkness, flashing a splendour on every side. Over a robe of soft white, her hair streamed in a cataract, black as the marble on which it fell... My frame quivered with conflicting consciousnesses, to analyse which I had no power. I was simultaneously attracted and repelled: each sensation seemed either.'[38]

Here Lilith is supremely an uncovering of the unconscious. She is sexual, destructive, eternal and changeable — like the black widow spider she mates with her men before consuming them. She is one of man's primal fears here embodied, and represents the terror at the heart of Vane, and indeed of every man — as opposed to every woman. The palace Vane wanders through is a mere extension of herself, while the room where Vane finds her, the black ellipsoid, is, paradoxically, Lilith's own brain: 'I knew that in the black ellipsoid I had been in the brain of the princess.'[39]

Lilith is his fear; he is a thought in her head. This is a variation on the Red King's dream in *Through the Looking Glass*, but magnified to terrifying proportions. Played out on the walls of the dark room are Lilith's shadowy thoughts, and Vane even sees a recounting of his story up to that point. Unlike her behaviour towards him in the wood, Lilith is sweet and tries to win Vane over, but he is repelled though tempted:

'Then first I noted on her left hand a large clumsy glove. In my mind's eye I saw hair and claws under it, but I knew it was a hand shut hard — perhaps badly bruised.'[40]

Lilith sucks Vane's blood once more, and persuades him to climb a tree, which he does, only to emerge by the fountain in his own garden at home.[41] Vane is naturally disconcerted by the sudden transition from one world to the other but, restored to the rationality of the everyday world, Mr Raven appears and gives Vane an explanation of everything that has been happening to him. Mr Raven accuses Vane of Hamlet's sin of procrastination:

'You lost your chance with the Lovers, Mr Vane! You speculated about them instead of helping them.'[42]

It seems that Vane has not sufficiently rid himself of his bookish habits. Mr Raven explains to him that the Little Ones need water to enable them to cry before they can grow. Mr Raven also suspects that Lilith has followed Vane out of the dream-world and discovers her in the guise of a Persian cat which he traps. He reveals something of Lilith's history to Vane:

> '...she poured out her blood to escape me, fled to the army of the aliens, and soon had so ensnared the heart of the great shadow that he became her slave, wrought her will, and made her queen of Hell... Vilest of God's creatures, she lives by the blood and lives and souls of men. She consumes and slays, but is powerless to destroy as to create.'[43]

Like other women, however, she is to be saved by her childbearing and so her own child Lona will prove to be the means of her salvation. Raven's speech shows something of the contradictory nature of Lilith. On one hand, she is a symbol of a revolt, appearing at a time when women were asserting themselves against the patriarchal order and demanding independence, careers, and the vote. She is a threat therefore to the male identity. On the other hand, the very processes she derides will save her.

Mr Raven offers Vane another chance to sleep at the House of Death, and gives him a horse in order to get there. But Vane is so infected with the power of the horse that he refuses the couch once again, and rides back to the Little Ones, noticing when he arrives that they have grown slightly. He now knows that the Little Ones have the power to destroy Lilith:

> 'For the terrible Lilith — woman or leopardess, I knew her one vulnerable point, her doom through her daughter, and the influence the ancient prophecy had upon the citizens.'[44]

It is also at this point that Vane discovers his love for 'The Lona, queen and mother and sister of them all...':[45]

> 'My every imagination flew to her; she was my heart's wife!'[46]

Lona is an image of womanly perfection, a child-bride and mother — the very opposite of Lilith, and yet like Lilith:

> '...but in Lona the dazzling beauty of Lilith was softened by childlikeness, and deepened by the sense of motherhood.'[47]

Lona did not appear in MacDonald's first draft of Lilith, but was written in after Lilia died. Lilia, MacDonald's favourite daughter, was, in a certain sense, very much a child-mother and MacDonald had already included a tentative incest motif in Weighed and Wanting where, with himself thinly disguised as Dr Christopher, he is to marry Hester Raymount, modelled on Lilia. MacDonald brought this idea to fruition in *Lilith* by portraying Lona and Vane as lovers, though even here they are not united until they reach Paradise. When Lona says, 'I do not remember ever being without a child to take care of...'[48] it sounds like something Lilia might have truthfully said. Through Lona, then, MacDonald paid homage to his beloved, lost daughter whom he hoped one day to see again.

Back in the dream-world Vane prepares the Little Ones as a holy army to war against Bulika, and the children ride there on the backs of bears and elephants to take the city by storm. Their hopes of finding mothers for themselves are cruelly dashed, however, when they see the brutal faces of the citizens staring at them. Lona alone does not give up hope and rushes to greet her mother, Lilith:

> '"Mother! mother!" cried Lona again, as she leaped on the dais, and flung her arms round the princess.
>
> An instant more and I should have reached them! — in that instant I saw Lona lifted high, and dashed on the marble floor. Oh, the horrible sound of her fall! At my feet she fell, and lay still. The princess sat down with the smile of a demoness.'[49]

Heartbroken, Vane takes his dead Lona and the captured princess from the evil city. He notices that the children have been frightened by something, unusual for them, and they say this is so because they have been attacked by the evil Shadow who is Lilith's henchman. One child says:

> 'It was the shadow that got into me, and hated him from inside me; it was not my own self me!'[50]

Vane, Lilith and the Little Ones set off for the House of Bitterness to find Mara, who lays Lilith on a couch, for at last the prophecy is about to be fulfilled, though Lilith must first repent. To do this she must see herself as she really is, as she has made herself. Up till now she has only gazed on an image of her own beauty flashed on a mirror in the black ellipsoid room. As Lilith is not the shape God intended her to be, she must literally re-form. Shadows and forms gather in the lamplit room, and Vane knows that something terrible is about to happen. He has, however, grown sufficiently in wisdom to trust Mara, and to be able to tell one of the Little Ones, who are all afraid of her:

'"My boy," I answered, "There is no harm in being afraid. The only harm is in doing what Fear tells you."'[51]

Suddenly a silvery worm crawls out of the cloudy presences that fill Mara's room and into the fire, from where it issues to enter the body of Lilith:

'. . . the creature had passed in by the centre of the black spot, and was piercing through the joints and marrow to the thoughts and intents of the heart. The princess gave one writhing, contorted shudder, and I knew that the worm was in her secret chamber.

"She is seeing herself?" said Mara; and laying her hand on my arm, she drew me three paces from the settle.'[52]

It is here that MacDonald probes the heart of repentance. If Teufelsbürst's regeneration in 'The Cruel Painter' is glib and swift, Lilith's is deeply agonizing, for she must give up her very self and realize that what she has been clinging to as life is, in fact, death. Her proud cry of, 'I will be myself and not another!' is useless, as she is not herself, that is, not as she was intended to be. Mara explains to Vane:

'The central fire of the universe is radiating into her the knowledge of good and evil, the knowledge of what she is. She sees at last the good she is not, the evil she is. She knows that she is herself the fire in which she is burning, but she does not know that the Light of Life is the heart of that fire. Her torment is that she is what she is.'[53]

With a start, Vane then realizes a truth about Lilith's existence, and indeed his own, which has passed him by until that moment:

'Then came the most fearful thing of all. I did not know what it was; I knew myself unable to imagine it; I knew only that if it came near me I should die of terror! I now know that it was *Life in Death* — life dead, yet existent; and I knew that Lilith had had glimpses, but only glimpses of it before: it had never been with her until now . . . She had killed her life and was dead — and knew it. She must *death* it for ever and ever!'[54]

Finally, after her terrifying ordeal, Lilith relents and chooses repentance, and outside refreshing rain begins to fall:

'For in the skirts of the wind had come the rain — the soft rain that heals the mown, the many-wounded grass — soothing it with the sweetness of all music, the hush that lives between music and silence. It bedewed the desert places around the cottage, and the sands of Lilith's heart heard it, and drank it in. When Mara returned to sit by her bed, her tears were flowing softer than the rain, and soon she was fast asleep.'[55]

Vane, Mara and the Little Ones take the shakily repentant Lilith from the House of Bitterness to the House of Death where Adam has prepared couches for them all. The Little Ones crawl eagerly under the white sheets to rest beside the bodies of sleeping women — 'The little orphans had adopted mothers!' exclaims Vane. They fall asleep immediately, but Lilith is unable to rest until she can open her hand which remains obstinately tight shut.[56] Try as she might, it remains clenched, and finally Adam severs it with the sword given to him by the angel who once guarded Paradise. He charges Vane to go on one last mission before he sleeps. Vane must bury the hand at the place where the waters flow strongest underground in order to make the rivers burst to the surface once again. Adam gives Vane his spade, and Vane sets off, encountering phantoms and horrors on his way who try to lure him from his task.

The last and greatest obstacle Vane meets is the Shadow, whose day of repentance must also come, and who stands in Vane's way:

'I had almost reached the other side when a Shadow — I think it was The Shadow, barred my way. He seemed to have a helmet upon his head, but as I drew closer I perceived it was the head itself I saw — so distorted as to bear but a doubtful resemblance to the human. A cold wind smote me, dank and sickening — repulsive as the air of a charnel house; firmness forsook my joints, and my limbs trembled as if they would drop in a helpless heap. I seemed to pass through him, but I think now that he passed through me: for a moment I was as one of the damned. Then a soft wind like the first breath of a new-born spring greeted me, and before me arose the dawn.'[57]

At last Vane is able to bury the hand, and the ensuing cataract drowns the evil brood of monsters that hatch from the ground of his unconscious. He returns to the House of Death having completed his mission, and now finally he can fall asleep. Despite his irresolution and impulsive behaviour throughout the book, Eve tells him: 'To our eyes...you were coming all the time.'[58]

Vane lies down beside his beloved Lona and begins to dream. There begins a whole series of dreams, culminating in Vane's and Lona's awakening and ascent to Paradise where:

'To be aware of a thing, was to know its life at once and mine, to know whence we came, and where we were at home — was to know that we are all what we are, because Another is what he is! Sense after sense, hitherto asleep, awoke in me — sense after sense indescribable, because no correspondent words, no likenesses or imaginations exist, wherewithal to describe them.'[59]

In Paradise, the earlier fluidity of things is replaced by a definite identity. Meaning is at last established and gains meaning from being in relation to other things round about it, replacing confusion with certainty, uniting words and things as living wholes:

'Life was a cosmic holiday . . . At last I was! I lived and nothing could touch my life! My darling walked beside me, and we were on our way home to the Father!'[60]

But they are also on their way home to their mothers:

'"I see my mother!" I cried.
"I see lots o' mothers!" said Luva.'[61]

As they approach Paradise they see that the light is made of angel faces, and a great angel bends down to say 'Welcome home!' Looking up, they catch sight of the splendid city of the New Jerusalem glittering with living gems:

'We stood for a moment at the gate whence issued roaring the radiant river. I know not whence came the stones that fashioned it, but among them I saw the prototypes of all the gems I had loved on earth — far more beautiful than they, for these were living stones — such in which I saw, not the intent alone, but the intender too; not the idea alone, but the imbodier present, the operant outsender: nothing in this kingdom was dead; nothing was mere; nothing only a thing.'[62]

It seems as if the approach to Paradise will signal the end of the book. At the climax of Vane's journey, however, just as he is scrambling up to the heavenly gate:

'At length we drew near the cloud, which hung down the steps like the borders of a garment, passed through the fringe, and entered the deep folds. A hand, warm and strong, laid hold of mine, and drew me to a little door with a golden lock. The door opened; the hand let mine go, and pushed me gently through — I turned quickly, and saw the board of a large book in the act of closing behind me. I stood alone in my library.'[63]

Back with his books, it appears that Vane has come full circle, but not quite — for now he is not sure whether his experience in the other world was a dream, or whether he is still asleep in the House of Death and the library is but a dream:

> 'Now and then, when I look round on my books, they seem to waver as if a wind rippled their solid mass, and another world were about to break through.'[64]

Vane's life finally has become a dream, and the book ends:

> 'But when I wake at last into that life which, as a mother her child, carries this life in its bosom, I shall know that I wake, and shall doubt no more.
>   I wait; asleep or awake, I wait.
> Novalis says, "Our life is not a dream, but it should and will perhaps become one."'[65]

So Vane is left to wake into that greater reality which will be his Home. *Lilith* is about many things and works on many levels. Driven by the two fundamental principles of Eros and Thanatos, the book maps out a myth depicting how to conquer and integrate the fears deepest to man. Lilith is death as well as sexual desire, and through coming to a knowledge of her true self she enables the landscape to be watered, irrigated by the power of Vane's subconscious. Vane moves on a journey from Hell to Paradise, from pride to humility, from ignorance to wisdom — he travels from a place where nothing is certain, and where the things there exist without signs, to a place where the signs and the things they signify become living wholes. The title of the final chapter of the book, *The Endless Ending*, shows how this process of change and appropriation must be a constant one. Vane finally occupies two places at once — the couch in the House of Death and the library. He is always arriving, always waiting, always learning — just as the reader must go on pondering the meaning of the myth and absorb it into his psyche.

Lilith is also a powerful spiritual book, taking seriously the saying of Christ that one must die in order to live, and that true life can only begin with the ending of self. MacDonald's tale is, then, very human, exploring primal human fears concerning sex, death and the meaning of existence. Vane does not understand what is happening to him most of the time because he cannot see the truth of the world he has stumbled upon — it is his own everyday world lifted into another dimension. For a time his pride prevents him from growing, until he is placed in a situation where his pride is no longer able to operate.

For MacDonald, *Lilith* was the culmination of his life's work, finally expelling from his system the myth he had been nurturing throughout all his books. Not only does he describe, with astonishing power, the dream-world and the matrix of archetypes — Lilith, Lona, Mara and Eve, all aspects of the feminine — the book represents for MacDonald himself the end of a quest. For he had long grappled with the loss of his own mother, taken from him when he was eight. In his writing there is a long parade of twisted mothers, summed up in Lilith, who is not only Lona's mother, but Vane's also. Freud claimed that a child bereaved of its mother could often construe her death as an abandonment, and then later project malevolent feelings onto a female figure, creating a destructive and evil mother-image. *Lilith* was the catharsis of those feelings, to the extent that the orphaned children are finally able to snuggle close to the corpses of their mothers, and Vane himself on the ascent to Paradise catches sight of his own mother. In dealing with the principles of life, death, sex and origin, MacDonald was able to integrate his unconscious anger and fear into a powerful myth, for at last even Lilith, MacDonald's own image of the betraying woman, does lie down in the House of Death and seek salvation.

In MacDonald's day, however, *Lilith* was simply an aberration, an irritating enigma. Instead of the usual rambling and uplifting novel, MacDonald had presented the public with something it could not stomach. As with *Phantastes* forty years earlier, the critics had no idea how to read it. *The Athenaeum* wrote:

'That some high purpose pervades this strange mystical farrago, we are willing to believe, but its method of presentment seems to be neither lucid nor edifying.'

The *Pall Mall Gazette* dismissed the book as 'a wild phantasmagoria of nonsense', and even MacDonald's friend, William Robertson-Nicoll, writing in the *British Weekly* found the book 'obscure'.[66] Most were disappointed and alarmed at what MacDonald had produced, and the book's reception may have been complicated by the fact that romantic sensationalism had become a popular genre, and supernatural pulp novels were then being written at great speed. The irrepressible Marie Corelli had shot to fame with *A Romance of Two Worlds* in 1886, in which she confused God and electricity, and she had published *The Soul of Lilith* in 1894, to which MacDonald's book was unfortunately if irrelevantly compared.

One reader who did admire *Lilith* was H.G. Wells, who thought that the use of the mirror to pass from one world to another was a compelling device.[67] *Lilith* was written before its time — it is a very modern book concerned with the nature of the mind, the subjectivity of all writing, even with its own textuality. It stands at a junction in literature from which emerged the three different strains: fantasy writing, science fiction, and the parable mode, used by writers such as Kafka and Borges who create other worlds that closely mirror our own. *Lilith*, then, is a pioneering book, a daring masterpiece, exploding the tenets of realistic fiction. Writing it was an audacious act for a man of MacDonald's age. MacDonald himself may have hoped that after years of his novels, his public would instinctively have known what *Lilith* was about, but he was proved wrong. All through his life he was painfully aware of the two kinds of mentality at odds with one another — represented by the Lovers and the Bags. MacDonald knew that the Lovers are only a small minority in the world, but it is only they, with their accepting child-like wisdom, who will even attempt to understand this difficult book.

CHAPTER THIRTY-THREE
The Final Chapter

MacDonald and Louisa began to inhabit a twilight world, and the strictures of the little English colony at Bordighera began to tell on them. In 1894 MacDonald wrote to Georgina Mount-Temple:

'Gradually we are shut in from the public, then the social relations are narrowed, then some, thank God, are shut up to their dear ones on this earth, then we are alone with the living one and have to take spoonfuls of life from his own hand; and there are some, doubtless, who call and think it, only nasty medicine.'[1]

Louisa carried on with the choir and organ at All Saints' Church, but she had been severely shaken by Lilia's death, and slumped once more in her bath chair, staying there for a good long time. The summer of 1892 was spent at Arth in Switzerland, therefore, to enable Louisa to have a good dose of clean air and time to regain her strength. She recovered, but both she and MacDonald were counting the days until they could go to join Lilia. MacDonald wrote to his daughter Winifred in 1893.

'Your mother is on the whole considerably better, but still liable to sudden attacks of which the great wear upon her nerves through having to go through so many sorrows and troubles is the cause.'[2]

Louisa's nerves were often a source of comment in Bordighera, where her sharp tongue and flaring temper made many of the English people there dislike her. It was a problem she had always had, but it grew worse in her later years. Only towards the end of her life did Greville diagnose an enlarged thyroid as a possible cause of her problem. By then it was too late to do anything for her, and Greville kept his diagnosis from his mother. To MacDonald, however, she was always devoted, and life carried on at Casa Coraggio, even if only as a shadow of its former self. The Wednesday afternoons and Sunday evenings continued, and attempts were made to revive *Pilgrim's Progress*, though with Lilia gone, these were none too successful. Eventually the curtains which had served them

385

so well were cut up and hung in the great room at Casa Coraggio. Theatricals continued at home thereafter, and as late as 1898 Louisa and her sister Charlotte Godwin were taking on roles at the respective ages of seventy-six and eighty-one. And Christmas remained a special time. Frank Troup, Robert Troup's son, spent the Christmas of 1891 at Casa Coraggio and wrote home to his brother James about his stay there:

'You see we have been at lots of picnics and drives and when not at that at long tramps among the hills. Saw last Sunday a little town perched on top of a hill near 3000 ft high — Church on the apex all in ruins lying just as it fell in the earthquake when 200 people were killed in it. . . . We dress for dinner every night which is nice when you are used to it. Play cards mostly after dinner. You have heard me "do the hen" I suppose. Cousin George is immensely fond of it and made me perform to a great company — in fact we had a regular farm yard. It was regarded as a grand success and something like a party was invited one evening to have a repetition of it. A brilliant idea occurred to me in the interval, which MacKay and I carried out successfully and with enormous eclat. I sung (sung — by george — what d'ye think of that?) sung "Ye banks and braes" but as if done by a *hen*. Cousin George nearly split himself laughing. I stuck about the last line and to finish ran in to "The keel row" a la chickie, which was if anything an improvement. I was encored and instead of trying another I apologised in Hen language — you never heard such a farce in all your born days — and there I am going about Bordighera meeting people at every turn who saw me making a perfect idiot of myself — my goodness — such is fame.'[3]

For a while MacDonald's industry remained unabated. He published his final volume of sermons *The Hope of the Gospel* in 1892, the same year that saw his *Collected Poems* appear in two volumes. *Heather and Snow* came out in 1893, *Lilith* in 1895 and *Salted with Fire* in 1897, but by then the fire had gone. *Salted with Fire* was little more than a worn-out replay of all his earlier themes. In addition to his writing, he decided to learn Dutch and Spanish and began studying those languages, but despite this burst of energy there was no doubt that he was tired. Lecturing and touring had lost their appeal, and MacDonald wrote to his friend and secretary William Carey Davies:

'. . . I have no impulse toward public work this year. I do not think I should feel at all sorry if I were told I should never preach or lecture again. . .'[4]

But there were compensations to this dreariness in friends and family. Their old friend Georgiana Burne-Jones, the wife of the painter, came to stay for six weeks in 1892, and both MacDonald and Louisa became very friendly with Violet and Hyacinth Cavendish Bentinck, the twin sisters of Lady Strathmore, and their mother Mrs Scott. They owned a villa in Florence, and there were several trips between Florence and Bordighera. MacDonald enjoyed driving out in the country and he would often allow himself to be taken for day trips through the countryside around Bordighera. Sometimes he would go to the little mountain towns built cheek by jowl on the sides of the hills such as Dolceaqua or Apricale, or else go along the coast to La Mortola where the Hanbury Gardens were open to the public twice a week. British visitors enjoyed the pleasing Mediterranean climate, and MacDonald's children darted in and out of Casa Coraggio, bringing more and more grandchildren with them.

Bernard's son Maurice was born in 1892 on St George's day, also Shakespeare's birthday, and MacDonald was delighted. He also became very fond of Ronald's daughter Ozella who was one of the few people who could coax him out of his increasingly withdrawn moods. There were more marriages in the family: Bob, christened Robert Falconer, married Mary St Johnstone in 1894, and the similarity of her name to Mary St John in *Robert Falconer* did not go unnoticed by the family; while in 1897 Ronald married for the second time, Constance Robertson the actress; MacKay married Blanche Bird, the sister of Bernard's wife; and Winifred married Edward Troup, the son of MacDonald's old friend Robert Troup and his cousin Margaret MacDonald. After the ceremony on 2 January at Bordighera, Winifred and Edward went to live at Earls Terrace where the MacDonalds had lived in the 1860s. That left only Irene at Bordighera out of the large clan of eleven, though Honey and Joan Desaint helped bolster the dwindling family. And though MacDonald was able to defend his friend Dr Goodchild in court in 1896[5] and give evidence in his favour, it was obvious that his powers were beginning to weaken. His mind began to lose its firmness and he would forget things. He became withdrawn, shuffling out of his study in his black velvet coat to eat and remaining in silence. Sometimes the clouds would clear for a moment and then he would suddenly drop one of his spiritual nuggets into the conversation, remarking for instance that:

'The lines in what we call Society are not perpendicular but horizontal. There are vulgar duchesses, and vulgar charwomen, and there are titled women who have the innate refinement and simplicity of soul which I have met with in some Scottish shepherds and Italian peasants.'[6]

Some guests found it disconcerting that MacDonald could pick up his spoon, mention the plum pudding and then in the same breath give a short discourse on the immortal soul. Confused, MacDonald begged Louisa to tell him that he was not going mad, a fear that he had always had, and she did her utmost to console and convince him that his wits were only 'ben the hoose' and that he was all right.[7] Yet he sensed that something was wrong, and withdrew even further. If inwardly life was becoming increasingly bewildering, outwardly he still paraded at parties at Casa Coraggio, entering the great room to thunderous applause in his velvet suit and cap — and still visitors lined up to see him, though more and more he did not recognize who they were. Life indeed was becoming a hazy dream, and MacDonald longed to wake from it. As his mind crumbled, worn out after many years of struggle, so his body too began to reveal the toll of the passing years. His eczema began to interfere with his sleep, and his doctor, who had forbidden him to work more than four hours a day, encouraged him to go lightly on smoking and alcohol. The doctor's earlier recommendation of exercise had never been followed, though MacDonald had tried a tricycle once or twice. Perhaps this slow descent was to be expected. In 1894 he wrote to John Stuart Blackie:

'This life is a lovely school-time, but I never was content with it. . . I think we do not yet know the joy of mere existence. To exist is to be a child of God; and to know it, to feel it, is to rejoice evermore. . . Next month I shall be 70 and I am humbler a good deal than when I was 20. To be rid of self is to have the heart bare to God and to the neighbour — to *have* all life ours, and possess all things.'[8]

At the same time, the strain of writing *Lilith* was very great. MacDonald had to steel himself to see the text through its many evolutionary stages and the effort involved in nurturing it through to publication was very taxing. The agitation of his mind broke out all over his body, and Greville MacDonald wrote:

'But early in that year (1897) my father, being then seventy-three, the eczema became alarming, so gravely did it interfere with sleep. It was a constant torture — no less — and my father's sadness increased. He realized that his brain sometimes would not respond to his imagination, though he set himself a course of reading as if to discipline his fatigue into some renewal of life. Then even this became difficult. . . My father's dejection was akin to Job's; and if at his worst, just before his deliverance from the evil thing came, he even echoed the words of his Master that God had forsaken him, his spirit was thereupon commended to God.'[9]

The nightmares that MacDonald endured are, perhaps, to be found in the pages of *Lilith*, and his 'deliverance' came swiftly and unexpectedly in the form of a stroke which clouded his mind and weakened his body. This happened while he and Louisa were spending the summer at Clammerhill in Surrey in 1898, just as MacDonald was trying to commit the whole of *In Memoriam* to memory. Greville wrote to Richard Watson Gilder:

> 'I have been away in Vienna or I should have answered your letter sooner. Father had been failing in many ways for the last year or two and during the whole of this spring and summer we have been very anxious about him. In a day of great heat he had an attack which appeared to be like a sunstroke; this prostrated him utterly for many weeks though he has been gradually improving since he returned to Bordighera — I do not consider there is any immediate cause for anxiety though I am pretty sure he will never be the same man again.'[10]

With his mind at rest, MacDonald's eczema cleared, and sleep came to him at last. He became like Vane, fast asleep on the couch, awaiting the grand resurrection, and in day-to-day life there was only a glimmer left of the powerful character he had once been. Louisa fought to nurse him, but she was not equal to the task and a man and woman were specially employed to take care of him. As the income from MacDonald's books dried up, Louisa was forced once more back on her own resources, especially as her own legacy had disappeared in 1891, and despite help from her children, she was obliged to take in recommended paying guests at Casa Coraggio. She remained wily and alert, silvery-haired under her perky bonnets and as late as 1899, the *Journal de Bordighera* reported:

> 'On Friday afternoon Mrs MacDonald gave an afternoon party in honour of the 84th birthday of her sister Mrs Godwin. The guests were asked to come in "Whitechapel Costume" and one well-known and respected resident appeared in such disreputable attire that even the natives of Whitechapel itself would have looked askance at him, while considerable doubts were expressed as to whether the gold watch in his possession was honestly acquired. Another excellent get-up was that of a sandwich man bearing a highly adorned but very clever likeness of Mrs Godwin, and one of our most popular residents not only dressed herself up as a "dirty old woman" but also mimicked the speech and action of a Whitechapel "lidy".'[11]

As for MacDonald, perhaps his signature can be seen at the end of his last story, 'Far above Rubies', published in the Christmas number of *The Sketch* in 1898. It is a tired story, rehashing many of MacDonald's own favourite incidents and preoccupations, and it ends:

> 'His legacy has long been spent, and he has often been in straits since; but he has always gathered good from those straits, and has never again felt as if slow walls were closing in upon him to crush him. And he has hopes, by God's help...of getting through at last, without ever having dishonoured his high calling.'[12]

In 1900 Bob, now an architect, planned and built a house for his parents at Haslemere in Surrey and named it St George's Wood. It 'had lovely gardens and three acres of woodland with superb beeches that overspread the wood'. There in the summer months while he was in England MacDonald would go for daily drives, dressed in a red cloak and white serge suit with a grey felt hat on his head, still looking a noble figure, though his keen eyes were now sad and vacant. Louisa was more than pleased with the new house and wrote to Winifred:

> 'I suppose you want me to tell you how we get on in this new house — The rooms are comfortable and well-arranged — and the aspect from the windows is beautiful — the sunsets are just as good as yours at Cullen or would be if Hindhead were removed and the vacant space filled up with blue sea. The water is good, the drainage excellent: and the tradespeople from Haslemere are most attentive.'[13]

In that same year a man called Percy Raymond was engaged to attend MacDonald, and remained with him right until the end. For there had begun what Greville MacDonald dubbed 'The Long Vigil' when Mac-Donald waited, like one of the characters out of his books, for the great good finally to come to him. Gradually, he subsided into silence until the power of speech seemed to abandon him completely. The few words he spoke attempted a feeble grasp at understanding what was happening to him. As Irene wrote to Winifred:

> 'Then after tea Greville and Winslow took him out in the chair and I walked with them. Father enjoyed it all and said so when he came in. As we came home he asked "Whose is this machine?" and when I told him it was his he seemed to be trying to understand. He looked as if he was waking up from a dream.'[14]

But MacDonald's dream became a nightmare for Louisa who found it hard to reconcile herself to her husband's condition and to the realization that she could do nothing for him. She never saw that each time she left the room, MacDonald's eyes would glance at the door, waiting and hoping for her return.

Back at Bordighera the one ray of light in these difficulties was their Golden Wedding celebrations held in 1901. The great room at Casa Coraggio was sumptuously decorated on 8 March with golden flowers and a feast was laid out.[15] Later that year in June there was another gathering at St George's Wood. Louisa was happy, surrounded by her children and the new generation of MacDonalds, but the only friend there from the old days seemed to be Octavia Hill. MacDonald watched the proceedings blankly from his Bath chair, though his gaze kept following Louisa as she moved to and fro in the crowd. This was the last of the happy times, and Greville MacDonald recorded Louisa's slow submission to despair:

> 'But a time came when my mother, worn out with clinging to hopes which increasingly failed her, and herself ailing with an internal affection, at last realized two things: one that he would never recover his power of speech, and the other that skilful and kind nurses could do more for him than she in her waning strength. She turned her face to the wall. Her own suffering and waywardness were great, and the devoted nursing of her one daughter, Irene, was their only mitigation.'[16]

Tired and defeated, Louisa died at Bordighera on 13 January 1902.[17] For some days afterwards, Winifred and Irene, who had been nursing Louisa, were afraid to break the news to MacDonald, fearing that he would not understand, but when they finally summoned enough courage to tell MacDonald, he broke down and wept. Louisa was laid to rest under a rough white stone cross in the Bordighera cemetery beside her daughters Lilia and Grace. There the cypress trees shade and protect them, the three stones that stand against the wall. Charlotte Godwin died at Casa Coraggio the following March, and so only Irene was left in Bordighera to tend MacDonald, and did so faithfully until her own marriage to the architect Cecil Brewer in May 1904.[18] They were married at Haslemere and MacDonald remained with them until January 1905 when he went to live with Winifred and Edward Troup, now living at Ashtead in Surrey. That May Irene and Cecil came to look after him while Winifred and Ronald went out to Italy to pack up Casa Coraggio, an enormous task that took them three weeks. They returned to find MacDonald quiet but sinking. As Octavia Hill wrote to Winifred:

> 'To have one we love with us, and not with us consciously, not to be able to reach them, and yet to see them here is a terrible feeling. One has to cling on to the knowledge of how the soul lives independent of the body, and how sure the future is for us all.'[19]

On 18 September, after a short two days' bout of pneumonia, with Edward Troup at his bedside, MacDonald died. He slipped away quietly, without a murmur, leaving only an aura of peace.[20]

The funeral took place three days later at Ashtead Parish Church on the 21st. It was a quiet affair, with only the family and a few close friends in attendance. Octavia Hill was there, and Arthur and Edward Hughes. The mourners walked bareheaded along the country lanes into the church and took their places. The oaken coffin was covered with flowers, Mary's silk pall, and a MacDonald tartan plaid, which MacDonald had much worn in his later years. Ronald, Bob, Bernard and MacKay carried the coffin into the church preceded by choirboys in white surplices and they all sang 'Thou art the Way' as Willie Nicholls played the organ. Kingsbury Jameson took the service. There was no pomp or show. The service was a simple, quiet affair, and perhaps the image of Mr Raven tugging the worm out of the earth to watch it soar into the air as a butterfly flashed through some minds. After the funeral was over, the coffin was taken by special train to Woking where MacDonald's body was cremated. For his journey was not yet over.

On 31 December 1905 Winifred and Edward drove from Menton to Bordighera where they met Irene. None of their brothers were able to be there, and the following day on 1 January the three of them entered the British cemetery and climbed the stone steps to the three graves, pausing in front of Louisa's white cross. The chaplain conducted a simple ceremony and MacDonald's ashes were placed into Louisa's grave, uniting them again in death as they had been inseparable in life.[21] They prayed. Winifred looked at the grave and thought of their years together — now ashes, now a white stone cross. She turned and walked away looking at the ground, at the graves and at the sky, the words filling her ears:

'They thought he was dead. I knew that he had gone to the back of the north wind.'

NOTES

In the notes each book cited is generally written out in full at least once in every chapter before being abbreviated. MacDonald's novels are identified by their initials. Thus *Robert Falconer* becomes *RF*, *Alec Forbes of Howglen* becomes *AF*, *Ranald Bannerman's Boyhood* becomes *RBB* and so on. ALS is the abbreviation for Autographed Letter Signed.

Generally speaking I have used first editions throughout, except for the fairy stories (where such a thing as a first edition is hard to define), *The Princess and Curdie* and *Lilith*.

CHAPTER ONE
The Blood-filled Glen

1 Quoted in *George MacDonald and His Wife* by Greville MacDonald, London, 1924 p.38.
2 The best modern book on the subject is *Glencoe: The Story of the Massacre* by John Prebble (London, 1966) from which I have drawn my facts.
3 *GMAW*, p.40.
4 See *Robert Falconer* Vol. I London 1868 p.66.
5 *GMAW*, p.39.
6 William's memory is elaborated, to some extent, in the character of Duncan MacPhail, the blind piper in MacDonald's novel *Malcolm*, London, 1875. See also *RF*, Vol. I, pp.64–66.
7 See footnote to *GMAW* p.39. He was registered only as Charles on the occasion of his marriage in 1778, but he was known always within the family as Charles Edward, named after the Young Pretender, and thus reinforcing his Roman Catholic origins. According to George MacDonald's elder brother Charles Francis, in his unpublished *Notes*, Charles Edward was the youngest of nineteen children.
8 See *GMAW*, p.25, p.39.

CHAPTER TWO
The MacDonald Descent

1 See *RF* Vol. I, pp.133, 302.
2 Mary Gray, 'A brief sketch of the life of George MacDonald', *Bookman*, November 1905.
3 'George MacDonald's Centenary

Address to Young Folk', *Huntly Express*, 12 December 1924. Isabella MacDonald may also have had other reasons for destroying the Chanter Kist. She may have wished to obliterate all traces of her husband's Roman Catholic past.
4 *RF*, Vol. I, p.293.
5 Robert Troup, *The Missionar Kirk*, (Huntly 1901).
6 *GMAW*, p.28.
7 *GMAW*, p.27.
8 *GMAW*, p.29.
9 *Ibid*.
10 *GMAW*, p.34.
11 This letter is now in the possession of Mrs Margaret Troup.
12 *GMAW*, pp.36–7.
13 *David Elginbrod* London 1863. Vol. I, pp.160–61.
14 Mary Gray: 'Sketch' *Bookman* (Brit) November 1905. It is clear that George MacDonald senior was a warm and good humoured man, unlike his more rigid brother, and he was certainly nothing of a bigot. In a letter to his son, George MacDonald (ALS Yale Huntly 31st May 1850) he wrote: 'Like you I cannot by any means give in to the extreme points either of *Calvinism* or *Arminianism*, nor can I bear to see that which is evidently *gospel* mystery torn to pieces by those who believe there is no mystery in the scriptures and therefore attempt to explain away what is evidently for the honour of God to conceal... As to the "New-faith" folks I believe they hold many important things in common with ourselves...'
15 The Farm is now known as Greenkirtle. The house was completed in 1826. It had

formerly been only a collection of farm buildings. The bleachfields and Dry-house were situated on the east bank of the river Bogie where the old road from the south came from Cocklarachy down to the ford over the river. As the MacDonalds lived on the far side of the Bogie from Huntly, they were in Drumblade Parish, and their family plot still stands in Drumblade Parish Cemetery.

16 See *RF*, Vol. II, p.260.

CHAPTER THREE
The Little Gray Town

1 *RF*, Vol. I, p.9.
2 *GMAW*, p.33.
3 'A Sketch of Individual Development', *Orts*, 1882, p.43.
4 Sources drawn on in this section include: Gray, *Recollections of Huntly*; Troup, *The Missionar Kirk*; *Statistical Account* of Huntly Parish 1792.
5 *Ranald Bannerman's Boyhood* London, 1871, p.16.
6 ibid. p.51.
7 ibid.
8 The flood is a recurring image in MacDonald's writing, appearing in *Sir Gibbie*, *Castle Warlock*, *Donal Grant*, *Paul Faber, Surgeon* and *The Princess and the Goblin*. The most detailed description of the Huntly floods is to be found in *Alec Forbes of Howglen*.
9 *RBB*, p.12.
10 *GMAW*, p.53. This account is taken from a letter from GMD senior to GMD 7 October 1850 (ALS Yale).
11 'The Hills', *Poems*, 1857.
12 *GMAW*, p.53.
13 First printed in *Good Words for the Young*, 1872, later included in the 1882 edition of *Adela Cathcart*.
14 *Huntly Express* 30 October 1872.
15 *Alec Forbes of Howglen*, London, 1865 Vol. I, p.59.
16 Charles Francis MacDonald, Unpublished *Notes*, now in the possession of Ian MacDonald.
17 *AF*, Vol. I, pp.56–57.
18 *AF*, Vol. I, p.26.
19 *GMAW*, p.60
20 The figure of the kindly schoolmaster appears in several of MacDonald's novels. There is Mr Innes in *Robert Falconer*, Mr Simon in *Castle Warlock* and Mr Graham in *The Marquis of Lossie*.
21 *GMAW*, p.63
22 *RBB*, p.236. Ranald Bannerman's career as a monitor is not very successful.
23 *GMAW*, p.63.
24 *Huntly Express*, 30 October 1872.

25 *GMAW*, p.65
26 *RBB*, p.54.
27 *RBB*, p.249.
28 *RF*, Vol. I, p.151.
29 *The Portent* London, 1864, pp.8–9.
30 Klopstock's eighteenth-century poem was translated several times into English. Edward Young (1684–1728) studied law and divinity and became chaplain to King George II. One of the so-called 'graveyard school' of poets, his gloomy religious verse to some extent fed the 'Gothic' literature of the late eighteenth/early nineteenth centuries.
31 *RBB*, p.287.
32 *RBB*, p.162.
33 *GMAW*, p.64.
34 ibid.
35 *GMAW*, pp.61–62 (ALS Yale).
36 'A notable Aberdeenshire Schoolmaster', By an Old Pupil, published at The Banffshire Journal Office, Banff, 1908.
37 Ibid. A letter, written from Earles Terrace, dated 31 October 1863. Quoted in 'A notable Aberdeenshire Schoolmaster'.
38 *Huntly Express*, 22 September 1905.
39 ibid.
40 *AF*, Vol. I, pp.232–236.
41 *RF*, Vol. I, p.154.
42 Application to Highbury Theological College, 1848. This document is now in Dr Williams Library, Gordon Square, London.
43 *RF*, p.244.
44 Now in the possession of Margaret Troup.
45 *GMAW*, p.66.
46 *GMAW*, p.53.
47 *RF*, Vol. II, p.19
48 *GMAW*, p.67
49 *RF*, Vol. II, p.25.
50 *RF*, Vol. II, p.26.
51 *RF*, Vol. II, p.48.

CHAPTER FOUR
The Crown of Stone

1 *RF*, Vol. II, p.51.
2 *The Life of Alexander Whyte*, C.F. Barbour, London, 1925.
3 *RF*, Vol. II, p.53.
4 ibid.
5 *RF*, Vol. II, pp.55–56.
6 *GMAW*, pp.67–68.
7 A provost is a mayor.
8 Neil Maclean, *Life at a Northern University*, Glasgow, 1874 p.66
9 *Castle Warlock*, London, 1882. Alec Forbes's descent into drunkenness and prostitution (*AF* Vol III p.86ff) is graphically written, leading some critics to believe that it is autobiographical. There is

no evidence, no family rumours or hints, for this. MacDonald abandoned Total Abstinence and drank wine and beer, rarely touching spirits. In his novels drinking whisky is always a moral evil.
10 Robert Troup, *The Missionar Kirk*.
11 GMD to GMD senior 28 October 1841 (ALS Yale), quoted in *GMAW*, p.69.
12 *CW*, Vol. II, p.117.
13 *AF*, Vol. II, p.1.
14 *GMAW*, p.68 (ALS Yale).
15 *GMAW*, p.69, (ALS Yale).
16 *GMAW*, p.78. Sir William Duguid Geddes (1828–1900) was the son of John Geddes, a farmer of Huntly. He was educated at Elgin Academy and King's College, Aberdeen, graduating with an MA. Became classics master at Aberdeen Grammar School and later rector (headmaster). Elected professor of Greek at King's College in 1855, in the same year he published a Greek grammar which became a standard text. Professor of Greek from 1860 to 1885, he was largely instrumental in reviving and reforming the study of Greek in Scottish universities. Elected principal and vice-chancellor of Aberdeen in 1885. Given the LLD by Edinburgh in 1876, Litt D. by Dublin in 1893, knighted in 1892.
17 *Weighed and Wanting* London, 1882, Vol. 1, p.47.
18 'The Disciple' 1867.
19 'A Sketch of Individual Development', *Orts*, pp.50–51.
20 *Alma Mater — Aberdeen University Magazine*, 18 October 1905.
21 Robert Troup, Unpublished *Notes*. In his last session Troup shared rooms with MacDonald's younger brother John Hill.
22 *GMAW*, pp.74–75.
23 Ronald MacDonald, *From a Northern Window*, Nisbet & Co, 1911.
24 *RF*, Vol. II, p.216.
25 Robert Troup, Unpublished *Notes*.
26 *GMAW* p.73.
27 Robert Troup, Unpublished *Notes*.
28 This missing session plagued MacDonald's son Greville MacDonald when writing his own biography of his father (see *GMAW* p.73n). Glenn Sadler's unpublished thesis *The Cosmic Vision* (Aberdeen 1966) pp.33–36, establishes reasonable circumstantial evidence that the 'nobleman's mansion' was Thurso Castle. Unfortunately the library was long ago disposed of and now no trace of MacDonald remains. In the *Roll of Alumni in Arts of the University and King's College of Aberdeen 1596–1860* pp.34–35 (Aberdeen 1900) edited by Peter John Anderson, MacDonald's name is on two lists of AM candidates, 1840–44 and

1841–45. 1842–43 is missing. Interestingly enough MacDonald's younger brother John Hill, also appears on two lists and it is clear that he missed a session from 1848–49. In a letter to his wife Louisa dated August 21st 1884 (ALS Yale), MacDonald stated 'Till Troup reminded me, I had forgotten altogether that John was some time at Eribol as tutor. James thought I was there before him, and *that it was there I got my hatred for Calvinism.*' There is another interesting letter, from Greville MacDonald to his brother-in-law Edward Troup (now in the possession of Ian MacDonald) dated 6 December 1922: 'Many thanks for your sending me on the result of Bob's [Troup] investigations. It is very good of him. The particulars of our great Uncle Charles' delinquencies . . . explain clearly enough, as you say, that father had to set to work in '42–'43. It is tragical to think that, once at least according to a letter of Uncle John's, grandfather was in need of a very few shillings.' Taken together these letters do suggest that MacDonald spent the session of 1842–43 tutoring because of financial constraints. Robert Troup whose *Notes* Greville MacDonald used for *GMAW* knew MacDonald and his brothers well, and the evidence points to Thurso Castle as the probable home of the library. Whether there was a flirt in the library or not, as some critics have suggested, remains a matter for conjecture.
29 *Wilfrid Cumbermede*, London, 1872, p.113. Wilfrid also sees: 'There a broad, low rock seemed to grow out of it, and upon the rock stood the lordliest house my childish eyes had ever beheld . . . Half castle, half old English country seat, it covered the rock with a huge square of building, from various parts of which rose towers, mostly square also, of different heights.' The image of half-house, half-castle is one that recurs many times in MacDonald's writing and is similar to contemporary prints of Thurso Castle.
30 *The Portent*, p.20 (Smith & Elder 1864).
31 *The Portent*, p.80
32 *GMAW*, p.74
33 Robert Troup, Unpublished *Notes*.
34 Alexander Gammie, *The Churches of Aberdeen: Historical and Descriptive*, Aberdeen Daily Journal Office, 1909. James Spence MA (1792–1843), educated at Marischal College, Aberdeen and Glasgow Theological Hall. He married MacDonald's aunt, Mary MacDonald, and after several charges ran a school in Newport, Isle of Wight from 1840 until his death.
35 See Glenn Sadler, *The Cosmic Vision*, unpublished thesis, Aberdeen 1966. John

Kennedy (1815–1900) was educated at King's College, Aberdeen, Edinburgh and at Glasgow Theological Hall (1834–36). Minister of Blackfriars Street from 1836–46, he then became minister of the Stepney Meeting in London. Professor of Apologetics at New College (the Congregationalist Theological College) 1872–76. Kennedy was the brother-in-law of John Stuart Blackie, a good friend of MacDonald's.

36 See Gammie, op. cit.

37 *Huntly Express*, 6 October, 1905.

38 See *GMAW*, p.69.

39 Robert Troup, Unpublished *Notes*.

40 Application to Highbury Theological College, 8 August 1848. This document is now in Dr Williams Library, Gordon Square, London.

41 MacDonald's medical ambitions were never fulfilled. In his novels, however, Alec Forbes attains his surgeon's diploma, and Robert Falconer goes on to study medicine (*RF* Vol. III p.36–37) and thinks of going to Germany (*RF* Vol. III p.23) — see also *CW* Vol. II p.117. Two of MacDonald's own sons, Greville and George MacKay, later entered the medical profession, and MacDonald entitled one novel after a doctor — *Paul Faber, Surgeon*.

CHAPTER FIVE
London

1 William Gregory (1803–58), born in Edinburgh and graduated as a doctor in 1828, made chemistry his speciality. He became professor of medicine and chemistry at King's College, Aberdeen in 1839, and in 1844 was elected to the Chair of Chemistry at Edinburgh. Gregory was very interested in magic and mesmerism, publishing *Letters to a Candid Inquirer on Animal Magnetism* in 1851. There are certain convincing links between this work and MacDonald's writing. Gregory's widow became a noted hostess for seances which often took place at her house in London.

2 *David Elginbrod*, Hurst & Blackett 1863, Vol. III p.53

3 *DE*, Vol. III, p.49.

4 *DE* Vol. III p.51

5 *RF*, Vol. III. p.49.

6 *RF* Vol. III, p.51.

7 *GMAW*, p.108 (ALS Yale).

8 Not the Morison who was the founder of the Evangelical Union.

9 GMD to GMD senior, 26 December 1845 (ALS Yale).

10 GMD to GMD senior, 12 January 1847 (ALS Yale).

11 GMD to GMD senior, 8 November, 1845 (ALS Yale).

12 *DE*, Vol. III, p.163.

13 GMD to GMD senior, 8 November 1845 (ALS Yale).

14 GMD to GMD senior, 11 April 1847 (ALS Yale).

15 *GMAW*, pp.97–99.

16 *GMAW*, p.100

17 *GMAW*, p.98. For a fuller account of the Powell household, see *GMAW*, pp.96–109.

18 *GMAW*, p.99.

19 It was thought at that time, by the religious circles that MacDonald moved in, that a beard was an unhealthy affirmation of the animal nature in man, and so beards were frowned on very severely indeed.

20 *GMAW*, p.98.

21 GMD to Louisa, 27 December 1850 (ALS Yale).

22 *What's Mine's Mine*, Kegan Paul, 1886, Vol. I, p.9.

23 Dated 27 March 1846 (ALS Yale).

24 *GMAW*, p.94 (ALS Yale).

25 GMD to Louisa (n.d.) (ALS Yale).

26 GMD to GMD senior, 11 April 1847 (ALS Yale).

27 James Legge (1815–1897), born in Huntly, attended the Missionar Kirk. Graduated from King's College, Aberdeen in 1835 and after training at Highbury Theological College in London, was one of the first missionaries to China. Later became the first Professor in Chinese at Oxford, where he counted among his friends Charles Dodgson, better known as Lewis Carroll. Translated Chinese classics into English.

28 GMD to GMD senior, 11 April 1847 (ALS Yale).

29 There is more insight into his theological questioning in a letter to his father dated 12 January 1847 (ALS Yale). He was already friendly with three students at Highbury and was not wholly impressed with what he had found at the college. MacDonald felt the need to know more Ecclesiastical History, and declared firmly, 'I would rather be of no sect than a sectarian.' Despite this he was disapproving of the Church of England: 'I do not know much, but what I do know chills my heart.'

In an extract from a letter written from GMD to Louisa Powell, 24 March 1848, copied out by Winifred Louisa MacDonald (*Notes* Yale) MacDonald wrote: '. . . my awakening spirit has so often struggled with the death which had so long bound it. It has not been in vain, Surely the morning is dawning, and the sky must ere long be clear, though even then the rain drops will be hanging from the thick leaves. But each drop will sparkle like a diamond in the beauty giving sun. I think faith can never have a greater victory than when it will trust even in the midst of darkness and doubt and temptation.'

CHAPTER SIX
Highbury

1 *Records of Highbury College*, Dr Williams Library, Gordon Square, London.
2 *Highbury College Minute Book*, Dr Williams Library, Gordon Square, London.
3 *GMAW*, pp.110−113.
4 GMD to James Powell, 19 October 1848 (ALS Yale).
John Christie wrote to Greville MacDonald (23 January 1911): 'Your mother was staying in my cousin's house when your father "proposed" to her. Mrs Powell happened to go suddenly into the drawing room and found your father in orthodox attitude — on bended knee — she therefore beat a hasty retreat.' (This letter is now in the possession of Mrs Rosemary MacDonald.)
5 GMD to James Powell, 21 October 1848 (ALS Yale).
6 Louisa to GMD, October 1848 (ALS Yale).
7 GMD to Louisa, 17 December 1848 (ALS Yale).
8 GMD to Louisa, 23 October 1848 (ALS Yale), quoted in *GMAW*, p.117. This letter is an example of Greville's editing. In *GMAW* he removed some lines without signifying he had done so. The full text of the letter is given here.
9 Robert Troup, Unpublished *Notes*.
10 John Mcleod Campbell (1800−72), a Scottish minister who found himself in trouble for preaching universalism.
11 Thomas Erskine of Linlathen (1788−1870), a mystic and theologian. Edward Irving (1792−1834), a famous preacher and founder of the Catholic Apostolic Church. For more on Campbell, Erskine and Irving see the chapter on MacDonald's theology, *God our Father and Mother*.
12 See the *Dictionary of National Biography* article on Scott.
13 Scott lectured on Dante, notably in September and October 1847 at the Manchester Athenaeum.
14 Louisa to GMD, 17 May 1849 (ALS Yale).

15 Louisa to GMD, 25 May 1849 (ALS Yale).
16 Louisa to GMD, 29 June 1849 (ALS Yale).
17 GMD senior to GMD, 7 October 1850 (ALS Yale).
18 GMD to GMD senior, 6 June 1849 (ALS Yale).

CHAPTER SEVEN
Home and Away

1 GMD to GMD senior, 25 July 1849 (ALS Yale).
2 Louisa to GMD, 26 July 1849 (ALS Yale).
3 Louisa to GMD, 1 August 1849 (ALS Yale).
4 See *GMAW*, pp.124−28.
5 GMD to Louisa, 5 February 1855 (ALS Yale).
6 Louisa to GMD, 24 August 1849 (ALS Yale).
7 *GMAW*, pp.120−21. See also *DE*, Vol. III pp.164−65 where Mrs Appleditch's horror at Hugh Sutherland's beard causes her to exclaim: 'As soon as the Apostles became Christians, they shaved. It was the sign of Christianity.'
8 Louisa to GMD, 4 October 1849. Written from Lynmouth. (ALS Yale).
9 Louisa to GMD, 5 October, 1849. Written from Lynmouth. (ALS Yale).
10 GMD to Louisa, 4 September 1853. (ALS Yale).
11 Robert Troup, Unpublished *Notes*. The Highbury College records also show clearly that MacDonald was never awarded a degree.
12 GMD senior to GMD, 29 April 1850 (ALS Yale).
13 GMD to Charles Francis MacDonald, 21 February 1850 (ALS Yale).
14 GMD to GMD senior, 23 February 1850 (ALS Yale).
15 GMD to GMD senior, 15 March 1850 (ALS Yale).
16 GMD to Caroline Chase Powell, 10 December (his birthday) 1850 (ALS Yale).
17 Louisa to GMD, 27 September 1850 (ALS Yale).
18 Louisa to GMD (n.d.) 1850 (ALS Yale).
19 Louisa to GMD, 27 August 1850 (ALS Yale).
20 James Powell to GMD, 30 August 1850 (ALS Yale).
21 GMD to GMD senior, 4 October 1850 (ALS Yale).
22 GMD to GMD senior, 16 October 1850 (ALS Yale).

CHAPTER EIGHT
Arundel

1 From 'All Things Bright and Beautiful.'
2 Margaret Oliphant, *Salem Chapel*, 1863.
Quoted in Amy Cruse, *The Victorians and their Books* Allen & Unwin 1935, p.72. See also chapter entitled 'The Chapel Folks.'
3 Joshua Wilson's paper, quoted in David M. Thompson, *Nonconformity in the Nineteenth Century*, Routledge & Kegan Paul, London, 1972, pp.63—65.
4 *GMAW*, p.139.
5 Owen Chadwick, *The Victorian Church* (1), Adam & Charles Black, London, 1966, p.400.
6 *Records of Arundel Chapel*, Dr Williams Library, Gordon Square, London. GMD to GMD senior, 16 October 1850 (ALS Yale).
7 Louisa to GMD, 24 October 1850 (ALS Yale).
8 GMD to Charles Francis MacDonald, 4 November 1850 (ALS Yale).
9 *GMAW*, p.144
10 GMD to GMD senior 11 December 1850 (ALS Yale).
11 GMD to GMD senior, 9 January 1851. This letter was written from The Limes.
12 GMD to Charles Francis MacDonald, 17 January 1851 (ALS Yale).

CHAPTER NINE
Marriage

1 *GMAW*, p.151.
2 GMD to Louisa, 23 May 1849 (ALS Yale).
3 *GMAW*, p.152.
4 *GMAW*, p.153.
5 *Annals of a Quiet Neighbourhood*, Hurst & Blackett, London, 1867, Vol. I, p.34.
6 *Annals*, Vol. I, p.304.
7 *Annals*, Vol. II, p.23.
8 *GMAW*, p.158
9 Robert Troup, Unpublished *Notes*.
10 Walter E. Houghton, *The Victorian Frame of Mind 1830—1870* Yale University Press, Yale, 1957, p.405. The poem quoted is Clough's 'In the Great Metropolis.'
11 *GMAW*, pp.156—57.
12 Robert Troup, Unpublished *Notes*.
13 GMD to GMD senior, 15 April 1851 (ALS Yale).
14 ibid.
15 GMD to his stepmother, Margaret McColl MacDonald, Autumn 1851 (ALS Yale).
16 GMD to Greville Matheson, 12 December 1851 (ALS Yale).
17 Thomas Toke Lynch's (1818—71), *Hymns for Heart and Voice: The Rivulet*,

first issued in 1855 was declared to be pantheistic and theologically unsound.

CHAPTER TEN
New Year, New Problems

1 Lilia was also the name of the half-child, half-woman in Tennyson's *The Princess* (1847) partly written to celebrate the founding of Queen's College for women in 1848 by the theologian F.D. Maurice.
2 GMD to GMD senior, 12 January 1852 (ALS Yale).
3 *GMAW*, p.159.
4 John H. MacDonald to GMD, 15 January 1852 (ALS Yale).
5 See *GMAW*, pp.179—80. This document still exist at the Beinecke Library, Yale. One non-doctrinal reason for MacDonald's problems with the deacons of the church was that 48, Tarrant Street, where the MacDonalds lived, was rented from one of the most influential of them. When MacDonald made some enquiries about the possibility of obtaining a larger house, which would have deprived this deacon of MacDonald's rent, the aggrieved deacon stirred up some trouble against him.
6 Handbill, Arundel, November 1852.
7 GMD to GMD senior, 27 July 1852 (ALS Yale).
8 *GMAW*, p.182
9 GMD to his sister Isabella, 19 January 1853 (ALS Yale).
10 GMD to GMD senior, 5 April 1853 (ALS Yale).
11 GMD to GMD senior, 9 April 1853 (ALS Yale).
12 GMD to Louisa, 21 March 1853 (ALS Yale).
13 GMD to Charles F. MacDonald, 7 March 1853 (ALS Yale).
14 GMD to John Godwin, 24 June 1853 (ALS Yale). MacDonald wrote to his father at this time (20 May 1853 — ALS Yale): 'You must not be surprised if you hear that I am not what is called *getting on*. Time will show what use the Father will make of me. I desire to be His — entirely — so sure am I that therein lies all things. If less than this were my hope. I should die.' Quoted at length in *GMAW*, *pp.184—85*.

CHAPTER ELEVEN
Manchester

1 GMD to Louisa, 1 July 1853 (ALS Yale).
2 GMD to Louisa, 4 July 1853 (ALS Yale).
3 Robert Spence d.1870. Educated at Aberdeen and Highbury Theological

College. Minister at Newington, Liverpool 1848–53, and Ward Chapel, Dundee, 1853–70. Died in London. Editor of *The Scottish Congregationalist* and chairman of the Congregation Union of Scotland in 1863. Newington, Liverpool, was something of a Scottish colony.

4 GMD to Louisa, 2 September 1853 (ALS Yale).

5 GMD to Louisa, 7 September 1853 (ALS Yale). Charles Edward MacDonald, George's cousin, the eldest son of James MacDonald senior died in Manchester in 1850(?).

6 GMD to GMD senior, 17 October 1853 (ALS Yale).

7 John Godwin to GMD, 27 June 1853 (ALS Yale).

8 GMD to John Godwin, 24 June 1853 (ALS Yale).

9 GMD to GMD senior, 17 October 1853 (ALS Yale).

10 GMD to GMD senior, 26 October 1853 (ALS Yale).

11 *GMAW*, p.203.

12 GMD to Louisa, 2 January 1854 (ALS Yale).

13 GMD to Louisa, January 1854 (ALS Yale).

14 GMD to Louisa (n.d.), probably January 1854 (ALS Yale).

15 ibid.

16 GMD to GMD senior, 6 February 1854 (ALS Yale).

17 *GMAW*, p.208.

18 GMD to GMD senior, 17 March 1854 (ALS Yale).

19 ibid.

20 'A Manchester Poem', *Poetical Works*.

21 GMD to Alphaeus Smith, 30 May 1854 (ALS Yale).

22 GMD to GMD senior, May 1854 (ALS Yale).

23 GMD to GMD senior, 16 September 1854 (ALS Yale).

24 GMD to Louisa, 1 November 1854 (ALS Yale).

25 GMD to Louisa, 8 January 1855 (ALS Yale).

26 GMD to Louisa, February 1855 (ALS Yale). Mention should also be made of MacDonald's friendship with Henry Septimus Sutton, a minor poet who wrote the *Evangel of Love* and who corresponded with Elizabeth Barrett Browning.

2 *Wilfrid Cumbermede*, Hurst & Blackett London, 1872, Vol. I, p.236.

3 This booklet is very rare. There is a copy in the Brander Library, Huntly.

4 *Heinrich von Ofterdingen*, New York 1964, p.25.

5 ibid.

6 *Orts*, p.245ff.

7 M.H. Abrams, *The Mirror and the Lamp*, Oxford University Press, 1953, p.22.

8 Plotinus, *Enneads*.

9 *England's Antiphon*, MacMillan, p.307.

10 Stephen Prickett, *Romanticism and Religion*, Cambridge University Press, 1976, p.33.

11 'The Imagination: Its Functions and Culture', *Orts*, p.2.

12 The MS of this poem is in the possession of Mrs Rosemary MacDonald, copied in another hand.

13 *GMAW*, p.81.

14 *GMAW*, p.95.

15 'David' is in *First Fruits and Fragments*, Houghton Library, Harvard.

16 The unpublished MS of *Gennaro* is in the Houghton Library, Harvard.

17 Amy Cruse, *The Victorians and their Books*, Allen & Unwin, London, 1935, p.92.

18 MacDonald copied out *In Memoriam* as a birthday present for Louisa in November 1850.

19 *England's Antiphon*, p.329.

20 The MS of *Within and Without* is in the Brander Library, Huntly.

21 There are echoes of Goethe's *Faust* here, as Gretchen and Faust are also reunited in heaven.

22 *Athenaeum*, 7 July 1855.

23 *Fraser's Magazine*, Vol. 54, 1856. *The Scotsman*, 21 July 1855 said: 'This is a very remarkable production of human intellect and human heart — for these are here united as they perhaps seldom have been before. The chief feature of the poem is its intense spirituality.'

24 *RF*, Vol. II, p.186.

25 'The Hills', *Poems*, 1857.

26 'The Earl o' Quarterdeck', *The Disciple and Other Poems*, 1867.

27 *The Disciple*.

28 *Poetical Works*, Vol. II.

29 ibid.

30 William Geddes, 'George MacDonald as a Poet', *Blackwoods Magazine* March, 1891.

CHAPTER TWELVE
Within and Without

1 Charles F. MacDonald, Unpublished *Notes*.

CHAPTER THIRTEEN
North Again

1 GMD to Louisa (n.d.), probably May/June 1855 (ALS Yale).

2 GMD to Louisa, 2 July 1855 (ALS Yale). This is the first of a long series of letters from MacDonald to Louisa while he was staying in Huntly. When they were parted they usually wrote to each other every day.

3 GMD to Louisa, 3 July 1855 (ALS Yale).
4 GMD to Louisa, 4 July 1855 (ALS Yale).
5 GMD to Louisa, 5 July 1855 (ALS Yale).
6 GMD to Louisa, 6 July 1855 (ALS Yale).
7 GMD to Louisa, 7 July 1855 (ALS Yale).
8 GMD to Louisa, 8 July 1855 (ALS Yale).
9 GMD to Louisa, 20 July 1855 (ALS Yale).
10 Louisa to GMD, 20 July 1855 (ALS Yale).
11 Louisa to GMD, 19 July 1855 (ALS Yale).
12 GMD to Louisa, 14 July 1855 (ALS Yale).
13 GMD to Louisa, 22 July 1855 (ALS Yale).
14 GMD to Louisa, 26 July 1855 (ALS Yale).
15 GMD to Louisa, 4 August (?) 1855 (ALS Yale).
16 GMD to GMD senior, August (?) 1855 (ALS Yale).
17 GMD to GMD senior (n.d.), possibly February/March 1855 (ALS Yale).
18 Lady Byron (1792–1860), born Anne Isabella Milbanke, married Byron in 1815. Their union was short, and they had one child.
19 GMD to GMD senior, August (?) 1855 (ALS Yale).
20 See the Dictionary of National Biography article on Lady Byron.
21 See Ethel Colburn Mayne, *The Life of Lady Byron* Constable & Co. London 1929, reprinted 1969, p.391ff.
22 See *The Vicar's Daughter*, London 1872, Vol. II, pp.92–93.
23 GMD to his stepmother Margaret McColl MacDonald, 26 August 1855 (ALS Yale).
24 *GMAW*, pp.252–53.
25 GMD to GMD senior, 30 December 1855 (ALS Yale).
26 GMD to Ann Ross, 2 January 1856. Quoted in Robert Troup's Unpublished *Notes*.
27 GMD to GMD senior, 21 January 1856 (ALS Yale).

CHAPTER FOURTEEN
North and South

1 GMD to Louisa, 24 January 1856 (ALS Yale).
2 GMD to GMD senior (n.d.),

Kingswear, Raven's Well (ALS Yale), see *GMAW*, pp.259–65.
3 GMD to GMD senior (n.d.), Lynmouth (ALS Yale).
4 GMD to Charlotte Powell Godwin, 8 August 1856 (ALS Yale).

CHAPTER FIFTEEN
Algiers

1 The information for the journey to Algiers comes from a short diary which Louisa kept. MacDonald Collection, Beinecke Library, Yale.
2 GMD to GMD senior, 28 November 1856 (ALS Yale), qu. *GMAW*, p.267.
3 ibid.
4 Barbara Leigh-Smith Bodichon (1827–91), Leigh-Smith's daughter, was benefactress of Girton College, Cambridge. She took a great interest in women's education and their position in society. She knew many leading Victorians and was an important connection, for through her MacDonald met Mrs Reid, founder of Bedford College, and so entered a circle of important nineteenth-century feminist thought.
5 GMD to Caroline Powell, 24 December 1856 (ALS Yale).
6 Louisa to Caroline Powell (n.d.), 1857, qu. *GMAW*, p.272. (ALS Yale).
7 GMD to James MacDonald, 24 December 1856 (ALS Yale).
8 GMD to Henry Septimus Sutton, 6 February 1857 (ALS Yale).
9 GMD to Caroline Powell, 24 December 1856 (ALS Yale).
10 GMD to GMD senior, (?) June 1857 (ALS Yale).
11 GMD to Louisa, Summer 1857 (ALS Yale).
12 ibid.
13 GMD to GMD senior, 15 October 1857 (ALS Yale).
14 *GMAW*, p.284
15 ibid.
16 GMD to GMD senior, 2 December 1857 (ALS Yale).
17 GMD to GMD senior, 2 January 1858 (ALS Yale).

CHAPTER SIXTEEN
Phantastes

1 GMD to GMD senior, 2 January 1858 (ALS Yale).
2 GMD to GMD senior (n.d.), January/February 1858 (ALS Yale).
3 Letter from Louisa (ALS Yale).

4 Stephen Prickett, *Victorian Fantasy* Harvester Press, London, 1979 p.10.
5 There was a play popular at this time called 'You Can't Marry Your Grandmother' by Thomas Bayley.
6 See *Victorian Fantasy*, Stephen Prickett, op. cit., p.175.
7 One of the interesting aspects of MacDonald's work is the way in which themes and symbols interconnect. MacDonald's only historical novel *St George and St Michael*, Vol. III, p.129 throws some light on MacDonald's conception of the Shadow. Vaughan (the poet) is talking: 'Shall I tell thee who hath possessed thee? for the demon hath a name that is known amongst men, though it frighteneth few, and draweth many, alas! His name is Self, and he is the shadow of thy own self. First he made thee love him, which was evil, and now he hath made thee hate him, which is evil also. But if he be cast out and never more enter into thy heart, but remain as a servant in thy hall, then wilt thou recover from this sickness, and be whole and sound, and shalt find the varlet serviceable.' This is uncannily close to Jung's idea that the shadow must be incorporated into the personality and not expunged on the journey towards wholeness.
8 Carl Jung, *The Archetypes and the Collective Unconscious*, Pantheon Books, 1959.
9 ibid.
10 Carl Jung, *Psychology and Religion: West and East*, Pantheon Books 1958.
11 Jung: *The Archetypes and the Collective Unconscious*, op.cit. p.251.
12 *Phantastes*.

CHAPTER SEVENTEEN
Another Farewell

1 GMD to GMD senior, 18 April 1858 (ALS Yale).
2 *GMAW*, p.291.
3 The Gurneys were already aware of MacDonald's work and perhaps this was a special meeting arranged by Lady Byron. MacDonald also met the sculptor Alexander Munro at Hastings. See *GMAW*, p.301. Munro (1825–71) was an important friend and introduced MacDonald to Arthur Hughes, the Rossettis and the painter Madox Ford.
4 GMD to GMD senior, 20 May 1858 (ALS Yale).
5 ibid.
6 GMD to GMD senior, (n.d.), June 1858 (ALS Yale).

7 'A Hidden Life', *The Disciple and Other Poems*.
8 *GMAW*, pp.292–93.
9 See *GMAW*, p.293. There is some confusion about the date: Greville MacDonald gives it as 24 August. Winifred MacDonald dated his death on 29 August. The telegram MacDonald received informing him of his father's death is dated 27 August however, and the funeral was set for Tuesday, 31 August. The letter that Greville dates as the 26th is, in fact, n.d. and so August 26th must be the correct date.
10 *GMAW*, p.293.
11 Telegram to GMD, 27 August 1858 (Yale).
12 *GMAW*, p.294.
13 GMD to Louisa (n.d.), Sunday Night, 29 August 1858 (ALS Yale).
14 From *The Disciple and Other Poems*.
15 MacDonald's father was sixty-six when he died, but he died suddenly and unexpectedly.
16 GMD to Margaret McColl MacDonald, 25 September 1858 (ALS Yale).

CHAPTER EIGHTEEN
From Hastings to London...

1 MacDonald also lectured there in 1860. See *GMAW, p.325*.
2 MacDonald's lectures at Hastings were favourably reviewed in the local *Hastings and St. Leonard's Chronicle and Fashionable Gazette* on 9 and 16 March 1859.
3 *The Diary of Henry Crabb Robinson — An Abridgement*, ed. Derek Hudson, Oxford University Press, 1967.
4 ibid 30 May 1859.
5 ibid 3 June, 1859.
6 ibid 8 June, 1860.
7 He must have felt that his hopes had been dashed as he had written to his stepmother in May: 'I am gradually getting more into the way of making money, though it is very scarce yet.' (ALS Yale).
8 David Masson (1822–1907) was a writer and academic.
9 GMD to Louisa, August (?) 1859, (ALS Yale).
10 ibid.
11 GMD to Lady Byron, 25 August 1859 qu. *GMAW*, p.309.
12 The house in Queen Square is now a hospital. The statue is now said to be of Queen Charlotte rather than of Queen Anne.
13 See *GMAW*, p.312. Greville MacDonald mentioned several features of Tudor Lodge including a Charles Lucy painting of King

Charles bidding farewell to his children
which Greville held in 'high dread' when
left alone at midday to rest on the sofa, and
the casts of the Elgin marbles on the walls of
the studio. There is a longer description of
Tudor Lodge in *The Vicar's Daughter*
Vol. I, p.49, where Ethelwyn Walton, now
married to Charles Percivale, a painter, goes
to live.
14 For a note on Thomas Lynch (1818–71)
see the notes on the chapter on Marriage.
15 MacDonald advertised in the autumn,
producing handbills about his Class of
English which he distributed. 'The class will
be held every Friday from 11am to 1pm till
the end of June 1861 with the omission of
December 28th and January 18th. Terms
Five Guineas payable in advance.'
16 *GMAW*, p.318: 'My mother once told
an admirer that when she asked my father
for the story's meaning, he said "You may
make of it what you like. If you see
anything in it, take it and I am glad you
have it; but I wrote it for the tale." Its
author received forty pounds for its serial
use, and thirty for the copyright of the
book.'
17 *GMAW*, p.313.
18 This list of names gives a glimpse of the
society in which MacDonald moved. Leigh
Hunt had been a friend of the romantic
poets; G.H. Lewes (1817–78) wrote the
standard *Life of Goethe* for his time, and
lived with George Eliot from 1854 onwards.
Leslie Stephen was the founder of the
Dictionary of National Biography and the
father of Virginia Woolf. Henry S. King
was a publisher and James Payn (1830–98)
was a minor novelist and editor of the
Cornhill Magazine from 1883–1896.
19 *GMAW*, p.321.
20 *GMAW*, p.300.
21 Octavia Hill appeared as Marion Clare
in *The Vicar's Daughter* (1872) and there is
more than a hint of her in the character of
Mary St. John in *Robert Falconer* (1868).
22 See Nancy Boyd, *Josephine
Butler/Octavia Hill/Florence Nightingale:
Three Victorian Women who changed their
World*, MacMillan, London 1982.
23 *GMAW*, p.312.
24 *Reminiscences of a Specialist*, Greville
MacDonald, Allen & Unwin, London
1932, p.23.
25 *Rems*, p.29 See *Lewis Carroll's Diaries*,
ed. Roger Lancelyn Green, MacMillan
(London 1953) for 5 July 1864: '...I
went with him [MacDonald] to bring home
Mrs M.D., Lily and Mary, who were at a
young ladies' school (Wesleyan) where
Lily and Mary take lessons, and where I
suppose he teaches...'

26 *Rems*, esp. pp.32–3.
27 *Rems*, pp.14–15.
28 *Rems*, p.27.
29 ibid.
30 *Rems*, p.28.
31 *Rems*, p.31.
32 *Rems*, p.15: 'To us he was *Uncle*
Dodgson though only by adoption.'

CHAPTER NINETEEN
Lewis Carroll

1 Charles Dodgson (1832–1898) began
his residence at Christ Church on 24
January 1851 and remained there until his
death.
2 *GMAW*, p.301.
3 This statue is now in Regent's Park
opposite the College of Physicians.
4 Stuart Dodgson Collingwood, *The Life
and Letters of Lewis Carroll*, Unwin,
London 1898, pp.83–4. Dodgson's diaries
for this period have been lost.
5 *GMAW*, p.343.
6 The Terrys were a famous acting family.
Lilia MacDonald was friendly with Kate
Terry (later Mrs Lewis) and the two families
met mainly through Dodgson. Roger
Manvell's biography, *Ellen Terry* (London
1968) gives more information on the family
and Dodgson's relationship with them.
7 Dodgson's *Diary*, 4 July 1864.
8 C. Dodgson to Mary MacDonald, 23
May 1864 (ALS Yale).
9 Powell had disapproved of
MacDonald's beard, and there was also
some dissent over it in the Missionar Kirk
congregation. A beard was thought to be
too strong a reminder of the animal nature
within man.
10 Dodgson's *Diary*, 24 July 1863.
11 ibid, 27 July 1863.
12 Dodgson came to photograph once
more, in 1870, when the MacDonalds were
living in a house known as The Retreat. His
Diary for 24 July (Sun) 1870 stated: 'After
leaving Mr Holiday, I had 2 days
photographing with the MacDonalds whom
I left on Sat. the 16th.'
13 Arthur Hughes also painted Mary at the
piano and Greville on his violin. See *Rems*,
facing p.48, for a reproduction of this
painting.
14 Dodgson's *Diary*, 5 February 1865.
15 ibid, 9 July 1862.
16 The reading was finished some time
before 10 February 1863.
17 *GMAW*, p.342.
18 *GMAW*, p.342–3.
19 See Raphael Shaberman's article 'George
MacDonald and Lewis Carroll', reprinted
in *North Wind 1* (1982) — the journal of the

George MacDonald Society. I am heavily indebted to this interesting article.

20 *Phantastes*, p.53.

21 Lewis Carroll, *Works*, The Nonesuch Press, London 1940, *Alice in Wonderland*, pp.48–9.

22 *Through the Looking Glass* in *Works*, pp.173–4.

23 *Orts*, 'The Imagination: Its Functions and Culture', p.4.

24 *Lewis Carroll, Works*, op. cit., p.272.

25 Dodgson's *Diary*, 16 January 1866.

26 *GMAW*, p.317.

27 *GMAW*, p.318.

28 *GMAW*, p.320. See also the letter quoted in *GMAW*, p.321: GMD to Charles Manby Smith, 7 September 1863: 'You gave me the Epitaph which was in a measure the germ of the whole. Please accept the result of its growth in my mind.'

29 MacDonald always referred to the *Scotch* language, though nowadays people prefer to talk about Scots.

30 *GMAW*, p.327.

31 *GMAW*, p.346.

32 C. Dodgson to Louisa 2 October 1863 (ALS Yale).

33 Margaret Oliphant (1828–97), a novelist and historical writer, she wrote a great deal for *Blackwoods Magazine* and her husband and her children were totally reliant on her writing to support them all. Her most successful novel was *Salem Chapel* (1863), mainly about Nonconformist life. Her major historical work was a *Life of Edward Irving* (2 Vols) (1862). She also wrote some tales of the supernatural. Her 'slavery to the pen' drove her to produce 125 separate publications. Superficially her work resembled that of George Eliot and Mrs Gaskell, but she has not found a lasting place in the twentieth century.

34 *The Autobiography and Letters of Margaret Oliphant*, ed. Mrs Harry Coghill, Leicester University Press (1974, originally published 1899), p.315. Greville MacDonald claimed (*GMAW*, p.322) that *David Elginbrod* was published through the efforts of Dinah Mulock, but presumably Margaret Oliphant's account is correct.

35 *Margaret Oliphant*, op. cit. p.190.

36 Dodgson recorded talking to MacDonald about *David Elginbrod* in *Diary*, 2 Feb 1863.

CHAPTER TWENTY
David Elginbrod

1 Amy Cruse, *The Victorians and their Books* Allen & Unwin London, 1935, p.80.

2 *Book News*, cxxvii, March 1893, p.304.

3 Walter E. Houghton, *The Victorian Frame of Mind 1830–1870*, Yale University Press, 1957, p.261.

4 See David Daiches, Thomas Green Lectures No. 4: *Carlyle and the Victorian Dilemma* (1963).

5 Thomas Carlyle, *Heroes*, Lect. 1, 13.

6 Houghton, op. cit. p.316.

7 'Art for Art's sake' was the motto of Oscar Wilde and the Aesthetic Movement.

8 Ronald MacDonald, 'George MacDonald: A Personal Note', *From a Northern Window* Nisbet and Co. 1911. See also *GMAW*, p.375: '"People," he once remarked, "find this great fault with me — that I turn my stories into sermons. They forget that I have a Master to serve first before I can wait upon the public."'

9 *David Elginbrod*, Vol. I, p.102.

10 *RF*, Vol. I, p.275.

11 *DE*, Vol. I, p.159.

12 *DE*, Vol. I, p.281.

13 *DE*, Vol. I, p.94.

14 *RF*, Vol. I, p.166.

15 *DE*, Vol. I, p.93.

16 *Alec Forbes of Howglen*, Vol. II, p.167.

17 Francis Russell Hart, *The Scottish Novel*, London, 1978, p.89.

18 *AF*, Vol. I, p.47.

19 *AF*, Vol. I, p.100 — see also p.239: 'There is not to be found a more thorough impersonation of his own theology than a Scotch schoolmaster of the rough old-fashioned type. His pleasure was law, irrespective of right or wrong, and the reward of submission to law was immunity from punishment.'

20 *AF*, Vol. I, p.237 and see p.244. In Annie Anderson's mind Malison becomes inseparably linked with God.

21 See Charles F. MacDonald: Unpublished *Notes* (in the possession of Ian MacDonald).

22 James MacDonald senior to GMD (n.d.) 1868 (ALS Yale).

23 See David Daiches: *The Paradox of Scottish Culture: The Eighteenth Century Experience* (Oxford University Press 1963).

24 See the journal *Seven*, Vol. II, 1981: 'The Abyss of His Mother-Tongue: Scotch Dialect in Novels by George MacDonald' by Roderick F. McGillis.

25 *AF*, Vol. I, p.73.

26 *DE*, Vol. I, p.108.

27 *RF*, Vol. II, pp.182–3.

28 MacDonald knew John Jamieson's 'Dissertation on the Origin of the Scottish Language' prefixed to his *Etymological Dictionary of the Scottish Language* (1808) which argues that Scotch is more than just a regional dialect. That MacDonald knew the

work is clear from remarks made in *The Elect Lady*, chapter 10.

29 'There grows a bonnie brier bush in our kail-yard, And white are the blossoms on't in our kail-yard.' These lines from Johnson's *Musical Museum*, printed at the beginning of *Beside the Bonnie Brier Bush* suggested to W.H. Millar the title for his article on 'The Literature of the Kailyard' in *The New Review* of 1895 and gave the Kailyard School its name. The three authors discussed were James Matthew Barrie (1860–1937), Samuel Rutherford Crockett (1859–1914) and John Watson (1850–1907) writing under the pen name of Ian Maclaren.

30 *RF*, Vol. III, p.121.

31 'Recent Scotch Novels' *Edinburgh Review*, April, 1876.

32 *Fortnightly Review*, Vol. 10.

33 GMD to William Cowper-Temple (Lord Mount-Temple), Porto Fino, 13 January 1879 (National Library of Scotland).

34 *Gutta Percha Willie*, p.38.

35 *RF*, Vol. I, p.243.

36 *Salted with Fire*, p.153.

37 Robert Colby: *Fiction with a Purpose* p.198 sees *Villette* by Charlotte Brontë as a kind of secular pilgrimage. On p.10, Colby comments: 'Early in the century religious educators like Mrs Barbauld and Hannah More appropriated fiction to their purposes in something like the way in which early Christianity adopted pagan ceremonies. Thereby they established a climate for the novel as a moral force. Charlotte Elizabeth Tonna, editor of *The Christian Lady's Magazine*, turned reluctantly to the novel to spread her gospel. Their better successors, like Charlotte Yonge and Elizabeth Missing Sewell, moved readily into fiction from Sunday School teaching. Dinah Mulock, one of the most popular of mid-Victorian novelists, thought of herself as a lay minister — one of her books, in fact, was called 'Sermons Outside of Church — with a wider congregation and a greater command over them.'

38 *AF*, Vol. II, p.120.

39 *The Cornhill Magazine*, August 1860 Vol. II, p.212.

40 ibid, p.221. Thackeray (the editor) footnoted p.211: 'As Editor of this Magazine, I can vouch for the good faith and honourable character of our correspondent, a friend of twenty-five years standing.'

41 *DE*, Vol. II, p.198. Later in *DE* Robert Falconer and Hugh Sutherland are sparked into a conversation over the seance by a letter on spiritualism in a newspaper.

Falconer comments: 'I hate the whole thing, Sutherland. It is full of impudence and irreverence.' MacDonald never doubted the existence of spirits, but questioned their morality and loathed the chicanery surrounding spiritualism. David Elginbrod's continuance as a force for good in the novel after his death vividly contrasts with the paraphernalia surrounding Funkelstein and his seance.

42 MacDonald's chemistry teacher at university, William Gregory, was very interested in phrenology, mesmerism, clairvoyance and somnambulism, and Gregory believed these phenomena could be explained scientifically. MacDonald may have used aspects of Gregory's work. For example, Gregory mentioned the hypnotic power of mirrors and crystals. Mirrors have an important part to play in *Phantastes* and *Lilith*, and a crystal ring in *David Elginbrod* heightens von Funkelstein's mesmeric powers. A somnambulist appears also in *Phantastes*, and both Lady Alice in *The Portent* and Euphrasia Cameron are afflicted with the same condition.

43 *DE*, Vol. II, p.233.

44 See David Punter: *The Literature of Terror: A History of Gothic Fictions from 1765 to the Present Day* Longman (London 1980) and *The Gothic Imagination: Essays in Dark Romanticism* ed G.R. Thompson (Washington 1974).

45 *TW*, Vol. II, p.255.

46 Julia Briggs: *Night Visitors: The Rise and Fall of the English Ghost Story* Faber and Faber (London 1977) goes into this question in greater detail.

47 *AF*, Vol. III, p.83.

48 *CW*, Vol. III, p.135.

49 *DE*, Vol. I, pp.248–9.

50 *F of S*, p.315.

51 *DE*, Vol. II, pp.285–6.

52 *DE*, Vol. II, pp.286–7.

53 *DE* Vol. II, p.307.

54 *Wilfrid Cumbermede*, Vol. II, p.287.

55 *WC*, Vol. III, p.216.

56 *AF*, Vol. II, p.51.

57 *F of S*, pp.213–4.

58 *WC*, Vol. I, p.314.

59 *Mary Marston*, Vol. II, p.82.

60 *WC*, Vol. I. p.26.

61 *PF*, Vol. II, p.246.

62 *DE*, Vol. I, p.321.

63 *AF*, Vol. II, pp.58–9.

64 *RF*, Vol. I, p.177.

65 There were still some witches alive when MacDonald was a boy, though they were 'mostly restricted to the dairy' and changed themselves into hares to gain access to byres. The last witches were burned in Huntly in the seventeenth century, but traditionally the area was famed for its warlocks. In the 1820s Gray in his *Recollections of Huntly* recalled: 'There were still a few warlocks extant, notably Willox in Buchan, who was usually consulted in cases where cows had unaccountably run dry or become affected with any occult complaint. In contrast with those of the witches, however, the operations of the warlocks were mostly beneficent — tending to counteract the machinations of the other sex.' References to warlocks come into MacDonald's work in *Castle Warlock* (1882) for example, and The Wizard's Room in *Malcolm* (1875).

The Horseman's Word was a cult centred on Huntly and active at least until the 1930s. Nearly every farm-hand was a member. Initiation took place around Martinmas (11 November) in an isolated barn. An odd number had to be present, usually 13, and the novices were led there blindfold. They were told that Cain was the first horseman and that they could invoke the Devil by reading certain verses of the Bible backwards — then they were given the Word. After this they shook hands with the devil's hoof (blindfolded again, they were given the hoof of a sheep or goat to shake), and towards dawn, after some story-telling and a 'communion' of whisky, bread and salt, the ceremonial Horseman's toast was drunk:
'Here's to the horse with the four white feet,
The chestnut tail and mane —
A star on his face and a spot on his breast,
And his master's name was Cain.'
The Horseman's Word was an interesting counterbalance to the eager church-going habits of the Huntly people, and it should be stressed that it was very widespread. The wizard, the devil and the horse are often inextricably linked in MacDonald's writing. Tractors and other machinery may have seen the number of working horses dwindle to almost nothing, but there are still those in Huntly today who have the Word.

66 *RF*, Vol. II, pp.203–4.
67 *T&B*, Vol. II, p.125.
68 *St. G & St. M.*, Vol. III. p.304.
69 *Eng's Ant.* p.61.

CHAPTER TWENTY-ONE
John Ruskin

1 Maria La Touche to Louisa, 10 October 1863 (ALS Yale).
2 Maria La Touche to GMD (n.d.) 1863 (ALS Yale).
3 MacDonald was also an admirer of Turner's work. GMD to Louisa, Highbury,

15 May 1849: 'What a strange picture of Turner's I saw yesterday at the Exhibition — a Rainbow over a stormy sea, ships far and near, boats and a buoy — I could make nothing of it at first. Only by degrees I awoke to the Truth and wonder of it. I lost much enjoyment however by going without any optical assistance.'
4 Ruskin's stress on artisanship perhaps turned MacDonald to his pursuit of bookbinding, noted by Ronald MacDonald in *From a Northern Window*. MacDonald's father-in-law was also a bookbinder. In *There and Back* John Tukes is a bookbinder with strong socialist principles. See also *Mary Marston* Vol. III, p.305: 'The day will come, and may I do something to help it hither, when the youth of our country will recognize that, taken in itself, it is a more manly, and therefore in the old true sense a more *gentle* thing, to follow a good handicraft, if it make the hands black as coal, than to spend the day in keeping books.'
5 *Praeterita*, Hart Davis, London 1949, p.494.
6 There was one break in Ruskin's relationship with the La Touches during this period. In 1862 some disagreement with the La Touches caused Ruskin to go off to the continent instead of spending time with them on their Harristown estate. He wrote to his friend, Lady Trevelyan: 'The Irish plan fell through in various unspeakable — somewhat sorrowful ways.'
7 Maria La Touche to GMD, postmarked Newbridge, 16 May 1863 (ALS Yale).
8 Maria La Touche to GMD, 13 July 1863.
9 Ruskin to Lady Mount-Temple, 24 January 1864, *The Letters of John Ruskin to Lord and Lady Mount-Temple*, ed. John Lewis Bradley, Ohio State University Press, 1964, p. 29.
10 Ruskin to Lady Mount-Temple, Mid-April 1864 (Bradley, op.cit.) p.31, p.33.
11 Ruskin to Lady Mount-Temple, 2 April 1868 (Bradley, op.cit.)
12 Maria La Touche to Louisa, 19 November 1863 (ALS Yale).
13 Maria La Touche to Louisa, 14 March 1865 (ALS Yale).
14 Ruskin to GMD, 30 June 1863 (ALS Yale).
15 Ruskin to GMD, 22 July 1863 (ALS Yale).
16 Ruskin to MacDonald, 13 April 1864 (ALS Yale).
17 Ruskin to MacDonald, 6 February 1865 (ALS Yale).
18 *GMAW*, p.330.
19 Ruskin to GMD, 8 November 1863.

CHAPTER TWENTY-TWO
Abroad

1 Ruskin to MacDonald, 22 July 1865 (ALS Yale).
2 MacDonald wrote a series of letters to Louisa from the continent, none of which he dated, but headed *Antwerp, Cologne, Basle* and so on. I have not footnoted these.
3 *RF*, Vol. III, p.10.
4 William Edmonstone Aytoun (1813–65), a Scottish poet, born in Edinburgh.
5 GMD to Mrs Scott, 25 August 1865 (ALS Yale).
6 John Stuart Blackie (1809–95), a Scottish professor and man of letters, translated Goethe's *Faust* in 1834. The first Regius Professor of Latin at Marischal College, Aberdeen in 1839, he later moved to the Greek Chair at Edinburgh where he was prominent in literary life.
7 John Stuart Blackie, *Testimonials* (Yale) — there is also a copy at the Brander Library, Huntly.
8 Ruskin, *Testimonials* 1865 (Yale) — there is also a copy at the Brander Library, Huntly.

CHAPTER TWENTY-THREE
On and Back

1 GMD to Mrs Scott, 9 February 1866 (Huntington Library, San Marino, California). See also *Chapters in the History of Owens College and of Manchester University 1851–1914* (Manchester 1937) by E. Fiddes.
2 See F.J.C. Hearnshaw, *The Centenary History of King's College, London* (London 1929) pp.257–8. The evening classes at King's were given a glowing report by Charles Dickens in his magazine *Household Words* 18 December 1858.
3 Edward Hayes Plumptre to GMD, 1 December 1866 (ALS Yale).
4 Ruskin to GMD, 13 February 1865 (ALS Yale).
5 GMD to Louisa (n.d.) July 1865. Second in the series sent to Louisa by MacDonald from his continental holiday.
6 Ruskin to Lady Mount-Temple (n.d.) 1866 (Bradley op.cit.).
7 Rose La Touche to Lady Mount-Temple, 10 October 1866, qu. *Ruskin, the Great Victorian*, Derrick Leon, London 1949, p.371.
8 *GMAW*, p.369.
9 *Rems*, p.34.
10 Ruskin to GMD, 3 September 1867 (ALS Yale).

11 *GMAW*, p.386.
12 Louisa to Lilia Scott MacDonald (n.d.) January 1868 (ALS Yale).
13 MacDonald and Louisa arrived in Aberdeen on 28 December 1867. MacDonald went first to Reid's studio at 199 King Street on Monday 30 December and made five subsequent visits. Reid's portrait of MacDonald was finished on 28 January and was sent to the exhibition at the Royal Scottish Academy where it was favourably criticized except for the *Scotsman*. Reid offered the portrait as a gift to Geddes on the condition that it be bequeathed to Aberdeen University. An engraving was made in 1869 and published by E. Graves and Son in May 1869. There are now portraits of MacDonald by Reid at the National Portrait Gallery in London and at Marischal College, Aberdeen. See also *GMAW*, p.313.
14 William Duguid Geddes to GMD, 29 February 1868 (ALS Yale).

CHAPTER TWENTY-FOUR
God our Father and Mother

1 GMD to GMD senior, 11 April 1847 (ALS Yale).
2 ibid.
3 MacDonald drew a portrait of F.D. Maurice in *DE*, Vol. III, p.197. And when Maurice left the Vere St. Chapel in 1869 he organized a testimonial to him which took the form of an oil painting by Lowes Dickinson, given to Queen's College (see *GMAW*, p.399).
4 Thomas Erskine of Linlathen (1788–1870), an advocate and theologian, was a nominal member of the Church of Scotland, while opposed to many of its Calvinist precepts. See *Erskine of Linlathen: Selections and Biography* (Edinburgh and London 1899) by Henry F. Henderson, and Erskine's own *True and False Religion*. D.J. Vaughan's article 'Scottish Influence upon English Theological Thought' in the *Contemporary Review* 32 (1878) p.457 is also helpful.
5 For more on Irving see *Edward Irving and His Circle* by Andrew Landale Drummond (London 1938).
6 Norman Macleod (1812–72) was one of the founders of the Evangelical Alliance in 1847. He was Moderator in 1869 and was active in social work among the poor, and became Chaplain to the Queen in 1857.
7 See *Mystics of the North-East* printed for the Third Spalding Club (Aberdeen

1934) ed. G.D. Henderson. In seventeenth century Aberdeen, three professors of Divinity at King's College turned, at differing times, from the weariness of outward controversy to the calmer reaches of inward reflection. John Forbes of Corse wrote his *Spiritual Exercises*, James Garden produced his *Comparative Theology*, and Henry Scougall worked on the classic *Life of God in the Soul of Man*. Scougall was a disciple of the Cambridge Platonists, and a friend of James Garden's elder brother, George, who preached Scougall's funeral sermon, and translated Forbes' *Spiritual Exercises* into Latin.

George Garden travelled widely on the continent, in Holland and in France, as was fashionable in those days, and became friendly with Poiret, Antoinette Bourignon, and the famous French mystic Madame Guyon, whose death bed he visited at Blois in 1717. It was through Poiret that Madame Guyon's works were introduced to those interested in mystical literature, and both George Garden and another man from the North-East, Dr James Keith, were drawn to her writings. Keith was part of a later circle who corresponded on theological and mystical subjects. He and others were a legacy of the 'Auld Alliance' between Scotland and France, Episcopalian Jacobites marooned in a country given over to Presbyterianism with their rightful King, James VII, exiled in France.

Keith corresponded freely with Lord Deskford who lived at Cullen House, the house MacDonald used as his model for the home of the Marquis of Lossie in *Malcolm*. When MacDonald was staying at Cullen in 1873 with Louisa and Octavia Hill, gathering material for his novel, Lord Seafield, who was then living at the house, gave MacDonald the keys to the garden and the house, and MacDonald may well have used the opportunity to leaf through the large collection of mystical volumes and correspondence housed there. It may be more than a coincidence that another of Deskford's circle was called Alexander Forbes, the Fourth Lord Forbes of Pitsligo, for MacDonald could easily have learned something of these men while he was still a student at King's College in Aberdeen.

8 Stopford Brooke published F.W. Robertson's *Life* in 1865. Owen Chadwick in *The Victorian Church*, Adam and Charles Black (London 1966) Vol. II, p.135 states: 'The book was important in the development of the broad church school. It was a drama of the intellectual conflict of the age. In October 1865, when it was published, the argument was raging between an incredible Christian orthodoxy and a scientific or philosophic materialism. The *Life* represented this conflict within a single soul of twenty years before, introspective and morbid and agonising, and at last rising triumphant with the banner of liberal Christianity... Robertson exercised far more influence dead than alive.'

9 MacDonald moved on from the stance he had taken as President of the Huntly Juvenile Temperance Society in 1837. He enjoyed beer and wine, though he rarely touched spirits, and the consumption of whisky in his novels is generally depicted as a moral evil. He hated the doctrinaire attitude of many of the promoters of Temperance, however, and while at Bradford on 13 April 1869 he complained in a letter to Louisa, 'There is nothing to drink but water at dinner.' Earlier that year he wrote to Louisa from Edinburgh: 'I *malted* at supper' — perhaps this meant that he drank whisky.

10 *Unspoken Sermons*, (3rd Series), pp.150−1.

11 *US 3*. p.3.

12 *US 3*, p.161.

13 MacDonald did not believe in pre-existence, as found in Wordsworth's *Intimations of Immortality*. Pre-existence is suggested in MacDonald's children's poem *Baby*, but MacDonald held the view that to be born out of God was better than to have lived a life previously with him and then to have descended to earth. He also rejected all notions of reincarnation. See also RF Vol I p.184.

14 See Geoffrey Rowell, *Hell and the Victorians* (Oxford University Press 1974) for an account of Logos Theology and Erskine of Linlathen. See also *Frederick Denison Maurice* by H.G. Wood (Cambridge University Press, 1950) p.77 for an account of Maurice's view of the Logos and other religions.

15 *There and Back*, Vol. II, p.224.

16 At the end of *Paul Faber, Surgeon* MacDonald wrote of Faber (Vol. III, p.282): 'He was growing and that is all we can require of any man.'

17 See Owen Chadwick, *The Victorian Church* Vol. II, p.35 and Wood (op.cit.) on Maurice — 'Christianity and the Religions of the World' (Chap. IV pp.73ff).

18 *PF*, Vol. I, p.54.

19 *Ranald Bannerman's Boyhood*, p.205.

20 See Edmund Gosse's *Father and Son*. Gosse's father, Philip Gosse, published a book called *Omphalos* (the Greek word for navel) claiming that God had created the

world with the fossils already buried in it.
21 *Unspoken Sermons* (First Series),
pp.52–3.
22 *US 3*, p.42.
23 *US 2*, p.149.
24 GMD to Louisa, 12 December 1846
(written into Winifred MacDonald's
notebook, now at Yale): 'Tho' not much of
a Greek scholar I was very glad on referring
to my Greek New Testament to find that
this is the real meaning of the words.'
Obviously, he was concerned with proper
exegesis from the outset of his theological
career.
25 *US 2*, p.36.
26 *US 2*, p.236. See also *WMM*, Vol. II,
p.211.
27 *The Elect Lady*, p.199.
28 *US 2*, pp.168–9.
29 See *MM*, Vol. II, pp.14–15.
30 *US 3*, pp.63–5.
31 *DE*, Vol. I, pp.163–4.
32 *The Miracles of Our Lord*, p.265.
33 *PF*, Vol. II, pp.182–3.
34 *US 1*, pp.17–19.
35 *US 3*, p.300.
36 *US 3*, p.196.
37 *Miracles*, p.245.
38 F.W. Robertson, *Sermons, 2nd Series*,
p.127, p.129. 'A miracle is commonly
defined to be a contravention of the laws of
nature. More properly speaking, it is only a
higher operation of those same laws, in a
form no more a suspension or contradiction
of the laws of nature than a hurricane or a
thunderstorm… Lastly, it is the intention
of a miracle to manifest the Divine in the
common and the ordinary.'
39 *Miracles*, p.227.
40 ibid. p.268.
41 *US 3*, p.211–12.
42 ibid. p.143.
43 ibid. p.96.
44 ibid. p.80.
45 *MM*, Vol. II, p.19. See also *US 1*, p.44;
and *US 3*, p.229.
46 See *MM*, Vol. II, p.336: Mary Marston
tells Hesper Redmain: 'But I have
sometimes thought — what if hell be just a
place where God gives everybody
everything she wants, and lets everybody
do whatever she likes, without once coming
nigh to interfere! What a hell that would be!
For God's presence in the very being, and
nothing else, is bliss.'
47 *US 1*, p.44.
48 *MM*, Vol. II, p.321.
49 *US 1*, p.88.
50 *US 1*, p.48.
51 *Salted with Fire*, p.325.
52 For more on MacDonald's doctrine of
hell see *GMAW*, p.398. One verse of the MS

of 'A Thanksgiving for F.D. Maurice'
omitted from the published version was:
'He taught that hell itself is yet within
The confines of thy kingdom; and its fires
The endless conflict of thy love with sin,
That even by horror works its pure desires.'
See also *Lilith A* p.124 — one of
MacDonald's last statements on hell:
'…and soon, with an occasional returning
heave or shudder now here, now there, the
slimy mess sank once more to rest. Then I
knew that one day the holy song of the
praising universe would enter in at the ears
of even the lost tribes of incorporated life.
And hell itself *would* pass away. And leave
her dolorous mansions to the peering day.'
53 *A Rough Shaking*, p.87.
54 *MM*, Vol. III, p.125.
55 *T&B*, Vol. III, pp.138–9.
56 MacDonald had a high view of the
body. See *US 1*, p.238, p.240.
57 *US 3*, p.207.
58 *TW*, Vol. III, p.150.
59 *US 2*, p.306.
60 *ARS*, p.287.
61 *US 2*, p.83.
62 *GMAW*, p.384.
63 He may well have possessed R.A.
Vaughan's *Hours with the Mystics*, which is
a guide to mysticism down the ages.
64 Thomas Erskine, *True and False
Religion*, p.46.
65 See *GMAW*, p.271. James John Garth
Wilkinson (1812–99) is best known as the
translator of Swedenborg's works into
English. More about his life can be found in
*James John Garth Wilkinson: A Memoir of
His Life with a Selection from His Letters*
by Clement John Wilkinson (London
1911). Greville MacDonald only makes one
brief mention of Wilkinson and there is no
mention of MacDonald in the *Memoir* on
Wilkinson. The fact that they knew each
other testifies once more, however, to
MacDonald's interest in the esoteric and
arcane.
66 See *Miracles*, p.158, and p.160: 'There
seems to me nothing unreasonable in the
supposition of the existence of spirits who,
having once had bodies such as ours, and
having abused the privileges of
embodiment, are condemned for a season to
roam about bodiless, ever mourning the loss
of their capacity for the only pleasures they
care for, and craving after them in their
imaginations.'
67 MacDonald held that the concept of the
family was very important. See *MM*. Vol.
III, p.150: 'Love and marriage are the
Father's most powerful means for the
making of his foolish little ones into sons
and daughters.'

68 GMD to his daughter, Mary Josephine MacDonald, 3 August 1869 (ALS Yale).
69 *WW*, Vol. III, pp.180−81. See also p.381.
70 Louisa to GMD, 19 November 1868 (ALS Yale).
71 GMD to Richard Watson Gilder, 8 August 1881 — Louisa added: 'Our dear Head and Lord and Master is so well, so much better for wintering on the Riviera.'
72 See Ray Strachey, *The Cause*, Virago, 1978, pp.71−6.
73 *The Seaboard Parish*, Vol. II, pp.91−2.
74 GMD to Louisa Stevenson, 27 April 1871 (Nat. Lib. Scotland).
75 *MM*, Vol. III, p.151.
76 *VD*, Vol. I, p.35.
77 See *Home Again* p.291: 'Man was made a little lower than the angels; he calls woman an angel, and then looks down upon her! Certainly, however, he has done his best to make her worthy of his condescension.'
78 *MM*, Vol. I, p.232.
79 *Adela Cathcart*, Vol. II, pp.76, 77.
80 *RF*, Vol. I, p.88.
81 See *GMAW*, pp.401−6 for Greville MacDonald's delineation of the differences between MacDonald and Maurice.
82 *RF*, Vol. III, p.181.
83 GMD to his cousin James MacDonald, 31 December 1893. (This letter is in the possession of Mrs Freda Levson). MacDonald also wrote to William Cowper-Temple, 17 February 1878: 'But I know more of the politics of the kingdom of heaven than I do of those of this world at least, if I do not, I am in evil case.' (Nat. Lib. Scotland)

CHAPTER TWENTY-FIVE
The Retreat

1 Charles Dodgson (Lewis Carroll) recorded visiting Kate Lewis on 27 May 1869 with Louisa and Lilia, but she was not at home. An amusing series of letters and apologies followed.
2 *GMAW*, pp.384−5.
3 GMD to Ruskin, 24 June 1868 (ALS Yale). See also *GMAW*, p.381 fn.
4 Charlotte Saunders Cushman (1816−76) played Lady Macbeth and Rosalind in London — only the second American actress to do so. The article on her in the American DNB states: 'There can be little doubt that Charlotte Cushman was the most powerful actress America has produced.'
5 GMD to Louisa, 26 November 1868 (ALS Yale).

6 GMD to Louisa, 21 October 1868 (ALS Yale).
7 GMD to Louisa, Thurs (1868?), (n.d.), (ALS Yale).
8 Louisa to GMD, 16 November 1868 (ALS Yale).
9 GMD to Louisa (n.d.), 1871 (ALS Yale).
10 GMD to Louisa, 11 June 1869 (ALS Yale).
11 See GMAW, p.392 where Greville MacDonald wrote: 'My mother declared they were afraid of him, lest his horrible suffering should be a visitation for his heresies.'
12 GMD to Louisa, prob. 21 June 1869 (ALS Yale). See *GMAW*, pp.392−3.
13 GMD to Louisa, (n.d.) 1869 (ALS Yale).
14 GMD to Louisa, 26 February 1871 (ALS Yale).
15 ibid. See *GMAW*, pp.411−12.
16 *Good Things for the Young of All Ages* ran until 1877. The title page of the volume for 1874 was 'A Feast of Good Things' and for 1875 'The Picturesque Annual.'
17 Louisa to Lilia Scott MacDonald, 23 April 1870 (ALS Yale).
18 GMD to Helen Powell, 17 September 1870.
19 GMD to Louisa, 20 July 1870 (ALS Yale).
20 *GMAW*, p.413.
21 The final payment of £100 was dated 2 August 1872.

CHAPTER TWENTY-SIX
St George and the Rose

1 Ruskin to GMD, 12 January 1866 (ALS Yale).
2 The engagement was broken off by 4 March 1868.
3 qu. *Ruskin, the Great Victorian* by Derrick Leon, p.416.
4 Ruskin to GMD, 7 March 1868 (ALS Yale).
5 *Rems*, p.100.
6 qu. Leon (op.cit.), p.409.
7 Ruskin to GMD, 1870 (ALS Yale).
8 qu. Leon (op.cit), pp.482−3.
9 Ruskin to GMD, 14 March 1870 (ALS Yale).
10 Rose La Touche to GMD, 20 April 1872 (ALS Yale).
11 Rose La Touche to GMD, 14 May 1872 (ALS Yale).
12 Rose La Touche to GMD, 18 June 1872.
13 Rose La Touche to Ruskin, 19 June 1872.
14 Ruskin to GMD, 5 July 1872 (Yale).
15 *Rems*, p.120.
16 Ruskin to GMD, Sunday 11 August 1872 (ALS Yale).

17 Ruskin to GMD, 10 September 1872: 'She returned my last letter unopened and I have no resource but you, as of old. My only fault had been letting her see I still had hope. I got the returned letter at the church door last Sunday, and walked home again — even Joanie couldn't go in. When the thing one meant to pray for turns out not with prayer — what is one to do?'

18 Ruskin to GMD, 8 September 1872 (ALS Yale).

19 Rose La Touche to Louisa (n.d.), Dublin Thursday (ALS Yale).

20 Ruskin to GMD, 25 February, 1875. (ALS Yale).

21 Ruskin to Carlyle, 4 June 1875, qu. Leon (op.cit.), p.500.

22 GMD to Ruskin, 30 May 1875 (ALS Yale).

23 Ruskin to GMD, 2 June 1875. (ALS Yale).

24 GMD to Louisa, 21 December 1875 (ALS Yale).

25 Ruskin to GMD, 21 February 1878 (ALS Yale). This letter is written in twisted, disturbing handwriting, disjointed across the page. The hallucination took place on February 20/21.

26 Maria La Touche visited the MacDonalds at Bordighera in Italy in 1885. MacDonald sent Ruskin a copy of his novel *What's Mine's Mine* in 1886. GMD to Ruskin, 23 June 1886: 'You think my highlanders impossible: they do not seem so to me; my own brothers who died both before thirty, were in my mind as I wrote. They were capable of all I say.' MacDonald also sent Ruskin a copy of *A Threefold Cord* on 20 July 1886.

CHAPTER TWENTY-SEVEN
America

1 James Redpath (1833–1891) journalist, editor and lecture promoter, was born in Britain at Berwick-on-Tweed of a Scottish father and an English mother. He founded the Boston Lyceum Bureau in 1868 to promote lecture tours which were then very popular. Among others, Emerson, Thoreau and Mark Twain worked with him.

2 GMD to R.W. Gilder, 10 December 1871 (ALS Yale). Richard Watson Gilder (1844–1909), assistant editor of *Scribner's Monthly Magazine*, was in charge of the arts features. His home was a centre for artistic and intellectual life. In 1881 he became editor of *Scribners'* successor, *The Century*.

3 James Thomas Fields (1817–81), head of Ticknor and Fields publishing business, was editor of the influential *Atlantic Monthly* from 1861–70, also an early member of the famous Saturday Club. He visited Europe several times and was friendly with many famous American and European writers.

4 Louisa to Lilia Scott MacDonald, 3 October 1872 (ALS Yale).

5 Louisa to Lilia Scott MacDonald, 13 October 1872 (ALS Yale).

6 Greville MacDonald to Winifred Louisa MacDonald, 15 October 1872 (ALS Yale).

7 Harriet Beecher Stowe (1811–96) had a Puritan upbringing — her father was a Congregationalist and strict Calvinist. Later she attended the Episcopalian Church, and after the death of her son became interested in spiritualism and corresponded with Elizabeth Barrett Browning on the subject. Her book *Uncle Tom's Cabin* caused a storm in 1852 when it was published, as it highlighted the evils of the slave trade. She came to public attention again when, in 1869, she published, in the *Atlantic Monthly* 'The True Story of Lady Byron's Life' laying the charge of incest against Byron, which she affirmed further in the publication of her book *Lady Byron Vindicated* in 1870.

8 Louisa to Lilia Scott MacDonald, 3 October 1872 (ALS Yale).

9 Louisa to Lilia Scott MacDonald, 5 October 1872 (ALS Yale).

10 Charlotte Saunders Cushman (1816–76) — see note in Chapter 25 'The Retreat'.

11 Oliver Wendell Holmes (1809–94), essayist, poet and teacher of anatomy. Became Parkman Professor of Anatomy and Physiology at the Harvard Medical School in 1847, and Dean from 1847–53. He wrote poetry, was a brilliant conversationalist, and reigned supreme in the Boston literary world. He named the *Atlantic Monthly* which first appeared in 1857 with Lowell as its editor, and was the last survivor of the New England group of writers which included Hawthorne, Emerson, Lowell, Morley, Longfellow and Whittier. He rebelled against his Calvinist background and wrote hymns. His fame never spread across the Atlantic and Leslie Stephen wrote of him in *Studies of a Biographer*, Vol. II p.167 '. . . few popular authors have had a narrower escape from obscurity.'

12 Louisa to Lilia Scott MacDonald, 10 October 1872 (ALS Yale).

13 See *GMAW*, p.423.

14 See *GMAW*, p.425.

15 Louisa to All Children, Sunday 20 October 1872 (ALS Yale).

16 Joshua Ballinger Lippincot (1813–86), an eminent publisher, began by producing Bibles and prayer books and then religious works before becoming the head of his own publishing house. He was also an animal-lover and for some time was President of the Society for the Prevention of Cruelty to Animals. He died leaving an estate valued at several million dollars.

17 John Greenleaf Whittier (1807–92), poet, abolitionist and Quaker, was influenced by Burns and wrote some poems in Scots when he was young. His fame increased following his contributions to the *Atlantic Monthly*. He wrote many abolitionist poems such as 'Massachusetts to Virginia.'

18 Louisa to Lilia Scott MacDonald, 30 October 1872 (ALS Yale), qu. *GMAW*, p.426.

19 Greville MacDonald to Winifred Louisa MacDonald, 14 November 1872 (ALS Yale).

20 Louisa to Lilia Scott MacDonald, 23 November 1872 (ALS Yale) qu. *GMAW*, p.428. FDM is a reference to F.D. Maurice.

21 Louisa to Lilia, 3 December 1872 (ALS Yale).

22 GMD to Lilia Scott MacDonald, 22 December (ALS Yale), qu. *GMAW*, p.432.

23 qu. *GMAW*, p.434.

24 GMD to Lilia Scott MacDonald, 3 January 1873 (ALS Yale).

25 *GMAW*, p.440.

26 Louisa to Lilia Scott MacDonald, (ALS Yale), qu. *GMAW*, p.441.

27 *GMAW*, p.442–3.

28 Louisa to Lilia Scott MacDonald, 30 January 1873 (ALS Yale), qu. *GMAW*, p.444.

29 Louisa to her daughters, 15 February 1873 (ALS Yale), qu. *GMAW*, p.446.

30 ibid.

31 Louisa to her children, 12 February 1873 (ALS Yale), qu. *GMAW*, p.447.

32 Louisa to all her children, 5 March 1873 (ALS Yale).

33 Louisa to Lilia Scott MacDonald, Sunday 6 April 1873 (ALS Yale), qu. *GMAW*, p.454.

34 Louisa to Mary Josephine MacDonald, 25 March 1873 (ALS Yale), qu. *GMAW*, p.453.

35 Louisa to Lilia Scott MacDonald, Sunday 19 April 1873 (ALS Yale), qu. *GMAW*, p.456.

36 *GMAW*, p.457.

37 *GMAW*, p.459.

38 *New York Daily Tribune*, Friday 23 May 1873.

CHAPTER TWENTY-EIGHT
In the Folds of Faërie

1 GMD to Helen Powell, 24 December 1883 (ALS Yale): 'I am often terribly hampered in my stories by sheer ignorance. I have seen so little of Scotland or any other place. Aberdeen, Banff, Cullen and Huntly are the *only* places I knew when I left at the age of twenty, and I have never been but once for as long as months in Scotland since. I have a shocking bad memory too. So I'm just driven back on bare-faced *leein'* . . .'

2 Originally printed as the preface to an American edition of *The Light Princess and Other Fairy Tales* in 1893, the essay was then included in *A Dish of Orts*. Also printed as part of the introduction to *The Gifts of the Christ Child and Other Stories*, ed. Glenn Sadler, Eerdmans & Co (1972).

3 *Nineteenth Century Children*, Gillian Avery (London 1965) p.40.

4 Dinah Mulock, *The Little Lame Prince* (London 1875) p.61.

5 *Nineteenth Century Children* op.cit. p.41.

6 'Frauds on the Fairies', *Household Words*, Saturday 1 October 1853, p.97.

7 ibid, p.98.

8 ibid.

9 The temper of the late Victorian period suffered perhaps from a distortion of romantic thought as regards children, and can be summed up in the last lines of Hans Andersen's *The Snow Queen*: 'The Grandmother sat in the warm sunshine, reading aloud from her Bible: "Whosoever shall not receive the Kingdom of Heaven as a little child shall not enter therein." Kai and Gerda looked into each other's eyes and now they understood the words from the Psalm.

Our roses bloom and fade away,
Our infant Lord abides alway,
May we be blessed his face to see
And ever little children be.'

It should be pointed out that this is a highly unusual moment in Andersen's writing — for here he strikes an 'evangelical note' uncharacteristic of his work.

10 Preface to *Dealings with the Fairies*, London 1867.

11 M.H. Abrams, *The Mirror and the Lamp* (Oxford University Press 1953) p.289.

12 *Selected Writings of Hoffmann* (Chicago 1969), ed. and trans. by Leonard J. Kent and Elizabeth C. Knight, pp.196–7.

13 'The Giant's Heart', for example, first appeared as 'Tell us a Story' in the

Christmas number of the *Illustrated London News* for December 1863, was incorporated into *Adela Cathcart* in 1864, and then went on to become part of the collections *Dealing with the Fairies* in 1867 and *Works of Fancy and Imagination* in 1871.

14 MacDonald also knew Sir Joseph Noël Paton RSA (1821–1901) who illustrated *The Water Babies* for Kingsley in 1863. Charles Dodgson asked MacDonald for an introduction to him when he was looking for an illustrator for *Through the Looking Glass* (1875).

15 *The Fantastic Imagination*, p.25.
  I realize that the definition of a fairy-tale is a difficult one — especially as many 'fairy-tales' have no fairies in them. My own feeling is that a story that combines traditional elements and draws on a firmly recognizable tradition as, say, *The Light Princess* or *The Giant's Heart* is a fairy-tale, while a visionary or symbolic work like *The Golden Key* is not. This definition is an elastic one — all of these tales by MacDonald are fantasy writing in the pure sense of the word, it is simply that some follow traditional models closely while others do not. The boundaries, however, are hard to draw.

16 *The Wise Woman*, Lion Publishing, 1980, p.82.
17 *The Golden Key*, Lion Publishing, p.11.
18 *The Fantastic Imagination*, op.cit. p.24.
19 ibid, pp.24–5.
20 ibid, p.28.
21 'The Giant's Heart', *The Light Princess*, Lion Publishing, 1980, p.78.
22 GMD to Louisa, early March 1861, (ALS Yale).
23 'The Cruel Painter', *The Gray Wolf*, Lion Publishing, 1980, p.44.
24 John Ruskin to GMD (n.d.), prob. July/August 1863 (ALS Yale).
25 *The Golden Key*, Lion Publishing, 1980, p.1.
26 ibid, p.16.
27 ibid, pp.26–7.
28 ibid, p.28.
29 ibid, p.35.
30 *MM*, Vol. III, p.312.
31 *A Rough Shaking*, p.105.
32 *At the Back of the North Wind*, p.1.
33 *ABNW*, p.114.
34 *ABNW*, p.20.
35 *ABNW*, p.37.
36 *ABNW*, p.59.
37 *ABNW*, p.129.
38 *ABNW*, p.114.
39 *ABNW*, p.113.
40 *ABNW*, p.212.

41 *ABNW*, p.345.
42 *ABNW*, pp.363–4.
43 *The Princess and the Goblin*, p.145.
44 See also *Lilith*, Lion Publishing, 1982, p.25.
45 *P&G*, p.235.
46 *P&G*, p.112.
47 *P&G*, pp.158–9.
48 *P&G*, p.119.
49 *P&G*, p.229.
50 *P&G*, p.47.
51 *P&G*, p.165. See Alice Chandler's *A Dream of Order: The Medieval Ideal in Nineteenth Century English Literature* (London 1971) p.195: 'Medievalism...has two major aspects in the eighteenth and nineteenth centuries. One is its naturalism — its identification with nature and the past and thus with simpler and truer modes of feeling and expression and nobler and more heroic codes of action. The other is its feudalism — its harmonious and stable social structure which reconciled freedom and order by giving each man an allotted place in society and an allotted leader to follow. The bridge between these two aspects of medievalism is chivalry, which made the spontaneous generosity of the natural man the guiding principle of man in society and which compensated for human frailty by having the strong protect the weak.'
52 *P&G*, p.115. Irene's thread, which is one of the most interesting motifs in the story, is not original to MacDonald, but was lifted and adapted from *The Gold Thread* by MacDonald's friend Norman Macleod in 1861. It is a rather tedious allegory about a boy who must follow a gold thread home to his father. The preface invites the reader: 'to learn the great lesson which [the book] is intended to teach; that lesson is, that we should always trust God and do what is right, and thus hold fast our gold thread in spite of every temptation and danger, being certain that in this way only will God lead us in safety and peace to His home.'
  Eric, the hero of the story, loses his thread when he yields to temptation, but instantly finds it again the moment he says his prayers. Like Irene he is reunited with his father at the end of the book. It is interesting to see how MacDonald transforms Macleod's idea. Unlike Macleod, he does not press home his point using crude allegory, but allows the child to draw his or her own conclusions about the nature and purpose of the thread.
53 *The Princess and Curdie*, p.17.
54 *P&C*, p.26.

55 *P&C*, p.25: 'It was the spinning wheel that first taught him to make verses, and to sing, and to think whether all was right inside him; or at least it had helped him in all these things. Hence it was no wonder he should know a spinning wheel when he heard it sing — even although as the bird of paradise to other birds was the song of that wheel to the song of his mother's.'
56 *P&C*, p.69.
57 *P&C*, p.70.
58 *P&C*, p.53.
59 *P&C*, p.104.
60 *P&C*, pp.156—7.
61 At the end of the nineteenth century the Pall Mall Gazette held a poll on the most popular of children's books for a ten-year-old and fairy literature came out top with *Alice* heading the list. As the reviewer commented: 'Of the list as a whole the most obvious point is the victory of fairy-tales.'

CHAPTER TWENTY-NINE
Home Again

1 *GMAW*, pp.465—6.
2 Mark Twain to GMD, 30 September 1873 (ALS Yale).
3 GMD to James T. Fields, 13 August 1874 (Houghton Library, Harvard).
4 GMD to Paine, 19 February 1874 (Houghton Lib. Harvard).
5 Edward Robert Hughes (1851— 1914), a London historical genre painter, studied at the RA Schools, and also with Holman Hunt and his uncle, Arthur Hughes. He exhibited at the RA from 1870—98 and also at international exhibitions at Venice, Munich and Düsseldorf. He painted mainly romantic pictures with subjects drawn from Boccaccio, and from novels. He later became Holman Hunt's assistant. He was engaged to Mary MacDonald from 1874 till her death in 1879, and the gravestone he made for her at Nervi was later copied for Lilia's and Grace's graves. He married after Mary's death and his friendship with the MacDonalds lasted until the end of his life.
6 Charles Dodgson to Mary Josephine MacDonald, 26 June 1874 (ALS Yale).
7 GMD to Louisa, 24 March 1875 (ALS Yale). 'Uncle's sale' refers to the sale after the death of MacDonald's uncle, MacIntosh MacKay, the Gaelic scholar.
8 Miss Jane and Miss Anne Cobden were the daughters of Richard Cobden (1804—65), a founder of the Anti-Corn Law League and a strong advocate of Free Trade. River Villa adjoined The Retreat. Lilia was very friendly with Jane Cobden and corresponded with her.

9 GMD to Richard Watson Gilder, 25 April 1876 (ALS Yale).
10 Georgina Mount-Temple, *Memorials* (1888), privately circulated 1890.
11 In the preface to *Dramatic Illustrations from John Bunyan's Pilgrim's Progress arranged by Mrs George MacDonald*, Winifred MacDonald wrote: 'The men and women were dressed in the costume of Bunyan's period. The allegorical and celestial persons wore simple Greek garments. Greatheart appeared in shining armour with a large red cross on the front of his white tabard.
   The music at the beginning and between the scenes was from Handel's *Messiah* and other classical works: only a piano was used. In most of the scenes there was a good deal of music...'
   The piece ended with Greatheart saying (with arms crossed): 'Thanks be unto God who giveth us the victory through our Lord Jesus Christ.'
12 GMD to Louisa, 2 November 1877 (ALS Yale). qu. *GMAW*, p.479.
13 Winifred MacDonald recalled an incident relating to MacDonald's first appearance as Greatheart in 1877: 'Some 25 years later at a Church army sale Mr Carlisle introduced me to her...' (Princess Louise) who told Winifred: 'I think that you would like to know that my mother — Queen Victoria, you know, gave that book to *every one* of her grandsons.'
14 GMD to Louisa, 30 October 1877 (ALS Yale).
15 GMD to Lady Mount-Temple, December 1877 (Nat. Lib. Scotland).
16 GMD to Lady Mount-Temple, December 1877 (Nat. Lib. Scotland).

CHAPTER THIRTY
Pilgrims

1 *GMAW*, p.485.
2 *GMAW*, p.486.
3 qu. *GMAW*, p.487.
4 GMD to Lord Mount-Temple, 13 January 1879 (Nat. Lib. Scotland).
5 GMD to his stepmother, Margaret McColl MacDonald, 18 August 1879 (ALS Yale).
6 Lilia Scott MacDonald to Nellie Matheson (n.d.) March 1879, written from Porto Fino (ALS Yale).
7 Ronald MacDonald to Greville M. MacDonald, 3 January 1932 (now in the possession of Rosemary MacDonald).
8 GMD to James T. Fields, 21 August 1879 (Houghton Library, Harvard). MacDonald wrote to Lady Mount-Temple,

20 March 1879 (Nat. Lib. Scotland): 'My wife says if we get this house we are looking for now she would like to put up in the hall "And they confessed that they were pilgrims and strangers on the earth." That is our mood, and may it last until we shall be no longer strangers or pilgrims, but at home. There are so many things that belong to home here — they must be strangers and pilgrims too somehow — Nothing comes to perfection. There is no time for anything but getting ready to go.'

9 Charles Dodgson (Lewis Carroll) to Lilia Scott MacDonald, 12 June 1879 (ALS Yale).

10 Mark Twain to GMD, 19 September 1882 (ALS Yale).

11 See Lewis Carroll's *Diary* 26 July (Sat.) 1879: 'In the second piece Mr Granite (son of the Lady Henry Gordon whom I met at Eastbourne) appeared — I cannot say acted.' Mr Granite was obviously Charley Granet. Lady Henry Gordon has not been identified.

12 Louisa to Richard Watson Gilder, 8 August 1881 (added to the end of a letter from MacDonald) (ALS Yale).

CHAPTER THIRTY-ONE
Bordighera

1 GMD to Lady Mount-Temple, 26 January 1880 (Nat. Lib. Scotland).

2 The MacDonalds 'adopted' several different people. *GMAW*, p.502 mentions Willie Nicholls (though not by name) who was taken in while the family still lived at The Retreat, and who went on to become a professor of Singing at the Royal Academy in London. Apart from Honey and Joan Desaint, Percy Harrat and his brother joined the household. Laura Ragg's acid article in *English ii* (1956) Summer, pp.59—63 suggests that the MacDonalds treated the Desaint girls as servants and the discussion over the fate of the foundling Theodora in *The Seaboard Parish* (London 1868) (who is to be brought up as a servant) could be used to support this view. Yet the girls continued their relationship with the family until their deaths, and seem to have been treated like younger sisters. With the MacDonalds' finances as they were, probably all the children were treated like servants at some time or other, and Honey and Joan were not singled out in any more disadvantageous way than any of the others.

3 Bordighera is known as *La città delle Palme* — the city of palms — and traditionally supplied the Vatican with palms for the Easter Celebrations.

4 Three thousand English people lived at Bordighera and the colony flourished until the 1930s. Many of the hotels still bear English names. The English cut down the olive-trees on the plain near the sea, slightly away from the old town which is crammed on to the hillside. The arrival of the railways influenced its popularity. The line from Nice to Ventigmilia (2½ miles from Bordighera) was opened in 1872. Travellers on the Great Tour had generally sailed from Nice to Genoa missing out that part of the coast. Other famous people associated with Bordighera were Charles Garnier, architect of the Paris Opera, and Monet, who painted there in 1884.

See also *The Meanderings of a Medico: A Record of Work and Travel in Many Lands* by James Linton Bogle MD, (Printed for Private Circulation 1928) p.164: 'One of the main causes of this big English colony was the influence of the MacDonald family, attracting visitors who knew his character and his books; another, also potent, was the English Church, its chaplain, and its supporters.' One of the mainstays of the English colony was Charles Bicknell (1842—1918) who had studied mathematics at Cambridge and then entered the church, only to abandon that career in the pursuit of natural science. He set up the Studia Liguria at Bordighera, examining flora, fauna and minerals in the area and identified some prehistoric markings.

5 GMD to Lady Mount-Temple, Sunday 30 September 1880 (National Library of Scotland).

6 C. Edmund Maurice, *Life of Octavia Hill*, (MacMillan London 1913) pp.438—9.

7 *GMAW*, pp.505—6.

8 MacDonald also took services, preached and prayed at All Saints' Church.

9 One photo of MacDonald kept at the Bibliotheca Nationale at Bordighera is entitled 'The Sage of Bordighera'.

10 GMD to James MacDonald, 5 November 1887 (in the possession of Mrs Freda Levson).

11 *GMAW*, p.508.

12 Georgina Mount-Temple, *Memorials* (1888/90), pp.78—9.

13 See *Bogle*, op.cit. He lived in Casa Grazia where the Jamesons had lived and recounted — p.138: 'The house had been built for the Rev. K. Jameson... whose wife was in delicate health, and it had been modified for her particular use. The ventilation was, even from a doctor's point of view, excessive. Tobin's tubes, ventilators over doors, windows and fireplaces — many windows, each opening

entirely to the air, folding doors between rooms, together with general high ceilings — these made it a cold dwelling-place not very comfortable in winter... In the bay window of the morning-room hooks were fixed where the hammock was slung in which Mrs Jameson used to lie for hours in the open-air and sunshine, whilst in the fine bedroom upstairs with its four windows the sun streamed in and gave her a continuous bath of warm light.'

14 GMD to Margaret Roberts, (n.d.) 1884 (ALS Yale).

15 The Chaplain's Book of All Saints' Church Bordighera recorded: 'Feb 23rd 1887: Violent shock of earthquake at 6.15a.m. damage in several places. A second about 7a.m. and the third at matins 9a.m. where about 20 people present — they went briefly out of church; later some returned. The plaster of the second wall was much shaken down — tower cracked. Some plaster by the East side fell — slighter shocks in the night. Great part of the people out of doors. At celebration an undulating motion in matins a similar one and there were about 40 people. On Feb 25th they collected 141 frs. On 23rd Feb. morning prayer at "Casa Coraggio." At that meeting is settled that the offertory was to be asked for the distressed in Bordighera and a committee consisting of the chaplain the churchwardens Canon Thornton... to state in which way the fund should be administered.'

16 Louisa to Anna Leigh-Smith, 24 February 1887 (ALS Yale).

17 *GMAW*, pp.514–5.

18 GMD to James MacDonald, 12 April 1887 (in the possession of Mrs Freda Levson).

19 Chaplain's Book for All Saints' Church Bordighera — 20 October 1887: 'Madame Desaint at the Casa Coraggio. She had been many years supported and lodged by Mr MacDonald; she was laid in the cemetery...'

20 GMD to Louisa, 5 March 1888 (ALS Yale). Greville MacDonald wrote in *Rems*, p.303: 'Year by year, as we grew older, our love for father and mother grew wiser and stronger: a fact none the less true that the severance from home introduced certain tragical misunderstandings that seemed insoluble.'

21 GMD to Louisa, 18 May 1889 (ALS Yale).

22 GMD to Lilia Scott MacDonald, 4 January 1891 (ALS Yale).

23 GMD to C. Edmund Maurice, 1 March 1891 (ALS Yale).

24 GMD to Louisa, 7 July 1891 (ALS Yale).

25 GMD to Louisa, 13 July 1891 (ALS Yale).

26 GMD to Louisa, 14 July 1891.

27 Two letters: GMD to Louisa, 21 October 1891 and 22 October 1891 (ALS Yale).

28 GMD to Louisa, 30 October 1891 (ALS Yale).

29 GMD to Louisa, 27 October 1891 (ALS Yale).

30 GMD to Louisa, 7 November 1891 (ALS Yale).

31 *Rems*, pp.308–9. Mr B- is probably Clarence Bicknell — see note 4 of this chapter.

32 *GMAW*, p.526.

33 GMD to Helen Powell, 16 April 1892 (ALS Yale).

34 GMD to Lilia Scott MacDonald, 4 January 1891 (ALS Yale).

CHAPTER THIRTY-TWO
Lilith

1 *GMAW*, p.548.

2 For details of the composition and evolution of *Lilith*, see appendix in this book, 'A Note on Lilith'.

3 *GMAW*, pp.551–2.

4 The strain of writing *Lilith* was great. See *Rems*, p.321. Greville MacDonald quotes from a letter from his father, 17 September 1894: '... I have been and am still going through a time of trial. That my book is not to be a success in the money way is not much of a trial thanks to you; but the conscious failing — the doubt if I shall ever write another book — is a trial that stirs up other mental and spiritual trials, one being the great dread of becoming a burden.'

A passage scored out in *Lilith B* p.27 perhaps gives some insight into MacDonald's state of mind at this time: 'One fear in especial I was delivered from. I had always had a right and wholesome horror of coming under the suggestive power of any but the power that had created me, and all the way we had been coming here I had been haunted with the wild, terrific notion, that I was under the mesmeric influence of a madman who was causing me to imagine all those things as objects, which were only suggestions and that not even of my own mind but wholly of his. Of this horrible fear I was now rid.'

5 Lilith's cry of 'Samoil' in Chap. XIX is MacDonald's only reference to this — probably Samoil is Satan.

6 *Lilith B*, p.137. Here Lilith is likened to Circe: 'I glanced up. She was waving her lovely arms over my head. "Is she changing me, like another Circe," I thought, "into some hideous animal? Alas, if there be beast enough in me to make that possible to her."'

7 *Malcolm*, Vol. II, p.189.

8 Lona is first called Bina, then Litha and Dalitha, before finally becoming *Lona* in *Lilith C*.

9 *Lilith*, Lion Publishing, 1982. All quotes are from this edition. p.173: 'To see her with any thoughtless, obstinate or irritable little one, was to think of a tender grandmother. I seemed to have known her for ages — for always — from before time began!'

See also *PF*, Vol. II, p.52: 'How many daughters have in their devotion of their tenderness, become as mothers to their own fathers.'

10 *GMAW*, p.554.

11 That the world through the mirror is an inner world is spelled out in *Lilith A* — see p.8 where Mr Crow tells Fane: '"But," he went on, "look here:" — and again he closed his eyes: — "What world is the image of your father I see him now as I see him with my heart swelling with love toward him?" "Oh, that's a world inside your own head!" I answered with a little laugh of amused unbelief. "Just so," he replied. "Then you allow there is at least one other world your hall-door does not open upon — the world of my thoughts?"'
In *Lilith A* p.38 the reference to Dante's Malebolge is made explicit: 'In a moment, swift as any in Dante's Malebolge, it threw itself upon me cold and clammy, smelling of the earth.'
And p.39:
'When in some after times I speculated on what, vision or reality, the thing might mean, I thought I knew that the ground of that moor outside the house of death was but the outissue of my own soul, the under soil of the vineyard of my own being, deep in which, unknown to myself, lay such nameless horrors.'
And in *Lilith B* p.48:
'"It is but a dream-sea!" I said to myself; "I will not fear that which only seems."'
And *Lilith B* p.50:
'... but how fares the human world in which the buried evil is alive still and ever ready to break forth ravening? for an inner eye had begun to open in me since I left the cottage.'

12 *L*, see p.243:
'Tin tin sonando con si dolce nota

Che' I ben disposto spirto d'amor turge' — *Del Paradiso* x.142.

13 ibid.

14 *L*, p.11. There was a mirror, as described in *Lilith*, with an eagle, ball and chain at Cullen House, home of the library of mystical volumes, and to which MacDonald had the key in 1873 when he was researching *The Marquis of Lossie*.

15 *L*, p.45. Mr Raven tells Vane: '... you and I use the same words with different meanings...'

16 In *Lilith B* Mr Raven tells Mr Vane: 'Nobody knows what anything is; he can only learn/try to find what it means. And that depends on the use he has been making of it.'

17 *L*, p.147.

18 *L*, p.22.

19 *L*, p.16. The identification of the garret with Vane's brain suggests that Vane is also his own house. The librarian could, to some extent, be seen as representing his conscience.

20 *L*, pp.46—7.

21 *L*, p.13.

22 *L*, p.82.

23 *L*, pp.12—13.

24 *L*, p.26.

25 *L*, p.79. See also *L*, p.55: 'Hitherto I had loved my Arab mare and my books more, I fear, than live man or woman; now at length my soul was athirst for human presence...'

26 *L*, p.48.

27 *L*, p.49.

28 There is a link here with Lilith's form as a Lamia, or serpent woman. It is also true that it is because someone has killed a serpent that she takes away the water.

There are further examples of this in *Lilith B*: p.49: 'But the most terrible sight of all, which however made no show of hurting me, was that of a woman-form that rose out of the ground like an exhalation, and came slowly toward me, with mouldy hair hanging over her white skin, moaning and lamenting as she came. She crossed my path in front of me, stopped for a moment and removing her right hand from her side, showed an open wound in her side, an old wound no longer bleeding, but no wise healed, then with a look in her decaying ey[es] that yet hardly shone in her otherwise beautiful face passed on her way to the other side. The sight of her woke in me no memory and no fear: she was to me but one of the indwelling horrors of the region.' Also *Lilith B*, p.110: 'Suddenly, as I held her up a little trying to place myself so that her head should rest on me as she lay, when those limp arms suddenly closed round my neck, and knotted there like serpents, or the arms of the iron torture-maiden. I could hold her no longer.' And *Lilith B*, p.123: 'Some said that she was hundreds of years old, and that she was the Princess of the Power of the Air.' Lilith is also described as a 'hag' and a 'sorceress' on *Lilith B*, p.203.

29 In *Lilith A* the egg that the princess has imprisoned the water in is seized by Fane. There are two accounts of the fate of this egg in *Lilith B*. One account, which MacDonald deleted, has Lilith opening her hand and dropping the egg, flooding the chamber of death. The second account is the one MacDonald finally used in the published version.

30 In *Lilith A* these dwarfs are a small, tiresome race of people whose growth and progress have been halted. Fane eventually takes their children away with him. In later versions these children became the Lovers while their parents became the Bags. The children (Lovers) first appear in *Lilith B*.

31 *L*, p.66.

32 *L*, p.67.

33 Mara is referred to as the Magdalene or Lady of Sorrows. In *Lilith B* she introduces herself as Lot's wife.

34 *L*, p.97.

35 *L*, p.110.

36 *L*, p.115.

37 *L*, p.122.

38 *L*, p.127.

39 *L*, p.137.

40 *L*, p.131.

41 In *Lilith B*, of the tree Vane climbs (p.146): 'It reminded me of that described by Dante in the Purgatorio, whose branches spread out the farther as they approached the top. She stood still under it, and I looked straight up through its branches.'

42 *L*, p.142.

43 *L*, p.148.

44 *L*, p.172.

45 *L*, p.177.

46 *L*, p.173.

47 *L*, p.165.

48 *L*, p.175.

49 *L*, p.184.

50 *L*, p.188.

51 *L*, p.195.

52 *L*, p.201.

53 *L*, pp.201–2.

54 *L*, pp.205–6.

55 *L*, p.207.

56 In *Letters to a Candid Inquirer on Animal Magnetism* (1851) by William Gregory, Gregory mentioned one sleeper whose hand clenched tight on contact with gold and refused to open. Perhaps MacDonald drew this motif from Gregory's work.

57 *L*, p.223.

58 *L*, p.229.

59 *L*, p.243.

60 *L*, p.244.

61 *L*, p.248.

62 *L*, p.250.

63 ibid.

64 *L*, p.251.

65 *L*, p.252. At the end of *Lilith B* MacDonald deleted: 'I used in after years to tell parts of this story, such as would not terrify them, to my children. They always listened with delight, but never thought it was other than what they called a think story. They are all gone before me, and now know better than I how much of it is true, and how much I have told so ill that it cannot be believed by those who read it.'

66 *Athenaeum*, 9 November 1895; 'Jim Jams', *Pall Mall Gazette*, 18 October 1895; *British Weekly*, 10 October 1895.

67 See *Rems*, pp.323–4: H.G. Wells to GMD, 24 September 1895: 'I have been reading your *Lilith* with exceptional interest. Curiously enough I have been at work on a book based on essentially the same idea, namely that, assuming more than three dimensions, it follows that there must be wonderful worlds nearer to us than breathing and closer than hands and feet. I have wanted to get into such kindred worlds for the purposes of romance for several years, but I've been bothered by the way. Your polarization and mirror business struck me as neat in the extreme.'

CHAPTER THIRTY-THREE
The Final Chapter

1 GMD to Lady Mount-Temple, 28 December 1894 (Nat. Lib. Scotland).

2 GMD to Winifred Louisa MacDonald, 14 June 1893 (ALS Yale).

3 *North Wind 4* (The journal of the George MacDonald Society), pp.32–5.

4 GMD to William Carey Davies, 15 June 1892.

5 See *The Meanderings of a Medico: A Record of Work and Travel in Many Lands* by James Linton Bogle MD — Printed for Private Circulation 1928: '. . .Dr Goodchild, a friend of George MacDonald, and, like him, a mystic; he lived at the Casa Grazia, and had his consulting-room in the same house, then occupied by Mr and Mrs Jameson. He was an eccentric being, and an unfortunate quarrel with another doctor, in which the sympathy of the English Colony was almost entirely with

Dr Goodchild, nevertheless re-acted upon him so strongly that he suffered from a nervous breakdown and gradually lost his practice.'

6 *English* (Oxford) XI, Summer 1956, p.62.

7 See also *Rems*, p.335. Louisa to Greville M. MacDonald, 30 October 1898: '. . . Suddenly Father exclaimed, "They say, don't they, my wits are all gone?" "No," I said, "the wits are out in the back premises at present. We all know that." Then that despairing look came into his face: "I know you are all going away from me and I'm going to be left in a strange house . . ." I with my arms round him told him *I* should never leave him and that Irene and I loved nothing in the world so much as to be with him. He really is not worse, only I think not having you, it seems worse for him and for us.'

8 GMD to John Stuart Blackie, 11 November 1894 (Nat. Lib. Scotland).

9 *GMAW*, p.558.

10 Greville MacDonald to Richard Watson Gilder, 9 December 1898 (New York Public Library).

11 *Journal de Bordighera*, Jeudi 19 Janvier 1899. This was a short newspaper, printed weekly in French, Italian and English during the winter months of each year.

12 *The Sketch*, Christmas No. (1898), p.38.

13 Louisa to Winifred L. MacDonald (now Troup), 22 August 1900 (ALS Yale).

14 Irene MacDonald to Winifred L. Troup, her sister, 27 May 1900 (ALS Yale).

15 *Journal de Bordighera*, 4 April 1901: Of the MacDonalds: '. . . They desire therefore, now to express their hearty and grateful thanks for the gifts of glorious golden fruit, of flowers golden and white, of lovely plants, of baskets of flowers, and graceful and gorgeous bouquets, with other golden treasures that were showered on them by their most good friends.'

16 *GMAW*, p.561. All this time Louisa still slept beside him.

17 Chaplain's Book of All Saints' Church, Bordighera recorded Louisa's funeral for 15 January 1902 and Charlotte Powell Godwin's (Louisa's sister) for 9 March. Charlotte is buried in the same row of graves as Louisa but a few stones to the right.

When Louisa died, the *Journal de Bordighera* recorded that: '. . . Casa Coraggio was the very heart of our common life, the centre of wise teaching, of open-handed hospitality, and of much intellectual pleasure and merry making.'

Louisa's last letter to Greville MacDonald was dictated and is recorded in *Rems*, p.356: '. . . I haven't written to you, Dearest, simply because I couldn't. If you come it will be lovely, divine . . . I don't fancy many more days can pass. Oh, to feel your hand once more! Dear, don't think I am miserable about the dying part of it — that is all right; and you and I will know it to be well, when it is decided for us . . .'

18 *GMAW*, p.562.

19 Octavia Hill to Winifred L. Troup (MacDonald), 4 July 1904 (ALS Yale).

20 There was a long obituary in *The Times* on 19 September 1905, and a stream of obituaries in other newspapers. See the *Westminster Gazette*, 19 September 1905; the *Daily News*, 19 and 20 September 1905; *The Standard*, 19 September 1905, Robertson Nicoll in the *Daily Express*, 19 September 1905; the *Daily Chronicle*, 20 September 1905, and *The British Weekly*, 21 September 1905. Most saw him as a grand old man with a spiritual vision who had gradually withdrawn from the world.

21 Entry for Chaplain's Book, All Saints' Church, Bordighera, 1 January 1906: 'The ashes of George MacDonald late of Casa Coraggio, Bordighera, who died during the summer in England and was cremated, were at 9.30 today buried by me in the grave of his Wife in the English cemetery.'

MACDONALD MSS

The bulk of the letters and papers relating to George MacDonald and his family are at Yale, housed in the Beinecke Library. This collection contains roughly 3,500 letters, 900 of which are by MacDonald himself and about 1,800 by Louisa. It was compiled and annotated by MacDonald's youngest daughter Winifred and stands very much as the family collection of letters. The Collection (Uncat MS 57) is uncatalogued and includes photographs, notebooks and scrapbooks as well as letters.

Outside of Yale there is not a substantial amount of material. There is an interesting collection of letters at the *National Library of Scotland* from MacDonald to the Mount-Temples. There are some letters at the *Houghton Library Harvard*, the Richard Watson Gilder papers at the *New York Public Library*, letters mainly to the Scotts at the *Huntington Library* San Marino California and some varied letters at the *University of California and Los Angeles*. *King's College Aberdeen* have some material as does the *Brander Library* Huntly while *Dr Williams Library*, Gordon Square London has interesting material relating to the Highbury period and the Royal Literary Fund London has several letters relating to MacDonald's applications for money and his sponsorships of others. The *Reading University Catalogue of 19th Century MSS* now lists scattered individual letters and there is still some material in the possession of the family.

Wherever possible I have put in brackets after the date of the letter where it is to be found.

MacDonald's daughter Winifred (Lady Troup) who died in 1946 was the last surviving member of the family and before she died she bequeathed her father's manuscripts very liberally to different libraries. In the list of MacDonald's works therefore, wherever possible, I have stated where the manuscript of the book can be found. MacDonald was careless with his MSS and many of them do not survive. They do give, however, a fascinating picture of his mind at work.

A NOTE ON *LILITH*

As the most complex and (arguably) the most important of all MacDonald's books, *Lilith* deserves further consideration as regards its composition and evolution. The eight pre-publication versions of *Lilith*, labelled A-H, are all to be found at the British Museum (Additional MS 46187), ranging from the first unbroken draft, dated 29 March 1890, to the second revise, bound and inscribed — 'Winifred Louisa MacDonald from her father to close the series of development May 1895.' Both the first and last versions are scarcely corrected.

Lilith A is very different from the published version, whose elements are contained in *Lilith* B. The Novalis quotation ending *Lilith* does not appear until the end of *Lilith* F where it is handwritten in, and the title of the last chapter, *The Endless Ending* first arises in *Lilith* E. The title *Lilith* does not appear at all in *Lilith* A where she is referred to only as 'the princess'. *Lilith* B has two titles scored out. One is *Anacosm*, meaning 'Between Worlds', and the other is *A Tale of the Seventh Dimension*. These are both typed, while *Lilith* is written in ink. 'Off, Lilith', the quotation from the *Kabbalah* first appears in *Lilith* C. Furthermore, *Lilith* B is divided into chapters (while *Lilith* A runs on without a break) and is written in typescript, heavily corrected in ink.

There is no major study of these manuscripts, though Roderick F. McGillis's two articles on 'Lilith: George MacDonald and the Lilith Legend in the Nineteenth Century' (*Mythlore*, Vol. 6, Winter 1979), and 'George MacDonald — The Lilith Manuscripts' (*Scottish Literary Journal*, Vol. 4, No. 2, December 1977) are indispensable. McGillis is very thorough, and he comments astutely on Robert Lee Wolff's mistakes regarding the *Lilith* MSS in *The Golden Key* (Yale 1961) and on Greville MacDonald's wayward paraphrase of *Lilith* A in the 1924 edition of *Lilith* to which Greville MacDonald wrote the introduction and touched on the composition of *Lilith*. Apposite quotations from *Lilith* A and *Lilith* B have been footnoted in the chapter on *Lilith*, as these are the two most interesting versions of *Lilith*, but more needs to be said of *Lilith* A.

Lilith A stresses three themes commonly found in MacDonald's work, but which are subordinated in the published version. These are:
1. The quest for the missing father.
2. The exploration of the inner world.
3. The need for work and obedience as a means to spiritual growth.

In addition, it should be stressed that *Lilith* A is eminently readable, flowing from line to line with little of MacDonald's usual digression. There are, however, many differences from the final version, some of which have already been pointed out. The transfer through the mirror, for example, is more scientific, as it takes place in Fane's father's laboratory where he has been experimenting with 'polarized light'. Fane is not an orphan. He has brothers, and the reader is introduced to his sister Imogen, and Fane falls in love with her beautiful friend. Lilith herself is in thrall to the Shadow, obviously Satan, who has more of a shape, and she hates herself and longs to repent:

'It was a terrible night for both of us; for me I was defending the princess from the longing of the demon to reenter where once he had been; and Astarte knew that if he entered again there would be the old horrible fight to fight once more, and all the good might be undone. But Astarte did not know that the best guard between the woman and the demon were the little ones that lay huddled like dead cherubs in the moonlight about her couch.'

Though a reference is made to 'the Steppes of Uranus' the planet seems to be Saturn (though this is denied in *Lilith* B) the equivalent to the Greek Kronos or time, the fourth dimension. There is much more space given in *Lilith* A to the stone she holds in her hand, which holds the waters of the country imprisoned, and which she throws at Fane who keeps it. It is like a blue pigeon egg. And there is nothing on Fane's culpability, or need for repentance, and less swopping of worlds. 'Fane' could mean 'Temple' — a very different interpretation of the hero's character from the later 'Vane' — which is likened to vanity, or like a directionless weather vane, echoing Anodos's meaning of 'pathless' or 'aimless'. The Little Ones are a race of rather tiresome dwarfs, including adults, likened to the Lilliputians, as Fane is to Gulliver, and are very different from the children of the later versions. There is no Lona. Fane's only companion is a leopard called Astarte.

Lilith A begins:

'When first I became aware that I was myself, I found myself one of a family . . .' the words incorporated into *Lilith* B as the beginning of Fane's father's manuscript, and it ends:

'I turned again — and lo, I stood in the morning room of the house where I was born, and my sister and her friend sat at the table at breakfast. They bade me good morning as if I had just come in from the garden. Afterward, when I told them some things, they said I had dreamed. But I have my own thoughts.

Life was rather dull for a while; but a comforter was given me, and the name of my comforter is Hope.'

A précis of *Lilith* A is here included, though McGillis's in *The Lilith Manuscripts* is longer and more detailed.

Mr Fane lives in a house with his brothers and sister. His mother is dead, and his father is either dead or has disappeared. One day, a man he has not seen before appears beside him in the library and explains some facts regarding his father's disappearance. He explains that Fane's father had been experimenting with 'polarized light' and he leads Fane to his father's laboratory where, by operating a mechanism, the light is thrown onto a door-shaped mirror, and Fane sees his father walking in a foreign landscape. Fane is fifteen years old at this time, and decides that the purpose of his life is 'to seek my father until I found him' (*Lilith* A p7). The librarian walks through the mirror into the landscape after talking of the fourth dimension, a sixth sense, and inner worlds, and at this sight Fane rushes in terror from the laboratory.

Fane has a sister called Imogen, and one morning he goes to pick primroses for her. As he does so, he finds himself in a different landscape, and sees a rook coming toward him. The rook (a bird from the front and the librarian from the back) tells him that he has entered the other world too soon, and urges him to go east through the wood. Fane follows his instructions and returns to a physical life of 'rowing, running and fencing' before going to college, taking his degree, and returning home with the hope of writing books. Meanwhile his sister Imogen has also grown, and Fane falls madly in love with her friend. Mr Rook makes another appearance just as a storm is beginning, and Fane finds himself once more in the other world. The rook takes Fane to his Sexton's Cottage where his wife is alternately a woman or a white pigeon.

'Does he wish to sleep?' said the woman.

'I think not,' replied her husband, 'he has not yet done his day's work.' Fane refuses to sleep and goes out into the night where he encounters monsters breaking out of the earth, and comes eventually to some shrubs which he realizes are miniature trees. 'I thought at first I had surely found the land of Lilliput' (*Lilith* A·p43). Here the people are dull dwarfs who take Fane for a god on account of his size.

Fane hears water running under the ground, and wonders if they are in need of water in order to grow, as there is none anywhere in the country. He leaves them and soon finds a ruined house or castle, all overgrown with ivy and a bed ready made to sleep in. Fane does so, and wakes to find skeletons dancing beneath him. He leaves the ruin and finds a naked, skeletal female body lying on the ground. Hoping that she might prove a companion for him, Fane dresses her and steeps her in a hot stream close by in order to bring her back to life. He begins to be bitten, and loses a lot of blood. His lady comes back to life, protesting that she has destroyed the leech that has been attacking him, but abandons Fane with tears crying that she is an 'evil thing' — '"Do not touch me," she cried in a low voice almost of agony that ended in a shriek' (*Lilith* A p84).

The woman throws the stone clasped in her hand at Fane, striking him senseless. It is blue, like a pigeon's egg, and when Fane awakes, he puts it in his pocket. Fane continues to the city where he is mocked by the children there and stoned as his apparent poverty is an offence. He seeks the princess, and makes friends with a leopard called Astarte, who becomes his constant companion. Meeting the princess once more, she tries to seduce Fane in an effort to regain the stone, and once more sucks his blood. Fane awakes back at the spot where he originally found the princess's body, skeletal now himself. He notices a tiny stream running from the stone and begins to realize its properties.

He returns to the land of the dwarfs who have grown (along with their trees) to a height of three feet. They do not notice their own growth, and take Fane for a trickster as he has diminished in size, and they treat him badly. They repudiate all Fane's efforts to help them and he bears their mistreatment patiently until one strikes him unconscious with a stone. He awakes to find that Astarte has massacred many of them. Fane and Astarte leave, and Astarte is then killed by a monster coming out of the earth. At that moment the rook appears and takes Fane back to his cottage where he at last lies down on a couch to sleep. When he wakes he returns to the dwarfs and takes their children along with Astarte (now restored to life) to the city to capture the princess. The army is joined by all sorts of animals on the way, and they carry the princess off. She is safe from the demon only when surrounded by the children, for then he cannot enter her, but Fane urges her to face him, which she does unsuccessfully. Nevertheless she does go to the House of Death and lie down, as do the children. Then the golden cock on the clock of the universe crows and the children all awake. They start the ascent to paradise and soon catch sight of the holy city:

'Never had I seen such glorious show of city. The moment it came in view, my father turned to me, and we fell in each other's arms.'

As they climb they are greeted by Cacourgos Heteros, the Colonel of the Guard, with 'Welcome home!' and the children swarm over the angel at the gate who sits looking like Albert Dürer's *Melancholia*. At this point a warm brotherly hand grasps Fane and he finds himself once more in the library. He enters to find his sister and her friend at breakfast. He tells them some things, but they say that he has been dreaming, and so finally he is left to wait on in hope.

Lilith A is much less threatening than the published version, as it is rational, coherent and ordered, with many props to help the reader understand the sequence of events. MacDonald deliberately removed these props in his revisions of the work in order to work towards a text where the reader would have to work to find a meaning rather than rest on the author's obvious intention. Though *Lilith* was written, according to MacDonald, on impulse from God, it cannot be read as an allegory or Christian parable. In the panorama of the seventh dimension, Vane's explorations show MacDonald at his most potent and enduring as a symbolic writer.

GEORGE MACDONALD: IMPORTANT DATES

1824   MacDonald born, 10 December.
1832   MacDonald's mother, Helen, dies.
1839   MacDonald's father marries Margaret McColl.
1840   MacDonald wins bursary to King's College, Aberdeen.
1842   Spends some time cataloguing a library. Teaches arithmetic.
1845   Receives M.A. Goes to London to tutor.
1846   Publishes first poem anonymously in the Scottish Congregational Magazine.
1848   Goes to Highbury Theological College. Becomes engaged to Louisa Powell.
1850   Called to Arundel. Severe haemorrhage in November.
1851   Marries Louisa Powell on 8 March. Gives translation of *Twelve of the Spiritual Songs of Novalis* to friends on Christmas Day.
1852   4 January, Lilia born. June, MacDonald's salary cut on account of his 'heresy'.
1853   May, resigns pulpit. 23 July, Mary Josephine born. Move to Manchester.
1854   16 September, Caroline Grace born.
1855   *Within and Without* published.
1856   20 January, Greville born. Lady Byron becomes MacDonald's patron. Winter in Algiers.
1857   31 August, Irene born. MacDonalds settle in Hastings.
1858   MacDonald's brother John dies in June. His father dies in August. *Phantastes* published. Winifred Louisa born, 6 November.
1859   Move to London. MacDonald accepts professorship of English Literature at Bedford College in October.
1860   Lady Byron dies. 27 October, Ronald born.
1862   Robert Falconer born.
1863   MacDonald family read Lewis Carroll's 'Alice' story. *David Elginbrod* published. Meets John Ruskin.
1864   Maurice born in February.
1865   MacDonald tries unsuccessfully for professorship of Rhetoric and Belles Lettres (literature) at Edinburgh. *Alec Forbes of Howglen* published. Bernard Powell born.
1867   MacDonalds move to The Retreat, Hammersmith. George MacKay born.
1868   *Robert Falconer* published. Awarded LLD by Aberdeen University.
1869   Accepts editorship of *Good Words for the Young*. Lecture tour of Scotland.
1871   *At the Back of the North Wind* published.
1872   Lecture tour of America. Climax of the Ruskin/La Touche affair. *Wilfrid Cumbermede* inspired by Ruskin/La Touche affair published. *The Princess and the Goblin* published.
1875   MacDonalds leave The Retreat.
1876   *Exotics* published.
1877   First trip to Italy. First performance of *Pilgrim's Progress*. MacDonald awarded a Civil List Pension.
1878   Mary Josephine dies.
1879   Maurice dies.
1880   The Family arrive in Bordighera.
1882   *The Princess and Curdie* published.
1884   Grace dies.
1890   First draft of *Lilith* completed.

1891 Lilia dies.
1895 *Lilith* published.
1897 *Salted with Fire*, his last novel, published. MacDonald's health deteriorates.
1898 MacDonald has a stroke and lapses into silence.
1901 The MacDonalds' Golden Wedding.
1902 13 January, Louisa dies at Bordighera.
1905 18 September, MacDonald dies at Ashtead in Surrey. He is cremated and his ashes buried at Bordighera beside those of his wife.

INDEX

176 DREAM / LIFE
368   ..   ..
382   "   "